Learning Core Data for iOS

 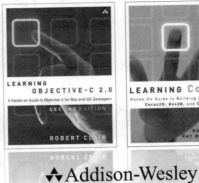  

Learning Core Data for iOS

Tim Roadley

✦✦ Addison-Wesley

Upper Saddle River, NJ • Boston • Indianapolis • San Francisco
New York • Toronto • Montreal • London • Munich • Paris • Madrid
Cape Town • Sydney • Tokyo • Singapore • Mexico City

The publisher offers excellent discounts on this book when ordered in quantity for bulk purchases or special sales, which may include electronic versions and/or custom covers and content particular to your business, training goals, marketing focus, and branding interests. For more information, please contact:

U.S. Corporate and Government Sales
(800) 382-3419
corpsales@pearsontechgroup.com

For sales outside the United States, please contact:

International Sales
international@pearsoned.com

Library of Congress Control Number: 2013946325

Visit us on the Web: informit.com/aw

ISBN-13: 978-0-321-90576-5
ISBN-10: 0-321-90576-8

Text printed in the United States on recycled paper at RR Donnelley in Crawfordsville, Indiana.

First printing: November 2013

Editor-in-Chief
Mark Taub

Senior Acquisitions Editor
Trina MacDonald

Senior Development Editor
Chris Zahn

Development Editor
Sheri Cain

Managing Editor
Kristy Hart

Senior Project Editor
Betsy Gratner

Copy Editor
Bart Reed

Indexer
Brad Herriman

Proofreader
Paula Lowell

Technical Reviewers
Carl Brown
Mark H. Granoff
Ricky O'Sullivan
Rich Warren

Publishing Coordinator
Olivia Basegio

Cover Designer
Chuti Prasertsith

Compositor
Nonie Ratcliff

❖

The more I learn, the more I learn I need to learn more.

I dedicate this book to my wonderful wife, Tracey, who has given up many nights and weekends with me to help make this book a reality. Finally, we can sit back and relax together again! I'm sure Tyler & Taliah will let us....

<3

❖

Contents at a Glance

Table of Contents

Acknowledgments

A resounding thank-you first goes out to Trina MacDonald for giving me the opportunity to write this book. Her guidance throughout the whole process has been invaluable, as has the assistance of the fantastic technical reviewers Rich Warren, Carl Brown, Mark Granoff, and Ricky O'Sullivan. You guys saved this book from a few bugs that crept through on those late nights and also provided some great insight and coding technique suggestions. Special thanks also go to Betsy Gratner, Olivia Basegio, Bart Reed, Sheri Cain, Chris Zahn, and Matt Vaznaian for your assistance in making this book a reality.

About the Author

Tim Roadley is a senior analytics software consultant at Emite Pty Ltd. He is primarily focused on delivering business intelligence dashboards, currently for one of Australia's major banks. Prior to Emite, Tim was Infrastructure Manager at Cuscal Pty Ltd, where he was heavily involved in designing and implementing a payments switch that drives 1,300+ ATMs throughout Australia. By night he is an avid iOS developer and tutorial writer, with several apps on the App Store, including Teamwork, iSoccer, and now Grocery Dude and Grocery Cloud. In his downtime, he enjoys spending time with his wonderful wife, Tracey, and two lovely children, Tyler and Taliah.

Preface

Every day, millions of Apple devices run applications, or apps, which rely on Core Data. This has led to a mature, stable, and incredibly fast platform for apps to access their data. Core Data itself is not a database. In fact, Core Data is a framework that, among other things, automates how you interact with a database. Instead of writing SQL code, you use Objective-C objects. All the associated SQL you would otherwise have to write yourself is generated automatically. This leaves you with all the benefits of a relational database without the headache of writing, testing, and optimizing SQL queries within your Objective-C code. The SQL code generated automatically "under the hood" is the product of years of refinement and optimization by Apple's masterful engineers. Using Core Data will not only speed up your own application development time, it will also significantly reduce the amount of code you have to write.

Here are some notable features of Core Data:

- Change management (undo and redo)
- Relationships
- Data model versioning and migration
- Efficient fetching (through batching and faulting)
- Efficient filtering (through predicates)
- Data consistency and validation

With this book, you'll be introduced to Core Data features and best practices. As you progress through the chapters, you'll also build a fully functional Core Data iPhone app from scratch. Each key piece of information will be explained in succinct detail so you can apply what you've learned straight away. The sample application built throughout this book has been especially designed to demonstrate as many aspects of Core Data as possible. At the same time it is a completely real-world application available on the App Store today. This should make it easier to absorb concepts as you relate them to real-life scenarios.

The arrival of iOS 7 has seen major improvements in the speed, reliability, and simplicity of Core Data integration with iCloud. I encourage anyone who has previously given up on this technology to give it another go, because you will be pleasantly surprised.

If you have feedback, bug fixes, corrections, or anything else you would like to contribute to a future edition, please contact me at timroadley@icloud.com. Finally, thank you for taking an interest in this book. I have put a lot of effort into meticulously crafting it, so I truly hope it helps you on your way to mastering this brilliant technology.

—Tim Roadley (*@TimRoadley*), September 2013

Who Is This Book For?

This book is aimed at Objective-C programmers who wish to learn how to efficiently manage data in their iOS apps. Prior experience with databases may help you pick up some topics faster, yet is not essential knowledge. As old habits die hard, some SQL programmers may find it more difficult to wrap their heads around some topics. Whatever your scenario, don't worry. Every step of the way will be explained and demonstrated clearly.

What You'll Need

As an Objective-C programmer, it is expected that you already have a reasonably modern Mac running Xcode 5 or above. You should also be quite familiar with Xcode and have an iOS device to test with. This is particularly true once you reach Chapter 10, "Performance," which is all about device performance.

You should already know what the Objective-C terms *property*, *method*, *delegate*, *class*, and *class instance* mean. If you're now uncertain that this book is for you, I suggest a detour via the following resources:

- *iOS Programming: The Big Nerd Ranch Guide* (search amazon.com)

- The iOS Newbie Tutorial Series (search timroadley.com)

- Learning Objective-C: A Primer (search apple.com)

How This Book Is Organized

This book takes you through the entire process of building the **Grocery Dude** and **Grocery Cloud** apps, which are available from the App Store today. Grocery Dude demonstrates Core Data integration with iCloud. Grocery Cloud demonstrates Core Data integration with StackMob. Each chapter in this book builds on the last, so you're introduced to topics in the order you need to implement them. Along the way you'll build helper classes that simplify redeployment of what you've learned into your own applications. In fact, the exercises at the end of Chapter 15, "Taming iCloud," guide you through a redeployment of these helper classes into an existing non–Core Data app. In next to no time, you'll have a fully functional Core Data app that is reliably integrated with iCloud.

Here's a brief summary of what you'll find in each chapter:

- **Chapter 1, "Your First Core Data Application"**—The groundwork is laid as the fundamental concepts of Core Data are introduced. You'll be shown what Core Data is, and just as importantly what it isn't. In addition, Core Data integration with an existing application is demonstrated as the `CoreDataHelper` class is implemented.

- **Chapter 2, "Managed Object Model Basics"**—Data models are introduced as parallels are drawn between traditional database schema design and Core Data. You'll be shown how to configure a basic managed object model as entities and attributes are discussed, along with accompanying advice on choosing the right data types. Inserting, fetching, filtering, sorting, and deleting managed objects is also covered and followed up with an introduction to fetch request templates.

- **Chapter 3, "Managed Object Model Migration"**—Experience lightweight migration, default migration, and using a migration manager to display migration progress. Learn how to make an informed decision when deciding between migration options for your own applications and become comfortable with the model-versioning capabilities of Core Data.

- **Chapter 4, "Managed Object Model Expansion"**—The true power of a relational data model is unlocked as different types of relationships are explained and added to Grocery Dude. Other model features such as abstract and parent entities are also covered, along with techniques for dealing with data validation errors.

- **Chapter 5, "Table Views"**—The application really comes to life as Core Data is used to drive memory-efficient and highly performing table views with a fetched results controller. Of course, most of the generic legwork is put into a reusable table view controller subclass called `CoreDataTVC`. By dropping this class into your own applications, you can easily deploy Core Data–driven table views yourself.

- **Chapter 6, "Views"**—Working with managed objects takes a front seat as you're shown how to pass them around the application. Objects selected on a table view are passed to a second view, ready for editing. The editing interface is added to Grocery Dude, demonstrating how to work with objects and then save them back to the persistent store.

- **Chapter 7, "Picker Views"**—As a nice touch, Core Data–driven picker views are added to the editing views. Picker views allow the user to quickly assign existing items to a unit of measurement, home location, or shop location. A special reusable text field subclass called `CoreDataPickerTF` is introduced, which replaces the keyboard with a Core Data picker view whenever an associated text field is tapped.

- **Chapter 8, "Preloading Data"**—Techniques for generating a persistent store full of default data from XML are explained and demonstrated in this chapter as the generic `CoreDataImporter` helper class is introduced. Once you have a persistent store to include with a shipping application, you'll then be shown how to determine whether a default data import is required or even desired by the user.

- **Chapter 9, "Deep Copy"**—A highly flexible and fine-grained alternative to `migratePersistentStore`, deep copy enables you to copy objects and relationships from selected entities between persistent stores. In this chapter, the `CoreDataImporter` helper class is enhanced with the deep copy capability.

- **Chapter 10, "Performance"**—Gain experience with Instruments as you identify and eliminate performance issues caused by the common pitfalls of a Core Data application. The camera functionality is introduced to highlight these issues and demonstrates just how important good model design is to a well-performing application.

- **Chapter 11, "Background Processing"**—Top-notch performance requires intensive tasks be offloaded to a background thread. Learn just how easy it is to run processes in the background as the example of photo thumbnail generation is added with a generic helper class called `Thumbnailer`. Also learn how to keep memory usage low with another helper class, called `Faulter`.

- **Chapter 12, "Search"**—Learn how to handle twin fetched results controllers in the one table view as you implement efficient search in `CoreDataTVC`.

- **Chapter 13, "Back Up and Restore with Dropbox"**—Create backups and synchronize them to Dropbox using their Sync API. Restore data to any iOS device using the same Dropbox account at the touch of a button.

- **Chapter 14, "iCloud"**—Enjoy the easiest, most reliable Core Data integration with iCloud yet. Handle multiple accounts and varying preferences on using iCloud without missing a beat.

- **Chapter 15, "Taming iCloud"**—Take iCloud integration to the next level with entity-level seeding and unique object de-duplication. Accurately emulate first-time iCloud use by resetting ubiquitous content globally, the right way.

- **Chapter 16, "Web Service Integration"**—Enable collaboration as cross-platform data sharing between multiple users is introduced with StackMob. StackMob has one of the best free Backend-as-a-Service (BaaS) offerings available, and its iOS API is native to Core Data. Thanks to StackMob for generously allowing its art assets to be used in this book and for its assistance with Chapter 16.

- **Appendix A, "Preparing Grocery Dude for Chapter 1"**—Every (non–Core Data) step involved in preparing the starting-point application for Chapter 1 is documented here for completeness.

- **Appendix B, "Preparing Grocery Cloud for Chapter 16"**—Every (non–Core Data) step involved in preparing the starting-point application for Chapter 16 is documented here for completeness.

Getting the Sample Code

The sample code built throughout this book is available for download from timroadley.com. Links are given in each chapter, or you can use Table P.1 as a reference, which is arranged in the order of implementation.

Table P.1 Grocery Dude Code

Final Code	Link
Appendix A	http://timroadley.com/LearningCoreData/GroceryDude-AfterAppendixA.zip
Chapter 1	http://timroadley.com/LearningCoreData/GroceryDude-AfterChapter01.zip
Chapter 2	http://timroadley.com/LearningCoreData/GroceryDude-AfterChapter02.zip

Final Code	Link
Chapter 3	http://timroadley.com/LearningCoreData/GroceryDude-AfterChapter03.zip
Chapter 4	http://timroadley.com/LearningCoreData/GroceryDude-AfterChapter04.zip
Chapter 5	http://timroadley.com/LearningCoreData/GroceryDude-AfterChapter05.zip
Chapter 6	http://timroadley.com/LearningCoreData/GroceryDude-AfterChapter06.zip
Chapter 7	http://timroadley.com/LearningCoreData/GroceryDude-AfterChapter07.zip
Chapter 8	http://timroadley.com/LearningCoreData/GroceryDude-AfterChapter08.zip
Chapter 9	http://timroadley.com/LearningCoreData/GroceryDude-AfterChapter09.zip
Chapter 10	http://timroadley.com/LearningCoreData/GroceryDude-AfterChapter10.zip
Chapter 11	http://timroadley.com/LearningCoreData/GroceryDude-AfterChapter11.zip
Chapter 12	http://timroadley.com/LearningCoreData/GroceryDude-AfterChapter12.zip
Chapter 13	http://timroadley.com/LearningCoreData/GroceryDude-AfterChapter13.zip
Chapter 14	http://timroadley.com/LearningCoreData/GroceryDude-AfterChapter14.zip
Chapter 15	http://timroadley.com/LearningCoreData/GroceryDude-AfterChapter15.zip
Chapter 15 "Mini-project"	http://timroadley.com/LearningCoreData/EasyiCloud.zip
Helper classes, for your own projects	http://timroadley.com/LearningCoreData/Generic%20Core%20Data%20Classes.zip
Appendix B	http://timroadley.com/LearningCoreData/GroceryCloud-AfterAppendixB.zip
Chapter 16	http://timroadley.com/LearningCoreData/GroceryCloud-AfterChapter16.zip

Note that occasionally lines of code in the chapters are too long to fit on the printed page. Where that occurs, a code-continuation arrow (➡) has been used to mark the continuation. For example:

```
[[NSURL fileURLWithPath:[self applicationDocumentsDirectory]]
➡URLByAppendingPathComponent:@"Stores"];
```

Editor's Note: We Want to Hear from You!

As the reader of this book, you are our most important critic and commentator. We value your opinion and want to know what we're doing right, what we could do better, what areas you'd like to see us publish in, and any other words of wisdom you're willing to pass our way.

You can email or write me directly to let me know what you did or didn't like about this book—as well as what we can do to make our books stronger.

Please note that I cannot help you with technical problems related to the topic of this book, and that due to the high volume of mail I receive, I might not be able to reply to every message.

When you write, please be sure to include this book's title and author as well as your name and phone number or email address. I will carefully review your comments and share them with the author and editors who worked on the book.

Email: trina.macdonald@pearson.com

Mail: Trina MacDonald
         Senior Acquisitions Editor
         Addison-Wesley/Pearson Education, Inc.
         75 Arlington St., Ste. 300
         Boston, MA 02116

1

Your First Core Data Application

If you can't explain it simply, you don't understand it well enough.

Albert Einstein

Kinesthetic learning, or learning by doing, is one of the best ways to absorb and retain information. The topic of Core Data has been a great hurdle for many seasoned programmers, so it's about time a book with a hands-on approach to Core Data was written. In order to avoid side tracking into deep topics too early, this chapter has many pointers to later chapters. First things first: It will give you a Core Data essentials primer, then dive right in and show how to add Core Data to the sample application. The sample application will be expanded over the course of this book as increasingly advanced topics are introduced.

What Is Core Data?

Core Data is a framework that enables you to work with your data as objects, regardless of how they're persisted to disk. This is useful to you as an Objective-C programmer, because you should be comfortable using objects in code already. To provide data objects, known as *managed objects*, Core Data sits between your application and a **persistent store**, which is the generic term given to a data file such as an SQLite database, XML file (which can't be used as a persistent store on iOS), or Binary (atomic) store. These files are called "persistent" because they can survive the underlying hardware being reset. Another (oddly named) persistent store option is the In-Memory store. Although it isn't really "persistent," an In-Memory store allows you to leverage all the functional benefits of Core Data to manage your data, such as change management and validation, not to mention performance.

To map data to a persistent store from managed objects, Core Data uses a **managed object model**, where you configure your application's data structure using an **object graph**. You can think of an object graph as a collection of cookie cutters used to make managed objects from. The "object" in object graph refers to something called an **entity**, which is used as a cookie cutter to make a customized managed object. Once you have managed objects, you're then free to manipulate them natively in Objective-C, without having to write any SQL code (assuming you're using SQLite as the persistent store, which is the most common scenario). Core Data will transparently map those objects back to a persistent store when you save to disk.

A managed object holds a copy of data from a persistent store. If you use a database as a persistent store, then a managed object might represent data from a table row in that database. If you use an XML file as a persistent store (Mac only), then a managed object would represent data found within certain data elements. A managed object can be an instance of NSManagedObject; however, it's usually an instance of a *subclass* of NSManagedObject. This is discussed in detail in Chapter 2, "Managed Object Model Basics."

All managed objects exist in a **managed object context**. A managed object context exists in high-speed volatile memory, also known as RAM. One reason a managed object context is required is the overhead involved with transferring data to and from disk. Disk is much slower than RAM, so you don't want to use it more than necessary. Having a managed object context allows access to data that has been previously retrieved from disk to be very fast. The downside, however, is that you need to call save: on the managed object context periodically to write changes back to disk. The managed object context exists also to track changes to its objects in order to provide full undo and redo support.

> **Note**
>
> "If you can't explain it simply, you don't understand it well enough" is a famous quote from the late great Albert Einstein. Each chapter of this book is headed by a famous Albert Einstein quote. Core Data can be a difficult topic to learn; however, that doesn't mean it cannot be broken down and explained in understandable chunks. Whenever I write technical tutorials or documentation, I remember this quote and strive for easy-to-read, highly informative material.

To help visualize how the main pieces of Core Data fit together, examine Figure 1.1.

Persistent Store Coordinator

On the left of Figure 1.1, a **persistent store coordinator** is shown containing a persistent store with table rows. When you set up a persistent store coordinator, you'll commonly choose an SQLite database as the persistent store. Other options for the persistent store are Binary, XML, and In-Memory stores. The thing to note about Binary and XML stores is that they are atomic. This means that even if you only want to change a small amount of data, you still have to write out the whole file to disk when you save. Of course, the same issue applies when reading an atomic store into memory in the first place. This can become problematic if you have a lot of data because it consumes valuable memory.

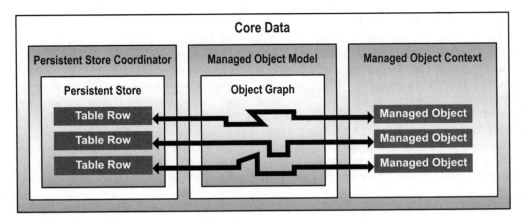

Figure 1.1   Core Data overview

An SQLite database, on the other hand, is updated incrementally as change logs, also known as *transaction logs,* are committed. As a result, the SQLite database memory footprint is comparably very small. For these reasons, you'll typically choose an SQLite database, especially when integrating Core Data with iCloud.

> **Note**
>
> Persistent stores should only ever be created by Core Data. You should not configure Core Data to use a database it did not originally create. If you need to use existing data, you should import it. This topic is covered in Chapter 8, "Preloading Data."

A persistent store coordinator can have multiple persistent stores. One situation where this may be appropriate is when Core Data is integrated with iCloud. By putting data that doesn't belong in iCloud into one store, and data that does in another, you will save network bandwidth and iCloud storage space. Even though you would then have two persistent stores, it does not mean that you need two separate object graphs. Using Core Data model configurations allows you to use separate stores, yet still have the one object graph. When you set up a Core Data model configuration, you can select what parts of the object graph belong in what persistent store. If you do use separate persistent stores, you'll need to ensure there's no requirement for a relationship between data in each store. Core Data configurations are discussed in Chapter 15, "Taming iCloud."

A persistent store is created from an instance of `NSPersistentStore` and a persistent store coordinator is created from an instance of `NSPersistentStoreCoordinator`.

Managed Object Model

In the middle of Figure 1.1, a **managed object model** is shown sitting between a persistent store coordinator and a managed object context. As its name suggests, a managed object model is the model or graphical representation of a data structure. It forms the basis on which managed objects are produced. This is similar to a database schema and is also referred to as an *object graph*. To create one, you'll use Xcode to configure entities and the relationships between them. An entity is similar to a table schema in a database. Entities don't contain data; they only dictate the properties that managed objects that are based on them will have. They're cookie cutters! Just as a database table has fields, similarly an entity has attributes. An attribute can have one of several data types, such as integer, string, or date. Chapter 2 and Chapter 4, "Managed Object Model Expansion," cover these topics in more detail.

A managed object model is created from an instance of NSManagedObjectModel.

Managed Object Context

On the right of Figure 1.1, a **managed object context** is shown with managed objects inside. A managed object context manages the lifecycle of objects within and provides powerful features such as faulting, change tracking, and validation. Faulting simply means that when you fetch data from a persistent store, only the parts you need are retrieved. Faulting is covered further in Chapter 10, "Performance." Change tracking is used for undo and redo support. Validation is the enforcement of rules set in the managed object model. For example, a minimum or maximum value rule can be enforced at an attribute level on an entity. Validation is discussed in Chapter 2.

Much like you can have multiple persistent stores, you may also have more than one managed object context. Typically you would use multiple contexts for background processing, such as saving to disk or importing data. When you call save: on a foreground context, you may notice user interface lag, especially when there are a lot of changes. An easy way to get around this issue is to simply call save: only when the home button is pressed and the application enters the background. Another more complicated yet flexible way is to use two managed object contexts. Remember that a managed object context is an area in high-speed memory. Well, you can actually configure a managed object context to save to *another* managed object context. Once you save a foreground context to a background context, you may then save the background context to disk asynchronously. This staged approach ensures the writes to disk never interfere with the user interface responsiveness.

The ability to configure a parent and child context hierarchy has been available since iOS 5. A child context treats its parent as a persistent store, when really the parent is another context that exists to process heavy workloads, such as saving in the background. This is discussed in further detail in Chapter 11, "Background Processing."

A managed object context is created from an instance of NSManagedObjectContext.

When to Use Core Data

Once your application outgrows trivial "settings" storage, such as `NSUserDefaults` and property lists, you're going to run into memory usage issues. The solution is to use a database either directly or instead indirectly with Core Data. If you choose Core Data, you'll save time otherwise spent coding a database interface. You'll also enjoy big performance gains, as well as some functional benefits such as undo and validation. The time you would have spent developing, testing, and generally speaking "reinventing the wheel," you'll free up to focus on more important areas of your application.

Now you might be thinking, "I just want to save lots of stuff to disk, so why does it have to be so complicated?" Well, it's not that difficult once a few key points are understood. Sure, you could write your own database interfaces and they would probably work great for a while. What happens, though, when your requirements change or you want to add, say, data synchronization between devices? How are your skills at building multithreaded data-import routines that don't impact the user interface? Would your code also support undo and validation yet still be fast and memory efficient on an old iPhone?

The good news for you is that all the hard work has already been done and is wrapped up in the tried and tested Core Data Framework. Even if your application's data requirements are minimal, it's still worth using Core Data to ensure your application is as scalable as possible without compromising performance.

Once you start using Core Data, you'll appreciate how robust and optimized it really is. The millions of people worldwide using Core Data applications every day has led to a mature feature set with performance to match. In short, you'll save more time learning Core Data than throwing it in the too-hard basket and writing your own database interfaces. You'll also benefit from loads of additional functionality for free.

> **Note**
>
> Before you continue, you should have at least Xcode 5 installed on your Mac. The code used in this book is targeted at iOS 7, so it won't work in lower versions of Xcode. It is also recommended that you become a member of the iOS Developer Program, so you can run the sample application on your device as required. Go to http://developer.apple.com for further information on becoming a member.

Introducing Grocery Dude

Grocery Dude is the sample iPhone application you'll create over the course of this book. As the features and best practices of Core Data are introduced, you can apply what you've learned to Grocery Dude. By the end of the book, you'll have created a fast and fully functional Core Data application that integrates seamlessly with iCloud. If you would like to see the end result upfront, head over to the App Store and download Grocery Dude now. Note that Grocery Dude is written only for iPhone. This is because Core Data doesn't care what size screen you display data on; the concepts are the same. Without further ado, it's time to begin!

Have you ever stood in front of the fridge, pantry, cupboard, or some other location at home wondering what you're forgetting to put on your shopping list? Then, when you get to the store, you can't find something because you have no idea what aisle it's in? To top it off, after zigzagging all the way from aisle 8 (and finally finding what you're looking for in aisle 2), you discover the next item you need is back in aisle 8!

Here's what Grocery Dude will do for you:

- Remind you what you *might* need by sorting potential items by their storage location in your house.

- Help you locate items at the grocery store by showing what aisle they're in.

- Group your list by aisle so you only need to visit each aisle once, and in order.

- Sync between your devices with iCloud.

- Help you learn Core Data!

> **Note**
>
> Appendix A, "Preparing Grocery Dude for Chapter 1," shows the steps required to create the master project "Grocery Dude" from scratch. You may run through those steps manually or alternatively download the starting point project from http://www.timroadley.com/LearningCoreData/GroceryDude-AfterAppendixA.zip. Once you have downloaded the project, you should open it in Xcode 5 or above.

Adding Core Data to an Existing Application

When you create an iOS Application project in Xcode, you can choose from various starting-point templates. Using Core Data in your project is as easy as ticking the **Use Core Data** check box during creation of a Master-Detail, Utility Application, or Empty Application template-based project. Adding Core Data manually is more educational, so the "Grocery Dude" project is created based on the **Single View Application** template, which doesn't include Core Data. To use the Core Data Framework, you'll need to link it to the project.

Update Grocery Dude as follows to link to the Core Data Framework:

1. Select the **Grocery Dude Target**, as shown in Figure 1.2.

2. Click the + found in the **Linked Frameworks and Libraries** section of the **General** tab and then link to the **CoreData.framework**, as shown in Figure 1.2.

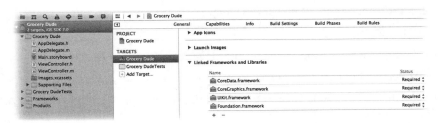

Figure 1.2   Linking the Core Data Framework

Introducing Core Data Helper

If you've ever examined the built-in Core Data–enabled templates, you may have noticed a lot of Core Data setup is done in the application delegate. So that you may apply the approach used in this book to your own projects, Core Data will be set up using a helper class. This keeps the Core Data components modular and portable. The application delegate will be used to lazily create an instance of the `CoreDataHelper` class. An instance of this class will be used to do the following:

- Initialize a managed object model
- Initialize a persistent store coordinator with a persistent store based on the managed object model
- Initialize a managed object context based on the persistent store coordinator

Update Grocery Dude as follows to create the `CoreDataHelper` class in a new Xcode group:

1. Right-click the **Grocery Dude** group in Xcode and then create a new group called **Generic Core Data Classes**, as shown in Figure 1.3.

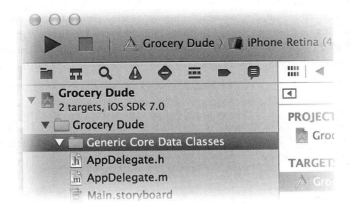

Figure 1.3   Xcode group for generic Core Data classes

2. Select the **Generic Core Data Classes** group.

3. Click **File > New > File...**.

4. Create a new **iOS > Cocoa Touch > Objective-C class** and then click **Next**.

5. Set **Subclass of** to `NSObject` and **Class** name to `CoreDataHelper` and then click **Next**.

6. Ensure the Grocery Dude target is ticked and then create the class in the Grocery Dude project directory.

Listing 1.1 shows new code intended for the `CoreDataHelper` header file.

Listing 1.1 **CoreDataHelper.h**

```
#import <Foundation/Foundation.h>
#import <CoreData/CoreData.h>

@interface CoreDataHelper :NSObject

@property (nonatomic, readonly) NSManagedObjectContext      *context;
@property (nonatomic, readonly) NSManagedObjectModel        *model;
@property (nonatomic, readonly) NSPersistentStoreCoordinator *coordinator;
@property (nonatomic, readonly) NSPersistentStore           *store;

- (void)setupCoreData;
- (void)saveContext;
@end
```

As an Objective-C programmer, you should be familiar with the purpose of header (`.h`) files. `CoreDataHelper.h` is used to declare properties for the context, model, coordinator and the store within it. The `setupCoreData` method will be called once an instance of `CoreDataHelper` has been created in the application delegate. The `saveContext` method may be called whenever you would like to save changes from the managed object context to the persistent store. This method can cause interface lag if there are a lot of changes to be written to disk. It is recommended that it only be called from the `applicationDidEnterBackground` and `applicationWillTerminate` methods of `AppDelegate.m`—at least until background save is added in Chapter 11.

Update Grocery Dude as follows to configure the `CoreDataHelper` header:

1. Replace all code in `CoreDataHelper.h` with the code from Listing 1.1. If you select `CoreDataHelper.m`, Xcode will warn that you haven't implemented the `setupCoreData` and `saveContext` methods, which is okay for now.

Core Data Helper Implementation

The helper class will start out with four main sections. These sections are FILES, PATHS, SETUP, and SAVING. For easy navigation and readability, these areas are separated by pragma marks. As shown in Figure 1.4, the pragma mark feature of Xcode allows you to logically organize your code and automatically provides a nice menu for you to navigate with.

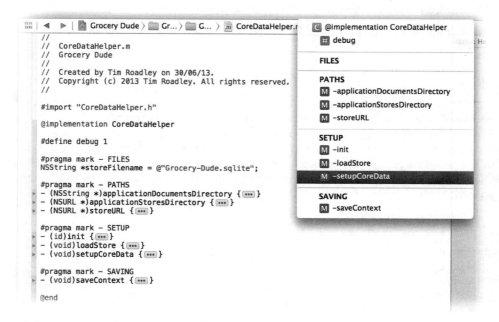

Figure 1.4   Pragma mark generated menu

Files

The FILES section of CoreDataHelper.m starts out with a persistent store filename stored in an NSString. When additional persistent stores are added later, this is where you'll set their filenames. Listing 1.2 shows the code involved along with a new #define statement, which will be used in most of the classes in Grocery Dude to assist with debugging. When debug is set to 1, debug logging will be enabled for that class. Most NSLog commands will be wrapped in an if (debug == 1) statement, which will only work when debugging is enabled.

Listing 1.2   **CoreDataHelper.m: FILES**

```
#define debug 1

#pragma mark - FILES
NSString *storeFilename = @"Grocery-Dude.sqlite";
```

Update Grocery Dude as follows to add the FILES section:

1. Add the code from Listing 1.2 to the bottom of CoreDataHelper.m before @end.

Paths

To persist anything to disk, Core Data needs to know where in the file system persistent store files should be located. Three separate methods help provide this information. Listing 1.3 shows the first method, which is called applicationDocumentsDirectory and returns an NSString representing the path to the application's documents directory. You'll also notice the first use of an if (debug==1) statement wrapping a line of code that shows what method is running. This NSLog statement is useful for seeing the order of execution of methods in the application, which is great for debugging.

Listing 1.3   **CoreDataHelper.m: PATHS**

```
#pragma mark - PATHS
- (NSString *)applicationDocumentsDirectory {
if (debug==1) {
    NSLog(@"Running %@ '%@'", self.class,NSStringFromSelector(_cmd));
}
return [NSSearchPathForDirectoriesInDomains(NSDocumentDirectory, NSUserDomainMask,YES)
➥lastObject];
}
```

Update Grocery Dude as follows to add the PATHS section:

1. Add the code from Listing 1.3 to the bottom of CoreDataHelper.m before @end.

The next method, applicationStoresDirectory, appends a directory called Stores to the application's documents directory and then returns it in an NSURL. If the Stores directory doesn't exist, it is created as shown in Listing 1.4.

Listing 1.4   **CoreDataHelper.m: applicationStoresDirectory**

```
- (NSURL *)applicationStoresDirectory {
if (debug==1) {
    NSLog(@"Running %@ '%@'", self.class, NSStringFromSelector(_cmd));
}
```

```
NSURL *storesDirectory =
[[NSURL fileURLWithPath:[self applicationDocumentsDirectory]
                               URLByAppendingPathComponent:@"Stores"];

NSFileManager *fileManager = [NSFileManager defaultManager];
if (![fileManager fileExistsAtPath:[storesDirectory path]]) {
    NSError *error = nil;
    if ([fileManager createDirectoryAtURL:storesDirectory
            withIntermediateDirectories:YES
                            attributes:nil
                                error:&error]) {
        if (debug==1) {
            NSLog(@"Successfully created Stores directory");}
        }
        else {NSLog(@"FAILED to create Stores directory: %@", error);}
    }
    return storesDirectory;
}
```

Update Grocery Dude as follows to add to the PATHS section:

1. Add the code from Listing 1.4 to the bottom of CoreDataHelper.m before @end.

The last method, which is shown in Listing 1.5, simply appends the persistent store filename to the store's directory path. The end result is a full path to the persistent store file.

Listing 1.5   **CoreDataHelper.m: storeURL**

```
- (NSURL *)storeURL {
if (debug==1) {
    NSLog(@"Running %@ '%@'", self.class, NSStringFromSelector(_cmd));
}
return [[self applicationStoresDirectory]
            URLByAppendingPathComponent:storeFilename];
}
```

Update Grocery Dude as follows to add to the PATHS section:

1. Add the code from Listing 1.5 to the bottom of CoreDataHelper.m before @end.

Setup

With the files and paths ready to go, it's time to implement the three methods responsible for the initial setup of Core Data. Listing 1.6 shows the first method, called init, which runs automatically when an instance of CoreDataHelper is created.

Listing 1.6   **CoreDataHelper.m: SETUP**

```
#pragma mark - SETUP
- (id)init {
if (debug==1) {
    NSLog(@"Running %@ '%@'", self.class, NSStringFromSelector(_cmd));
}
    self = [super init];
    if (!self) {return nil;}

    _model = [NSManagedObjectModel mergedModelFromBundles:nil];
    _coordinator = [[NSPersistentStoreCoordinator alloc]
                            initWithManagedObjectModel:_model];
    _context = [[NSManagedObjectContext alloc]
                            initWithConcurrencyType:NSMainQueueConcurrencyType];
    [_context setPersistentStoreCoordinator:_coordinator];
    return self;
}
```

The _model instance variable points to a managed object model. The managed object model is initiated from all available data model files (object graphs) found in the main bundle by calling mergedModelFromBundles and passing nil. At the moment, there are no model files in the project; however, one will be added in Chapter 2. It is possible to pass an NSArray of NSBundles here in case you wanted to merge multiple models. Usually you won't need to worry about this.

> **Note**
>
> Another way to initialize a managed object model is to specify the exact model file to use. This takes over twice the amount of code, as opposed to just merging bundles. Here's how you would manually specify the model to use: _model = [[NSManagedObjectModel alloc] initWithContentsOfURL: [[NSBundle mainBundle] URLForResource:@"Model" withExtension:@"momd"]];.

The _coordinator instance variable points to a persistent store coordinator. It is initialized based on the _model pointer to the managed object model that has just been created. So far, the persistent store coordinator has no persistent store files because they will be added later by the setupCoreData method.

The _context instance variable points to a managed object context. It is initialized with a concurrency type that tells it to run on a "main thread" queue. You'll need a context on the main thread whenever you have a data-driven user interface. Once the context has been initialized, it is configured to use the existing _coordinator pointer to the persistent store coordinator. Chapter 8 will demonstrate how to use multiple managed object contexts, including a background (private queue) concurrency type. For now, the main thread context will do.

Update Grocery Dude as follows to add the SETUP section:

1. Add the code from Listing 1.6 to the bottom of CoreDataHelper.m before @end.

The next method required in the SETUP section is loadStore and is shown in Listing 1.7.

Listing 1.7   **CoreDataHelper.m: loadStore**

```
- (void)loadStore {
if (debug==1) {
NSLog(@"Running %@ '%@'", self.class, NSStringFromSelector(_cmd));
}
    if (_store) {return;} // Don't load store if it's already loaded
    NSError *error = nil;
    _store = [_coordinator addPersistentStoreWithType:NSSQLiteStoreType
                                        configuration:nil
                                                  URL:[self storeURL]  .
                                              options:nil error:&error];
    if (!_store) {NSLog(@"Failed to add store. Error: %@", error);abort();}
    else        {if (debug==1) {NSLog(@"Successfully added store: %@", _store);}}
}
```

The loadStore method is straightforward. Once a check for an existing _store has been performed, a pointer to a nil NSError instance is created as error. This is then used when setting the _store instance variable to capture any errors that occur during setup. If _store is nil after an attempt to set it up fails, an error is logged to the console along with the content of the error.

When the SQLite persistent store is added via addPersistentStoreWithType, a pointer to the persistent store is held in _store. The storeURL of the persistent store is the one returned by the methods created previously.

Update Grocery Dude as follows to add to the SETUP section:

1. Add the code from Listing 1.7 to the bottom of CoreDataHelper.m before @end.

Finally, it's time to create the setupCoreData method. With the other supporting methods in place, this is a simple task. Listing 1.8 shows the contents of this new method, which at this stage only calls loadStore. This method will be expanded later in the book as more functionality is added.

Listing 1.8   **CoreDataHelper.m: setupCoreData**

```
- (void)setupCoreData {
if (debug==1) {
    NSLog(@"Running %@ '%@'", self.class, NSStringFromSelector(_cmd));
}
    [self loadStore];
}
```

Update Grocery Dude as follows to add to the SETUP section:

1. Add the code from Listing 1.8 to the bottom of CoreDataHelper.m before @end.

Saving

The next puzzle piece is a method called whenever you would like to save changes from the _context to the _store. This is as easy as sending the context a save: message, as shown in Listing 1.9. This method will be placed in a new SAVING section.

Listing 1.9   **CoreDataHelper.m: SAVING**

```
#pragma mark - SAVING
- (void)saveContext {
if (debug==1) {
    NSLog(@"Running %@ '%@'", self.class, NSStringFromSelector(_cmd));
}
    if ([_context hasChanges]) {
        NSError *error = nil;
        if ([_context save:&error]) {
            NSLog(@"_context SAVED changes to persistent store");
        } else {
            NSLog(@"Failed to save _context: %@", error);
        }
    } else {
        NSLog(@"SKIPPED _context save, there are no changes!");
    }
}
```

Update Grocery Dude as follows to add the SAVING section:

1. Add the code from Listing 1.9 to the bottom of CoreDataHelper.m before @end.

The Core Data Helper is now ready to go! To use it, a new property is needed in the application delegate header. The CoreDataHelper class also needs to be imported into the application delegate header, so it knows about this new class. The bold code shown in Listing 1.10 highlights the changes required to the application delegate header.

Listing 1.10   **AppDelegate.h**

```
#import <UIKit/UIKit.h>
#import "CoreDataHelper.h"
@interface AppDelegate : UIResponder <UIApplicationDelegate>
@property (strong, nonatomic) UIWindow *window;
@property (nonatomic, strong, readonly) CoreDataHelper *coreDataHelper;
@end
```

Update Grocery Dude as follows to add `CoreDataHelper` to the application delegate:

1. Replace all code in `AppDelegate.h` with the code from Listing 1.10.

The next step is to update the application delegate implementation with a small method called cdh, which returns a non-nil `CoreDataHelper` instance. In addition, a `#define debug 1` statement needs to be added for debug purposes, as shown in Listing 1.11.

Listing 1.11   **AppDelegate.m: cdh**

```
#define debug 1

- (CoreDataHelper*)cdh {
if (debug==1) {
    NSLog(@"Running %@ '%@'", self.class, NSStringFromSelector(_cmd));
}
    if (!_coreDataHelper) {
        _coreDataHelper = [CoreDataHelper new];
        [_coreDataHelper setupCoreData];
    }
    return _coreDataHelper;
}
```

Update Grocery Dude as follows to add the cdh method to the application delegate:

1. Add the code from Listing 1.11 to `AppDelegate.m` on the line after `@implementation AppDelegate`.

The final step required is to ensure the context is saved each time the application enters the background or is terminated. This is an ideal time to save changes to disk because the user interface won't lag during save as it is hidden. Listing 1.12 shows the code involved in saving the context.

Listing 1.12   **AppDelegate.m: applicationDidEnterBackground**

```
- (void)applicationDidEnterBackground:(UIApplication *)application {
    [[self cdh] saveContext];
}
- (void)applicationWillTerminate:(UIApplication *)application {
    [[self cdh] saveContext];
}
```

Update Grocery Dude as follows to ensure the context is saved when the application enters the background or is terminated:

1. Add `[[self cdh] saveContext];` to the bottom of the applicationDidEnterBackground method in `AppDelegate.m`.

2. Add `[[self cdh] saveContext];` to the bottom of the `applicationWillTerminate` method in `AppDelegate.m`.

Run Grocery Dude on the iOS Simulator and examine the debug log window as you press the home button (**Shift+⌘+H** or **Hardware > Home**). The log is initially blank because Core Data is set up on demand using the `cdh` method of the application delegate. The first time Core Data is used is during the `save:` that's triggered when the application enters the background. As the application grows, the `cdh` method will be used earlier. Figure 1.5 shows the order of method execution once you press the home button.

```
▼  ▶  II  ⟳  ↥  ↧  ◀  | ▭ Grocery Dude
2013-07-01 07:20:06.654 Grocery Dude[61842:a0b] Running AppDelegate 'cdh'
2013-07-01 07:20:06.656 Grocery Dude[61842:a0b] Running CoreDataHelper 'init'
2013-07-01 07:20:06.657 Grocery Dude[61842:a0b] Running CoreDataHelper 'setupCoreData'
2013-07-01 07:20:06.657 Grocery Dude[61842:a0b] Running CoreDataHelper 'loadStore'
2013-07-01 07:20:06.657 Grocery Dude[61842:a0b] Running CoreDataHelper 'storeURL'
2013-07-01 07:20:06.658 Grocery Dude[61842:a0b] Running CoreDataHelper 'applicationStoresDirectory'
2013-07-01 07:20:06.658 Grocery Dude[61842:a0b] Running CoreDataHelper 'applicationDocumentsDirectory'
2013-07-01 07:20:06.668 Grocery Dude[61842:a0b] Successfully created Stores directory
2013-07-01 07:20:06.673 Grocery Dude[61842:a0b] Successfully added store: <NSSQLCore: 0xe973200> (URL: file:///Users/
Timbo/Library/Application%20Support/iPhone%20Simulator/7.0/Applications/4DBD86E3-BB1D-4D71-BEDD-47520E97F67B/Documents/
Stores/Grocery-Dude.sqlite)
2013-07-01 07:20:06.673 Grocery Dude[61842:a0b] Running CoreDataHelper 'saveContext'
2013-07-01 07:20:06.674 Grocery Dude[61842:a0b] SKIPPED _context save, there are no changes!
```

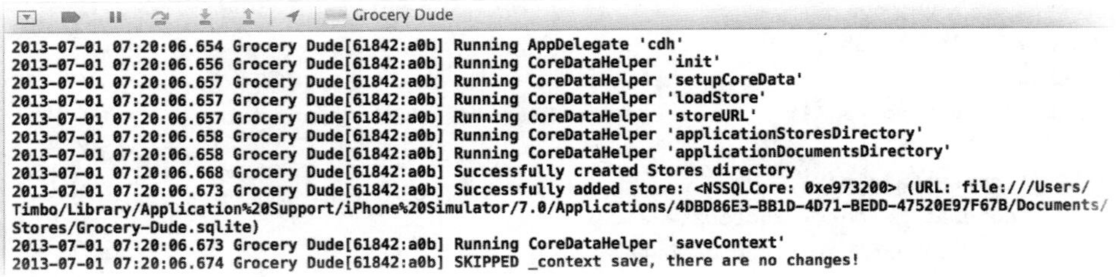

Figure 1.5   The debug log window showing order of execution

Summary

You've now been introduced to the key components of Core Data. The sample application Grocery Dude has been updated to include an SQLite persistent store, persistent store coordinator, managed object model, and managed object context. The data model has not been configured, so the application isn't very interesting yet. Chapter 2 is where the real fun begins with the introduction of data models. If you're still unclear on the role some parts of Core Data play, don't worry too much at this stage. As you come to use each component more, it should become easier to understand how they fit together.

Exercises

Why not build on what you've learned by experimenting?

1. Add the following code to the top of each method in the application delegate to assist with debugging:

```
if (debug==1) {
    NSLog(@"Running %@ '%@'", self.class, NSStringFromSelector(_cmd));
}
```

2. Examine the console log to compare the different locations persistent store files are saved to when running the application on a device versus running on the iOS Simulator. This is useful information when it comes time to open the persistent store for troubleshooting.

3. Change the persistent store type in the `loadStore` method of `CoreDataHelper.m` from `NSSQLStoreType` to `NSXMLStoreType` and try running the application. You won't be able to run the application because this store type is not available on iOS.

2

Managed Object Model Basics

The only source of knowledge is experience.

Albert Einstein

In Chapter 1, "Your First Core Data Application," the fundamental Core Data building blocks were added to the Grocery Dude sample application. You configured a persistent store, coordinator, model, and context; however, the object graph remained empty. This means that although all the ingredients are ready to make cookies, you're missing the cookie cutters! This chapter explains managed object model basics and takes you through the process of configuring an object graph for the sample application.

What Is a Managed Object Model?

A managed object model represents a data structure. The terms *data structure, schema, object graph, data model*, and *managed object model* may all be used interchangeably because they all mean more or less the same thing. If you were designing a new database without Core Data, you might configure a database schema and refer to it as a "data model." With Core Data, the focus is (managed) objects. Therefore, instead of calling the schema a data model, you may refer to it as a managed object model. That said, it's still perfectly appropriate to call it a data model, object graph, schema, or data structure, too!

> **Note**
>
> To continue building the sample application, you'll need to have added the previous chapter's code to Grocery Dude. Alternatively, you may download, unzip, and use the project up to this point from http://www.timroadley.com/LearningCoreData/GroceryDude-AfterChapter01.zip. Any time you start using an Xcode project from a ZIP file, it's good practice to click **Product** > **Clean**. This practice ensures there's no residual cache from previous projects using the same name.

Adding a Managed Object Model

In Chapter 1, you initialized a managed object model in `CoreDataHelper.m` using the `mergedModelFromBundles` method. The issue now, however, is that there are actually no models to merge! This renders Core Data pretty useless, so it's about time to create a model file. The model file will primarily contain an object graph representing the application's data structure and some other bits and pieces that will make your life easier, which will be explained later on.

Update Grocery Dude as follows to add a data model file:

1. Right-click the existing **Grocery Dude** group and then select **New Group**.

2. Set the new group name to **Data Model**.

3. Select the **Data Model** group.

4. Click **File > New > File...**.

5. Select **iOS > Core Data > Data Model** and then click **Next**.

6. Ensure the Grocery Dude target is selected, leave the default filename as **Model**, and then click **Create**.

7. Select **Model.xcdatamodeld**, as shown in Figure 2.1.

Figure 2.1   The Xcode Data Model Designer

Figure 2.1 shows the Xcode Data Model Designer, which is used to configure a data model. At first glance, some items you see in the model designer may be alien to you and raise a few questions. Entities and Fetch Requests are discussed in this chapter. Configurations are discussed in Chapter 15, "Taming iCloud."

Entities

A managed object model is made up of a collection of entity description objects called **entities**. You can think of an entity as an individual cookie cutter used to create managed objects. Once you have managed objects, you can work with data natively in code.

A managed object model can have one or more entities, which varies between applications. Before you can produce managed objects, you'll first need to design each cookie cutter (entity) appropriately. Designing an entity is similar to traditional database table design.

When designing a database table, you would do the following:

- Configure a table name.
- Configure fields and set a data type for each one.

When designing an entity, you do this:

- Configure an entity name.
- Configure attributes and set a data type for each one.
- Configure an NSManagedObject subclass based on the entity (optional).

Whereas a table in a database has fields, an entity has attributes. An attribute must have a data type specified (for example, a string or integer). When it comes time to produce a managed object from an entity, you'll usually create an NSManagedObject subclass based on the entity; however, this is not mandatory. Using an NSManagedObject subclass does have some advantages, though, such as enabling dot notation for your managed objects, which makes your code easier to read. From NSManagedObject or an NSManagedObject subclass, you create instances to begin working with data as managed objects. In database terms, managed object instances are like a row in a database table. The name of the entity and the name of the NSManagedObject subclass you create from it are usually the same. Whatever attributes you configure in an entity will become properties of the managed objects created from them. Figure 2.2 shows how entities are used to map between a persistent store's database and managed objects.

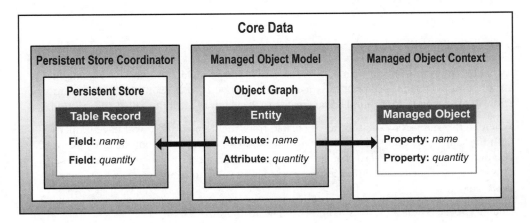

Figure 2.2   Core Data entity mapping

Entities are the foundation of a managed object model because they are used to logically group data that belongs together. One of the most important things to think about when designing a managed object model is the name you give each entity. The name you choose for an entity needs to describe (in a word or two) the data that the entity represents. For Grocery Dude, there's a requirement to put things on a list. When you're out shopping, you may want to put apples and oranges on the list. With this in mind, perhaps "fruit" is a good name for the entity representing things you might put on a list.

When you configure an entity, be careful to use a name that is generic enough to be flexible, yet specific enough that it's obvious what it represents. Sometimes it's easy to work out; sometimes it's a delicate balancing act that forces you to think hard about your application's purpose—now and in future releases. A shopping list is prone to containing more than just fruit, so perhaps "Item" is a better name for the entity representing things that could be put on a shopping list.

Update Grocery Dude as follows to add an Item entity:

1. Select **Model.xcdatamodeld**.

2. Click **Add Entity**.

3. Rename the new entity to **Item**.

Attributes

An **attribute** is a property of an entity. In the sample application, the Item entity represents things you can put on a shopping list. To work out what attributes are appropriate for the Item entity, you should think about things all shopping list items have in common. As a reasonable starting point, you might come up with a list similar to this:

- Item **name**
- Item **quantity**

Attribute names must begin with a lowercase letter. They should also not have a name that is already in use by NSObject or NSManagedObject methods. Xcode won't let you break this rule and will warn you if, for example, you create an illegal entity attribute called "description."

When an NSManagedObject subclass is created from the Item entity, it will have properties with the same name as the equivalent entity attributes. As with other objects in Objective-C, you may refer to class properties of an NSManagedObject subclass using dot notation. This will make code easier to read as you get property values directly via item.name and item.quantity.

Update Grocery Dude as follows to add two new attributes:

1. Add a **name** and **quantity** attribute to the **Item** entity by clicking **Add Attribute** while the **Item** entity is selected. The expected result is shown in Figure 2.3.

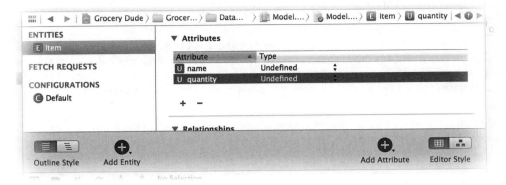

Figure 2.3   Attributes with undefined types

When you add an attribute to an entity, you must specify the *type* of data it represents. The default attribute type is **Undefined**. The data type you choose for each attribute will vary and will require some forward thinking. There are several attribute types to choose from and as an Objective-C programmer, you may already be familiar with some of them.

Integer 16/32/64

Each of these similar attribute data types represents a whole number, without a decimal point. The only difference between them is how big or small that number can be. Core Data uses *signed* integers, so their range starts in the negative instead of with zero:

- **Integer 16** ranges from –32768 to 32767
- **Integer 32** ranges from –2147483648 to 2147483647
- **Integer 64** ranges from –9223372036854775808 to 9223372036854775807

The bigger a number, the more memory is needed to hold it. When choosing between the three options for integers, you need to think about the lowest and highest value that may ever be needed by this attribute. If you're not quite sure which size to choose, it's generally a safe bet to go with Integer 32. Just beware that if you get it wrong and it turns out that you need a bigger number, you will need to upgrade the attribute to Integer 64. This type of change requires an upgrade to the managed object model, which is discussed in Chapter 3, "Managed Object Model Migration."

Integers use the base-2 number system, better known as binary. Calculations using integers are faster than those with floating-point numbers. This is because there's no need to handle the remainder left over after a calculation. For example, if you divide 10 by 3, then the result is 3 and the remainder of 1 is lost. The term for this is **low precision**. If you choose to use integers to represent money, it is highly recommended that 1 = 1 cent. This way, there are no rounding errors if you need to do financial calculations.

> **Note**
>
> The minimum and maximum values for standard integers can be seen in `stdint.h`. Type `INT32_MAX` in any class file in Xcode, right-click it, then select **Jump to Definition**. You will then see various definitions for minimum and maximum integers. You may notice unsigned integers have higher maximums because they don't go below zero. Core Data only uses signed integers, which means they can be positive or negative numbers at the cost of a lower maximum.

When an `NSManagedObject` subclass is created from an entity containing an Integer 16, Integer 32, or Integer 64 attribute, the resulting property is an `NSNumber`.

Float and Double

These two similar attribute data types can be thought of as non-integers with a decimal point. They are both used to represent real numbers; however, they have some limitations in doing so. Floats and doubles use the base-2 (binary) number system, which is a CPU native number system prone to rounding errors. Consider the fraction 1/5. In decimal this can be represented exactly as 0.2. In binary it can only ever be represented by an approximation. The more digits you have after the decimal point, the higher the precision and more accurate the approximation is. Higher precision comes at the cost of more memory to store that precision.

Compared to a float, a double is just that—double the amount of bits. A float takes 32 bits to store and a double takes 64 bits. They are both stored in scientific notation. That is, there is a number (called a mantissa) and an exponent (power of) that are put together to form a floating-point number. Having 64 bits means a double has a larger range of values and higher precision than a float.

The biggest float on iOS is 340282346638528859811704183484516925440.000000. Floats and doubles are also stored with a sign bit, so this means that the lowest possible float on iOS is –340282346638528859811704183484516925440.000000. The biggest double is much larger than the biggest float. At the end of this chapter, the exercises will provide code to display the minimum and maximum values for each of the numerical data types.

When deciding between float and double, you should consider the characteristics of the attribute you are configuring. What are the smallest and largest values you need? Do you really need more than the ~7 digits of precision float offers? If you don't, then you should stick with floats on iOS because they're better matched to the underlying processor prior to the 64-bit iPhone 5S. Although it may seem inconsequential for a handful of properties to all be doubles, be aware that databases will amplify the storage requirements because they potentially have thousands of rows. Given the power and capacity of modern devices these days, you could get away with using a double for most scenarios. On the other hand, if you need to increase the speed of floating-point calculations and precision isn't too critical, a float may be more appropriate. You shouldn't use a float or double to represent dollars and cents for financial calculations because rounding errors might cause money to go missing!

When an NSManagedObject subclass is created from an entity containing either a float or double attribute, the resulting property is an NSNumber.

Decimal

Decimal is the recommended attribute data type for working with money and other scenarios where base-10 arithmetic is appropriate. Base-10 is not a CPU native number system like base-2 (binary). This means substantial processor overhead is incurred when working with decimals. Much like floats and doubles, decimals are made up of an integer mantissa, exponent, and sign. At the cost of extra memory and processing time, decimal provides excellent calculation accuracy. With this system, numbers such as 0.1 can be represented exactly. In essence, the decimal type stores this example as $1 / 10$ ^ 1.

The largest decimal isn't as big as the largest double; however, the precision is much higher and in some cases perfect. At the end of this chapter, the exercises will provide code to display an example of the precision achievable by each of the numerical data types.

When an NSManagedObject subclass is created from an entity containing a decimal attribute, the resulting property is an NSDecimalNumber. When you perform calculations with an NSDecimalNumber, it is imperative you only use its built-in methods to ensure you retain the precision.

String

The String attribute data type is used to store an array of characters, or plain old text. Being an Objective-C programmer, odds are you're quite familiar with strings already. When an NSManagedObject subclass is created from an entity containing a string attribute, the resulting property is an NSString.

Boolean

The Boolean attribute data type is used to store a yes or no value. When an NSManagedObject subclass is created from an entity containing a Boolean attribute, the resulting property is an NSNumber. To get the Boolean value back out of the NSNumber, simply send a boolValue message to the NSNumber instance. When setting a Boolean value in an NSNumber, use the numberWithBool method.

Date

The Date attribute data type is self-explanatory. It is used to store a date and time. When an NSManagedObject subclass is created from an entity containing a date attribute, the resulting property is an NSDate.

Binary Data

If you need to store photos, audio, or some other contiguous BLOB of zeros and ones, you should use the Binary Data attribute type. When an `NSManagedObject` subclass is created from an entity containing a binary data attribute, the resulting property type is `NSData`. Depending on the data you're storing, the approach in converting your data to and from `NSData` will differ. One common scenario is storing photos. To store a photo, you convert a `UIImage` to `NSData` using `UIImagePNGRepresentation()` or `UIImageJPEGRepresentation()`. To retrieve a photo, you convert the `NSData` to `UIImage` using the `UIImage` class method `imageWithData`. Binary Data is a good choice for large files because they can be seamlessly stored outside the database using the **Allows External Storage** attribute setting. With this setting enabled, Core Data will decide whether it is more efficient to store the file inside or outside of the database.

Transformable

The Transformable attribute data type is used to store an Objective-C object. This attribute type is a flexible option that allows you to store an instance of any class. An example of a transformable attribute is an instance of `UIColor`. When an `NSManagedObject` subclass is created from an entity containing a transformable attribute, the resulting property type is `id`. For the `id` object to make it into the store (and back again), you'll need to use an instance of `NSValueTransformer` or an instance of a subclass of `NSValueTransformer`. This class helps transparently convert the attribute to `NSData` and back again. This is a reasonably simple process, especially when the class you want to store implements the `NSCoding` protocol. If it does, the system provides a default transformer that already knows how to archive and un-archive specific objects.

Update Grocery Dude as follows to configure its attributes:

1. Set the **name** attribute type to **String**.

2. Set the **quantity** attribute type to **Float**.

3. Add an attribute called **photoData** to the **Item** entity and set its type to **Binary Data**. This attribute will store the image data of an item's photo. (Note: The **Allows External Storage** setting won't be enabled until later in the book.)

4. Add an attribute called **listed** to the **Item** entity and set its type to **Boolean**. This attribute will be used to indicate whether an item is on the shopping list.

5. Add an attribute called **collected** to the **Item** entity and set its type to **Boolean**. This attribute will be used to indicate whether an item has been collected and therefore ticked off the shopping list.

The data model should now match Figure 2.4, as each attribute now has a data type configured.

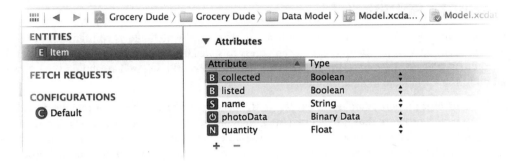

Figure 2.4   Grocery Dude's data model in Table editor style

In preparation for an increasingly complicated data model, it is good to be aware you can switch to a graphical view. To change to graph editor mode, simply toggle the **Editor Style** button shown in the middle at the bottom of Figure 2.5. The left side of Figure 2.5 shows what the editor looks like in Graph style.

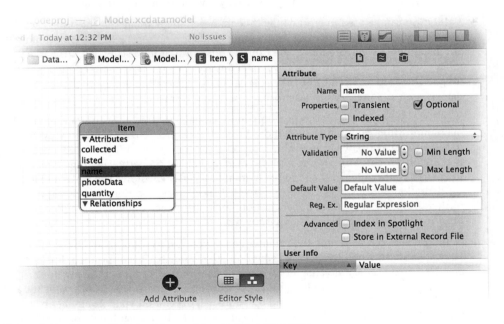

Figure 2.5   Grocery Dude's data model in Graph editor style

Attribute Settings

On the right of Figure 2.5 the Data Model Inspector is shown, which allows configuration of attribute settings beyond their type. You can access this area by pressing **Option+⌘+3** when an attribute is selected. The options presented vary depending on the selected attribute's type. Not all options are available to all attributes:

- **Transient** properties are never written to the persistent store. Although it may seem odd to have a property that is never persisted, there are scenarios where you need a property only in the managed object context. For example, you may wish to calculate a value on the fly and then store the result in a transient property. Being in a context allows those properties to benefit from features such as undo and redo.

- **Optional** properties aren't required to have a value. All properties are originally created as optional. When a property is not optional, you won't be able to save the managed object back to the store until the non-optional properties have a valid value.

- **Indexed** properties are optimized for search efficiency at the cost of additional storage space in the underlying persistent store. This additional space required for the index will range in size depending on how much data needs indexing. If you're not going to search on a particular attribute, you can save space by not indexing the attribute.

- **Validation** can be used to ensure illogical data never enters the persistent store. Each of the numerical attribute types has the same validation options, which are minimum and maximum values. Similarly, you can set constraints around string lengths and date ranges, too. It is perfectly fine to have invalid values in a managed object context; as long as these are resolved before `save:` is called. It's generally a good practice to validate data as soon as a user tries to take focus off an input element, such as a `UITextfield`.

- **Reg. Ex.** is short for **Regular Expression** and goes beyond validating a minimum or maximum string length. Although it can be used to enforce length, it is primarily used to test that an attribute's string value matches a certain pattern. When Reg Ex validation is configured for an attribute, any related managed object property values must match the pattern; otherwise, they cannot be written to a persistent store. The pattern match configuration options must conform to the ICU Reg Ex specification. You can find further information about this specification, including valid configuration options, at http://userguide.icu-project.org/strings/regexp.

- **Default** values can be set for all attributes types except transformable and binary data. They are a starting point value used when no other value has been specified. It is best practice to have a default value set on numerical attributes because of the way the backend SQLite database handles null values. Setting an appropriate default value for a string attribute will be situational and therefore will depend on your requirements. For the date attribute type, you unfortunately cannot configure a default date of "now" in the model editor.

- **Allows External Storage** is used to permit large binary data attribute values to be stored outside the persistent store. It is recommended that you enable this option when storing large media such as photos, audio, or video. Core Data will automatically store attribute values over 1MB outside an SQLite persistent store when this option is enabled. This option has no effect when the underlying persistent store is XML (remember, this type of store isn't supported on iOS).

- **Index in Spotlight** doesn't do anything for an iOS application. It is used to integrate a Core Data–based Mac application with Spotlight. Spotlight is the search facility available via the magnifying glass in the top-right corner of the screen on a Mac. When a Mac application's Core Data attribute is indexed in Spotlight, its values are able to appear in the results of a Spotlight search. When performing the search index, Spotlight looks for the hidden, zero-length files Core Data created that represent records from the persistent store. As indexed attribute values change in the persistent store, the equivalent files outside the store are updated automatically.

- **Store in External Record File** duplicates data from the persistent store into an XML representation outside the store. When used in conjunction with Index in Spotlight, this setting causes the index files created for Spotlight to be populated with values. It's not recommended that you use this option unless you have a specific need to, such as for debugging purposes. If you choose to use external records to feed data to another application, note that the directory structure containing the records is subject to change.

- **Name** properties (of transformable attributes) are used to specify the name of the specific `NSValueTransformer` subclass that knows how to convert from any class into `NSData` and back again.

Update Grocery Dude as follows to configure indexing and defaults:

1. Set the **name** attribute to **Indexed**.
2. Set the **name** attribute **Default Value** to **New Item**.
3. Set the **quantity** attribute **Default Value** to **1**.
4. Set the **listed** attribute **Default Value** to **YES**. This will ensure newly created items show up on the shopping list.
5. Set the **collected** attribute **Default Value** to **NO**. This will ensure newly created items aren't ticked off the shopping list as soon as they're created.

Subclassing `NSManagedObject`

With a basic managed object model in place, it's time to create an `NSManagedObject` subclass based on the Item entity. These subclass files will let you work with data objects directly in code using dot notation, without any SQL queries. Whenever the model is updated in the future, you will need to regenerate these files again using the procedure you're about to follow. Although it is possible to add methods to these generated files, you should avoid doing so directly because changes you've made will be lost if they're ever regenerated. If you need to add custom methods, you're better off subclassing or creating a category for the generated files.

Update Grocery Dude as follows to generate NSManagedObject subclass files:

1. Select the **Item** entity.

2. Click **Editor > Create NSManagedObject Subclass....**

3. Ensure the **Model** is selected and then click **Next.**

4. Ensure the **Item** entity is selected and then click **Next.**

5. Ensure the **Grocery Dude target** is ticked.

6. Ensure that **Use scalar properties for primitive data types** is not ticked.

7. Ensure the files will be saved into the Grocery Dude project directory and then click **Create.**

There will now be two new files in the Xcode project: Item.h and Item.m. These files were generated based on the Item entity, as is shown in Listing 2.1. The order the properties are listed in may vary.

Listing 2.1   **Item.h**

```
#import <Foundation/Foundation.h>
#import <CoreData/CoreData.h>

@interface Item : NSManagedObject

@property (nonatomic, retain) NSString * name;
@property (nonatomic, retain) NSNumber * listed;
@property (nonatomic, retain) NSNumber * quantity;
@property (nonatomic, retain) NSNumber * collected;
@property (nonatomic, retain) NSData * photoData;

@end
```

Notice the slight differences between the entity attribute types and the resulting class property types. Here's a summary of how entity attributes translate to managed object properties:

- A Date attribute becomes an NSDate property.

- A String attribute becomes an NSString property.

- A Decimal attribute becomes an NSDecimalNumber property and all other numerical data types become an NSNumber property.

- A Binary Data attribute becomes an NSData property.

- A Transformable attribute becomes an id property.

When you examine the contents of `Item.m`, notice its implementation just lists each property as `@dynamic`. This is Core Data's way of indicating that it has dynamically generated the required methods to allow getting and setting values, so you don't have to.

Scalar Properties for Primitive Data Types

When you created an `NSManagedObject` subclass for the Item entity, you came across the option **Use scalar properties for primitive data types**. This option allows the resulting `NSManagedObject` subclass to use object properties only when it has no other recourse. Here's a summary of how entity attributes translate to managed object properties when this option is selected:

- A Date attribute becomes an `NSTimeInterval`.

- A Double attribute becomes a `double`.

- A Float attribute becomes a `float`.

- An Integer 16/32/64 attribute becomes an `int16_t`, `int32_t`, or `int64_t`, respectively.

- A Boolean attribute becomes a `BOOL`.

This option has no effect on String, Decimal, Binary Data, or Transformable attributes, so their resulting property will still be an object pointer. Using scalar properties for primitive data types generates different "getter" methods in the `NSMangedObject` subclass files, so you don't have to unbox the scalar values before using them in code.

Snippet Demo Method

Throughout this book there's code that demonstrates a point and yet isn't required in the final application. Listing 2.2 shows a new `demo` method along with an updated `applicationDidBecomeActive` method that calls `demo` after ensuring Core Data is ready with `[self cdh]`.

Listing 2.2 **AppDelegate.m: demo**

```
- (void)demo {
    if (debug==1) {
        NSLog(@"Running %@ '%@'", self.class, NSStringFromSelector(_cmd));
    }
}
- (void)applicationDidBecomeActive:(UIApplication *)application
{
    if (debug==1) {
        NSLog(@"Running %@ '%@'", self.class, NSStringFromSelector(_cmd));
    }
```

```
    [self cdh];
    [self demo];
}
```

Update Grocery Dude as follows to implement the `demo` method:

1. Add the `demo` method from Listing 2.2 to the top of `AppDelegate.m` on the line after `#define debug 1`.

2. Replace the `applicationDidBecomeActive` method of `AppDelegate.m` with the `applicationDidBecomeActive` method from Listing 2.2.

Creating a Managed Object

Everything is now in place to create some new managed objects. New objects are based off the `NSEntityDescription` of a particular entity, specified by name. In addition to specifying the entity to base an object on, you'll also need to provide a pointer to a managed object context where the new managed object will go. In the application delegate, access to an appropriate context is achieved via the `context` property of `[self cdh]` or `_coreDataHelper`.

The code in Listing 2.3 demonstrates how to insert a new managed object based on an entity into a context. Inserting a new managed object is as simple as calling the `insertNewObjectForEntityForName` method of the `NSEntityDescription` class and then passing it an appropriate entity name and context pointer.

Once a new Item-based managed object is created, you can then manipulate its values directly in code. The `NSLog` command at the end of Listing 2.3 demonstrates this when `newItem.name` is passed in as a string variable. The dot notation shown is a particularly clean way of working with objects because it makes your code easier to read.

Listing 2.3 **AppDelegate.m: demo (Inserting)**

```
NSArray *newItemNames =
[NSArray arrayWithObjects:
 @"Apples", @"Milk", @"Bread", @"Cheese", @"Sausages", @"Butter",
 @"Orange Juice", @"Cereal", @"Coffee", @"Eggs", @"Tomatoes", @"Fish",
 nil];

for (NSString *newItemName in newItemNames) {
    Item *newItem =
    [NSEntityDescription insertNewObjectForEntityForName:@"Item"
                         inManagedObjectContext:_coreDataHelper.context];
    newItem.name = newItemName;
    NSLog(@"Inserted New Managed Object for '%@'", newItem.name);
}
```

Update Grocery Dude as follows to practice inserting managed objects:

1. Add `#import "Item.h"` to the top of `AppDelegate.m`.

2. Add the code from Listing 2.3 to the bottom of the `demo` method of `AppDelegate.m`.

Run the application, and you should see managed object names listed in the console. If you can, give yourself a pat on the back because you're successfully using Core Data! Figure 2.6 shows the expected result.

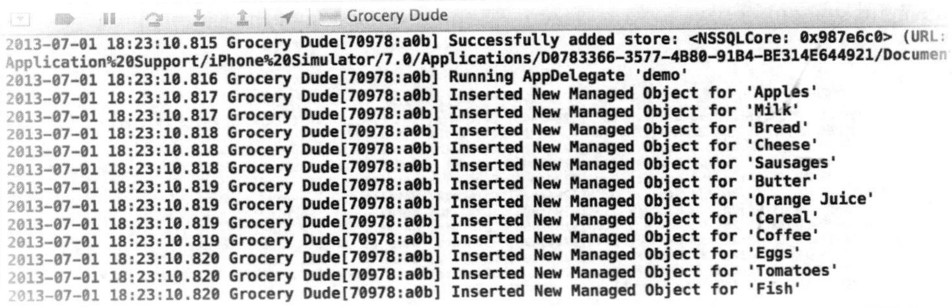

```
2013-07-01 18:23:10.815 Grocery Dude[70978:a0b] Successfully added store: <NSSQLCore: 0x987e6c0> (URL:
Application%20Support/iPhone%20Simulator/7.0/Applications/D0783366-3577-4B80-91B4-BE314E644921/Documen
2013-07-01 18:23:10.816 Grocery Dude[70978:a0b] Running AppDelegate 'demo'
2013-07-01 18:23:10.817 Grocery Dude[70978:a0b] Inserted New Managed Object for 'Apples'
2013-07-01 18:23:10.817 Grocery Dude[70978:a0b] Inserted New Managed Object for 'Milk'
2013-07-01 18:23:10.818 Grocery Dude[70978:a0b] Inserted New Managed Object for 'Bread'
2013-07-01 18:23:10.818 Grocery Dude[70978:a0b] Inserted New Managed Object for 'Cheese'
2013-07-01 18:23:10.818 Grocery Dude[70978:a0b] Inserted New Managed Object for 'Sausages'
2013-07-01 18:23:10.819 Grocery Dude[70978:a0b] Inserted New Managed Object for 'Butter'
2013-07-01 18:23:10.819 Grocery Dude[70978:a0b] Inserted New Managed Object for 'Orange Juice'
2013-07-01 18:23:10.819 Grocery Dude[70978:a0b] Inserted New Managed Object for 'Cereal'
2013-07-01 18:23:10.819 Grocery Dude[70978:a0b] Inserted New Managed Object for 'Coffee'
2013-07-01 18:23:10.820 Grocery Dude[70978:a0b] Inserted New Managed Object for 'Eggs'
2013-07-01 18:23:10.820 Grocery Dude[70978:a0b] Inserted New Managed Object for 'Tomatoes'
2013-07-01 18:23:10.820 Grocery Dude[70978:a0b] Inserted New Managed Object for 'Fish'
```

Figure 2.6   Inserting managed objects

> **Note**
>
> If you've been launching the project between adding each attribute, you may have run up against an error stating "The model used to open the store is incompatible with the one used to create the store." If you get this error, you'll need to delete the application and re-run it to install a fresh copy. If that doesn't fix it, you should also click **Product** > **Clean**. Graceful model upgrades are discussed and implemented in Chapter 3.

Backend SQL Visibility

At face value, examining the console logs for Core Data results is rather underwhelming. How do you know what's really going on under the covers? What is Core Data actually doing to get your data into the persistent store? Is it doing its job properly? What SQL queries are being generated to provide the seamless Core Data experience? Are duplicate objects being inserted every time you run the app in the simulator?

These questions can be answered with an extremely verbose debug option that provides plenty of information regarding what's going on under the hood. The debug option will expose the auto-generated SQL queries and give some great insight to the workings of Core Data.

Update Grocery Dude as follows to enable SQL Debug mode:

1. Click **Product** > **Scheme** > **Edit Scheme....**

2. Ensure **Run Grocery Dude** and the **Arguments** tab is selected.

3. Add a new argument by clicking + in the **Arguments Passed On Launch** section.

4. Enter `-com.apple.CoreData.SQLDebug 3` as a new argument and then click **OK**.

Now that you've enabled SQL Debug mode level 3, run the application again. Press the home button (**Shift+⌘+H** or **Hardware** > **Home**) and reexamine the logs. Look at all those INSERT statements you didn't have to write! Figure 2.7 shows a fraction of the expected results.

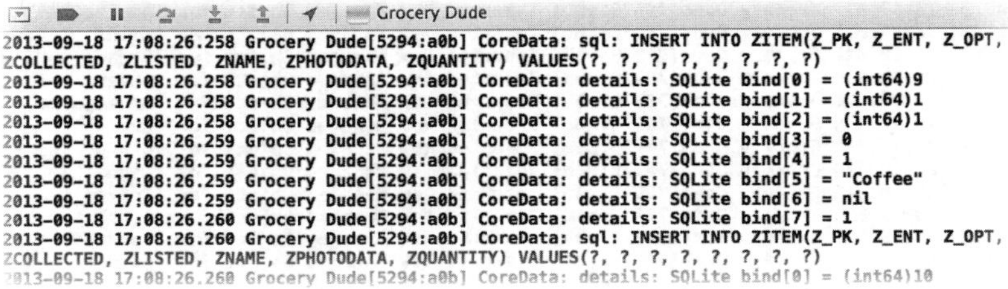

```
2013-09-18 17:08:26.258 Grocery Dude[5294:a0b] CoreData: sql: INSERT INTO ZITEM(Z_PK, Z_ENT, Z_OPT,
ZCOLLECTED, ZLISTED, ZNAME, ZPHOTODATA, ZQUANTITY) VALUES(?, ?, ?, ?, ?, ?, ?, ?)
2013-09-18 17:08:26.258 Grocery Dude[5294:a0b] CoreData: details: SQLite bind[0] = (int64)9
2013-09-18 17:08:26.258 Grocery Dude[5294:a0b] CoreData: details: SQLite bind[1] = (int64)1
2013-09-18 17:08:26.258 Grocery Dude[5294:a0b] CoreData: details: SQLite bind[2] = (int64)1
2013-09-18 17:08:26.259 Grocery Dude[5294:a0b] CoreData: details: SQLite bind[3] = 0
2013-09-18 17:08:26.259 Grocery Dude[5294:a0b] CoreData: details: SQLite bind[4] = 1
2013-09-18 17:08:26.259 Grocery Dude[5294:a0b] CoreData: details: SQLite bind[5] = "Coffee"
2013-09-18 17:08:26.259 Grocery Dude[5294:a0b] CoreData: details: SQLite bind[6] = nil
2013-09-18 17:08:26.260 Grocery Dude[5294:a0b] CoreData: details: SQLite bind[7] = 1
2013-09-18 17:08:26.260 Grocery Dude[5294:a0b] CoreData: sql: INSERT INTO ZITEM(Z_PK, Z_ENT, Z_OPT,
ZCOLLECTED, ZLISTED, ZNAME, ZPHOTODATA, ZQUANTITY) VALUES(?, ?, ?, ?, ?, ?, ?, ?)
2013-09-18 17:08:26.260 Grocery Dude[5294:a0b] CoreData: details: SQLite bind[0] = (int64)10
```

Figure 2.7   Core Data–generated SQL queries

Each of the SQLite binds shown in Figure 2.7 is a variable used to form an INSERT statement. The purpose of the statement is to insert managed object property values into a row of the ZITEM table found in the persistent store. The ZITEM table is associated with the Item entity. You can tell which entity attributes relate to what database fields by their name. The Z prefix is just a Core Data standard naming convention.

To verify managed objects are being persisted to an SQLite persistent store, you can actually look inside using a third-party utility. Be aware that altering a database directly isn't recommended. Figure 2.8 shows where you can find the iOS Simulator working directory containing Grocery-Dude.sqlite. The Library directory is hidden, so you may have to right-click **Finder**, select **Go to Folder**, and then type the directory name in manually. The exact location (with a substituted username, of course) is **/Users/*Username*/Library/Application Support/iPhone Simulator/**. The directory name under **Applications** will vary because it is a randomly generated GUID.

Alongside Grocery-Dude.sqlite are two accompanying files ending with -wal and -shm. These are the result of a new default database journaling mode introduced in iOS 7. This journaling mode is discussed in further detail in Chapter 8, "Preloading Data." For the time being, this journaling mode needs to be disabled so you can examine the contents of Grocery-Dude. sqlite. Disabling the default journaling mode requires that a new option be passed when adding the persistent store.

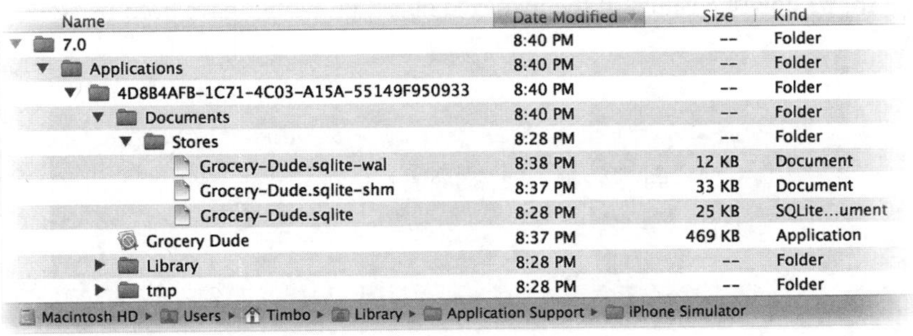

Name	Date Modified	Size	Kind
▼ 🖿 7.0	8:40 PM	--	Folder
▼ 🖿 Applications	8:40 PM	--	Folder
▼ 🖿 4D8B4AFB-1C71-4C03-A15A-55149F950933	8:40 PM	--	Folder
▼ 🖿 Documents	8:40 PM	--	Folder
▼ 🖿 Stores	8:28 PM	--	Folder
🖹 Grocery-Dude.sqlite-wal	8:38 PM	12 KB	Document
🖹 Grocery-Dude.sqlite-shm	8:37 PM	33 KB	Document
🖹 Grocery-Dude.sqlite	8:28 PM	25 KB	SQLite...ument
🔍 Grocery Dude	8:37 PM	469 KB	Application
▶ 🖿 Library	8:28 PM	--	Folder
▶ 🖿 tmp	8:28 PM	--	Folder

🖥 Macintosh HD ▶ 🖿 Users ▶ 🏠 Timbo ▶ 🖿 Library ▶ 🖿 Application Support ▶ 🖿 iPhone Simulator

Figure 2.8   The iOS Simulator's Grocery Dude SQLite database

Update Grocery Dude as follows to disable the default journaling mode:

1. Add the following code to the `loadStore` method of `CoreDataHelper.m` on the line before `NSError *error = nil`:

```
NSDictionary *options =
@{NSSQLitePragmasOption: @{@"journal_mode": @"DELETE"}};
```

2. Replace `options:nil` with `options:options` in the `addPersistentStoreWithType` call found in the `loadStore` method of `CoreDataHelper.m`.

3. Run the application again and the `-wal` file should disappear, which means that all the data will now be located in `Grocery-Dude.sqlite`. The `-shm` file can be deleted or ignored.

To open an SQLite database file, you can use one of many freely available SQLite database browser utilities found by searching Google. There's a good one on Sourceforge called **SQLite Database Browser** you may wish to try, so take a moment now to download and install it. This application isn't signed, so you will need to "Allow applications downloaded from Anywhere" in **System Preferences > Security & Privacy > General**. If you're not comfortable allowing this, search the Mac App Store for **extension:sqlite** to find another suitable signed application that can open `.sqlite` files.

Even though browsing the contents of a database is great for debugging purposes, you should not code your application to rely on the internal, private schema of a Core Data–managed database because Apple could change it without notice.

> **Note**
>
> Given that the Library folder is hidden, it's easier opening `Grocery-Dude.sqlite` by right-clicking it, selecting **Open With**, and then selecting **SQLite Database Browser**. Be careful not to have the SQLite file already open with the database browser while Xcode is running Grocery Dude. If you do, the application may time out when attempting to open the database.

Figure 2.9 shows how the values of the managed object properties have been persisted to the store.

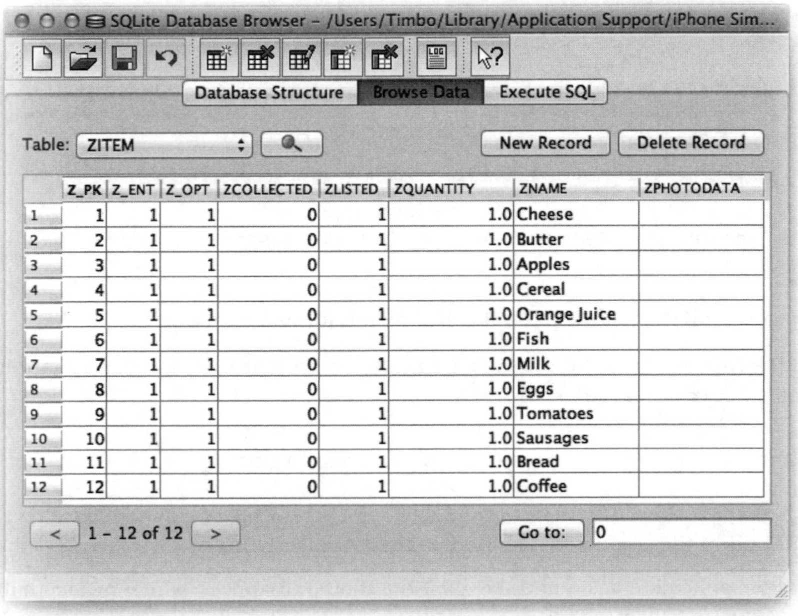

Figure 2.9   Browsing the Grocery Dude SQLite persistent store

If you have duplicate entries, they are a result of the context being saved more than once. At the moment, the only time a context is saved is when the home button is pressed. This, alongside the `demo` method inserting new objects every time the application is launched, can cause duplication. Don't worry if you have duplicates; you'll soon be shown how to delete managed objects.

Update Grocery Dude as follows to avoid further data duplication:

1. Remove everything from within the `demo` method of `AppDelegate.m` except the `NSLog` code.

Fetching Managed Objects

To work with existing data from a managed object context, you'll first need to fetch it. If the data isn't already in a context when fetched, it will be retrieved from the underlying persistent store transparently. To fetch, you'll need an instance of `NSFetchRequest`, which will return an

`NSArray` of managed objects. When the fetch is executed, every managed object for the specified entity will be returned in the resulting array. In SQL database terms, a fetch is similar to a `SELECT` statement. The code involved is shown in Listing 2.4.

Listing 2.4 `AppDelegate.m`: demo **(Fetch Request)**

```
NSFetchRequest *request =
[NSFetchRequest fetchRequestWithEntityName:@"Item"];
[_coreDataHelper.context executeFetchRequest:request error:nil];
```

Update Grocery Dude as follows to fetch all the Item entity instances:

1. Add the code from Listing 2.4 to the `demo` method of `AppDelegate.m`.

Run the application to examine the logs and you'll see a dozen similar lines showing each managed object that has been retrieved from the database. This number may vary depending on whether you have any duplicated data. Figure 2.10 shows the expected result.

```
                       Grocery Dude
2013-07-01 20:41:34.465 Grocery Dude[74177:a0b] CoreData: annotation: sql connection fetch time: 0.0004s
2013-07-01 20:41:34.466 Grocery Dude[74177:a0b] CoreData: annotation: fetch using NSSQLiteStatement <0xa04eee0> on entity 'Item' with
sql text 'SELECT 0, t0.Z_PK, t0.Z_OPT, t0.ZCOLLECTED, t0.ZLISTED, t0.ZNAME, t0.ZPHOTODATA, t0.ZQUANTITY FROM ZITEM t0 ' returned 12
rows with values: (
    "<Item: 0x8b3c950> (entity: Item; id: 0x8b3a470 <x-coredata://01BC77D7-EE27-45B0-A70A-ED7349AB89DB/Item/p1> ; data: <fault>)",
    "<Item: 0x8b3c330> (entity: Item; id: 0x8b3c500 <x-coredata://01BC77D7-EE27-45B0-A70A-ED7349AB89DB/Item/p2> ; data: <fault>)",
    "<Item: 0x8b3e370> (entity: Item; id: 0x8b23aa0 <x-coredata://01BC77D7-EE27-45B0-A70A-ED7349AB89DB/Item/p3> ; data: <fault>)",
    "<Item: 0x8b3e3b0> (entity: Item; id: 0x8b25720 <x-coredata://01BC77D7-EE27-45B0-A70A-ED7349AB89DB/Item/p4> ; data: <fault>)",
    "<Item: 0x8b3e410> (entity: Item; id: 0x8b379c0 <x-coredata://01BC77D7-EE27-45B0-A70A-ED7349AB89DB/Item/p5> ; data: <fault>)",
    "<Item: 0x8b3e460> (entity: Item; id: 0x8b416d0 <x-coredata://01BC77D7-EE27-45B0-A70A-ED7349AB89DB/Item/p6> ; data: <fault>)",
    "<Item: 0x8b3e4b0> (entity: Item; id: 0x8b3c5e0 <x-coredata://01BC77D7-EE27-45B0-A70A-ED7349AB89DB/Item/p7> ; data: <fault>)",
    "<Item: 0x8b3e500> (entity: Item; id: 0x8b41c20 <x-coredata://01BC77D7-EE27-45B0-A70A-ED7349AB89DB/Item/p8> ; data: <fault>)",
    "<Item: 0x8b3e560> (entity: Item; id: 0x8b40ee0 <x-coredata://01BC77D7-EE27-45B0-A70A-ED7349AB89DB/Item/p9> ; data: <fault>)",
    "<Item: 0x8b3e5c0> (entity: Item; id: 0x8b40ef0 <x-coredata://01BC77D7-EE27-45B0-A70A-ED7349AB89DB/Item/p10> ; data: <fault>)",
    "<Item: 0x8b3e610> (entity: Item; id: 0x8b40db0 <x-coredata://01BC77D7-EE27-45B0-A70A-ED7349AB89DB/Item/p11> ; data: <fault>)",
    "<Item: 0x8b40550> (entity: Item; id: 0x8b40dc0 <x-coredata://01BC77D7-EE27-45B0-A70A-ED7349AB89DB/Item/p12> ; data: <fault>)"
)
2013-07-01 20:41:34.466 Grocery Dude[74177:a0b] CoreData: annotation: total fetch execution time: 0.0018s for 12 rows.
```

Figure 2.10   Fetched managed objects

To see the property values of each managed object, you can use a `for` loop to iterate through the `NSArray` and log the value of the item's `name`. The code involved is shown in Listing 2.5.

Listing 2.5 `AppDelegate.m`: demo **(Fetching)**

```
NSFetchRequest *request =
[NSFetchRequest fetchRequestWithEntityName:@"Item"];
NSArray *fetchedObjects =
[_coreDataHelper.context executeFetchRequest:request error:nil];
for (Item *item in fetchedObjects) {
    NSLog(@"Fetched Object = %@", item.name);
}
```

Update Grocery Dude as follows to configure item names to display in the console log:

1. Update the `demo` method of `AppDelegate.m` to match Listing 2.5. Feel free to keep or remove the `NSLog` statement from the start of the method.

Run the application again to examine the logs, and you should see each of the managed object's name property values listed in the console window. Figure 2.11 shows the expected result.

```
▼  ➡  II  ⇄  ⬇  ⬆  ⚡ |  Grocery Dude
2013-07-01 20:48:15.600 Grocery Dude[74391:a0b] CoreData: annotation: total fetch execution time: 0.0017s for 12 rows.
2013-07-01 20:48:15.600 Grocery Dude[74391:a0b] Fetched Object = Cheese
2013-07-01 20:48:15.601 Grocery Dude[74391:a0b] Fetched Object = Butter
2013-07-01 20:48:15.601 Grocery Dude[74391:a0b] Fetched Object = Apples
2013-07-01 20:48:15.601 Grocery Dude[74391:a0b] Fetched Object = Cereal
2013-07-01 20:48:15.602 Grocery Dude[74391:a0b] Fetched Object = Orange Juice
2013-07-01 20:48:15.602 Grocery Dude[74391:a0b] Fetched Object = Fish
2013-07-01 20:48:15.602 Grocery Dude[74391:a0b] Fetched Object = Milk
2013-07-01 20:48:15.602 Grocery Dude[74391:a0b] Fetched Object = Eggs
2013-07-01 20:48:15.603 Grocery Dude[74391:a0b] Fetched Object = Tomatoes
2013-07-01 20:48:15.603 Grocery Dude[74391:a0b] Fetched Object = Sausages
2013-07-01 20:48:15.603 Grocery Dude[74391:a0b] Fetched Object = Bread
2013-07-01 20:48:15.604 Grocery Dude[74391:a0b] Fetched Object = Coffee
```

Figure 2.11   Fetched managed object names

Fetch Request Sorting

An `NSFetchRequest` returns an `NSArray`, which by nature supports being sorted. As such, you may optionally configure an `NSFetchRequest` with a sort descriptor configured to order managed objects in a certain way. Sort descriptors are passed to an `NSFetchRequest` as an instance of `NSSortDescriptor`. In SQL database terms, a sort descriptor is similar to an `ORDER BY` statement. Listing 2.6 shows the code involved.

Listing 2.6   **AppDelegate.m: demo (Sorting)**

```
NSFetchRequest *request =
[NSFetchRequest fetchRequestWithEntityName:@"Item"];

NSSortDescriptor *sort =
[NSSortDescriptor sortDescriptorWithKey:@"name" ascending:YES];
[request setSortDescriptors:[NSArray arrayWithObject:sort]];

NSArray *fetchedObjects =
[_coreDataHelper.context executeFetchRequest:request error:nil];
for (Item *item in fetchedObjects) {
    NSLog(@"Fetched Object = %@", item.name);
}
```

Update Grocery Dude as follows to ensure the fetch is sorted:

1. Insert the bold code from Listing 2.6 into the equivalent place within the `demo` method of `AppDelegate.m`.

Run the application again to examine the logs, and you should see the managed object names are now sorted in alphabetical order. Figure 2.12 shows the expected result.

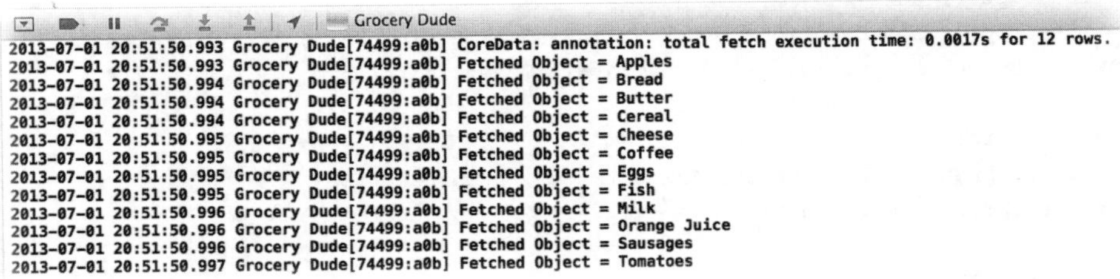

```
            II                 Grocery Dude
2013-07-01 20:51:50.993 Grocery Dude[74499:a0b] CoreData: annotation: total fetch execution time: 0.0017s for 12 rows.
2013-07-01 20:51:50.993 Grocery Dude[74499:a0b] Fetched Object = Apples
2013-07-01 20:51:50.994 Grocery Dude[74499:a0b] Fetched Object = Bread
2013-07-01 20:51:50.994 Grocery Dude[74499:a0b] Fetched Object = Butter
2013-07-01 20:51:50.994 Grocery Dude[74499:a0b] Fetched Object = Cereal
2013-07-01 20:51:50.995 Grocery Dude[74499:a0b] Fetched Object = Cheese
2013-07-01 20:51:50.995 Grocery Dude[74499:a0b] Fetched Object = Coffee
2013-07-01 20:51:50.995 Grocery Dude[74499:a0b] Fetched Object = Eggs
2013-07-01 20:51:50.995 Grocery Dude[74499:a0b] Fetched Object = Fish
2013-07-01 20:51:50.996 Grocery Dude[74499:a0b] Fetched Object = Milk
2013-07-01 20:51:50.996 Grocery Dude[74499:a0b] Fetched Object = Orange Juice
2013-07-01 20:51:50.996 Grocery Dude[74499:a0b] Fetched Object = Sausages
2013-07-01 20:51:50.997 Grocery Dude[74499:a0b] Fetched Object = Tomatoes
```

Figure 2.12   Fetched managed object names (sorted)

Fetch Request Filtering

When it isn't appropriate to fetch everything possible for an entity, you can filter fetches using a predicate. A predicate is defined for a fetch request using an instance of `NSPredicate` and then passing it to an instance of `NSFetchRequest`. Using a predicate will limit the number of managed objects returned in the fetched results based on the criteria specified. Predicates are persistent store agnostic, so you can use the same predicates regardless of the backend store. That said, there are some corner cases where particular predicates won't work with certain stores. For example, the **matches** operator works with in-memory filtering; however, it does not with an SQLite store. In SQL database terms, a predicate is similar to a `WHERE` clause.

A predicate is evaluated against each potential managed object as a part of fetch execution. The predicate evaluation result is a Boolean value. If `YES`, the predicate criteria are satisfied and the managed object will be a part of the fetched results. If `NO`, the predicate criteria are not satisfied and the managed object will not be a part of the fetched results.

Once you have the `NSArray` of fetched results from executing an `NSFetchRequest`, it is possible to filter the array again if you wish. To do this you can use the `filteredArrayUsingPredicate` method of `NSArray`, or filter "in place" using the `filterUsingPredicate` method of `NSMutableArray`.

In Grocery Dude, let's say you wanted to exclude items with the name "Coffee." When you create the `NSPredicate` that will be passed to the `NSFetchrequest`, you would specify that **name** is not equal to the string "Coffee". In code, this predicate is written as `name != @"Coffee"`. Because predicates support variable substitution, a string could also be passed to the predicate at runtime, as shown in bold in Listing 2.7. Building predicates can be a complicated topic, depending on your requirements. For further information, search http://developer.apple.com for the **Predicate Programming Guide**.

Listing 2.7   `AppDelegate: demo` (Filtering)

```
NSFetchRequest *request =
[NSFetchRequest fetchRequestWithEntityName:@"Item"];

NSSortDescriptor *sort =
[NSSortDescriptor sortDescriptorWithKey:@"name" ascending:YES];
[request setSortDescriptors:[NSArray arrayWithObject:sort]];

NSPredicate *filter =
[NSPredicate predicateWithFormat:@"name != %@", @"Coffee"];
[request setPredicate:filter];

NSArray *fetchedObjects =
[_coreDataHelper.context executeFetchRequest:request error:nil];
for (Item *item in fetchedObjects) {
    NSLog(@"Fetched Object = %@", item.name);
}
```

Update Grocery Dude as follows to add a predicate to filter the fetch:

1. Add the bold code from Listing 2.7 into the equivalent place within the demo method of AppDelegate.m.

Run the application again to examine the logs and you should see the list of item names now excludes Coffee. Figure 2.13 shows the expected results.

```
2013-07-01 20:59:39.235 Grocery Dude[74664:a0b] CoreData: annotation: total fetch execution time: 0.0021s for 11 rows.
2013-07-01 20:59:39.235 Grocery Dude[74664:a0b] Fetched Object = Apples
2013-07-01 20:59:39.236 Grocery Dude[74664:a0b] Fetched Object = Bread
2013-07-01 20:59:39.236 Grocery Dude[74664:a0b] Fetched Object = Butter
2013-07-01 20:59:39.236 Grocery Dude[74664:a0b] Fetched Object = Cereal
2013-07-01 20:59:39.236 Grocery Dude[74664:a0b] Fetched Object = Cheese
2013-07-01 20:59:39.237 Grocery Dude[74664:a0b] Fetched Object = Eggs
2013-07-01 20:59:39.237 Grocery Dude[74664:a0b] Fetched Object = Fish
2013-07-01 20:59:39.237 Grocery Dude[74664:a0b] Fetched Object = Milk
2013-07-01 20:59:39.238 Grocery Dude[74664:a0b] Fetched Object = Orange Juice
2013-07-01 20:59:39.238 Grocery Dude[74664:a0b] Fetched Object = Sausages
2013-07-01 20:59:39.238 Grocery Dude[74664:a0b] Fetched Object = Tomatoes
```

Figure 2.13   Fetched managed object names (sorted and filtered)

Fetch Request Templates

Determining the correct predicate format to use for every fetch can become laborious. Thankfully, the Xcode Data Model Designer supports predefining fetch requests. These reusable templates are easier to configure than predicates and reduce repeated code. Fetch request templates are configured using a series of drop-down boxes and fields specific to the application's model. Unfortunately, given their simplicity they aren't as powerful as predicates. If you need features such as custom AND/OR combinations, they're missing and you'll have to revert to predicate programming.

Update Grocery Dude as follows to create a fetch request template:

1. Select **Model.xcdatamodeld**.

2. Click **Editor > Add Fetch Request**.

3. Set the name of the fetch request template to **Test**.

4. Click + and configure the **Test** fetch request template, as shown in Figure 2.14.

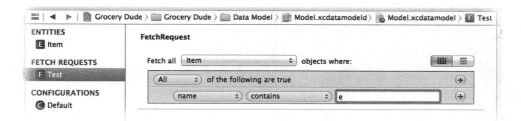

Figure 2.14   Fetch request template configuration

To use a fetch request template, you'll need to send a message to the managed object model, telling it the name of the template to use. This will give you an NSFetchRequest to work with. Because the fetch request has been created from a template, there's no longer a need to pass in a predicate for filtering. To modify the fetch request in any way (for example, to sort it), you must first copy the fetch request. This is because a fetch request template comes from an immutable (unchangeable) model. Listing 2.8 shows the code involved.

Listing 2.8   `AppDelegate: demo` **(Fetch Request Template)**

```
NSFetchRequest *request =
[[[_coreDataHelper model] fetchRequestTemplateForName:@"Test"] copy];

NSSortDescriptor *sort =
[NSSortDescriptor sortDescriptorWithKey:@"name" ascending:YES];
[request setSortDescriptors:[NSArray arrayWithObject:sort]];

NSArray *fetchedObjects =
[_coreDataHelper.context executeFetchRequest:request error:nil];
```

```
for (Item *item in fetchedObjects) {
    NSLog(@"Fetched Object = %@", item.name);
}
```

Update Grocery Dude as follows to use the Test fetch request template:

1. Replace the existing code in the `demo` method of `AppDelegate.m` with the code from Listing 2.8. The new code is shown in bold and the predicate code has been removed.

Run the application again to examine the logs, and you'll see the sorted managed object names all contain the letter *e*, as configured in the fetch request template. Figure 2.15 shows the expected results.

```
⊡ ▶ ‖ ⌂ ⌄ ⌃ ◢ | Grocery Dude
2013-07-01 21:11:14.527 Grocery Dude[74928:a0b] CoreData: annotation: total fetch execution time: 0.0061s for 9 rows.
2013-07-01 21:11:14.528 Grocery Dude[74928:a0b] Fetched Object = Apples
2013-07-01 21:11:14.528 Grocery Dude[74928:a0b] Fetched Object = Bread
2013-07-01 21:11:14.528 Grocery Dude[74928:a0b] Fetched Object = Butter
2013-07-01 21:11:14.528 Grocery Dude[74928:a0b] Fetched Object = Cereal
2013-07-01 21:11:14.529 Grocery Dude[74928:a0b] Fetched Object = Cheese
2013-07-01 21:11:14.529 Grocery Dude[74928:a0b] Fetched Object = Coffee
2013-07-01 21:11:14.529 Grocery Dude[74928:a0b] Fetched Object = Orange Juice
2013-07-01 21:11:14.530 Grocery Dude[74928:a0b] Fetched Object = Sausages
2013-07-01 21:11:14.530 Grocery Dude[74928:a0b] Fetched Object = Tomatoes
```

Figure 2.15   Fetched managed object names (filtered via template)

Did you also notice the SQL statement generated for this fetch? You can see all the elements required to retrieve (`SELECT`) a filtered (`WHERE`) and sorted (`ORDER BY`) set of results. Figure 2.16 shows the expected results.

```
⊡ ▶ ‖ ⌂ ⌄ ⌃ ◢ | Grocery Dude
2013-07-01 21:11:14.522 Grocery Dude[74928:a0b] CoreData: annotation: fetch using NSSQLiteStatement <0x8b80470> on entity 'Item'
with sql text 'SELECT 0, t0.Z_PK, t0.Z_OPT, t0.ZCOLLECTED, t0.ZLISTED, t0.ZNAME, t0.ZPHOTODATA, t0.ZQUANTITY FROM ZITEM t0 WHERE
NSCoreDataStringSearch( t0.ZNAME, ?, 0, 0) ORDER BY t0.ZNAME' returned 9 rows with values: (
    "<Item: 0x8b844f0> (entity: Item; id: 0x8b82bd0 <x-coredata://01BC77D7-EE27-45B0-A70A-ED7349AB89DB/Item/p3> ; data: <fault>)",
    "<Item: 0x8b84700> (entity: Item; id: 0x8b82be0 <x-coredata://01BC77D7-EE27-45B0-A70A-ED7349AB89DB/Item/p11> ; data: <fault>)",
    "<Item: 0x8b84740> (entity: Item; id: 0x8b82bf0 <x-coredata://01BC77D7-EE27-45B0-A70A-ED7349AB89DB/Item/p2> ; data: <fault>)",
    "<Item: 0x8b84780> (entity: Item; id: 0x8b82c00 <x-coredata://01BC77D7-EE27-45B0-A70A-ED7349AB89DB/Item/p4> ; data: <fault>)",
    "<Item: 0x8b847c0> (entity: Item; id: 0x8b82c10 <x-coredata://01BC77D7-EE27-45B0-A70A-ED7349AB89DB/Item/p1> ; data: <fault>)",
    "<Item: 0x8b84800> (entity: Item; id: 0x8b82c20 <x-coredata://01BC77D7-EE27-45B0-A70A-ED7349AB89DB/Item/p12> ; data: <fault>)",
    "<Item: 0x8b84840> (entity: Item; id: 0x8b82c30 <x-coredata://01BC77D7-EE27-45B0-A70A-ED7349AB89DB/Item/p5> ; data: <fault>)",
```

Figure 2.16   Automatically generated SQL

Deleting Managed Objects

Deleting a managed object is as easy as calling `deleteObject` or `deleteObjects` on a containing context. Note that the deletion isn't permanent until you also call `save:` on the context. The code involved is shown in Listing 2.9.

Listing 2.9 **AppDelegate: demo (Deleting)**

```
NSFetchRequest *request =
[NSFetchRequest fetchRequestWithEntityName:@"Item"];

NSArray *fetchedObjects =
[_coreDataHelper.context executeFetchRequest:request error:nil];

for (Item *item in fetchedObjects) {
    NSLog(@"Deleting Object '%@'", item.name);
    [_coreDataHelper.context deleteObject:item];
}
```

Update Grocery Dude as follows to delete all the objects:

1. Replace all code in the demo method with the code from Listing 2.9.

2. Run the application.

3. Press the home button (**Shift+⌘+H** or **Hardware > Home**) to save the changes to the context.

Did you notice all the SQL statements calling DELETE that were logged to the console once you pressed the home button to trigger a save? By now you should have a reasonable level of comfort that Core Data is taking care of the backend SQL for you. Turn off SQLDebug and remove all code from the demo method before heading to Chapter 3.

Summary

You've now been introduced to the steps required to configure a basic managed object model. Entities and attributes have been discussed, along with some advice on choosing the right data types. Inserting, fetching, filtering, sorting, and deleting managed objects have all been covered, followed up with an introduction to fetch request templates. The covers have also been lifted off Core Data to give you some insight into what it's doing for you under the hood.

Exercises

Why not build on what you've learned by experimenting?

1. Insert some new managed objects and set their name and quantity.

2. Alter the **Test** fetch request template and experiment with other filtering options.

3. Open Grocery-Dude.sqlite in **SQLite Database Browser** then click the **Database Structure** button. Notice the existence of ZITEM_ZNAME_INDEX? That's where the indexing for the **name** attribute is stored since you ticked the **Indexed** check box.

4. Temporarily run the code from Listing 2.10 in the demo method. Examine the range limitations of the numerical data types.

Listing 2.10   **Numerical Attribute Ranges**

```
NSLog(@"Integer 16 Range: %d to %d", INT16_MIN, INT16_MAX);
NSLog(@"Integer 32 Range: %d to %d", INT32_MIN, INT32_MAX);
NSLog(@"Integer 64 Range: %lld to %lld", INT64_MIN, INT64_MAX);
NSLog(@"Float Range = %f to %f", -FLT_MAX, FLT_MAX);
NSLog(@"Double Range = %f to %f", -DBL_MAX, DBL_MAX);
NSLog(@"Decimal Range = %@ to %@",
[NSDecimalNumber minimumDecimalNumber],
[NSDecimalNumber maximumDecimalNumber]);

NSLog(@"  Float 1/3 = %@", [NSNumber numberWithFloat:1.0f/3]);
NSLog(@" Double 1/3 = %@", [NSNumber numberWithDouble:1.0/3]);
NSLog(@"Decimal 1/3 = %@",
[[NSDecimalNumber one] decimalNumberByDividingBy:
[NSDecimalNumber decimalNumberWithString:@"3"]]);
```

Managed Object Model Migration

Anyone who has never made a mistake has never tried anything new.

Albert Einstein

In Chapter 2, "Managed Object Model Basics," the fundamentals of managed object models were introduced, yet you were constrained to just one entity and a few attributes. The next logical step is to add more to the model; however, this requires a number of preliminary steps in order to prevent crashes caused by these changes. This chapter will show how to add model versions and model mappings, as well as demonstrate different migration techniques you can choose when upgrading a model.

Changing a Managed Object Model

As an application evolves, its managed object model will probably need to change, too. Simple changes, such as attribute defaults, validation rules, and fetch request templates can be modified without consequence. Other more structural changes require that persistent stores be migrated to new model versions. If a persistent store doesn't have the appropriate mappings and settings required to migrate data, the application will crash.

> **Note**
>
> To continue building the sample application, you'll need to have added the previous chapter's code to Grocery Dude. Alternatively, you may download, unzip, and use the project up to this point from http://www.timroadley.com/LearningCoreData/GroceryDude-AfterChapter02.zip. Any time you start using an Xcode project from a ZIP file, it's good practice to click **Product** > **Clean**. This practice ensures there's no residual cache from previous projects using the same name. It is recommended that you use the iOS Simulator when following this chapter so you can inspect the contents of the SQLite database files easily.

Update Grocery Dude as follows to generate a model incompatibility error:

1. Run Grocery Dude once to ensure the existing model has been used to create the persistent store. You should see the words "Successfully added store" in the console log.

2. Select **Model.xcdatamodeld** in Xcode.

3. Add a new entity called **Measurement**.

4. Select the **Measurement** entity and add an attribute called **abc**. Set its type to **String**.

5. Re-run the application and examine the console log. You should now have generated arguably one of the most common Core Data errors, as shown in Figure 3.1. If this error has not appeared, delete the application and then click **Product > Clean** and retry from Step 1.

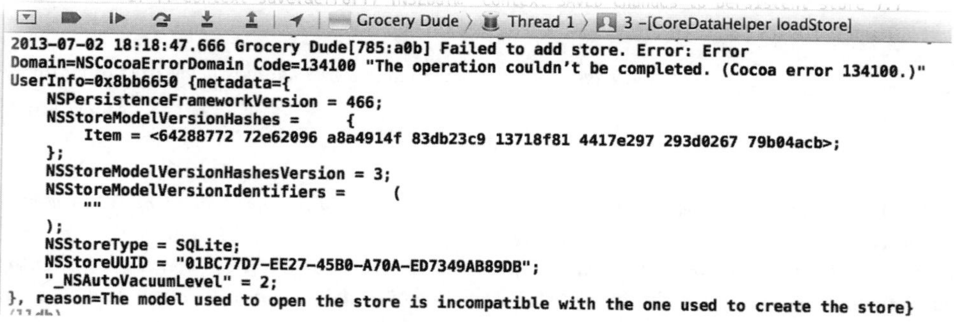

```
▼   ▶   I▶   ⇆   ⬇   ⬆   ⤴  │  ▬ Grocery Dude  〉 🗐 Thread 1 〉 🧍 3 -[CoreDataHelper loadStore]
2013-07-02 18:18:47.666 Grocery Dude[785:a0b] Failed to add store. Error: Error
Domain=NSCocoaErrorDomain Code=134100 "The operation couldn't be completed. (Cocoa error 134100.)"
UserInfo=0x8bb6650 {metadata={
    NSPersistenceFrameworkVersion = 466;
    NSStoreModelVersionHashes =    {
        Item = <64288772 72e62096 a8a4914f 83db23c9 13718f81 4417e297 293d0267 79b04acb>;
    };
    NSStoreModelVersionHashesVersion = 3;
    NSStoreModelVersionIdentifiers =    (
        ""
    );
    NSStoreType = SQLite;
    NSStoreUUID = "01BC77D7-EE27-45B0-A70A-ED7349AB89DB";
    "_NSAutoVacuumLevel" = 2;
}, reason=The model used to open the store is incompatible with the one used to create the store}
```

Figure 3.1   Model changes make persistent stores incompatible.

This crash isn't an issue when an application is in its initial development phase. To get past it, you can just delete the application and run it again. When the application is run for the first time after being deleted, the persistent store will be created based on the latest model. This will make the store compatible with the model, so the application won't crash anymore. *However,* it won't have any old data in it. As such, this scenario is unacceptable for any application already available on the App Store. There are a few approaches to migrating existing persistent stores, and the migration path you choose will be driven by the complexity of the changes and whether or not you're using iCloud. Whatever you do, you'll first need to become familiar with model versioning.

Update Grocery Dude as follows to revert to the original model:

1. Select **Model.xcdatamodeld**.

2. Delete the **Measurement** entity.

3. Re-run the application, which now should not crash.

Adding a Model Version

To avoid the crash previously demonstrated in Figure 3.1, you'll need to create a new model version *before* making changes to the model. Ongoing, you should not remove old versions of a model. Old model versions are needed to help migrate older persistent stores to the current model version. If there are no existing persistent stores on customer devices, you can ignore model versioning until your application is on the App Store.

Update Grocery Dude as follows to add a model version:

1. Select **Model.xcdatamodeld**.

2. Click **Editor > Add Model Version...**.

3. Click **Finish** to accept **Model 2** as the version name.

You should now have two model versions, as shown in Figure 3.2.

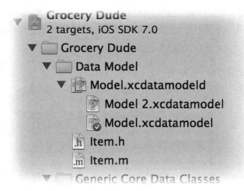

Figure 3.2   Multiple model versions

The new model **Model 2.xcdatamodel** will start out as a replica of **Model.xcdatamodel**. This makes it easy to modify the wrong version unintentionally. Before you edit a model, you should triple-check you have selected the correct one. You may wish to get into the habit of taking a snapshot, or even backing up the whole project prior to editing a model.

Update Grocery Dude as follows to reintroduce the **Measurement** entity:

1. Optionally take a snapshot or back up the Grocery Dude project.

2. Select **Model 2.xcdatamodel**.

3. Create a new entity called **Measurement**.

4. Select the **Measurement** entity, create an attribute called **abc**, and then set its type to **String**.

After you've added the new model version, you still need to set it as the current version before it will be used by the application.

Update Grocery Dude as follows to change the current model version:

1. Select **Model.xcdatamodeld**.

2. Click **View > Utilities > Show File Inspector** (or press **Option+⌘+1**).

3. Set the **Current Model Version** to **Model 2**, as shown in Figure 3.3.

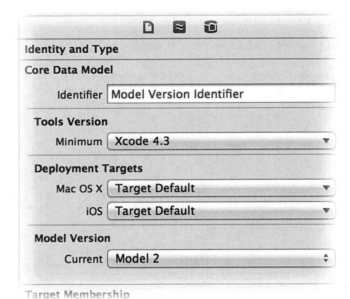

Figure 3.3   Setting the current model

Before you can successfully launch the application, you'll need to configure migration options to tell Core Data how to migrate. Feel free to launch it again to generate the "Store is incompatible" error in the meantime.

Lightweight Migration

Whenever a new model is set as the current version, existing persistent stores must be migrated to use them. This is because the persistent store coordinator will try to use the latest model to open the existing store, which will fail if the store was created using a previous version of the model. The process of store migration can be handled automatically by passing the following options to a persistent store coordinator in an NSDictionary as a store is added to it:

- When NSMigratePersistentStoresAutomaticallyOption is YES and passed to a persistent store coordinator, Core Data will automatically attempt to migrate lower versioned (and hence incompatible) persistent stores to the latest model.

- When NSInferMappingModelAutomaticallyOption is YES and passed to a persistent store coordinator, Core Data will automatically attempt to infer a best guess at what attributes from the *source model entities* should end up as attributes in the *destination model entities*.

Using those persistent store coordinator options together is called **lightweight migration** and is demonstrated in bold in Listing 3.1. These options are set in an updated loadStore method of CoreDataHelper.m. Note that if you're using iCloud, this is your only choice for migration.

Listing 3.1 **CoreDataHelper.m: loadStore**

```
if (debug==1) {
    NSLog(@"Running %@ '%@'", self.class, NSStringFromSelector(_cmd));
}
    if (_store) {return;} // Don't load store if it's already loaded
    NSDictionary *options =
    @{
        NSMigratePersistentStoresAutomaticallyOption:@YES
        ,NSInferMappingModelAutomaticallyOption:@YES
        ,NSSQLitePragmasOption: @{@"journal_mode": @"DELETE"}
    };
    NSError *error = nil;
    _store = [_coordinator addPersistentStoreWithType:NSSQLiteStoreType
                                        configuration:nil
                                                  URL:[self storeURL]
                                              options:options error:&error];
    if (!_store) {NSLog(@"Failed to add store. Error: %@", error);abort();}
    else         {NSLog(@"Successfully added store: %@", _store);}
```

Update Grocery Dude as follows to enable lightweight migration:

1. Replace all existing code in the loadStore method of CoreDataHelper.m with the code from Listing 3.1. For reference, the bold code shows the new changes.

2. Re-run the application, which should not crash.

From now on, any time you set a new model as the current version and lightweight migration is enabled, the migration should occur seamlessly.

Before other migration types can be demonstrated, some test data needs to be generated. Listing 3.2 contains code that generates managed objects based on the **Measurement** entity.

Listing 3.2 `AppDelegate.m:` demo (Inserting Test Measurement Data)

```
- (void)demo {
if (debug==1) {
    NSLog(@"Running %@ '%@'", self.class, NSStringFromSelector(_cmd));
}
    for (int i = 1; i < 50000; i++) {
        Measurement *newMeasurement =
        [NSEntityDescription insertNewObjectForEntityForName:@"Measurement"
                            inManagedObjectContext:_coreDataHelper.context];

        newMeasurement.abc =
        [NSString stringWithFormat:@"-->> LOTS OF TEST DATA x%i",i];
        NSLog(@"Inserted %@",newMeasurement.abc);
    }
    [_coreDataHelper saveContext];
}
```

Update Grocery Dude as follows to generate test data:

1. Create an `NSManagedObject` subclass of the **Measurement** entity. As discussed in Chapter 2, this is achieved by first selecting the entity and then clicking **Editor > Create NSManagedObject Subclass...** and following the prompts. When it comes time to save the class file, don't forget to tick the Grocery Dude target.

2. Add `#import "Measurement.h"` to the top of `AppDelegate.m`.

3. Replace the `demo` method in `AppDelegate.m` with the code from Listing 3.2.

4. Run the application once. This will insert quite a lot of test data into the persistent store, which you can monitor by examining the console log. This may take a little while, depending on the speed of your machine. Please be patient as these objects are inserted. It's important to have a fair amount of data in the persistent store to demonstrate the speed of migrations later.

The test data should now be in the persistent store, so there's no need to reinsert it each time the application is launched. Note that the Items table view will still remain blank because it has not yet been configured to display anything.

The next step is to reconfigure the `demo` method to show some of what's in the persistent store. The code shown in Listing 3.3 fetches a small sample of **Measurement** data. Notice that a new option is included that limits fetched results to 50. This is great for limiting how many results are fetched from large data sets, and even more powerful when mixed with sorting to generate a Top-50, for example.

Listing 3.3   `AppDelegate.m:` demo **(Fetching Test Measurement Data)**

```
- (void)demo {
if (debug==1) {
    NSLog(@"Running %@ '%@'", self.class, NSStringFromSelector(_cmd));
}
    NSFetchRequest *request =
    [NSFetchRequest fetchRequestWithEntityName:@"Measurement"];
    [request setFetchLimit:50];
    NSError *error = nil;
    NSArray *fetchedObjects =
    [_coreDataHelper.context executeFetchRequest:request error:&error];

    if (error) {NSLog(@"%@", error);}
    else {
        for (Measurement *measurement in fetchedObjects) {
            NSLog(@"Fetched Object = %@", measurement.abc);
        }
    }
}
```

Update Grocery Dude as follows to prevent duplicate test data from being inserted:

1. Replace the demo method in `AppDelegate.m` with the code from Listing 3.3.

2. Run the application.

3. Examine the contents of the `Grocery-Dude.sqlite` file using **SQLite Database Browser**, as explained previously in Chapter 2. Figure 3.4 shows the expected results.

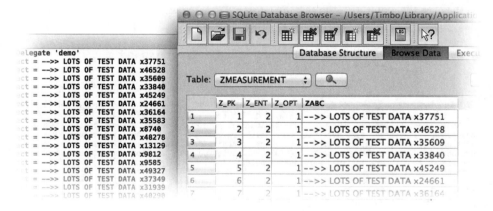

Figure 3.4   Test data ready for the next parts of this chapter

Ensure you close SQLite Database Browser before continuing.

Default Migration

Sometimes, you need more control than what lightweight migration offers. Let's say, for instance, you want to replace the **Measurement** entity with another entity called **Amount**. In addition, you want the **abc** attribute from the **Measurement** entity to end up as an **xyz** attribute in the **Amount** entity. Any existing **abc** data should also be migrated to the **xyz** attribute. To achieve these requirements, you'll need to create a model mapping to manually specify what maps to where. When the persistent store option `NSInferMappingModelAutomaticallyOption` is set to `YES`, Core Data still checks to see if there are any model-mapping files it should use before trying to infer automatically. It is recommended that you disable this setting while you're testing a mapping model. This way, you can be certain that the mapping model is being used and is functioning correctly.

Update Grocery Dude as follows to disable automatic model mapping:

1. Set the `NSInferMappingModelAutomaticallyOption` option in the `loadStore` method of `CoreDataHelper.m` to `@NO`.

Update Grocery Dude as follows to add a new model in preparation for the migration from the **Measurement** entity to the **Amount** entity:

1. Optionally take a snapshot or back up the project.

2. Add a new model version called **Model 3** based on **Model 2**.

3. Select **Model 3.xcdatamodel**.

4. Delete the **Measurement** entity.

5. Add a new entity called **Amount** with a String attribute called **xyz**.

6. Create an `NSManagedObject` subclass of the **Amount** entity. When it comes time to save the class file, don't forget to tick the Grocery Dude target.

7. Set **Model 3** as the current model version.

8. Run the application, which should crash with the error shown in Figure 3.5.

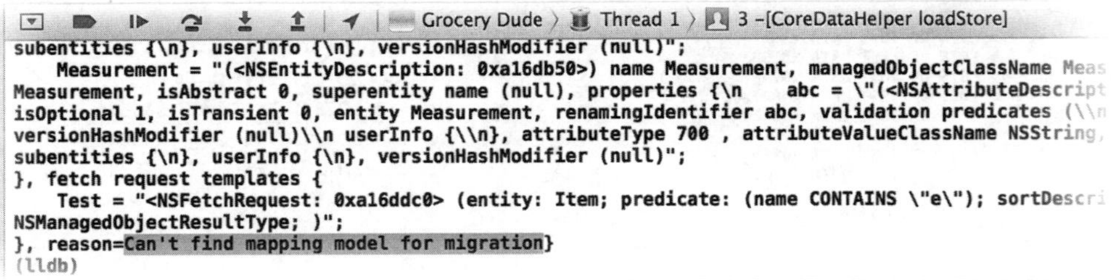

```
       ▼   ▶   ▶   ⟳   ⤓   ⤒   ⟋  │  Grocery Dude ⟩ Thread 1 ⟩ 3 –[CoreDataHelper loadStore]
subentities {\n}, userInfo {\n}, versionHashModifier (null)";
      Measurement = "(<NSEntityDescription: 0xa16db50>) name Measurement, managedObjectClassName Meas
Measurement, isAbstract 0, superentity name (null), properties {\n     abc = \"(<NSAttributeDescript
isOptional 1, isTransient 0, entity Measurement, renamingIdentifier abc, validation predicates (\\n
versionHashModifier (null)\\n userInfo {\\n}, attributeType 700 , attributeValueClassName NSString
subentities {\n}, userInfo {\n}, versionHashModifier (null)";
}, fetch request templates {
      Test = "<NSFetchRequest: 0xa16ddc0> (entity: Item; predicate: (name CONTAINS \"e\"); sortDescri
NSManagedObjectResultType; )";
}, reason=Can't find mapping model for migration}
(lldb)
```

Figure 3.5   A mapping model is required when mapping is not inferred.

To resolve the error shown in Figure 3.5, you need to create a mapping model that shows what fields map where. Specifically, the requirement is to map the old Measurement **abc** attribute to the new Amount **xyz** attribute.

Update Grocery Dude as follows to add a new mapping model:

1. Ensure the **Data Model** group is selected.

2. Click **File > New > File...**.

3. Select **iOS > Core Data > Mapping Model** and then click **Next**.

4. Select **Model 2.xcdatamodel** as the **Source Data Model** and then click **Next**.

5. Select **Model 3.xcdatamodel** as the **Target Data Model** and then click **Next**.

6. Set the mapping model name to save as **Model2toModel3**.

7. Ensure the Grocery Dude target is ticked and then click **Create**.

8. Select **Model2toModel3.xcmappingmodel**.

You should now be presented with the model-mapping editor, as shown in Figure 3.6.

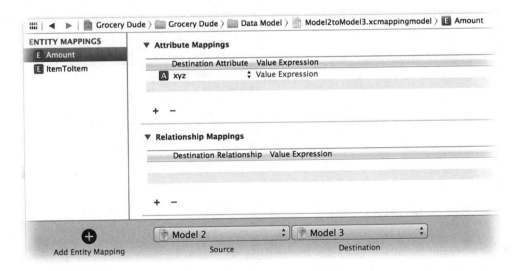

Figure 3.6   The model-mapping editor

The mappings you're presented with will be a best guess based on what Core Data can infer on its own. On the left you should see **Entity Mappings**, showing what source entities map to what destination entities. You should also see as in Figure 3.6 how the source **Item** entity has already inferred that it should map to the destination **Item** entity, which is a fair assumption. The naming standard of an entity mapping is **SourceToDestination**. With this in mind, notice the **Amount** entity doesn't seem to have a source entity because it never existed in the source model.

Update Grocery Dude as follows to map the old Measurement entity to the new Amount entity:

1. Ensure **Model2toModel3.xcmappingmodel** is selected.

2. Select the **Amount** entity mapping.

3. Click **View > Utilities > Show Mapping Model Inspector** (if that's not visible in the menu system, press **Option+⌘+3**). You need to be able to see the pane shown in Figure 3.7.

4. Set the **Source** of **Amount** entity mapping to **Measurement**. The expected result is shown in Figure 3.7.

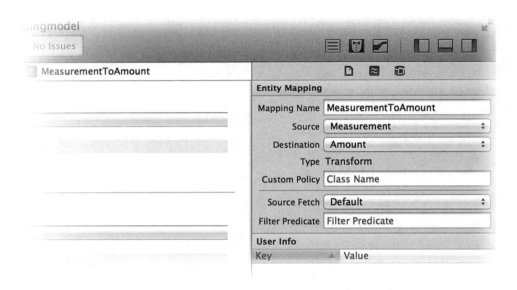

Figure 3.7   Custom entity mapping of measurement to amount

Because **Measurement** was selected as the source entity for the **Amount** destination entity, the Entity Mapping Name was automatically renamed to **MeasurementToAmount**. In addition, the mapping type changed from **Add** to **Transform**. For more complex implementations, you can specify a custom policy in the form of an NSEntityMigrationPolicy subclass. By overriding createDestinationInstancesForSourceInstance in the subclass, you can manipulate the data that's migrated. For example, you could intercept the values of the **abc** attribute, set them all to title case, and then migrate them to the **xyz** attribute.

The Source Fetch option shown at the bottom of Figure 3.7 allows you to limit the migrated data to the results of a predicated (filtered) fetch. This is useful if you only want a subset of the existing data to be migrated. The predicate format you use here is the same as the format you would use when normally configuring a predicate, except you use $source variables. An example of a predicate that would filter out nil source data from the **abc** attribute is $source.abc != nil.

Select the **ItemToItem** entity mapping shown previously in Figure 3.6 and examine its attribute mappings. Notice how each destination attribute has a **Value Expression** set. Now examine the **MeasurementToAmount** entity mapping. Notice there's no value expression for the **xyz** destination attribute. This means that the **xyz** attribute has no source attribute, and you'll need to set one using the same format used in the **ItemToItem** entity mapping. The original requirement was to map the **abc** attribute to the **xyz** attribute, so that's what needs configuring here.

Update Grocery Dude as follows to set an appropriate value expression for the **xyz** destination attribute:

1. Set the **Value Expression** for the **xyz** destination attribute of the **MeasurementToAmount** entity mapping to **$source.abc**.

The mapping model is now ready to go; however, the demo method still fetches from the Measurement entity, which doesn't exist under the new model.

Update Grocery Dude as follows to refer to the Amount entity instead of the Measurement entity:

1. Replace `#import "Measurement.h"` with `#import "Amount.h"` at the top of `AppDelegate.m`.

2. Replace the code in the demo method of `AppDelegate.m` with the code from Listing 3.4. Similar to the code being replaced, this code simply fetches a small sample of **Amount** data instead of **Measurement** data.

3. Run the application. The loading screen might display longer than usual due to the migration, depending on the speed of your machine.

Listing 3.4 `AppDelegate.m`: demo (Fetching Test Amount Data)

```
NSFetchRequest *request =
[NSFetchRequest fetchRequestWithEntityName:@"Amount"];
[request setFetchLimit:50];
NSError *error = nil;
NSArray *fetchedObjects =
[_coreDataHelper.context executeFetchRequest:request error:&error];

if (error) {NSLog(@"%@", error);}
else {
    for (Amount *amount in fetchedObjects) {
        NSLog(@"Fetched Object = %@", amount.xyz);
    }
}
```

So long as the migration has been successful, the application won't crash and you should see the expected result in the console log, as shown in Figure 3.8.

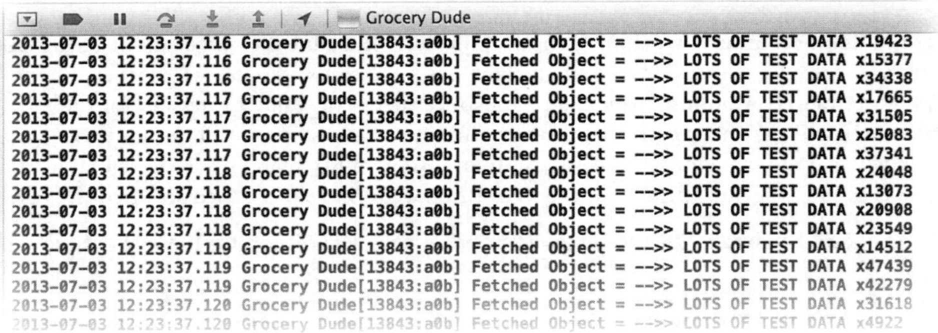
Grocery Dude
2013-07-03 12:23:37.116 Grocery Dude[13843:a0b] Fetched Object = -->> LOTS OF TEST DATA x19423
2013-07-03 12:23:37.116 Grocery Dude[13843:a0b] Fetched Object = -->> LOTS OF TEST DATA x15377
2013-07-03 12:23:37.116 Grocery Dude[13843:a0b] Fetched Object = -->> LOTS OF TEST DATA x34338
2013-07-03 12:23:37.117 Grocery Dude[13843:a0b] Fetched Object = -->> LOTS OF TEST DATA x17665
2013-07-03 12:23:37.117 Grocery Dude[13843:a0b] Fetched Object = -->> LOTS OF TEST DATA x31505
2013-07-03 12:23:37.117 Grocery Dude[13843:a0b] Fetched Object = -->> LOTS OF TEST DATA x25083
2013-07-03 12:23:37.117 Grocery Dude[13843:a0b] Fetched Object = -->> LOTS OF TEST DATA x37341
2013-07-03 12:23:37.118 Grocery Dude[13843:a0b] Fetched Object = -->> LOTS OF TEST DATA x24048
2013-07-03 12:23:37.118 Grocery Dude[13843:a0b] Fetched Object = -->> LOTS OF TEST DATA x13073
2013-07-03 12:23:37.118 Grocery Dude[13843:a0b] Fetched Object = -->> LOTS OF TEST DATA x20908
2013-07-03 12:23:37.118 Grocery Dude[13843:a0b] Fetched Object = -->> LOTS OF TEST DATA x23549
2013-07-03 12:23:37.119 Grocery Dude[13843:a0b] Fetched Object = -->> LOTS OF TEST DATA x14512
2013-07-03 12:23:37.119 Grocery Dude[13843:a0b] Fetched Object = -->> LOTS OF TEST DATA x47439
2013-07-03 12:23:37.119 Grocery Dude[13843:a0b] Fetched Object = -->> LOTS OF TEST DATA x42279
2013-07-03 12:23:37.120 Grocery Dude[13843:a0b] Fetched Object = -->> LOTS OF TEST DATA x31618
2013-07-03 12:23:37.120 Grocery Dude[13843:a0b] Fetched Object = -->> LOTS OF TEST DATA x4922

Figure 3.8 Results of a successfully mapped model

To verify the migration has persisted to the store, examine the contents of the `Grocery-Dude.sqlite` file using the techniques discussed in Chapter 2. The expected result is shown in Figure 3.9, which illustrates the new ZAMOUNT table (that is, Amount entity) with the data from the old Measurement entity.

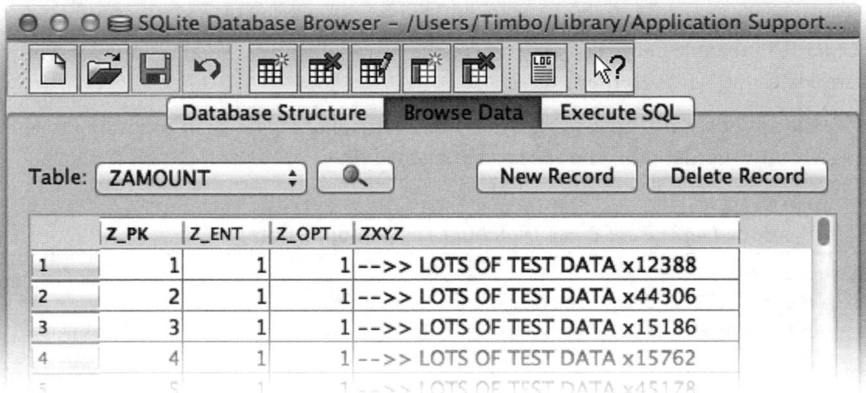
SQLite Database Browser - /Users/Timbo/Library/Application Support...
Database Structure
Browse Data
Execute SQL
Table: ZAMOUNT
New Record
Delete Record
Z_PK
Z_ENT
Z_OPT
ZXYZ
1 1 1 1 -->> LOTS OF TEST DATA x12388
2 2 1 1 -->> LOTS OF TEST DATA x44306
3 3 1 1 -->> LOTS OF TEST DATA x15186
4 4 1 1 -->> LOTS OF TEST DATA x15762

Figure 3.9 A successfully mapped model

Make sure you close the SQLite Database Browser before continuing.

Migration Manager

Instead of letting a persistent store coordinator perform store migrations, you may wish to use a migration manager. Using a migration manager gives you total control over the files created during a migration and thus the flexibility to handle each aspect of a migration in your own way. One example of a benefit of using a migration manager is that you can report on the progress of a migration, which is useful for keeping the user informed (and less cranky) about a slow launch. Although most migrations should be quite fast, some large databases requiring complex changes can take a while to migrate. To keep the user interface responsive, the migration must be performed on a background thread. The user interface has to be responsive in order to provide updates to the user. The challenge is to prevent the user from attempting to use the application during the migration. This is because the data won't be ready yet, so you don't want the user staring at a blank screen wondering what's going on. This is where a migration progress View Controller comes into play.

Update Grocery Dude as follows to configure a migration View Controller:

1. Select **Main.storyboard**.

2. Drag a new **View Controller** onto the storyboard, placing it above the existing Navigation Controller.

3. Drag a new **Label** and **Progress View** onto the new View Controller.

4. Position the **Progress View** in the center of the View Controller and then position the **Label** above it.

5. Widen the **Label** and **Progress View** to the width of the View Controller margins, as shown on the left in Figure 3.10.

6. Configure the **Label** with **Centered** text that reads **Migration Progress 0%**, as shown on the left in Figure 3.10.

7. Configure the **Progress View** progress to 0.

8. Set the **Storyboard ID** of the View Controller to migration using **Identity Inspector (Option+⌘+3)** while the View Controller is selected.

9. Click **Editor > Resolve Auto Layout Issues > Reset to Suggested Constraints in View Controller**. Figure 3.10 shows the expected result.

The new migration View Controller has UILabel and UIProgressView interface elements that will need updating during a migration. This means a way to refer to these interface elements in code is required. A new UIViewController subclass called MigrationVC will be created for this purpose.

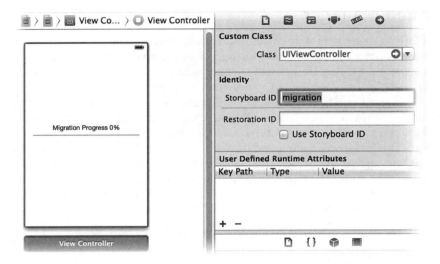

Figure 3.10   Migration View Controller

Update Grocery Dude as follows to add a `MigrationVC` class in a new group:

1. Right-click the existing **Grocery Dude** group and then select **New Group**.

2. Set the new group name to **Grocery Dude View Controllers**.

3. Select the **Grocery Dude View Controllers** group.

4. Click **File > New > File....**

5. Create a new **iOS > Cocoa Touch > Objective-C class** and then click **Next**.

6. Set **Subclass of** to `UIViewController` and **Class** name to `MigrationVC` and then click **Next**.

7. Ensure the Grocery Dude target is ticked and then create the class in the Grocery Dude project directory.

8. Select **Main.storyboard**.

9. Set the **Custom Class** of the new migration View Controller to `MigrationVC` using **Identity Inspector (Option+⌘+3)** while the View Controller is selected. This is in the same place as where the **Storyboard ID** was set.

10. Show the **Assistant Editor** by clicking **View > Assistant Editor > Show Assistant Editor** (or pressing **Option+⌘+Return**).

11. Ensure the **Assistant Editor** is automatically showing `MigrationVC.h`. The top-right of Figure 3.11 shows what this looks like. If you need to, just click **Manual** or **Automatic** while the migration View Controller is selected and select `MigrationVC.h`.

12. Hold down **Control** while dragging a line from the migration progress label to the code in `MigrationVC.h` before `@end`. When you let go of the left mouse button, a pop-up will appear. In the pop-up, set the **Name** of the new `UILabel` property to **label** and ensure the **Storage** is set to **Strong** before clicking **Connect**. Figure 3.11 shows the intended configuration.

13. Repeat the technique in step 12 to create a linked `UIProgressView` property from the progress view called **progressView**.

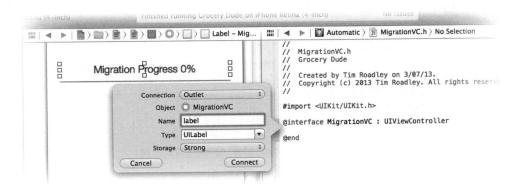

Figure 3.11   Creating storyboard-linked properties to `MigrationVC.h`

To report migration progress, a pointer to the migration View Controller is required in `CoreDataHelper.h`.

Update Grocery Dude as follows to add a new property:

1. Show the **Standard Editor** by clicking **View > Standard Editor > Show Standard Editor** (or pressing ⌘+**Return**).

2. Add `#import "MigrationVC.h"` to the top of `CoreDataHelper.h`.

3. Add `@property (nonatomic, retain) MigrationVC *migrationVC;` to `CoreDataHelper.h` beneath the existing properties.

To handle migrations manually, you'll need to work out whether a migration is necessary each time the application is launched. To make this determination, you'll need to know the URL of the store you're checking to see that it actually exists. Providing that it does, you then compare the store's model metadata to the new model. The result of this model comparison is used to determine whether the new model is compatible with the existing store. If it's not, migration is required. The `isMigrationNecessaryForStore` method shown in Listing 3.5 demonstrates how these checks translate into code.

Listing 3.5 **CoreDataHelper.m: isMigrationNecessaryForStore**

```
#pragma mark - MIGRATION MANAGER
- (BOOL)isMigrationNecessaryForStore:(NSURL*)storeUrl {
if (debug==1) {
    NSLog(@"Running %@ '%@'", self.class, NSStringFromSelector(_cmd));
}
if (![[NSFileManager defaultManager] fileExistsAtPath:[self storeURL].path]) {
    if (debug==1) {NSLog(@"SKIPPED MIGRATION: Source database missing.");}
    return NO;
}
NSError *error = nil;
NSDictionary *sourceMetadata =
[NSPersistentStoreCoordinator metadataForPersistentStoreOfType:NSSQLiteStoreType
 URL:storeUrl error:&error];
NSManagedObjectModel *destinationModel = _coordinator.managedObjectModel;
if ([destinationModel isConfiguration:nil
 compatibleWithStoreMetadata:sourceMetadata]) {
if (debug==1) {
    NSLog(@"SKIPPED MIGRATION: Source is already compatible");}
    return NO;
}
return YES;
}
```

Update Grocery Dude as follows to implement a new MIGRATION MANAGER section:

1. Add the code from Listing 3.5 to the bottom of CoreDataHelper.m before @end.

Provided migration is necessary, the next step is to perform migration. Migration is a three-step process, as shown by the comments in Listing 3.6.

Listing 3.6 **CoreDataHelper.m: migrateStore**

```
- (BOOL)migrateStore:(NSURL*)sourceStore {
if (debug==1) {
    NSLog(@"Running %@ '%@'", self.class, NSStringFromSelector(_cmd));
}
    BOOL success = NO;
    NSError *error = nil;

    // STEP 1 - Gather the Source, Destination and Mapping Model
    NSDictionary *sourceMetadata = [NSPersistentStoreCoordinator
    metadataForPersistentStoreOfType:NSSQLiteStoreType
                        URL:sourceStore
                      error:&error];
```

```objc
NSManagedObjectModel *sourceModel =
[NSManagedObjectModel mergedModelFromBundles:nil
                           forStoreMetadata:sourceMetadata];

NSManagedObjectModel *destinModel = _model;

NSMappingModel *mappingModel =
[NSMappingModel mappingModelFromBundles:nil
                       forSourceModel:sourceModel
                      destinationModel:destinModel];

// STEP 2 - Perform migration, assuming the mapping model isn't null
if (mappingModel) {
    NSError *error = nil;
    NSMigrationManager *migrationManager =
  [[NSMigrationManager alloc] initWithSourceModel:sourceModel
                                  destinationModel:destinModel];
    [migrationManager addObserver:self
                       forKeyPath:@"migrationProgress"
                          options:NSKeyValueObservingOptionNew
                          context:NULL];

    NSURL *destinStore =
    [[self applicationStoresDirectory]
      URLByAppendingPathComponent:@"Temp.sqlite"];

    success =
    [migrationManager migrateStoreFromURL:sourceStore
            type:NSSQLiteStoreType options:nil
                        withMappingModel:mappingModel
                        toDestinationURL:destinStore
                         destinationType:NSSQLiteStoreType
                      destinationOptions:nil
                                   error:&error];
    if (success) {
        // STEP 3 - Replace the old store with the new migrated store
        if ([self replaceStore:sourceStore withStore:destinStore]) {
            if (debug==1) {
            NSLog(@"SUCCESSFULLY MIGRATED %@ to the Current Model",
                                                sourceStore.path);}
                [migrationManager removeObserver:self
                                      forKeyPath:@"migrationProgress"];
        }
    }
    else {
        if (debug==1) {NSLog(@"FAILED MIGRATION: %@",error);}
    }
```

```
    }
    else {
        if (debug==1) {NSLog(@"FAILED MIGRATION: Mapping Model is null");}
    }
    return YES; // indicates migration has finished, regardless of outcome
}
```

STEP 1 involves gathering the things you need to perform a migration, which are as follows:

- A **source model**, which you get from the metadata of a persistent store through its coordinator via metadataForPersistentStoreOfType

- A **destination model**, which is just the existing _model instance variable

- A **mapping model**, which is determined automatically by passing nil as the bundle along with the source and destination models

STEP 2 is the process of the actual migration. An instance of NSMigrationManager is created using the source and destination models. Before migrateStoreFromURL is called, a destination store is set. This destination store is just a temporary store that's only used for migration purposes.

STEP 3 is only triggered when a migration has succeeded. The replaceStore method is used to clean up after a successful migration. When migration occurs, a new store is created at the destination; yet, this is no good to Core Data until the migrated store has the same location and filename as the old store. In order to use the newly migrated store, the old store is deleted and the new store is put in its place. In your own projects you may wish to copy the old store to a backup location first. The option to keep a store backup is up to you and would require slightly modified code in the replaceStore method. If you do decide to back up the old store, be aware that you'll double your application's storage requirements in the process.

The migration process is made visible to the user by an observeValueForKeyPath method that is called whenever the migration progress changes. This method is responsible for updating the migration progress View Controller whenever it sees a change to the migrationProgress property of the migration manager.

The code involved in the observeValueForKeyPath and replaceStore methods is shown in Listing 3.7.

Listing 3.7   **CoreDataHelper.m: observeValueForKeyPath and replaceStore**

```
- (void)observeValueForKeyPath:(NSString *)keyPath
                      ofObject:(id)object
                        change:(NSDictionary *)change
                       context:(void *)context {

    if ([keyPath isEqualToString:@"migrationProgress"]) {
```

```
        dispatch_async(dispatch_get_main_queue(), ^{

            float progress =
            [[change objectForKey:NSKeyValueChangeNewKey] floatValue];
            self.migrationVC.progressView.progress = progress;
            int percentage = progress * 100;
            NSString *string =
            [NSString stringWithFormat:@"Migration Progress: %i%%",
                                            percentage];

            NSLog(@"%@",string);
            self.migrationVC.label.text = string;
        });
    }
}
- (BOOL)replaceStore:(NSURL*)old withStore:(NSURL*)new {

    BOOL success = NO;
    NSError *Error = nil;
    if ([[NSFileManager defaultManager]
         removeItemAtURL:old error:&Error]) {

        Error = nil;
        if ([[NSFileManager defaultManager]
             moveItemAtURL:new toURL:old error:&Error]) {
            success = YES;
        }
        else {
            if (debug==1) {NSLog(@"FAILED to re-home new store %@", Error);}
        }
    }
    else {
        if (debug==1) {
            NSLog(@"FAILED to remove old store %@: Error:%@", old, Error);
        }
    }
    return success;
}
```

Update Grocery Dude as follows to continue implementing the MIGRATION MANAGER section:

1. Add the code from Listing 3.7 and then Listing 3.6 to the MIGRATION MANAGER section at the bottom of CoreDataHelper.m before @end.

To start a migration in the background using a migration manager, the method shown in Listing 3.8 is needed.

Listing 3.8   **CoreDataHelper.m: performBackgroundManagedMigrationForStore**

```
- (void)performBackgroundManagedMigrationForStore:(NSURL*)storeURL {
if (debug==1) {
    NSLog(@"Running %@ '%@'", self.class, NSStringFromSelector(_cmd));
}

    // Show migration progress view preventing the user from using the app
    UIStoryboard *sb = [UIStoryboard storyboardWithName:@"Main" bundle:nil];
    self.migrationVC =
    [sb instantiateViewControllerWithIdentifier:@"migration"];
    UIApplication *sa = [UIApplication sharedApplication];
    UINavigationController *nc =
    (UINavigationController*)sa.keyWindow.rootViewController;
    [nc presentViewController:self.migrationVC animated:NO completion:nil];

    // Perform migration in the background, so it doesn't freeze the UI.
    // This way progress can be shown to the user
    dispatch_async(
    dispatch_get_global_queue(
    DISPATCH_QUEUE_PRIORITY_BACKGROUND, 0), ^{
        BOOL done = [self migrateStore:storeURL];
        if(done) {
            // When migration finishes, add the newly migrated store
            dispatch_async(dispatch_get_main_queue(), ^{
                NSError *error = nil;
                _store =
                [_coordinator addPersistentStoreWithType:NSSQLiteStoreType
                                           configuration:nil
                                                     URL:[self storeURL]
                                                 options:nil
                                                   error:&error];
                if (!_store) {
                    NSLog(@"Failed to add a migrated store. Error: %@",
                    error);abort();}
                else {
                    NSLog(@"Successfully added a migrated store: %@",
                    _store);}
                [self.migrationVC dismissViewControllerAnimated:NO
                                                     completion:nil];
                self.migrationVC = nil;
            });
        }
    });
}
```

The performBackgroundManagedMigrationForStore method uses a storyboard identifier to instantiate and present the migration view. Once the view is blocking user interaction, the migration can begin. The migrateStore method is called on a background thread. Once migration is complete, the coordinator then adds the store as usual, the migration view is dismissed, and normal use of the application can resume.

Update Grocery Dude as follows to continue implementing the MIGRATION MANAGER section:

1. Add the code from Listing 3.8 to the MIGRATION MANAGER section at the bottom of CoreDataHelper.m before @end.

The best time to check whether migration is necessary is just before a store is added to a coordinator. To orchestrate this, the loadStore method of CoreDataHelper.m needs to be updated. If a migration is necessary, it will be triggered here. Listing 3.9 shows the code involved.

Listing 3.9 **CoreDataHelper.m: loadStore**

```
if (debug==1) {
    NSLog(@"Running %@ '%@'", self.class, NSStringFromSelector(_cmd));
}
    if (_store) {return;} // Don't load store if it's already loaded

    BOOL useMigrationManager = YES;
    if (useMigrationManager &&
        [self isMigrationNecessaryForStore:[self storeURL]]) {
        [self performBackgroundManagedMigrationForStore:[self storeURL]];
    } else {
        NSDictionary *options =
        @{
          NSMigratePersistentStoresAutomaticallyOption:@YES
          ,NSInferMappingModelAutomaticallyOption:@NO
          ,NSSQLitePragmasOption: @{@"journal_mode": @"DELETE"}
          };
        NSError *error = nil;
        _store = [_coordinator addPersistentStoreWithType:NSSQLiteStoreType
                                            configuration:nil
                                                      URL:[self storeURL]
                                                  options:options
                                                    error:&error];
        if (!_store) {
            NSLog(@"Failed to add store. Error: %@", error);abort();
        }
        else            {NSLog(@"Successfully added store: %@", _store);}
    }
```

Update Grocery Dude as follows to finalize the Migration Manager:

1. Replace all existing code in the `loadStore` method of `CoreDataHelper.m` with the code from Listing 3.9.

2. Add a model version called **Model 4** based on **Model 3**.

3. Select **Model 4.xcdatamodel**.

4. Delete the **Amount** entity.

5. Add a new entity called **Unit** with a String attribute called **name**.

6. Create an `NSManagedObject` subclass of the **Unit** entity. When it comes time to save the class file, don't forget to tick the Grocery Dude target.

7. Set **Model 4** as the current model.

8. Create a new mapping model with **Model 3** as the source and **Model 4** as the target. When it comes time to save the mapping model file, don't forget to tick the Grocery Dude target and save the mapping model as **Model3toModel4**.

9. Select **Model3toModel4.xcmappingmodel**.

10. Select the **Unit** entity mapping.

11. Set the **Source** of the **Unit** entity to **Amount** and the **Value Expression** of the **name** destination attribute to **$source.xyz**. You should see the **Unit** entity mapping automatically renamed to **AmountToUnit**, as shown in Figure 3.12.

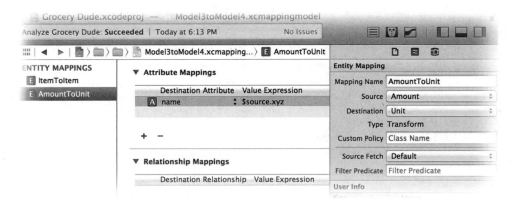

Figure 3.12   Mapping model for AmountToUnit

You're almost ready to perform a migration; however, the fetch request in the `demo` method still refers to the old Amount entity.

Update Grocery Dude as follows to refer to the Unit entity instead of the Amount entity:

1. Replace `#import "Amount.h"` with `#import "Unit.h"` at the top of `AppDelegate.m`.

2. Replace the code in the `demo` method of `AppDelegate.m` with the code shown in Listing 3.10. This code just fetches 50 **Unit** objects from the persistent store.

Listing 3.10   `AppDelegate.m: demo` (Fetching Test Unit Data)

```
NSFetchRequest *request =
[NSFetchRequest fetchRequestWithEntityName:@"Unit"];
[request setFetchLimit:50];
NSError *error = nil;
NSArray *fetchedObjects =
[_coreDataHelper.context executeFetchRequest:request error:&error];

if (error) {NSLog(@"%@", error);}
else {
    for (Unit *unit in fetchedObjects) {
        NSLog(@"Fetched Object = %@", unit.name);
    }
}
```

The migration manager is finally ready! Run the application and *pay close attention*! You should see the migration manager flash before your eyes, alerting you to the progress of the migration. The progress will also be shown in the console log.

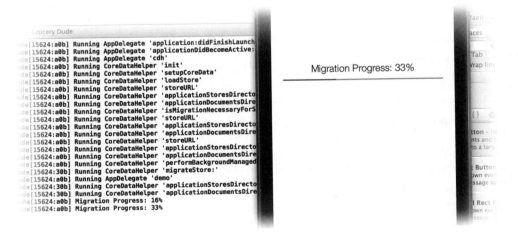

Figure 3.13   Visible migration progress

Examine the contents of the ZUNIT table in the `Grocery-Dude.sqlite` file using the techniques discussed in Chapter 2. The expected result is shown in Figure 3.14. If you notice a `-wal` file in the Stores directory and you're sure that the default journaling mode is disabled, you might need to click **Product > Clean** and run the application again to examine the contents of the `sqlite` file.

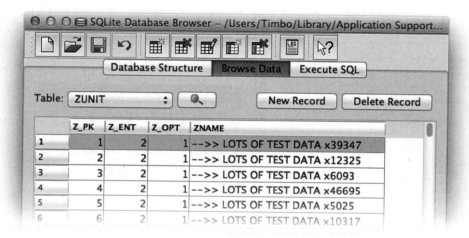

Figure 3.14   Successful use of the Migration Manager

If you've reproduced the results shown in Figure 3.14, give yourself a pat on the back because you've successfully implemented three types of model migration! The rest of the book will use lightweight migrations, so it needs to be re-enabled.

Update Grocery Dude as follows to re-enable lightweight migration:

1. Set the `NSInferMappingModelAutomaticallyOption` option in the `loadStore` method of `CoreDataHelper.m` to `@YES`.

2. Set `useMigrationManager` to `NO` in the `loadStore` method of `CoreDataHelper.m`.

3. Remove all code from the `demo` method of `AppDelegate.m`.

The old mapping models and `NSManagedObject` subclasses of entities that don't exist anymore are no longer needed. Although you could remove them, leave them in the project for reference sake.

Summary

You've now experienced lightweight migration, default migration, and using a Migration Manager to display progress. You should now be able to make an informed decision when determining between migration options for your own applications. Don't forget that the only migration option for iCloud-enabled Core Data applications is lightweight migration. Adding model versions should now be a familiar procedure because the model has changed several times already.

Exercises

Why not build on what you've learned by experimenting?

1. Set the current model version to **Model 3** and run the application. It should not crash because the downgrade of data is inferred automatically. Note that this is only because `NSInferMappingModelAutomaticallyOption` has been re-enabled. In reality, you would need a **Model4toModel3** mapping model to map attributes properly.

2. Examine the contents of the ZAMOUNT table in `Grocery-Dude.sqlite` and you'll notice something critical: Where has all the data gone? There was no mapping model, so all the ZUNIT data was lost during the downgrade!

3. Set the current model to **Model 4** and re-enable the migration manager in the `loadStore` method of `CoreDataHelper.m` by setting `useMigrationManager` to YES.

4. Run the application to witness another manual migration, which will be extremely fast because there is no data in the store. Set `useMigrationManager` to NO before continuing to the next chapter.

4

Managed Object Model Expansion

Black holes are where God divided by zero.

Albert Einstein

In Chapter 3, "Managed Object Model Migration," you learned how to manage a changing model with versioning, mappings, and migration techniques. This chapter will exercise your newfound migration knowledge as it introduces further changes to the model. The topics will cover expanding beyond one or two entities with the introduction of relationships, and at the end of the chapter, entity inheritance. The implications of delete rules will be discussed, along with the impact some of them can have on data validation. Following that, you'll be shown how to handle data validation errors and, worst case, how to terminate gracefully and give users an error code to report back to you.

Relationships

Relationships link entities. Using relationships in the managed object model introduces a powerful means to connect logical areas of data represented by entities. Using relationships can significantly reduce the capacity requirements of a database. Instead of duplicating the same data in multiple entities, a relationship can be put in place as a pointer to a piece of data so it only needs to be stored once. Although de-duplication is one advantage, the true power of relationships is their ability to allow connections between complex data types.

Consider the existing Item and Unit entities found in Grocery Dude's model. Instances of the Item entity will represent things you can put on a shopping list, such as the following:

- Chocolate
- Potatoes
- Milk

Instances of the Unit entity will represent units of measurement (g, Kg, and ml), appended to an item quantity. For example:

- 250g chocolate
- 4Kg potatoes
- 500ml milk

If you really wanted to, you could simply have a string attribute in the Item entity called **unit**. For each item object, you could then populate the string representing the unit with something like **g**, **Kg**, or **ml**. The problem with that approach is that you're wasting space in the database because you repeatedly duplicate the data for every Item's unit. In addition to wasting all that space, you're also going to have a hard time updating a unit for all items. If you wanted to use *kilogram* instead of *Kg*, you would have to iterate through all items with the string **Kg** and rename it to **kilogram**, item by item. This is highly inefficient and would make for a very slow application. The solution is to instead use a relationship to a Unit entity, thereby just using a pointer to a single Kg object. This not only reduces the amount of storage space required, it also means you only have to update the unit name in one place to change a unit's name.

> **Note**
>
> To continue building the sample application, you'll need to have added the previous chapter's code to Grocery Dude. Alternatively, you may download, unzip, and use the project up to this point from http://www.timroadley.com/LearningCoreData/GroceryDude-AfterChapter03.zip. It is recommended that you use the iOS Simulator when following this chapter so you can inspect the contents of the SQLite database files easily.

Update Grocery Dude as follows to prepare for this chapter:

1. Delete the application from the iOS Simulator.
2. Click **Product** > **Clean** to ensure there's no residual cache from previous incarnations of the project.
3. Run the application once on the iOS Simulator to generate an empty persistent store.

Update Grocery Dude as follows to create a relationship:

1. Optionally take a snapshot or back up the project.
2. Add a model version named **Model 5** based on **Model 4** using the techniques from Chapter 3.
3. Set **Model 5** as the **Current Model**.
4. Select **Model 5.xcdatamodel**.
5. Change the **Editor Style** to **Graph**, as shown in Figure 4.1.

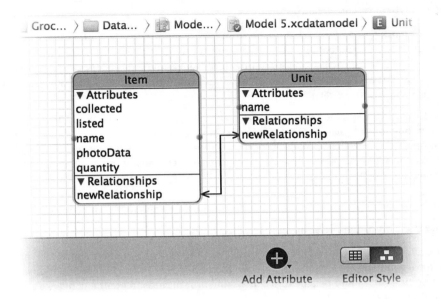

Figure 4.1   A new relationship

6. If the **Item** and **Unit** entities are sitting on top of each other, drag them apart.

7. Hold down **Control** and drag a line from the **Item** entity to the **Unit** entity. The expected result is shown in Figure 4.1.

By creating a relationship between two entities using the Graph Editor Style, you've created an **inverse relationship**, which is two relationships in opposite directions between two entities. In this case, one relationship is from Item to Unit and the other is from Unit to Item. If instead you created a relationship using the Table Editor Style, the result would only be a one-way relationship. You need to manually add inverse relationships when using the Table Editor Style, provided that is what you want.

With an inverse relationship in place, you can now do the following:

- Associate Item managed objects to Unit managed objects.
- Associate Unit managed objects to Item managed objects.

This newfound association allows access to the attributes of the related entity through the relationship (for example, `item.newRelationship.name`). You next need to consider whether each direction of the relationship is **To-Many** or **To-One**. The answer to this question should also help you rename the relationship appropriately. A To-Many relationship allows a potentially unlimited number of destination objects, whereas the alternative limits the allowable number of destination objects to one.

Consider the Item-to-Unit relationship:

- Configuring a To-Many relationship from the Item entity to the Unit entity would allow an item to have potentially unlimited units of measurement. This is not ideal because items on a shopping list only need one unit of measurement (such as Kg or pound). Note also that it is possible to configure a maximum number of related objects allowable through a To-Many relationship.

- Configuring a To-One relationship from the Item entity to the Unit entity would mean only one unit of measurement can be assigned to an item. This is ideal because items on a shopping list only need one unit of measurement. A good name for the relationship in this direction would therefore be **unit**. With this new relationship name, you could then use `item.unit.name` to reference the related unit's name through the item object.

When you create an inverse relationship, you need to think about *both* directions.

Consider the Unit-to-Item relationship:

- Configuring a To-One relationship from the Unit entity to the Item entity will prevent a unit from being used by more than one item. This is not ideal because many items on a shopping list should be able to use the same unit of measurement (such as 2Kg of onions and 1Kg of corn).

- Configuring a To-Many relationship from the Unit entity to the Item entity will allow a unit to be used by potentially unlimited items. This is ideal because many items on a shopping list will need to use the same unit of measurement. A good name for the relationship in this direction would therefore be **items**. If you wanted to list all objects related to a particular unit, it's as easy as fetching `unit.items` to retrieve an `NSSet` with pointers them all!

Update Grocery Dude as follows to configure the relationships:

1. Rename the **newRelationship** in the **Item** entity to **unit**.

2. Rename the **newRelationship** in the **Unit** entity to **items**.

3. Change the **items** relationship **Type** to **To-Many**, as shown in Figure 4.2.

As you've now been shown, the name of a relationship should reflect something in line with what it provides access to. With the unit and items relationships now configured, you can access relationship destination properties in code via `item.unit` and `unit.items`. That said, you first need new `NSManagedObject` subclasses of these entities before you can use this dot notation.

Update Grocery Dude as follows to refresh the existing `NSManagedObect` subclasses:

1. Ensure **Model 5.xcdatamodel** is selected.

2. Create an `NSManagedObject` subclass of the **Item** and **Unit** entities using techniques discussed in the previous chapters. On the **Select the entities you would like to manage** page, ensure both the Item and Unit entities are ticked. When it comes time to save the class file, don't forget to tick the Grocery Dude target. Replace the existing files when prompted.

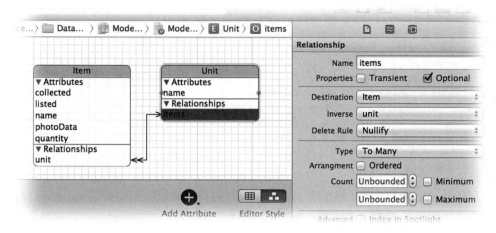

Figure 4.2   The unit and items relationships

Examine Unit.h and look for the new NSSet items property. The items property represents a To-Many relationship, so the "many" is provided as an NSSet that also comes with associated helper methods for adding and removing objects. The thing to know about an NSSet is that the objects within are not ordered, as opposed to an NSOrderedSet or NSArray. The ordering of fetched objects is usually done with a sort descriptor passed to a fetch request, which, in contrast, returns an NSArray. If you tick the "Ordered" relationship setting available with a To-Many relationship, the resulting NSManagedObject property type is an NSOrderedSet. Another difference between an NSSet and NSArray to keep in mind is that an NSSet cannot contain duplicate objects.

Examine Item.h, and you should notice a new unit property of type Unit. The unit property represents a To-One relationship, so the "one" is simply the class type of the target entity.

Inserting a couple of items and setting both their unit attributes to the same thing is now a clear-cut exercise, as shown in Listing 4.1.

Listing 4.1   **AppDelegate.m: demo (Relationship Creation)**

```
if (debug==1) {
    NSLog(@"Running %@ '%@'", self.class, NSStringFromSelector(_cmd));
}
    Unit *kg =
    [NSEntityDescription insertNewObjectForEntityForName:@"Unit"
                         inManagedObjectContext:[[self cdh] context]];
    Item *oranges =
    [NSEntityDescription insertNewObjectForEntityForName:@"Item"
                         inManagedObjectContext:[[self cdh] context]];
```

```
Item *bananas =
[NSEntityDescription insertNewObjectForEntityForName:@"Item"
                     inManagedObjectContext:[[self cdh] context]];
kg.name = @"Kg";
oranges.name = @"Oranges";
bananas.name = @"Bananas";
oranges.quantity = [NSNumber numberWithInt:1];
bananas.quantity = [NSNumber numberWithInt:4];
oranges.listed = [NSNumber numberWithBool:YES];
bananas.listed = [NSNumber numberWithBool:YES];
oranges.unit = kg;
bananas.unit = kg;

NSLog(@"Inserted %@%@ %@",
     oranges.quantity, oranges.unit.name, oranges.name);
NSLog(@"Inserted %@%@ %@",
     bananas.quantity, bananas.unit.name, bananas.name);
[[self cdh] saveContext];
```

Update Grocery Dude as follows to insert new items with a common unit:

1. Populate the demo method of AppDelegate.m with the code from Listing 4.1.

2. Run the application once. The expected console log results are shown in Figure 4.3.

3. Delete all code from the demo method of AppDelegate.m.

```
⊡ ▶ ‖ ⟲ ⬇ ⬆ ◀ | ▦ Grocery Dude
2013-07-05 08:06:31.627 Grocery Dude[50785:a0b] Successfully added store: <NSSQLCore: 0x8e815e0> (URL:
file:///Users/Timbo/Library/Application%20Support/iPhone%20Simulator/7.0/Applications/
80DFF82E-8FB1-4A1C-8684-3FAB242E5608/Documents/Stores/Grocery-Dude.sqlite)
2013-07-05 08:06:31.627 Grocery Dude[50785:a0b] Running AppDelegate 'demo'
2013-07-05 08:06:31.627 Grocery Dude[50785:a0b] Running AppDelegate 'cdh'
2013-07-05 08:06:31.628 Grocery Dude[50785:a0b] Running AppDelegate 'cdh'
2013-07-05 08:06:31.628 Grocery Dude[50785:a0b] Running AppDelegate 'cdh'
2013-07-05 08:06:31.629 Grocery Dude[50785:a0b] Inserted 1Kg Oranges
2013-07-05 08:06:31.630 Grocery Dude[50785:a0b] Inserted 4Kg Bananas
2013-07-05 08:06:31.630 Grocery Dude[50785:a0b] Running AppDelegate 'cdh'
2013-07-05 08:06:31.630 Grocery Dude[50785:a0b] Running CoreDataHelper 'saveContext'
2013-07-05 08:06:31.633 Grocery Dude[50785:a0b] _context SAVED changes to persistent store
```

Figure 4.3   Successful insertion of items with a relationship to the same unit

To prove there is only one row in the database representing the Kg object, examine the contents of the Grocery-Dude.sqlite file using the techniques discussed in Chapter 2, "Managed Object Model Basics." The expected result is shown in Figure 4.4.

Ensure you close SQLite Database Browser before continuing.

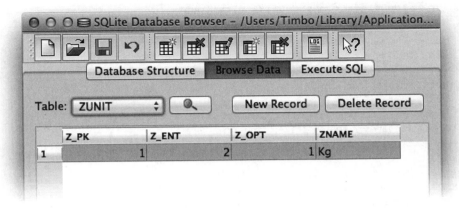

Figure 4.4   The Unit entity in the SQLite database as ZUNIT

Delete Rules

An important relationship setting to be aware of is **Delete Rule**. When an object is deleted, this setting determines what happens to related objects, as detailed here:

- The **Nullify** delete rule is a good default for most situations. When an object is deleted and this rule is in place, related objects nil out their relationship to the deleted object. For example, assume a **unit** object named **Kg** is related to some **item** objects. If a **Nullify** delete rule was set on the **items** relationship and the Kg unit object was deleted, the related **item** objects would set their **unit** property to nil.

- The **Cascade** delete rule propagates deletions through the relationship. For example, assume a **unit** object named **Kg** is related to some **item** objects. If a **Cascade** delete rule was set on the **items** relationship and the Kg **unit** object was deleted, all the related **item** objects would be deleted, too.

- The **Deny** delete rule prevents the deletion of an object if it still has related objects. For example, assume a **unit** object named **Kg** is related to some **item** objects. If a **Deny** delete rule was set on the **items** relationship and the Kg unit object was deleted, the existence of related **item** objects would cause a validation error when the context was saved. When you use a **Deny** delete rule, you need to ensure that there are no related objects at the relationship destination before deleting the source object.

- The **No Action** delete rule is a strange one that will actually leave your object graph in an inconsistent state. If you use this delete rule, it is up to you to manually set the inverse relationship to something valid. Only corner-case situations call for this delete rule.

In order to test the results of object deletion, a new method is required that displays a count of unit and item objects in the persistent store. Listing 4.2 shows the code involved.

Listing 4.2 **AppDelegate.m: showUnitAndItemCount**

```
- (void)showUnitAndItemCount {
    // List how many items there are in the database
    NSFetchRequest *items =
    [NSFetchRequest fetchRequestWithEntityName:@"Item"];
    NSError *itemsError = nil;
    NSArray *fetchedItems =
    [[[self cdh] context] executeFetchRequest:items error:&itemsError];
    if (!fetchedItems) {NSLog(@"%@", itemsError);}
    else {NSLog(@"Found %lu item(s) ",(unsigned long)[fetchedItems count]);}

    // List how many units there are in the database
    NSFetchRequest *units =
    [NSFetchRequest fetchRequestWithEntityName:@"Unit"];
    NSError *unitsError = nil;
    NSArray *fetchedUnits =
    [[[self cdh] context] executeFetchRequest:units error:&unitsError];
    if (!fetchedUnits) {NSLog(@"%@", unitsError);}
    else {NSLog(@"Found %lu unit(s) ",(unsigned long)[fetchedUnits count]);}
}
```

Update Grocery Dude as follows to prepare for delete rule testing:

1. Add the `showUnitAndItemCount` method from Listing 4.2 to `AppDelegate.m`, just above the existing `demo` method.

2. Replace all code in the `demo` method of `AppDelegate.m` with `[self showUnitAndItemCount];`.

3. Run the application. The expected console log results are shown in Figure 4.5.

```
2013-07-05 11:42:53.957 Grocery Dude[53517:a0b] Successfully added store: <NSSQLCore: 0x8e6bd80> (URL: file:///
Users/Timbo/Library/Application%20Support/iPhone%20Simulator/7.0/Applications/F81E31EF-15EB-4A3B-A535-
D33C79EE1129/Documents/Stores/Grocery-Dude.sqlite)
2013-07-05 11:42:53.957 Grocery Dude[53517:a0b] Running AppDelegate 'cdh'
2013-07-05 11:42:53.959 Grocery Dude[53517:a0b] Found 2 item(s)
2013-07-05 11:42:53.959 Grocery Dude[53517:a0b] Running AppDelegate 'cdh'
2013-07-05 11:42:53.960 Grocery Dude[53517:a0b] Found 1 unit(s)
```

Figure 4.5   A count of item(s) and unit(s) in the persistent store

The expected result shows there are two item objects and one unit object in the persistent store. The two item objects are **oranges** and **bananas**, which were inserted as a part of implementing Listing 4.1. The only unit object is Kg, which both items are related to. It's time to see what happens when the Kg unit is deleted when a **Deny** delete rule is in play.

Update Grocery Dude as follows to configure a **Deny** delete rule:

1. Select the **items** relationship in the **Unit** entity of **Model 5**.

2. Set the **items** relationship **Delete Rule** to **Deny** using Data Model Inspector (**Option+⌘+3**).

The code to delete a **unit** object named Kg is shown in Listing 4.3.

Listing 4.3   **AppDelegate.m: demo (Unit Deletion)**

```
NSLog(@"Before deletion of the unit entity:");
[self showUnitAndItemCount];

NSFetchRequest *request =
[NSFetchRequest fetchRequestWithEntityName:@"Unit"];
NSPredicate *filter =
[NSPredicate predicateWithFormat:@"name == %@", @"Kg"];
[request setPredicate:filter];
NSArray *kgUnit =
[[[self cdh] context] executeFetchRequest:request error:nil];
for (Unit *unit in kgUnit) {
    [_coreDataHelper.context deleteObject:unit];
    NSLog(@"A Kg unit object was deleted");
}

NSLog(@"After deletion of the unit entity:");
[self showUnitAndItemCount];
```

Update Grocery Dude as follows to implement the code to delete a Kg unit object:

1. Replace the existing code in the demo method of AppDelegate.m with the code from Listing 4.3.

2. Run the application. The expected console log results are shown in Figure 4.6.

```
2013-07-05 11:52:22.196 Grocery Dude[53732:a0b] Running AppDelegate 'cdh'
2013-07-05 11:52:22.197 Grocery Dude[53732:a0b] Found 2 item(s)
2013-07-05 11:52:22.198 Grocery Dude[53732:a0b] Running AppDelegate 'cdh'
2013-07-05 11:52:22.198 Grocery Dude[53732:a0b] Found 1 unit(s)
2013-07-05 11:52:22.199 Grocery Dude[53732:a0b] Running AppDelegate 'cdh'
2013-07-05 11:52:22.271 Grocery Dude[53732:a0b] A Kg unit object was deleted
2013-07-05 11:52:22.272 Grocery Dude[53732:a0b] After deletion of the unit entity:
2013-07-05 11:52:22.272 Grocery Dude[53732:a0b] Running AppDelegate 'cdh'
2013-07-05 11:52:22.273 Grocery Dude[53732:a0b] Found 2 item(s)
2013-07-05 11:52:22.273 Grocery Dude[53732:a0b] Running AppDelegate 'cdh'
2013-07-05 11:52:22.274 Grocery Dude[53732:a0b] Found 0 unit(s)
```

Figure 4.6   The Deny delete rule doesn't work?

Upon examining the console log, it appears that the Deny delete rule hasn't worked. What's going on here? Why are there no units anymore? Shouldn't the Deny rule have prevented the Kg unit object from being deleted because oranges and bananas are related to it? They're all good questions; however, the key point here is that the delete rule is only enforced when it comes time to save the context.

Update Grocery Dude as follows to save the context after the deletion:

1. Add `[[self cdh] saveContext];` to the bottom of the `demo` method of `AppDelegate.m`.

2. Re-run the application, which will fail to save the context as shown in Figure 4.7.

```
▽  ▶  ▷  ⟳  ⬇  ⬆  ◀  ━ Grocery Dude › ⛁ Thread 1 › ⬛ 3 –[CoreDataHelper saveContext]
2013-07-05 11:59:33.129 Grocery Dude[53885:a0b] Found 0 unit(s)
2013-07-05 11:59:33.129 Grocery Dude[53885:a0b] Running AppDelegate 'cdh'
2013-07-05 11:59:33.129 Grocery Dude[53885:a0b] Running CoreDataHelper 'saveContext'
2013-07-05 11:59:33.133 Grocery Dude[53885:a0b] Failed to save _context: Error Domain=NSCocoaErrorDomain
Code=1600 "The operation couldn't be completed. (Cocoa error 1600.)" UserInfo=0xe943480
{NSValidationErrorObject=<Unit: 0xa087f30> (entity: Unit; id: 0xa03dbf0 <x-coredata://122F1084-2759-415A-
B699-807C7B29FDC5/Unit/p1> ; data: {
    items =     (
        "0xe93f4f0 <x-coredata://122F1084-2759-415A-B699-807C7B29FDC5/Item/p2>",
        "0xe93f4e0 <x-coredata://122F1084-2759-415A-B699-807C7B29FDC5/Item/p1>"
    );
    name = Kg;
}), NSValidationErrorKey=items, NSLocalizedDescription=The operation couldn't be completed. (Cocoa error
1600.), NSValidationErrorValue=Relationship 'items' on managed object (0xa087f30) <Unit: 0xa087f30> (entity:
Unit; id: 0xa03dbf0 <x-coredata://122F1084-2759-415A-B699-807C7B29FDC5/Unit/p1> ; data: {
```

Figure 4.7   The Deny delete rule works.

The delete rule only comes into effect when a context save is attempted. Any breach of the delete rule will generate an `NSCocoaErrorDomain` error 1600. To get around this error, you'll need to check that the unit object can be safely deleted *before* deleting it.

If it is not safe to delete the object, you could do either of the following:

- Tell the user the deletion is denied and skip deletion.

- Nil out all `unit.items` first and then delete the `unit` object.

In reality, this type of issue would probably come up after a user swipes to delete a unit from a table view. When a Deny delete rule is in place, you should use a method available from the super class `NSManagedObject` called `validateForDelete`. This method returns `YES` if it's safe to delete the object in question. Listing 4.4 shows this method in some sample code.

Listing 4.4   **AppDelegate.m: demo (Validate for Delete)**

```
NSError *error;
if ([unit validateForDelete:&error]) {
    NSLog(@"Deleting '%@'", unit.name);
    [_coreDataHelper.context deleteObject:unit];
```

```
} else {
    NSLog(@"Failed to delete %@, Error: %@",
    unit.name, error.localizedDescription);
}
```

Update Grocery Dude as follows to perform validation prior to deletion:

1. Replace all code within the existing `for` loop of the `demo` method of `AppDelegate.m` with the code from Listing 4.4.

2. Run the application again. The expected result is that the Kg unit is not deleted, which is shown in Figure 4.8.

```
2013-07-05 12:09:48.252 Grocery Dude[54046:a0b] Found 1 unit(s)
2013-07-05 12:09:48.252 Grocery Dude[54046:a0b] Running AppDelegate 'cdh'
2013-07-05 12:09:48.255 Grocery Dude[54046:a0b] Failed to delete Kg, Error: The operation couldn't be completed.
(Cocoa error 1600.)
2013-07-05 12:09:48.255 Grocery Dude[54046:a0b] After deletion of the unit entity:
2013-07-05 12:09:48.256 Grocery Dude[54046:a0b] Running AppDelegate 'cdh'
2013-07-05 12:09:48.256 Grocery Dude[54046:a0b] Found 2 item(s)
2013-07-05 12:09:48.256 Grocery Dude[54046:a0b] Running AppDelegate 'cdh'
2013-07-05 12:09:48.257 Grocery Dude[54046:a0b] Found 1 unit(s)
2013-07-05 12:09:48.257 Grocery Dude[54046:a0b] Running AppDelegate 'cdh'
2013-07-05 12:09:48.257 Grocery Dude[54046:a0b] Running CoreDataHelper 'saveContext'
2013-07-05 12:09:48.258 Grocery Dude[54046:a0b] SKIPPED _context save, there are no changes!
```

Figure 4.8   Validate that objects are safe to delete before deleting them.

The next step is to make validation errors visible to the user, even though this is a last resort that they should never have to experience.

Validation Errors

Before objects can be saved to a persistent store, they must pass validation. If an object fails validation, an `NSError` from the `NSCocoaErrorDomain` will be thrown. There are just over a dozen types of validation errors, which you can see by jumping to the definition of `NSManagedObjectValidationError` in Xcode. This jump will take you to `CoreDataErrors.h`, which defines the validation errors that are also shown in Table 4.1.

Table 4.1   **Possible Validation Errors**

Code	Constant
1560	NSValidationMultipleErrorsError
1570	NSValidationMissingMandatoryPropertyError
1580	NSValidationRelationshipLacksMinimumCountError
1590	NSValidationRelationshipExceedsMaximumCountError

Code	Constant
1600	NSValidationRelationshipDeniedDeleteError
1610	NSValidationNumberTooLargeError
1620	NSValidationNumberTooSmallError
1630	NSValidationDateTooLateError
1640	NSValidationDateTooSoonError
1650	NSValidationInvalidDateError
1660	NSValidationStringTooLongError
1670	NSValidationStringTooShortError
1680	NSValidationStringPatternMatchingError

The application currently can't save due to error 1600. A validateForDelete was put in place to at least ensure the save isn't attempted. Because it's likely this type of validation logic could be forgotten in other areas of the application, it's good to put in some graceful "last-resort" error alerting. This way, an end user could contact the developer to pass on the error code received. Listing 4.5 shows the code required to cause a validation error.

Listing 4.5   **CoreDataHelper.m: demo (Unit Deletion)**

```
NSLog(@"Before deletion of the unit entity:");
[self showUnitAndItemCount];

NSFetchRequest *request =
[NSFetchRequest fetchRequestWithEntityName:@"Unit"];
NSPredicate *filter =
[NSPredicate predicateWithFormat:@"name == %@", @"Kg"];
[request setPredicate:filter];
NSArray *kgUnit =
[[[self cdh] context] executeFetchRequest:request error:nil];
for (Unit *unit in kgUnit) {
    [[[self cdh] context] deleteObject:unit];
    NSLog(@"A Kg unit object was deleted");
}

NSLog(@"After deletion of the unit entity:");
[self showUnitAndItemCount];
[[self cdh] saveContext];
```

Update Grocery Dude as follows to ensure the application fails to save again:

1. Replace all code in the demo method of AppDelegate.m with the code from Listing 4.5.

2. Run the application again, which should fail to save with error 1600.

To show the validation error to the user, a new showValidationError method will inter-cept validation errors and present an appropriate alert. To begin with, the new method will only have increased information regarding error code 1600. As per Table 4.1, error code 1600 means an NSValidationRelationshipDeniedDeleteError occurred. Listing 4.6 shows the showValidationError method that will catch and alert on this error.

Listing 4.6 **CoreDataHelper.m: showValidationError**

```
#pragma mark - VALIDATION ERROR HANDLING
- (void)showValidationError:(NSError *)anError {

    if (anError && [anError.domain isEqualToString:@"NSCocoaErrorDomain"]) {
        NSArray *errors = nil;  // holds all errors
        NSString *txt = @""; // the error message text of the alert

    // Populate array with error(s)
    if (anError.code == NSValidationMultipleErrorsError) {
        errors = [anError.userInfo objectForKey:NSDetailedErrorsKey];
    } else {
        errors = [NSArray arrayWithObject:anError];
    }
    // Display the error(s)
    if (errors && errors.count > 0) {
    // Build error message text based on errors
        for (NSError * error in errors) {
        NSString *entity =
      [[[error.userInfo objectForKey:@"NSValidationErrorObject"]entity]name];

        NSString *property =
        [error.userInfo objectForKey:@"NSValidationErrorKey"];

        switch (error.code) {
        case NSValidationRelationshipDeniedDeleteError:
        txt = [txt stringByAppendingFormat:
@"%@ delete was denied because there are associated %@\n(Error Code
➥%li)\n\n"
        , entity, property, (long)error.code];
        break;
        default:
        txt = [txt stringByAppendingFormat:
        @"Unhandled error code %li in showValidationError method"
        , (long)error.code];
        break;
        }
    }
    // display error message txt message
```

```
        UIAlertView *alertView =
        [[UIAlertView alloc] initWithTitle:@"Validation Error"

        message:[NSString stringWithFormat:@"%@Please double-tap the home button
➥and close this application by swiping the application screenshot
➥upwards",txt]
                                delegate:nil
                        cancelButtonTitle:nil
                        otherButtonTitles:nil];
            [alertView show];
            }
        }
    }
```

The `showValidationError` method starts by breaking apart the detailed contents of an
`NSError` and then putting single errors into an `errors` array. Provided the resulting array isn't
empty, the method then iterates through the array and builds an error message string. Once
the string is created, it is passed to a `UIAlertView` that is shown to the user.

Update Grocery Dude as follows to warn the user of the validation error:

1. Add the code from Listing 4.6 to the bottom of `CoreDataHelper.m`, just before `@end`.

2. Add `[self showValidationError:error];` to the `saveContext` method of
   `CoreDataHelper.m` on the line after `Failed to save`.

3. Run the application. The expected result is shown in Figure 4.9.

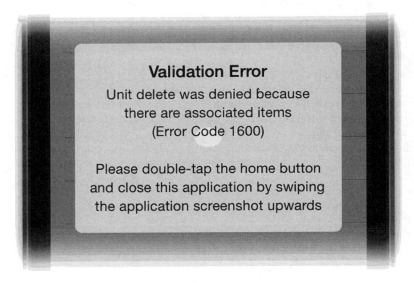

Figure 4.9   An alert view is more user friendly than an outright crash.

From now on, when a context is saved and data validation fails, at least there's a nice error displaying what happened. Adding descriptions for the other validation failures is as easy as updating the switch-case statement in the showValidationError method, as shown in Listing 4.7.

Listing 4.7 **CoreDataHelper.m: showValidationError (Additional Cases)**

```
case NSValidationRelationshipLacksMinimumCountError:
txt = [txt stringByAppendingFormat:
@"the '%@' relationship count is too small (Code %li)."
, property, (long)error.code];
break;
case NSValidationRelationshipExceedsMaximumCountError:
txt = [txt stringByAppendingFormat:
@"the '%@' relationship count is too large (Code %li)."
, property, (long)error.code];
break;
case NSValidationMissingMandatoryPropertyError:
txt = [txt stringByAppendingFormat:
@"the '%@' property is missing (Code %li).", property, (long)error.code];
break;
case NSValidationNumberTooSmallError:
txt = [txt stringByAppendingFormat:
@"the '%@' number is too small (Code %li).", property, (long)error.code];
break;
case NSValidationNumberTooLargeError:
txt = [txt stringByAppendingFormat:
@"the '%@' number is too large (Code %li).", property, (long)error.code];
break;
case NSValidationDateTooSoonError:
txt = [txt stringByAppendingFormat:
@"the '%@' date is too soon (Code %li).", property, (long)error.code];
break;
case NSValidationDateTooLateError:
txt = [txt stringByAppendingFormat:
@"the '%@' date is too late (Code %li).", property, (long)error.code];
break;
case NSValidationInvalidDateError:
txt = [txt stringByAppendingFormat:
@"the '%@' date is invalid (Code %li).", property, (long)error.code];
break;
case NSValidationStringTooLongError:
txt = [txt stringByAppendingFormat:
@"the '%@' text is too long (Code %li).", property, (long)error.code];
break;
case NSValidationStringTooShortError:
txt = [txt stringByAppendingFormat:
```

```
@"the '%@' text is too short (Code %li).", property, (long)error.code];
break;
case NSValidationStringPatternMatchingError:
txt = [txt stringByAppendingFormat:
@"the '%@' text doesn't match the specified pattern (Code %li)."
, property, (long)error.code];
break;
case NSManagedObjectValidationError:
txt = [txt stringByAppendingFormat:
@"generated validation error (Code %li)", (long)error.code];
break;
```

Update Grocery Dude to enhance the validation error alert descriptions:

1. Add the additional cases from Listing 4.7 to the existing switch-case statement found in the `showValidationErrors` method of `CoreDataHelper.m` on the line before `default`.

2. Remove all code from the `demo` method of `AppDelegate.m`.

3. Run the application again, which should not display a validation error alert view.

Entity Inheritance

Similar to classes, entities have the ability to inherit from a parent. This useful feature allows you to simplify the data model. Child entities automatically inherit the attributes of their parent entity. In an underlying SQLite store, all entities involved in a parent-child hierarchy reside in the same table.

The sample application is centered on the understanding that grocery items could live in one of two locations: the shop or your house. This means entity inheritance could be leveraged to allow attributes common to a shop location and home location to be inherited from a parent location. For example, let's say an entity called **Location** has an attribute called **summary**. If another entity such as **LocationAtHome** or **LocationAtShop** inherits from Location, it will automatically have the **summary** attribute. This behavior is similar to class inheritance.

To prevent the Location entity from ever being instantiated, you have the option of making it abstract. You would do this only if it doesn't make sense to have instances of the Location entity in your code.

Update Grocery Dude as follows to configure entities with inheritance:

1. Add a new model version named **Model 6** based on **Model 5**.

2. Set **Model 6** as the **Current Model**.

3. Ensure **Model 6.xcdatamodel** is selected.

4. Add a new entity called **Location** with a **String** attribute called **summary**.

5. Select the **Location** entity and open up the **Data Model Inspector** in the **Utilities** pane, as shown in Figure 4.10.

6. Tick **Abstract Entity**, which triggers a warning that the Location entity has no children.

7. Create a new entity called **LocationAtHome** with a **String** attribute called **storedIn**.

8. Create a new entity called **LocationAtShop** with a **String** attribute called **aisle**.

9. Click the **LocationAtHome** entity and then set its parent entity to **Location** using Data Model Inspector (**Option+⌘+3**).

10. Click the **LocationAtShop** entity and then set its parent entity to **Location**.

11. Change the **Editor Style** to **Graph** (if it isn't already) and then arrange the entities as shown in Figure 4.10. If you can't see all the entities, you might need to scroll to them.

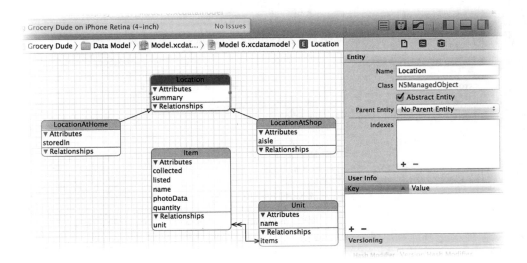

Figure 4.10   Location as an abstract, parent entity

With the new parent and child entities in place, it's time to link them to the Item entity so items can be related to a home or shop location.

Update Grocery Dude as follows to configure the "location at home" relationships:

1. Hold down **Control** while dragging a line from the **LocationAtHome** entity to the **Item** entity.

2. Rename **newRelationship** in the **LocationAtHome** entity to **items**.

3. Set the **items** relationship in the **LocationAtHome** entity to **To-Many**.

4. Rename **newRelationship** in the **Item** entity to **locationAtHome**.

Update Grocery Dude as follows to configure the "location at shop" relationships:

1. Hold down **Control** while dragging a line from the **LocationAtShop** entity to the **Item** entity.

2. Rename **newRelationship** in the **LocationAtShop** entity to **items**.

3. Set the **items** relationship in the **LocationAtShop** entity to **To-Many**.

4. Rename **newRelationship** in the **Item** entity to **locationAtShop**.

The model should now match the one shown in Figure 4.11. Notice how the double-headed arrows indicate a To-Many relationship.

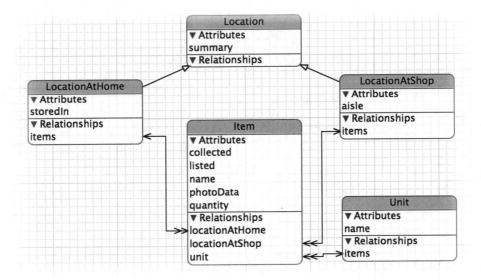

Figure 4.11   The new model adds support for item locations

Update Grocery Dude as follows to ensure dot notation can be used with the new entities in code:

1. Create an NSManagedObject subclass of all entities in **Model 6**, replacing any existing files. Remember to select the Grocery Dude target when you save.

When generating subclass files, you may come across a chicken-and-egg situation. This situation causes a To-One relationship to be generated as an NSManagedObject property, instead of a property named after the target instance. Figure 4.12 shows an incorrectly generated subclass Item.h.

```
#import <Foundation/Foundation.h>
#import <CoreData/CoreData.h>

@class Unit;

@interface Item : NSManagedObject

@property (nonatomic, retain) NSNumber * collected;
@property (nonatomic, retain) NSNumber * listed;
@property (nonatomic, retain) NSString * name;
@property (nonatomic, retain) NSData * photoData;
@property (nonatomic, retain) NSNumber * quantity;
@property (nonatomic, retain) Unit *unit;
@property (nonatomic, retain) NSManagedObject *locationAtHome;
@property (nonatomic, retain) NSManagedObject *locationAtShop;

@end
```

Figure 4.12   An incorrectly generated `NSManagedObject` subclass

Just which files have these base-level properties may vary depending on the order of subclass generation. To fix this issue, all you have to do is generate the subclass files again the same way you did previously. Figure 4.13 shows a correctly generated subclass, `Item.h`. You may want to get into the habit of generating `NSManagedObject` subclasses twice to avoid this issue so you don't have to check whether or not it happened.

```
#import <Foundation/Foundation.h>
#import <CoreData/CoreData.h>

@class LocationAtHome, LocationAtShop, Unit;

@interface Item : NSManagedObject

@property (nonatomic, retain) NSNumber * collected;
@property (nonatomic, retain) NSNumber * listed;
@property (nonatomic, retain) NSString * name;
@property (nonatomic, retain) NSData * photoData;
@property (nonatomic, retain) NSNumber * quantity;
@property (nonatomic, retain) Unit *unit;
@property (nonatomic, retain) LocationAtHome *locationAtHome;
@property (nonatomic, retain) LocationAtShop *locationAtShop;

@end
```

Figure 4.13   A correctly generated `NSManagedObject` subclass

Update Grocery Dude as follows to ensure the correct subclass files exist:

1. Again, create an `NSManagedObject` subclass of all entities in **Model 6**, overwriting any existing files.

Summary

You've now been shown how to create and configure relationships between entities. As the benefits of using relationships were discussed, the key relationship settings such as To-Many, To-One, and Delete Rules were covered, too. As the model was expanded, new location-centric entities were introduced that demonstrated abstract entities as parents in a new entity inheritance hierarchy. This hierarchy was related back to the items entity, which now enables items to have a shop location and home location.

Any issues due to data validation errors will now display what went wrong before the user is told to close the application. This should put you on a resolution path faster than the alternative. To prevent validation issues in the first place, the validation methods existing in all `NSManagedObject` files were brought to light.

The foundation has now been laid, so it's time to bring the application to life with the introduction of table views, which are discussed in the next chapter.

Exercises

Why not build on what you've learned by experimenting?

1. Insert a new **Item**, **ShopLocation**, and **HomeLocation**.

2. Set the new **item.shopLocation** and **item.homeLocation** to be the **ShopLocation** and **HomeLocation** objects. (Hint: Use Listing 4.1 as a cheat sheet.)

3. Set the delete rule on the **items** relationship of the **Unit** entity to **Cascade** instead of **Deny**. Delete a unit. What happens to the related items after you save the context?

4. Examine the contents of the location table in `Grocery-Dude.sqlite` to see how the location entities translate to database tables. Notice how the **storedIn** and **aisle** attributes from the **Location** child entities are all in the ZLOCATION table.

Change the delete rule on the **items** relationship of the **Unit** entity to **Nullify** once you finish testing.

5

Table Views

If we knew what it was we were doing, it would not be called research, would it?

Albert Einstein

In Chapter 4, "Managed Object Model Expansion," you tapped into the flexibility that relationships and entity inheritance add to a managed object model. Up until now, the demonstrations were constrained to the console log. It's now time to move closer to the end user experience as you're shown how to efficiently present Core Data–fetched results in a table view. This chapter will begin with a brief refresher on table views and then dive right in to constructing a Core Data–driven Table View Controller subclass. This reusable subclass will be leveraged to populate two new table views—one for preparing a shopping list and one for shopping with.

Table Views 101

Arguably one of the most common iOS interface elements is the table view. Based on UIScrollView, this powerful part of UIKit offers a highly customizable way to display a list of information in a single column. Even if you're new to Core Data, you may already be familiar with creating table views populated using an NSArray. In case you're unfamiliar, this section will outline the basics of table views.

Figure 5.1 shows the main components of a table view, in which the section header title and table view cell (row) locations should be apparent. The section index is the small, vertical text shown down the right side. Tapping or dragging the section index allows you to jump quickly between sections within the table view.

Figure 5.1   Fundamental table view components

To populate a table view, you would usually create a UITableViewController subclass adopting the UITableViewDataSource protocol. You would then assign the subclass to a Table View Controller on a storyboard. The UITableViewDataSource protocol requires that a couple of mandatory methods be implemented to allow the table to be populated with data:

- **numberOfRowsInSection** is where you would specify how many rows each table view section has. For example, you might configure this method to return [someArray count], so the number of objects in the data source array matches the number of rows in the table view.

- **cellForRowAtIndexPath** is where you would specify what will be displayed in each cell. It's common to heavily customize this method. If you use the built-in cell styles, there are some default properties available with a standard UITableViewCell to be aware of. For example, the text shown in each row of Figure 5.1 appears because the textLabel. text property has been set. For a complete list of properties, you can jump to the definition of UITableViewCell in Xcode.

Other optional methods are available by adopting the UITableViewDataSource protocol. These methods may be used to configure editing, reordering, deleting, headers, footers, the index, and more. Most of them will be covered later in this chapter.

Core Data Table Views

As previously mentioned, if you weren't using Core Data, you might populate a table view using an `NSArray` as the data source. A key problem with this approach, which you may have experienced first hand, is that performance can suffer when the array is too big and consumes too much memory. Up until now, you've performed Core Data fetches using an `NSFetchRequest`, which produces an `NSArray`. Although you could use this array directly to populate a table view, there is a better way. To populate a table view, you'll still fetch with an `NSFetchRequest`; however, this time you'll configure additional options such as `setFetchBatchSize` to stagger the fetch. This small option can have a huge impact on the memory footprint and consequently improve overall performance. The batch size you set should be a bit larger than the number of rows visible on the screen at any one time.

The best way to efficiently manage fetched data between Core Data and a table view is with an `NSFetchedResultsController`. If you were to otherwise use the array returned by a fetch request directly without a fetched results controller, there's a chance that when the underlying data changes, the objects in the array could become invalid. This could lead to a crash.

Setting a table view as a delegate of a fetched results controller enables change tracking, which will help update the table view automatically when fetched objects change in the underlying context. The performance of a fetched results controller–backed table view can also be increased by setting a cache, which is as easy as specifying a unique name for the cache. Using a cache will minimize unnecessary repeated fetches. As well as the performance and change-tracking benefits, a fetched results controller has a number of convenient properties that make it trivial to wire up a Core Data table view.

> **Note**
>
> To continue building the sample application, you'll need to have added the previous chapter's code to Grocery Dude. Alternatively, you may download, unzip, and use the project up to this point from http://www.timroadley.com/LearningCoreData/GroceryDude-AfterChapter04.zip. Any time you start using an Xcode project from a ZIP file, it's good practice to click **Product** > **Clean**. This practice ensures there's no residual cache from previous projects using the same name. Also, delete any existing copy of Grocery Dude from your device or the iOS Simulator.

Introducing `CoreDataTVC`

`CoreDataTVC` will be a reusable subclass that underpins all Core Data table views in Grocery Dude. It will also be generic enough to reuse in your own applications. To create `CoreDataTVC`, you'll create a `UITableViewController` subclass with an `NSFetchedResultsController` instance variable.

Update Grocery Dude as follows to create `CoreDataTVC`:

1. Select the **Generic Core Data Classes** group.

2. Click **File > New > File....**

3. Create a new **iOS > Cocoa Touch > Objective-C class** and then click **Next**.

4. Set **Subclass of** to `UITableViewController` and **Class** name to `CoreDataTVC` and then click **Next**.

5. Ensure the Grocery Dude target is ticked and then click **Create** to create the class in the Grocery Dude project directory.

Figure 5.2 shows the expected results.

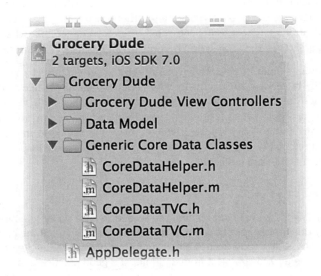

Figure 5.2   CoreDataTVC

Select `CoreDataTVC.m` and then click inside the class editor window. Xcode will warn that `CoreDataTVC.m` isn't configured properly. You may safely ignore these warnings for the moment.

> **Note**
>
> The `CoreDataTVC` class name was chosen against `CoreDataTableViewController` to mini-mize the amount of repeated text throughout this book. This goes against standard Objective-C naming conventions and would otherwise be discouraged. Class names should be expressive, clear, and unambiguous. For example, TVC could be confused for Table View Cell instead of Table View Controller.

The CoreDataTVC class will simply be a UITableViewController subclass that adopts the NSFetchedResultsControllerDelegate protocol and contains a property for an NSFetchedResultsController named frc. As shown in Listing 5.1, it will also have a method named performFetch. This method will be responsible for fetching data and refreshing the table view, with some error reporting just in case the fetch fails.

Listing 5.1 **CoreDataTVC.h**

```
#import <UIKit/UIKit.h>
#import "CoreDataHelper.h"
@interface CoreDataTVC : UITableViewController
<NSFetchedResultsControllerDelegate>
@property (strong, nonatomic) NSFetchedResultsController *frc;
- (void)performFetch;
@end
```

Update Grocery Dude as follows to configure the CoreDataTVC header:

1. Replace all code in CoreDataTVC.h with the code from Listing 5.1. Continue to ignore the Xcode warnings.

The CoreDataTVC class implementation has three main sections. For easy navigation and readability, they're separated by pragma marks.

- FETCHING

- DATASOURCE: UITableView

- DELEGATE: NSFetchedResultsController

Fetching

As shown in Listing 5.2, the FETCHING section of CoreDataTVC.m implements the performFetch method. As previously mentioned, this method is responsible for fetching data and refreshing the table view. If errors occur during the fetch, they'll be logged to the console.

Listing 5.2 **CoreDataTVC.m: FETCHING**

```
#import "CoreDataTVC.h"
@implementation CoreDataTVC
#define debug 1

#pragma mark - FETCHING
- (void)performFetch {
if (debug==1) {
    NSLog(@"Running %@ '%@'", self.class, NSStringFromSelector(_cmd));
}
```

```
    if (self.frc) {
        [self.frc.managedObjectContext performBlockAndWait:^{

            NSError *error = nil;
            if (![self.frc performFetch:&error]) {

                NSLog(@"Failed to perform fetch: %@", error);
            }
            [self.tableView reloadData];
        }];
    } else {
        NSLog(@"Failed to fetch, the fetched results controller is nil.");
    }
}
@end
```

Update Grocery Dude as follows to configure the `CoreDataTVC` implementation:

1. Replace all code in `CoreDataTVC.m` with the code from Listing 5.2. The warnings should now have disappeared.

DATASOURCE: UITableView

`CoreDataTVC` inherits from `UITableViewController`, so it adopts the `UITableViewDataSource` protocol by default. By adopting this protocol, `CoreDataTVC` or one of its subclasses is responsible for implementing the previously mentioned mandatory methods `numberOfRowsInSection` and `cellForRowAtIndexPath`. Without these methods, the table view would remain empty with no visible data. The `cellForRowAtIndexPath` method will be implemented later within a subclass of `CoreDataTVC` because it will always be unique.

There are nine optional `UITableViewDataSource` protocol methods; four of them are generic enough to be implemented in `CoreDataTVC`. A fetched results controller can easily provide the values they need to return.

- **numberOfSectionsInTableView** indicates how many sections the table view has. The default value is 1 if this method isn't implemented. When an instance of a fetched results controller is created, you have an opportunity to configure a `sectionNameKeyPath`, which organizes results into sections. To handle all cases of fetched result sections appropriately, you simply need to configure this method to return `[[self.frc sections] count]`. This will ensure that when multiple sections are required by the fetched results controller, that the Table View Controller can automatically handle it.

- **sectionForSectionIndexTitle** indicates what section a particular section title belongs to. A fetched results controller has a method specifically to help populate this table view data source method. This means returning `[self.frc sectionForSectionIndexTitle: title atIndex:index]` is all that's required here.

- **titleForHeaderInSection** indicates what text title should be shown in a particular section. Generally, returning [[[self.frc sections] objectAtIndex:section] name] will suffice to provide appropriate section information with respect to any sectionNameKeyPath you may have configured.

- **sectionIndexTitlesForTableView** indicates the text title of each index that should be shown in the table view. A fetched results controller has a property specifically to help populate this table view data source method. This means returning [self.frc sectionIndexTitles] is all that's required here.

As shown in Listing 5.3, the code to populate a table view using the UITableViewDataSource protocol methods is trivial. You may wish to override methods such as the header title later on in a CoreDataTVC subclass; however, this is a great starting point for now.

Listing 5.3   **CoreDataTVC.m: DATASOURCE: UITableView**

```
#pragma mark - DATASOURCE: UITableView
- (NSInteger)tableView:(UITableView *)tableView
numberOfRowsInSection:(NSInteger)section {
if (debug==1) {
    NSLog(@"Running %@ '%@'", self.class, NSStringFromSelector(_cmd));
}
    return [[self.frc.sections objectAtIndex:section] numberOfObjects];
}
- (NSInteger)numberOfSectionsInTableView:(UITableView *)tableView {
if (debug==1) {
    NSLog(@"Running %@ '%@'", self.class, NSStringFromSelector(_cmd));
}
    return [[self.frc sections] count];
}
- (NSInteger)tableView:(UITableView *)tableView
sectionForSectionIndexTitle:(NSString *)title
atIndex:(NSInteger)index {
if (debug==1) {
    NSLog(@"Running %@ '%@'", self.class, NSStringFromSelector(_cmd));
}
    return [self.frc sectionForSectionIndexTitle:title atIndex:index];
}
- (NSString *)tableView:(UITableView *)tableView
titleForHeaderInSection:(NSInteger)section {
if (debug==1) {
    NSLog(@"Running %@ '%@'", self.class, NSStringFromSelector(_cmd));
}
    return [[[self.frc sections] objectAtIndex:section] name];
}
```

```
- (NSArray *)sectionIndexTitlesForTableView:(UITableView *)tableView {
if (debug==1) {
    NSLog(@"Running %@ '%@'", self.class, NSStringFromSelector(_cmd));
}
    return [self.frc sectionIndexTitles];
}
```

Update Grocery Dude as follows to update the CoreDataTVC implementation:

1. Add the code from Listing 5.3 to the bottom of CoreDataTVC.m before @end.

DELEGATE: NSFetchedResultsController

You can tell by looking in its header file that CoreDataTVC adopts the
NSFetchedResultsControllerDelegate protocol, which means optional
methods can now be implemented to ensure the Table View Controller correctly
handles moves, deletes, updates, and insertions. Whenever you need to make
a change to a table view, you need to tell it to beginUpdates, and when you're done,
endUpdates. When you're using a fetched results controller, you need to call these
methods from controllerWillChangeContent and controllerDidChangeContent,
respectively, as shown in Listing 5.4.

Listing 5.4   **CoreDataTVC.m Content Changes**

```
#pragma mark - DELEGATE: NSFetchedResultsController
- (void)controllerWillChangeContent:(NSFetchedResultsController *)controller
{if (debug==1) {
    NSLog(@"Running %@ '%@'", self.class, NSStringFromSelector(_cmd));
}
    [self.tableView beginUpdates];
}
- (void)controllerDidChangeContent:(NSFetchedResultsController *)controller
{if (debug==1) {
    NSLog(@"Running %@ '%@'", self.class, NSStringFromSelector(_cmd));
}
    [self.tableView endUpdates];
}
```

Update Grocery Dude as follows to update the CoreDataTVC implementation:

1. Add the code from Listing 5.4 to the bottom of CoreDataTVC.m before @end.

The next two fetched results controller delegate protocol methods handle moves, deletes,
updates, and insertions, depending on the given change type. Listing 5.5 shows the
code involved. Note that NSFetchedResultsChangeUpdate in the didChangeObject
method has no row animation as opposed to other change types in the same method.

This speeds up user interaction with table view cells. In the case of Grocery Dude, when someone ticks an item off the shopping list, the tick should appear immediately. The chosen animation option makes sure there's no fade-in delay. You may wish to set this to `UITableViewRowAnimationAutomatic` if you adapt this code to your own projects.

Listing 5.5   **CoreDataTVC.m: DELEGATE: NSFetchedResultsController**

```
- (void)controller:(NSFetchedResultsController *)controller
  didChangeSection:(id <NSFetchedResultsSectionInfo>)sectionInfo
           atIndex:(NSUInteger)sectionIndex
     forChangeType:(NSFetchedResultsChangeType)type {

if (debug==1) {
NSLog(@"Running %@ '%@'", self.class, NSStringFromSelector(_cmd));
}
switch(type) {
case NSFetchedResultsChangeInsert:
[self.tableView insertSections:[NSIndexSet indexSetWithIndex:sectionIndex]
             withRowAnimation:UITableViewRowAnimationFade];
break;
case NSFetchedResultsChangeDelete:
[self.tableView deleteSections:[NSIndexSet indexSetWithIndex:sectionIndex]
              withRowAnimation:UITableViewRowAnimationFade];
break;
}
}
- (void)controller:(NSFetchedResultsController *)controller
   didChangeObject:(id)anObject
       atIndexPath:(NSIndexPath *)indexPath
     forChangeType:(NSFetchedResultsChangeType)type
      newIndexPath:(NSIndexPath *)newIndexPath {

if (debug==1) {
    NSLog(@"Running %@ '%@'", self.class, NSStringFromSelector(_cmd));
}
UITableView *tableView = self.tableView;
switch(type) {
case NSFetchedResultsChangeInsert:
[tableView insertRowsAtIndexPaths:[NSArray arrayWithObject:newIndexPath]
                withRowAnimation:UITableViewRowAnimationAutomatic];
break;
case NSFetchedResultsChangeDelete:
[tableView deleteRowsAtIndexPaths:[NSArray arrayWithObject:indexPath]
                withRowAnimation:UITableViewRowAnimationAutomatic];
break;
case NSFetchedResultsChangeUpdate:
if (!newIndexPath) {
```

```
        [tableView reloadRowsAtIndexPaths:[NSArray arrayWithObject:indexPath]
                        withRowAnimation:UITableViewRowAnimationNone];
    } else {
        [tableView deleteRowsAtIndexPaths:[NSArray arrayWithObject:indexPath]
                        withRowAnimation:UITableViewRowAnimationNone];
        [tableView insertRowsAtIndexPaths:[NSArray arrayWithObject:newIndexPath]
                        withRowAnimation:UITableViewRowAnimationNone];
    }
    break;
    case NSFetchedResultsChangeMove:
    [tableView deleteRowsAtIndexPaths:[NSArray arrayWithObject:indexPath]
                    withRowAnimation:UITableViewRowAnimationAutomatic];
    [tableView insertRowsAtIndexPaths:[NSArray arrayWithObject:newIndexPath]
                    withRowAnimation:UITableViewRowAnimationAutomatic];
    break;
    }
}
```

Update Grocery Dude as follows to update the `CoreDataTVC` implementation:

1. Add the code from Listing 5.5 to the bottom of `CoreDataTVC.m` before `@end`.

`CoreDataTVC` is now ready to be subclassed. There will be five table views in Grocery Dude. This means there will also be five separate `CoreDataTVC` subclasses, one for each customized table view, all with similar code:

- **PrepareTVC** will list items that can be put on the shopping list.
- **ShopTVC** will list items that are on the shopping list.
- **UnitsTVC** will list units that items are measured by (for example, Kg, g, or liters). This class will be implemented in the next chapter.
- **LocationsAtHomeTVC** will list the possible locations items can be stored in at home. This class will be implemented in the next chapter.
- **LocationsAtShopTVC** will list the possible aisle locations items can be in at a shop. This class will be implemented in the next chapter.

The `PrepareTVC` and `ShopTVC` table views will be Grocery Dude's primary views. The application will need a Tab Bar Controller to allow switching between them.

Update Grocery Dude as follows to add a Tab Bar Controller:

1. Select **Main.storyboard**.

2. Drag a **Tab Bar Controller** onto the storyboard to the left of the existing **Navigation Controller**.

3. Delete the two default view controllers connected to the **Tab Bar Controller**.

4. Hold down **Control** and drag a line from the **Tab Bar Controller** to the existing **Navigation Controller** and then select **Relationship Segue > view controllers**.

5. Set the **Tab Bar Controller** as the initial view controller using **Attributes Inspector** (**Option+⌘+4**), as shown in Figure 5.3.

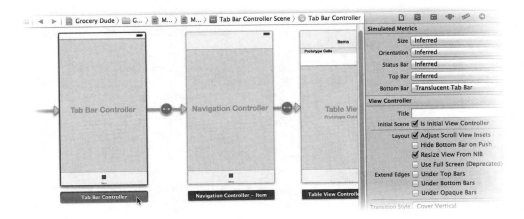

Figure 5.3   A Tab Bar Controller will be used to toggle table views.

A Tab Bar Controller isn't any good with just one tab, so another needs to be added for the upcoming `ShopTVC` table view. Before that can happen, the `ShopTVC` table view itself needs to be created.

Update Grocery Dude as follows to add a new table view connected to the tab bar:

1. Select **Main.storyboard**.

2. Drag a new **Table View Controller** onto the storyboard beneath the existing **Navigation Controller**.

3. Ensure that the new **Table View Controller** is selected and then click **Editor > Embed In > Navigation Controller**.

4. Set the **Navigation Item Title** of the new **Table View Controller** to **Grocery Dude** using **Attributes Inspector** (**Option+⌘+4**).

5. Click the **Prototype Table View Cell** of the new **Table View Controller** and set the **Reuse Identifier** to `Shop Cell`. This identifier will be referred to in `ShopTVC`'s `cellForRowAtIndexPath` method as it populates these cells with data.

6. Hold down **Control** and drag a line from the **Tab Bar Controller** to the new **Navigation Controller**; then select **Relationship Segue > View controllers**.

7. Vertically center the **Tab Bar Controller** so it lines up nicely, as shown in Figure 5.4.

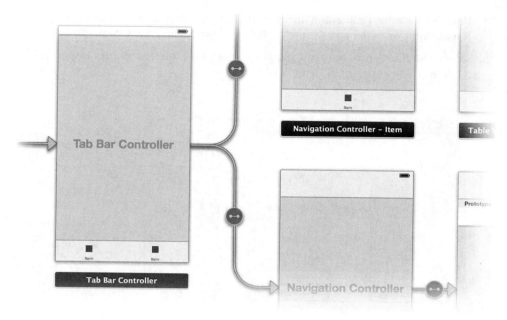

Figure 5.4   The Tab Bar Controller now has two tabs.

The Tab Bar Controller now has two tabs that will be used to cycle between the PrepareTVC and ShopTVC table views. Before those subclasses are created and assigned to the table views, final touches are needed to help identify the tabs properly.

Update Grocery Dude as follows to add tab bar icons:

1. Download and extract the tab bar icons from the following URL: http://www.timroadley. com/LearningCoreData/TabBarIcons.zip.

2. Select the **Images.xcassets** asset catalog.

3. Drag the tab bar icons into the asset catalog beneath **LaunchImage**, as shown in Figure 5.5.

Update Grocery Dude as follows to configure the tabs:

1. Select **Main.storyboard**.

2. Select the **Tab Bar Item** on the **Navigation Controller** next to the **Items** table view.

3. Set the **Bar Item Title** to **Prepare** and **Bar Item Image** to **prepare**, as shown in Figure 5.6.

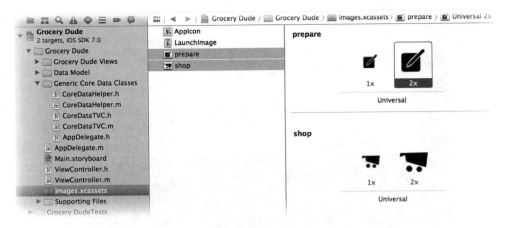

Figure 5.5   The Tab Bar Controller icons

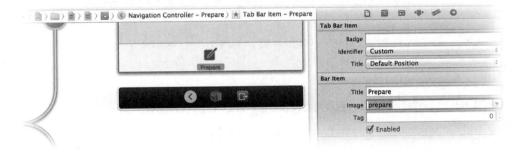

Figure 5.6   The Prepare tab

4. Select the **Tab Bar Item** on the **Navigation Controller** next to the **Grocery Dude** table view.

5. Set the **Bar Item Title** to **Shop** and **Bar Item Image** to **shop** using the technique from step 3.

6. Run the application. You should be able to switch between table views, as shown in Figure 5.7. There won't be any data in the tables just yet. If the Prepare and Shop tabs are in the wrong order, you can drag them to the correct order using the Tab Bar Controller on the storyboard.

Figure 5.7   Grocery Dude's Tab Bar Controller allows table view toggling

AppDelegate's `CoreDataHelper` Instance

Frequently throughout the application, access will be required to the shared instance of `CoreDataHelper`. This means that the existing `cdh` code found in `AppDelegate.m` needs to be exposed through `AppDelegate.h`. Listing 5.6 shows the code required to expose `cdh`.

Listing 5.6   **AppDelegate.h: cdh**

```
- (CoreDataHelper*)cdh;
```

Update Grocery Dude as follows to expose the `cdh` method:

1. Add the code from Listing 5.6 to the bottom of `AppDelegate.h` before `@end`.

The existing implementation of `cdh` is intended to return the shared instance of `CoreDataHelper`. At present, this method isn't thread-safe because there's no guarantee that `CoreDataHelper` won't be instantiated more than once from separate threads. An updated version of `cdh` is shown in Listing 5.7. This updated method wraps the instantiation of `CoreDataHelper` in `dispatch_once` to resolve the thread safety issue. It does this by guaranteeing that `CoreDataHelper` can only be instantiated once for the lifetime of the application.

Listing 5.7 **AppDelegate.m: cdh**

```
- (CoreDataHelper*)cdh {
if (debug==1) {
    NSLog(@"Running %@ '%@'", self.class, NSStringFromSelector(_cmd));
}
    if (!_coreDataHelper) {
        static dispatch_once_t predicate;
        dispatch_once(&predicate, ^{
            _coreDataHelper = [CoreDataHelper new];
        });
        [_coreDataHelper setupCoreData];
    }
    return _coreDataHelper;
}
```

Update Grocery Dude as follows to implement a thread-safe cdh method:

1. Replace the existing cdh method in AppDelegate.m with the code from Listing 5.7.

Introducing **PrepareTVC**

To provide data to the table view shown on the **Prepare** tab, a new class named PrepareTVC will be created as a subclass of CoreDataTVC. This subclass will configure a fetch request and display items that can be put on a shopping list.

Update Grocery Dude as follows to add PrepareTVC:

1. Right-click the existing **Grocery Dude** group and create a new group called **Grocery Dude Table View Controllers**.

2. Ensure the new **Grocery Dude Table View Controllers** group is selected.

3. Click **File > New > File...**.

4. Create a new **iOS > Cocoa Touch > Objective-C class** and then click **Next**.

5. Set **Subclass of** to CoreDataTVC and **Class** name to PrepareTVC. Click **Next**.

6. Ensure the Grocery Dude target is ticked and then click **Create** to create the class in the Grocery Dude project directory.

There isn't much to the PrepareTVC header. As shown in Listing 5.8, the only thing worth noting is that this class adopts the UIActionSheetDelegate protocol. In addition, there's an instance variable that will hold an action sheet. To put an item on the shopping list (the Shop tab), a user will simply tap an item on the Prepare tab. To completely clear the shopping list, a Clear button will be implemented on the Prepare tab. To prevent the shopping list from being accidentally cleared, an action sheet is needed to confirm that a shopping list should be cleared. This is the sole purpose of the `clearConfirmActionSheet` property shown in Listing 5.8.

Listing 5.8   **PrepareTVC.h**

```
#import <UIKit/UIKit.h>
#import "CoreDataTVC.h"
@interface PrepareTVC : CoreDataTVC <UIActionSheetDelegate>
@property (strong, nonatomic) UIActionSheet *clearConfirmActionSheet;
@end
```

Update Grocery Dude as follows to configure `PrepareTVC`:

1. Replace all code in `PrepareTVC.h` with the code from Listing 5.8.

The implementation files of the upcoming subclasses of `CoreDataTVC` will all have sections for DATA, VIEW, and INTERACTION.

Data

The DATA section of the `PrepareTVC` implementation contains only a `configureFetch` method. This method creates a fetched results controller based on a customized `NSFetchRequest`. It also sets `PrepareTVC` as a delegate of the fetched results controller. The delegate methods are already implemented in the superclass `CoreDataTVC`, so you don't have to worry about repeating that code. The code involved is shown in Listing 5.9.

Listing 5.9   **PrepareTVC.m: DATA**

```
#import "PrepareTVC.h"
#import "CoreDataHelper.h"
#import "Item.h"
#import "Unit.h"
#import "AppDelegate.h"

@implementation PrepareTVC
#define debug 1

#pragma mark - DATA
- (void)configureFetch {
if (debug==1) {
    NSLog(@"Running %@ '%@'", self.class, NSStringFromSelector(_cmd));
}
    CoreDataHelper *cdh =
    [(AppDelegate *)[[UIApplication sharedApplication] delegate] cdh];
```

```
    NSFetchRequest *request =
    [NSFetchRequest fetchRequestWithEntityName:@"Item"];

    request.sortDescriptors =
    [NSArray arrayWithObjects:
     [NSSortDescriptor sortDescriptorWithKey:@"locationAtHome.storedIn"
                                    ascending:YES],
     [NSSortDescriptor sortDescriptorWithKey:@"name"
                                    ascending:YES],
     nil];
    [request setFetchBatchSize:50];
    self.frc =
    [[NSFetchedResultsController alloc] initWithFetchRequest:request
                                       managedObjectContext:cdh.context
                          sectionNameKeyPath:@"locationAtHome.storedIn"
                                         cacheName:nil];
    self.frc.delegate = self;
}
@end
```

Most of the code in `configureFetch` should be familiar because it primarily involves the creation of an `NSFetchRequest`, as discussed in Chapter 2, "Managed Object Model Basics." The remaining code staggers the fetch into batches with `setFetchBatchSize` and also configures `self.frc` with an instance of `NSFetchedResultsController`. To create the fetched results controller, you need four things:

- An instance of `NSFetchRequest`. In this case, `request` was created at the start of the `configureFetch` method using techniques from previous chapters.

- An instance of `NSManagedObjectContext`. In this case, the `cdh` convenience method of the `AppDelegate` is leveraged to provide this.

- A string representing a `sectionNameKeyPath`. This string value represents an entity attribute key and is used to group the table view into sections. In this case, `locationAtHome.storedIn` indicates the table view should be grouped into sections representing the location where items are stored in the user's home. It's important to note that the attribute specified here must also be the first sort descriptor in the fetch request.

- A string representing a cache. Although it's not provided in this case, if it were it should be a string that's unique across the entire application.

Update Grocery Dude as follows to implement the DATA section in `PrepareTVC`:

1. Replace all code in `PrepareTVC.m` with the code from Listing 5.9.

View

The VIEW section of PrepareTVC.m is where most of the action happens. This section mostly consists of table view data source methods and a viewDidLoad method. The code involved is shown in Listing 5.10.

Listing 5.10 **PrepareTVC.m: VIEW**

```
#pragma mark - VIEW
- (void)viewDidLoad {
if (debug==1) {
    NSLog(@"Running %@ '%@'", self.class, NSStringFromSelector(_cmd));
}
    [super viewDidLoad];
    [self configureFetch];
    [self performFetch];
    self.clearConfirmActionSheet.delegate = self;

  [[NSNotificationCenter defaultCenter] addObserver:self
                                     selector:@selector(performFetch)
                                         name:@"SomethingChanged"
                                       object:nil];
}
- (UITableViewCell *)tableView:(UITableView *)tableView
        cellForRowAtIndexPath:(NSIndexPath *)indexPath {
if (debug==1) {
NSLog(@"Running %@ '%@'", self.class, NSStringFromSelector(_cmd));
}
    static NSString *cellIdentifier = @"Item Cell";
    UITableViewCell *cell =
    [tableView dequeueReusableCellWithIdentifier:cellIdentifier
                                   forIndexPath:indexPath];
    cell.accessoryType = UITableViewCellAccessoryDetailButton;
    Item *item = [self.frc objectAtIndexPath:indexPath];
    NSMutableString *title = [NSMutableString stringWithFormat:@"%@%@ %@",
                               item.quantity, item.unit.name, item.name];
    [title replaceOccurrencesOfString:@"(null)"
                          withString:@""
                             options:0
                               range:NSMakeRange(0, [title length])];
    cell.textLabel.text = title;

    // make selected items orange
    if ([item.listed boolValue]) {
```

```
        [cell.textLabel setFont:[UIFont
                 fontWithName:@"Helvetica Neue" size:18]];
        [cell.textLabel setTextColor:[UIColor orangeColor]];
    }
    else {
        [cell.textLabel setFont:[UIFont
                 fontWithName:@"Helvetica Neue" size:16]];
        [cell.textLabel setTextColor:[UIColor grayColor]];
    }
    return cell;
}
- (NSArray*)sectionIndexTitlesForTableView:(UITableView *)tableView {
if (debug==1) {
    NSLog(@"Running %@ '%@'", self.class, NSStringFromSelector(_cmd));
}
return nil; // we don't want a section index.
}
```

The **viewDidLoad** method is responsible for configuring and performing the fetch that drives the table view. It also configures the table view as an action sheet delegate, which will be used later to verify that a user wants to clear the entire shopping list. The final code in this method configures the table view to listen for a SomethingChanged notification. This enables other areas of the application to trigger a re-fetch if required (for example, when the Core Data Stack is completely reset).

The **cellForRowAtIndexPath** method is responsible for wiring up the data that is displayed in each table view cell. Table view cell creation is optimized using dequeueReusableCell-WithIdentifier. The method continues on to color-code items depending on whether or not they're listed on the Shop tab. There is also logic involved in removing ugly **(null)** values encountered when a user doesn't enter an item name.

The **sectionIndexTitlesForTableView** method is overridden from CoreDataTVC to return nil. Returning nil disables the index. If you don't override this method, the superclass implementation enables the section index.

Update Grocery Dude as follows to implement the VIEW section:

1. Add the code from Listing 5.10 to the bottom of PrepareTVC.m before @end.

2. Select **Main.storyboard**.

3. Select the **Items** Table View Controller.

4. Set the **Custom Class** of the **Items** Table View Controller to PrepareTVC using **Identity Inspector (Option+⌘+3)**, as shown in Figure 5.8.

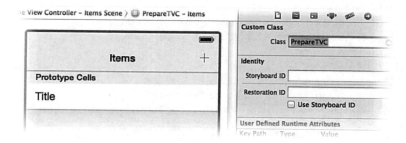

Figure 5.8   `PrepareTVC` Table View Controller

The `PrepareTVC` is now in a position to display data, yet there's nothing in the persistent store to show because the application should have been deleted at the beginning of this chapter.

Update Grocery Dude as follows to insert some test objects:

1. Add `#import "LocationAtHome.h"` to the top of `AppDelegate.m`.

2. Add `#import "LocationAtShop.h"` to the top of `AppDelegate.m`.

3. Replace all code in the `demo` method of `AppDelegate.m` with the code shown in Listing 5.11. This code inserts test data using techniques discussed in the previous chapters.

Listing 5.11   `AppDelegate.m: demo`

```
CoreDataHelper *cdh = [self cdh];
NSArray *homeLocations = [NSArray arrayWithObjects:
@"Fruit Bowl",@"Pantry",@"Nursery",@"Bathroom",@"Fridge",nil];
NSArray *shopLocations = [NSArray arrayWithObjects:
@"Produce",@"Aisle 1",@"Aisle 2",@"Aisle 3", @"Deli",nil];
NSArray *unitNames = [NSArray arrayWithObjects:
@"g",@"pkt",@"box",@"ml",@"kg",nil];
NSArray *itemNames = [NSArray arrayWithObjects:
@"Grapes",@"Biscuits",@"Nappies",@"Shampoo",@"Sausages",nil];
    int i = 0;
    for (NSString *itemName in itemNames) {
        LocationAtHome *locationAtHome =
        [NSEntityDescription
                insertNewObjectForEntityForName:@"LocationAtHome"
                inManagedObjectContext:cdh.context];
        LocationAtShop *locationAtShop =
        [NSEntityDescription
                insertNewObjectForEntityForName:@"LocationAtShop"
                inManagedObjectContext:cdh.context];
        Unit *unit =
        [NSEntityDescription insertNewObjectForEntityForName:@"Unit"
```

```
                         inManagedObjectContext:cdh.context];
    Item *item =
    [NSEntityDescription insertNewObjectForEntityForName:@"Item"
                         inManagedObjectContext:cdh.context];


    locationAtHome.storedIn = [homeLocations objectAtIndex:i];
    locationAtShop.aisle = [shopLocations objectAtIndex:i];
    unit.name = [unitNames objectAtIndex:i];
    item.name = [itemNames objectAtIndex:i];


    item.locationAtHome = locationAtHome;
    item.locationAtShop = locationAtShop;
    item.unit = unit;


    i++;
}
[cdh saveContext];
```

4. Run the application once to insert the test data. The expected result is shown in Figure 5.9.

Figure 5.9   PrepareTVC table view with test data

5. Remove all code within the `demo` method of `AppDelegate.m` to prevent further inserts of the same data.

Congratulations! The fundamental components of a Core Data–driven table view are now in place. The next steps for `PrepareTVC` involve adding the basic features a user would expect from this application, such as the ability to delete items or add them to the Shop tab when they're selected.

Two additional table view data source methods are required:

- **`commitEditingStyle`** is responsible for handling item deletion, which happens when a user swipes a table view cell. Not only does it delete the item in question, it also ensures the table view row is removed, too.

- **`didSelectRowAtIndexPath`** is responsible for toggling whether or not an item is listed and thereby shown on the Shop tab. It also ensures items freshly set as listed are not set as collected. When an item is marked as collected, it will be "ticked off" yet still visible in the Shop tab. When a user taps Clear on the Shop tab, any item marked as collected will be removed from the Shop tab.

Listing 5.12 shows the two new methods required in the VIEW section.

Listing 5.12   PrepareTVC.m: VIEW (Selection and Deletion)

```
- (void)tableView:(UITableView *)tableView
       commitEditingStyle:(UITableViewCellEditingStyle)editingStyle
       forRowAtIndexPath:(NSIndexPath *)indexPath {
if (debug==1) {
    NSLog(@"Running %@ '%@'", self.class, NSStringFromSelector(_cmd));
}
if (editingStyle == UITableViewCellEditingStyleDelete) {
 Item *deleteTarget = [self.frc objectAtIndexPath:indexPath];
 [self.frc.managedObjectContext deleteObject:deleteTarget];
 [self.tableView reloadRowsAtIndexPaths:[NSArray arrayWithObject:indexPath]
                     withRowAnimation:UITableViewRowAnimationFade];
}
}
- (void)tableView:(UITableView *)tableView
       didSelectRowAtIndexPath:(NSIndexPath *)indexPath {
if (debug==1) {
    NSLog(@"Running %@ '%@'", self.class, NSStringFromSelector(_cmd));
}
NSManagedObjectID *itemid =
[[self.frc objectAtIndexPath:indexPath] objectID];
```

```
Item *item =
(Item*)[self.frc.managedObjectContext existingObjectWithID:itemid
                                        error:nil];
if ([item.listed boolValue]) {
    item.listed = [NSNumber numberWithBool:NO];
} else {
    item.listed = [NSNumber numberWithBool:YES];
    item.collected = [NSNumber numberWithBool:NO];
}
[self.tableView reloadRowsAtIndexPaths:[NSArray arrayWithObject:indexPath]
                  withRowAnimation:UITableViewRowAnimationNone];
}
```

Update Grocery Dude as follows to add to the existing VIEW section:

1. Add the code from Listing 5.12 to the bottom of the VIEW section of `PrepareTVC.m`.

2. Select **Main.storyboard**.

3. Select the **Prototype Table View Cell** of the **Items** Table View Controller and then open **Attributes Inspector (Option+⌘+4)**, as shown in Figure 5.10.

4. Set the Table View Cell **Selection** to **None**, as shown in Figure 5.10.

5. Set the Table View Cell **Accessory** to **Detail Disclosure**, as shown in Figure 5.10.

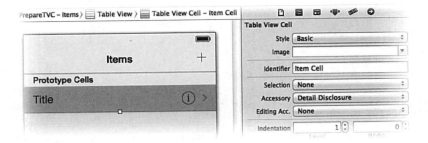

Figure 5.10   The Items table view prototype cell

Run the application again to see the new application behaviors. First, when an item is selected on the Prepare tab, it goes orange or gray. Once the ShopTVC table view is configured later in this chapter, orange items on the Prepare tab will be visible on the Shop tab. This is how an item is "added" to the shopping list.

The second new behavior is the ability to delete items by swiping them. Test this out by deleting the biscuits. Note that deletions won't be saved to the persistent store until `save` is called on the context.

Interaction

The INTERACTION section of PrepareTVC is used to handle the new **Clear** button on the Prepare tab. This button will be used to remove all items displayed on the Shop tab. Because this button could be pressed accidentally, an action sheet will be used to confirm the action.

The ShopTVC table view will display the shopping list items, which means it will only show items where item.listed = YES. This calls for a new fetch request template to be created that will not only be used to populate the ShopTVC table view, it will also be used to unlist listed items when the Clear button is pressed.

Update Grocery Dude as follows to create the shopping list fetch request template:

1. Select **Model 6.xcdatamodel**.

2. Rename the existing **Test** fetch request template to **ShoppingList** and configure it as shown in Figure 5.11. This fetch request will only fetch items flagged as listed. As per usual for Boolean attributes, 1 is equal to YES.

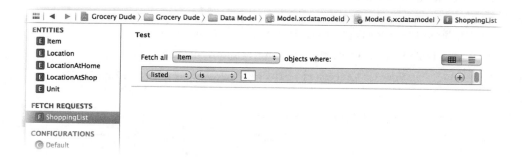

Figure 5.11   ShoppingList only fetches listed items.

The INTERACTION section will have three methods:

- **clear** is an interface builder action that will be linked to a new Clear button on the Items table view. Pressing this button will present a "Clear entire shopping list?" action sheet, provided there is at least one listed item.

- **actionSheet** is an action sheet delegate method used to handle the confirmation or cancellation of the clear action.

- **clearList** will iterate through all listed items, marking them as unlisted. This will have the effect of "removing" the items from the Shop tab.

Listing 5.13 shows these three new methods required in the INTERACTION section.

Listing 5.13   `PrepareTVC.m`: INTERACTION

```
#pragma mark - INTERACTION
- (IBAction)clear:(id)sender {
if (debug==1) {
    NSLog(@"Running %@ '%@'", self.class, NSStringFromSelector(_cmd));
}

    CoreDataHelper *cdh =
    [(AppDelegate *)[[UIApplication sharedApplication] delegate] cdh];
    NSFetchRequest *request =
    [cdh.model fetchRequestTemplateForName:@"ShoppingList"];
    NSArray *shoppingList =
    [cdh.context executeFetchRequest:request error:nil];

    if (shoppingList.count > 0) {

        self.clearConfirmActionSheet =
        [[UIActionSheet alloc] initWithTitle:@"Clear Entire Shopping List?"
                                    delegate:self
                           cancelButtonTitle:@"Cancel"
                      destructiveButtonTitle:@"Clear"
                           otherButtonTitles:nil];
        [self.clearConfirmActionSheet
         showFromTabBar:self.navigationController.tabBarController.tabBar];
    }
    else {
        UIAlertView *alert =
        [[UIAlertView alloc] initWithTitle:@"Nothing to Clear"
                                   message:@"Add items to the Shop tab by
➡tapping them on the Prepare tab. Remove all items from the Shop
➡tab by clicking Clear on the Prepare tab"
                                  delegate:nil
                         cancelButtonTitle:@"Ok"
                         otherButtonTitles:nil];
        [alert show];
    }
    shoppingList = nil;
}
- (void)actionSheet:(UIActionSheet *)actionSheet
clickedButtonAtIndex:(NSInteger)buttonIndex {
```

```
        if (actionSheet == self.clearConfirmActionSheet) {
            if (buttonIndex == [actionSheet destructiveButtonIndex]) {
                [self performSelector:@selector(clearList)];
            }
            else if (buttonIndex == [actionSheet cancelButtonIndex]){
                [actionSheet dismissWithClickedButtonIndex:
                [actionSheet cancelButtonIndex] animated:YES];
            }
        }
    }
}
- (void)clearList {
if (debug==1) {
    NSLog(@"Running %@ '%@'", self.class, NSStringFromSelector(_cmd));
}

    CoreDataHelper *cdh =
    [(AppDelegate *)[[UIApplication sharedApplication] delegate] cdh];
    NSFetchRequest *request =
    [cdh.model fetchRequestTemplateForName:@"ShoppingList"];
    NSArray *shoppingList =
    [cdh.context executeFetchRequest:request error:nil];

    for (Item *item in shoppingList) {
        item.listed = [NSNumber numberWithBool:NO];
    }
}
```

Update Grocery Dude as follows to implement the INTERACTION section:

1. Add the code from Listing 5.13 to the bottom of PrepareTVC.m before @end and then save the class file (press ⌘+S).

2. Select **Main.storyboard**.

3. Drag a **Bar Button Item** to the top left of the **Items** table view.

4. Set the new **Bar Item Title** to **Clear** using **Attributes Inspector** (**Option+⌘+4**), as shown in Figure 5.12.

5. Hold down **Control** and drag a line from the Clear button to the yellow circle at the bottom of the Items table view. Then select **Sent Actions > clear:** from the pop-up menu. This will link the Clear button to the clear method.

Run the application again to see the new application behaviors. If you press the Clear button and nothing is selected, a notification will tell you to select items before pressing Clear. If items are selected (orange) and Clear is pressed, you will have a chance to confirm or cancel that action. If you confirm the action, then all orange items will return to gray. Throughout all of this, the Shop tab will remain empty because it hasn't yet been configured.

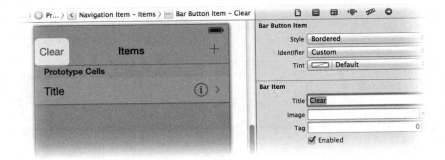

Figure 5.12   The Clear button will remove items from the shopping list

Introducing ShopTVC

The purpose of the ShopTVC table view is to show a shopping list sorted by where items are located in a shop. ShopTVC will be so similar to the PrepareTVC that some method implementations are exactly the same.

Update Grocery Dude as follows to create the ShopTVC class:

1. Ensure the **Grocery Dude Table View Controllers** group is selected.

2. Click **File > New > File...**.

3. Create a new **iOS > Cocoa Touch > Objective-C class** and then click **Next**.

4. Set **Subclass of** to CoreDataTVC and **Class** name to ShopTVC. Click **Next**.

5. Ensure the Grocery Dude target is ticked and then click **Create** to create the class in the Grocery Dude project directory.

6. Select **Main.storyboard**.

7. Set the **Custom Class** of the Table View Controller titled **Grocery Dude** to ShopTVC using the same approach shown previously in Figure 5.8.

The ShopTVC header will remain unchanged; however, the implementation file will need updating. The DATA, VIEW, and INTERACTION sections will be used again.

Data

The DATA section of the ShopTVC implementation contains only a configureFetch method. The code is the same as the equivalent PrepareTVC code, with the only difference being that a fetch request template is used to constrain the fetch results to listed items. Notice that the fetched results controller uses a copy of the fetch request template. This is because you can't edit an existing fetch request template, which you need to do when specifying a sort descriptor. Everything else in the method shown in Listing 5.14 should be familiar.

Listing 5.14   **ShopTVC.m: DATA**

```objc
#import "ShopTVC.h"
#import "CoreDataHelper.h"
#import "Item.h"
#import "Unit.h"
#import "AppDelegate.h"

@implementation ShopTVC
#define debug 1

#pragma mark - DATA
- (void)configureFetch {
if (debug==1) {
    NSLog(@"Running %@ '%@'", self.class, NSStringFromSelector(_cmd));
}

    CoreDataHelper *cdh =
    [(AppDelegate *)[[UIApplication sharedApplication] delegate] cdh];
    NSFetchRequest *request =
    [[cdh.model fetchRequestTemplateForName:@"ShoppingList"] copy];

    request.sortDescriptors =
    [NSArray arrayWithObjects:
     [NSSortDescriptor sortDescriptorWithKey:@"locationAtShop.aisle"
                                   ascending:YES],
     [NSSortDescriptor sortDescriptorWithKey:@"name"
                                   ascending:YES],
     nil];
    [request setFetchBatchSize:50];

    self.frc =
    [[NSFetchedResultsController alloc] initWithFetchRequest:request
                                 managedObjectContext:cdh.context
                               sectionNameKeyPath:@"locationAtShop.aisle"
                                            cacheName:nil];
    self.frc.delegate = self;
}
@end
```

Update Grocery Dude as follows to implement the DATA section in ShopTVC:

1. Replace all code in ShopTVC.m with the code from Listing 5.14.

View

The VIEW section is a familiar sight because the methods involved are again similar to the existing PrepareTVC methods. Here are the only differences:

- The **viewDidLoad** method doesn't configure an action sheet delegate because it's not required in ShopTVC.

- The **cellForRowAtIndexPath** method shows listed items in green with a tick if they're marked as collected (otherwise in orange).

- The **sectionIndexTitlesForTableView** method hasn't changed.

- The **didSelectRowAtIndexPath** method toggles whether or not an item is marked as collected. To a user, tapping a row ticks items off the shopping list.

- The **commitEditingStyle** method is not implemented in ShopTVC, which prevents a user from deleting items from the Shop tab. It may have been otherwise confusing to the user how to properly tick an item off the shopping list.

Listing 5.15 shows the VIEW section code.

Listing 5.15   **ShopTVC.m: VIEW**

```
#pragma mark - VIEW
- (void)viewDidLoad {
if (debug==1) {
    NSLog(@"Running %@ '%@'", self.class, NSStringFromSelector(_cmd));
}

    [super viewDidLoad];
    [self configureFetch];
    [self performFetch];

    // Respond to changes in underlying store
    [[NSNotificationCenter defaultCenter] addObserver:self
                                    selector:@selector(performFetch)
                                        name:@"SomethingChanged"
                                      object:nil];

}
- (UITableViewCell *)tableView:(UITableView *)tableView
cellForRowAtIndexPath:(NSIndexPath *)indexPath {
if (debug==1) {
NSLog(@"Running %@ '%@'", self.class, NSStringFromSelector(_cmd));
}
    static NSString *cellIdentifier = @"Shop Cell";
    UITableViewCell *cell =
    [tableView dequeueReusableCellWithIdentifier:cellIdentifier
                            forIndexPath:indexPath];

    Item *item = [self.frc objectAtIndexPath:indexPath];
    NSMutableString *title = [NSMutableString stringWithFormat:@"%@%@ %@",
                            item.quantity, item.unit.name, item.name];
    [title replaceOccurrencesOfString:@"(null)"
                    withString:@""
```

```
                                  options:0
                                    range:NSMakeRange(0, [title length])];
    cell.textLabel.text = title;

    // make collected items green
    if (item.collected.boolValue) {
        [cell.textLabel setFont:[UIFont
                    fontWithName:@"Helvetica Neue" size:16]];
        [cell.textLabel setTextColor:
        [UIColor colorWithRed:0.368627450
                        green:0.741176470
                         blue:0.349019607 alpha:1.0]];
        cell.accessoryType = UITableViewCellAccessoryCheckmark;
    }
    else {
        [cell.textLabel setFont:[UIFont
                    fontWithName:@"Helvetica Neue" size:18]];
        cell.textLabel.textColor = [UIColor orangeColor];
        cell.accessoryType = UITableViewCellAccessoryDetailButton;
    }
    return cell;
}
- (NSArray*)sectionIndexTitlesForTableView:(UITableView *)tableView {
if (debug==1) {
    NSLog(@"Running %@ '%@'", self.class, NSStringFromSelector(_cmd));
}
    return nil; // prevent section index.
}
- (void)tableView:(UITableView *)tableView
didSelectRowAtIndexPath:(NSIndexPath *)indexPath  {
if (debug==1) {
    NSLog(@"Running %@ '%@'", self.class, NSStringFromSelector(_cmd));
}
    Item *item = [self.frc objectAtIndexPath:indexPath];
    if (item.collected.boolValue) {
        item.collected = [NSNumber numberWithBool:NO];
    }
    else {
        item.collected = [NSNumber numberWithBool:YES];
    }
    [self.tableView reloadRowsAtIndexPaths:
                        [NSArray  arrayWithObject:indexPath]
                        withRowAnimation:UITableViewRowAnimationNone];
}
```

Update Grocery Dude as follows to add the VIEW section:

1. Add the code from Listing 5.15 to the bottom of ShopTVC.m before @end.

Interaction

The INTERACTION section of ShopTVC is used to handle another Clear button. The difference between the Clear buttons on each tab is that the one on the Prepare tab clears the whole shopping list, whereas the one on the Shop tab clears only collected items. Again, a clear method will be executed when the Clear button is tapped. As shown in Listing 5.16, this method either clears collected items or alerts the user that there's nothing to clear.

Listing 5.16   **ShopTVC.m: INTERACTION**

```
#pragma mark - INTERACTION
- (IBAction)clear:(id)sender {
if (debug==1) {
    NSLog(@"Running %@ '%@'", self.class, NSStringFromSelector(_cmd));
}
    if ([self.frc.fetchedObjects count] == 0) {

        UIAlertView *alert =
        [[UIAlertView alloc] initWithTitle:@"Nothing to Clear"
                                   message:@"Add items using the Prepare tab"
                                   delegate:nil
                          cancelButtonTitle:@"Ok" otherButtonTitles:nil];
        [alert show];
        return;
    }
    BOOL nothingCleared = YES;
    for (Item *item in self.frc.fetchedObjects) {

        if (item.collected.boolValue)
        {
            item.listed = [NSNumber numberWithBool:NO];
            item.collected = [NSNumber numberWithBool:NO];
            nothingCleared = NO;
        }
    }
    if (nothingCleared) {
        UIAlertView *alert =
        [[UIAlertView alloc] initWithTitle:nil message:
         @"Select items to be removed from the list before pressing Clear"
         delegate:nil cancelButtonTitle:@"Ok" otherButtonTitles:nil];
        [alert show];
    }
}
```

Update Grocery Dude as follows to implement the INTERACTION section:

1. Add the code from Listing 5.16 to the bottom of ShopTVC.m before @end and then save the class file (press ⌘+S).

2. Select **Main.storyboard**.

3. Drag a **Bar Button Item** to the top left of the **Grocery Dude** table view and then set its **Bar Item Title** to **Clear** using the same approach used with the Clear button on the Items view.

4. Hold down **Control** and drag a line from the new Clear button to the yellow circle at the bottom of the Grocery Dude table view. Then select **Sent Actions > clear:** from the pop-up menu. This will link the Clear button to the clear method.

5. Select the **Prototype Table View Cell** on the **Grocery Dude** Table View Controller.

6. Set the Table View Cell **Style** to **Basic**.

7. Set the Table View Cell **Selection** to **None**.

8. Set the Table View Cell **Accessory** to **Detail Disclosure**.

Run the application and ensure some items on the Prepare tab are orange. Change to the Shop tab and notice these items have appeared sorted by aisle! Tap items on the Shop tab and they will go green and ticked. Press the Clear button on the Shop tab to remove the ticked items from the Shop tab. Return to the Prepare tab and notice the bought items (collected and cleared) aren't orange anymore.

Summary

The application has really started to take shape as core functionality has been implemented. Already you can see the Prepare and Shop tabs listing potential items and shopping list items, respectively. To get to this point, certain repeatable design patterns were followed as you've seen with the implementation of the PrepareTVC and ShopTVC classes. By modifying the configureFetch method, you'll be able to leverage these design patterns in your own projects. Note that debug is enabled in all of the TVC classes, so performance of the application will be slower than usual for the time being.

Exercises

Why not build on what you've learned by experimenting?

1. Try changing the sectionNameKeyPath and the sort descriptor in the configureFetch method of PrepareTVC.m to **name**. If implemented correctly, this will group the data into sections by name.

2. Delete the sectionIndexTitlesForTableView method from PrepareTVC.m and then run the application. You should see a section index in the Items table view.

3. Reinstate the code from Listing 5.11 into the demo of AppDelegate. Run the application three times to insert triplicate data. Examine the console log as you scroll up and down in the Items table view. As you scroll, you should notice the methods cellForRowAtIndexPath and titleForHeaderInSection repeatedly appearing in the console log. This is the table view efficiently reusing cells to give the illusion that all data is in memory and waiting to be displayed.

Reverse any changes you've made to the project during the exercises before continuing to the next chapter.

6

Views

A man should look for what is, and not for what he thinks should be.

Albert Einstein

Chapter 5, "Table Views," demonstrated how to create Core Data–backed table views. During this process, the benefits of a fetched results controller were explained as one was implemented in `CoreDataTVC`. This helpful `UITableViewController` subclass was itself subclassed as you customized the Prepare and Shop tabs to display different information. The application now looks a lot more like a real iOS application, and less like an exercise in Core Data theory. This chapter shows how to pass selected managed objects from a table view to a view. A custom view will also be configured to edit the selected managed object. In the process, you'll be shown how to configure a `UITextField` to allow editing of a managed object's property values.

Overview

The most common standard iOS interface element is the `UIView`. Based on `UIResponder`, this powerful part of `UIKit` offers a highly customizable way to display things onscreen. Interface elements such as `UIPickerView`, `UITextField`, `UIButton`, and `UIScrollView` are all derived from `UIView`. Although the `UITableView` is great for displaying or deleting data, a `UIView` offers a better starting point for editing data. By adding a `UIKit` component such as a `UITextField` to a view, the user can modify object properties. Typically, a customized `UIView` concentrates on editing one managed object at a time, which will be the case for Grocery Dude.

When designing a `UIView` for editing, think about what the user might be doing outside the application when performing edits. In the case of Grocery Dude, the user will probably be pushing a grocery cart, collecting an item, or rummaging through the house determining what he or she needs to buy. This means a user only has one hand free to interact with the application. By favoring interface elements that minimize user interaction, you'll produce an application that's easy to use. An example of such a decision might be choosing to use a picker-view-enabled `UITextField` instead of a `UITextField` on its own. Even the choice of keyboard that's displayed when a `UITextField` is tapped can go a long way to improve the user experience.

> **Note**
>
> To continue building the sample application, you'll need to have added the previous chapter's code to Grocery Dude. Alternatively, you may download, unzip, and use the project up to this point from http://www.timroadley.com/LearningCoreData/GroceryDude-AfterChapter05.zip. Any time you start using an Xcode project from a ZIP file, it's good practice to click **Product** > **Clean**. This practice ensures there's no residual cache from previous projects using the same name.

The Target View Hierarchy

Currently, the view hierarchy has a tab bar controller at the root, with table views at the next level. Deeper into the view hierarchy is a blank **Item** view controller, which will become central to the editing of an item. Figure 6.1 shows a high-level overview of the target view hierarchy that will be in place by the end of this chapter.

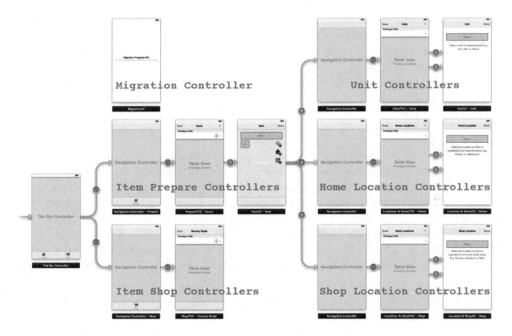

Figure 6.1   A high-level overview of the target view hierarchy

You should already be familiar with the Prepare and Shop tabs, which display the `PrepareTVC` and `ShopTVC` table views. When the **+** in the top-right corner of the `PrepareTVC` table view is tapped, a segue to the Item view controller occurs. In this segue, a new managed object needs to be created and its `objectID` passed to the Item view controller. When the accessory detail button is tapped on the `PrepareTVC` table view, the existing managed object's `objectID` will be passed to the Item view controller. Note that when passing managed objects around an application, you don't necessarily need to use the `objectID` unless you're passing the object between threads. If you get into the habit of using object IDs, you don't need to consider whether there will be threading issues.

Introducing `ItemVC`

A managed object from the Item entity has several properties that the user will need to edit, such as item name, quantity, and so on. To enable this functionality, a new `UIViewController` subclass named `ItemVC` will be created. This new class will be connected to various interface elements and will enable the user to edit an item.

Update Grocery Dude as follows to add a new `UIViewController` subclass called `ItemVC`:

1. Select the **Grocery Dude View Controllers** group.

2. Click **File > New > File...**.

3. Create a new **iOS > Cocoa Touch > Objective-C class** and then click **Next**.

4. Set **Subclass of** to `UIViewController` and **Class** name to `ItemVC` and then click **Next**.

5. Ensure the Grocery Dude target is ticked and then click **Create** to create the class in the Grocery Dude project directory.

The expected result is shown in Figure 6.2.

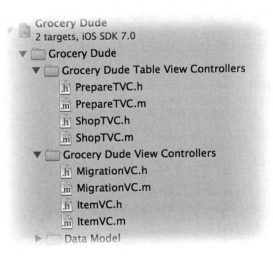

Figure 6.2   View Controller and Table View Controller subclasses

> **Note**
>
> Similar to `CoreDataTVC`, the `ItemVC` class name was chosen against `ItemViewController`
> to minimize the amount of repeated text throughout this book. This goes against standard
> Objective-C naming conventions and would otherwise be discouraged. Class names should be
> expressive, clear, and not ambiguous.

Keeping Reference to a Selected Item

To edit an existing item, users will select the accessory detail button for an item on the
`PrepareTVC` or `ShopTVC` table view. To prepare the `ItemVC` view, a `selectedItemID` property
in `ItemVC` will be populated with the `objectID` of the selected item. Listing 6.1 shows this new
property among the new header file code for `ItemVC`.

Listing 6.1 `ItemVC.h`

```
#import <UIKit/UIKit.h>
#import "CoreDataHelper.h"
@interface ItemVC : UIViewController <UITextFieldDelegate>
@property (strong, nonatomic) NSManagedObjectID *selectedItemID;
@end
```

Update Grocery Dude as follows to configure the `ItemVC` header:

1. Replace the existing code in `ItemVC.h` with the code from Listing 6.1.

Passing a Selected Item to `ItemVC`

An item will be passed to `ItemVC` in Grocery Dude in two ways. For new items, the
`prepareForSegue` method in `PrepareTVC` will be used. For existing items, the
`accessoryButtonTappedForRowWithIndexPath` method of `PrepareTVC` and
`ShopTVC` will be used. Both methods are shown in Listing 6.2.

Listing 6.2 `PrepareTVC.m` and `ShopTVC.m`: `prepareForSegue` and
`accessoryButtonTappedForRowWithIndexPath`

```
#pragma mark - SEGUE
- (void)prepareForSegue:(UIStoryboardSegue *)segue sender:(id)sender {
if (debug==1) {
    NSLog(@"Running %@ '%@'", self.class, NSStringFromSelector(_cmd));
}
    ItemVC *itemVC = segue.destinationViewController;
    if ([segue.identifier isEqualToString:@"Add Item Segue"])
    {
        CoreDataHelper *cdh =
```

```
    [(AppDelegate *)[[UIApplication sharedApplication] delegate] cdh];
    Item *newItem =
    [NSEntityDescription insertNewObjectForEntityForName:@"Item"
                                inManagedObjectContext:cdh.context];
        NSError *error = nil;
        if (![cdh.context
                obtainPermanentIDsForObjects:[NSArray arrayWithObject:newItem]
                error:&error]) {
            NSLog(@"Couldn't obtain a permanent ID for object %@", error);
        }
        itemVC.selectedItemID = newItem.objectID;
    }
    else {
        NSLog(@"Unidentified Segue Attempted!");
    }
}
- (void)tableView:(UITableView *)tableView
accessoryButtonTappedForRowWithIndexPath:(NSIndexPath *)indexPath {
if (debug==1) {
    NSLog(@"Running %@ '%@'", self.class, NSStringFromSelector(_cmd));
}
    ItemVC *itemVC =
    [self.storyboard instantiateViewControllerWithIdentifier:@"ItemVC"];
    itemVC.selectedItemID =
    [[self.frc objectAtIndexPath:indexPath] objectID];
    [self.navigationController pushViewController:itemVC animated:YES];
}
```

When a new item is inserted as a part of the Add Item Segue, an immediate call to obtain a permanent ID for the object is made. This prevents issues down the track when multiple contexts, iCloud, and web service integration are introduced.

Update Grocery Dude as follows to configure the `PrepareTVC` and `ShopTVC` implementations:

1. Add #import "ItemVC.h" to the top of `PrepareTVC.m` and `ShopTVC.m`. This is required so these views know what `ItemVC` is in order to transition to it.

2. Add the code from Listing 6.2 to the bottom of `PrepareTVC.m` before @end.

3. Add the code from Listing 6.2 to the bottom of `ShopTVC.m` before @end.

4. Delete the `prepareForSegue` method from `ShopTVC.m`. It's not required in this class because new items aren't created on the Shop tab.

Configuring the Scroll View and Text Fields

At first, the focus will be on the `UITextField` objects used to edit the name and quantity values. In the next chapter, custom `UITextField` objects with the ability to present a `UIPickerView` will be added. Those special `UITextField` objects will be used to select an item's `unit.name`, `locationAtHome.storedIn`, and `locationAtShop.aisle` from a picker. The target layout of the Item view for this chapter is shown in Figure 6.3. All of the fields shown will be contained within a Scroll View to allow scrolling up and down within the view. The buttons will lead to other views used to add and edit units, home locations, and shop locations.

Figure 6.3   The target Item View Controller

The easiest way to create properties linked to a view is to configure the interface elements on the storyboard. You can then drag them into the appropriate class header or implementation file, depending on whether they should be public or private properties.

Update Grocery Dude as follows to add a Scroll View:

1. Select **Main.storyboard**.

2. Select the Item view controller and untick **Extend Edges Under Top Bars** using **Attributes Inspector (Option+⌘+4)**.

3. Drag a **Scroll View** onto the existing **Item** view, centering it exactly so it takes up the whole view.

4. While the **Scroll View** is selected, click **Editor > Resolve Auto Layout Issues > Add Missing Constraints**. This ensures the Scroll View will stretch when the device is rotated.

5. If it's hidden, show the **Document Outline** by clicking **Editor > Show Document Outline**.

6. While the **Scroll View** is selected, click **Editor > Reveal in Document Outline** and then check constraints were applied to the Scroll View, as shown in Figure 6.4.

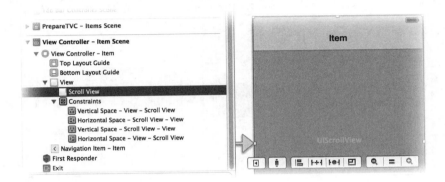

Figure 6.4   A new Scroll View using Auto Layout

Update Grocery Dude as follows to add the **Name** and **Quantity** text fields:

1. Drag a **Text Field** anywhere onto the new **Scroll View** and then configure it as follows using **Attributes Inspector (Option+⌘+4)**:
   - Set **Font** to **System Bold 17.0**.
   - Set **Text Alignment** to **Center**.
   - Set **Placeholder** Text to **Name**.
   - Set **Border Style** to the **Line** (represented by a rectangle).
   - Set **Capitalization** to **Sentences**.
   - Set **Background** to **Other** > **Crayons** > **Mercury** (the second lightest gray crayon).

2. Configure the **Height** of the text field to **48** using **Size Inspector (Option+⌘+5)**.

3. Duplicate the text field by holding **Option** while dragging downward.

4. Configure the duplicated text field as follows using **Attributes Inspector (Option+⌘+4)**:
   - Set **Placeholder** Text to **Qty**.
   - Set **Keyboard** to **Decimal Pad**.
   - Tick **Clear when editing begins**.

5. Configure the **Width** of the **Qty** text field to **60** using **Size Inspector (Option+⌘+5)**.

6. Widen the **Name** text field to the edge guides and then arrange the text fields to the edge guides, as shown in Figure 6.5.

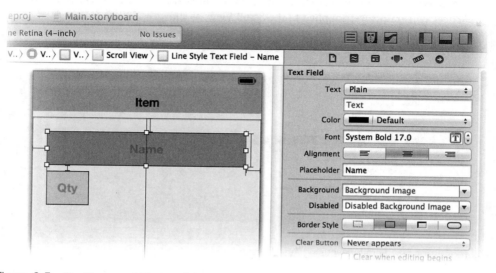

Figure 6.5   The Name and Qty text field arrangement

7. Select both text fields at once (⌘+**click**) and then click **Editor > Resolve Auto Layout Issues > Add Missing Constraints**. This ensures the text fields resize when the device is rotated. The expected result is shown in Figure 6.5.

To make the connection from the scroll view and text fields into code, the **Custom Class** of the Item view controller needs to be set. After that's done, you'll be able to drag these user interface elements straight into the ItemVC header using the Assistant Editor.

Update Grocery Dude as follows to configure the Item view:

1. Select the **Item** View Controller.

2. Set both the **Custom Class** and **Storyboard ID** of the **Item** View Controller to ItemVC using **Identity Inspector (Option+⌘+3)**. The Storyboard ID will be used to reference this view when the detail disclosure is tapped on the Items table view. The expected result is shown in Figure 6.6.

Update Grocery Dude as follows to create properties for the Name and Qty text fields:

1. With the **Item** View Controller selected, show the Assistant Editor (**Option+⌘+Return**).

2. Set the Assistant Editor to **Automatic > ItemVC.h**, as shown in the top right of Figure 6.7.

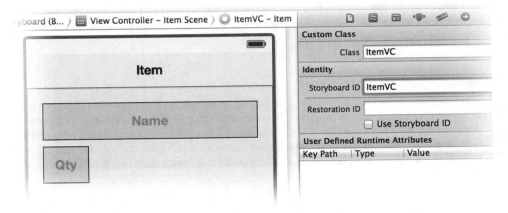

Figure 6.6   The Item View Controller uses the `ItemVC` class

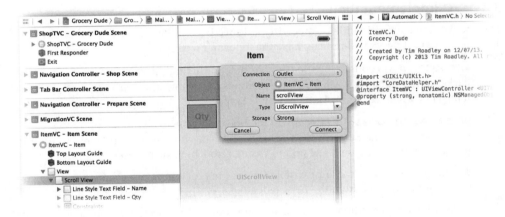

Figure 6.7   Creating properties from storyboard elements

3. If it's hidden, show the **Document Outline** by clicking **Editor > Show Document Outline**.

4. Expand **ItemVC - Item Scene**, as shown in Figure 6.7 on the left.

5. Hold down **Control** and drag a line from the **Scroll View** to `ItemVC.h` before `@end` and then set the property **Name** to `scrollView`, as shown in the middle of Figure 6.7. Double-check the **Type** is `UIScrollView` and the **Storage** is **Strong**.

6. Hold down **Control** and drag a line from the **Line Style Text Field - Name** to `ItemVC.h` before `@end`. Set the new property **Name** to `nameTextField`. Double-check the **Type** is `UITextField` and the **Storage** is **Strong**.

7. Hold down **Control** and drag a line from the **Line Style Text Field - Qty** to `ItemVC.h` before `@end`. Set the new property **Name** to `quantityTextField`. Double-check the **Type** is `UITextField` and the **Storage** is **Strong**.

> **Note**
>
> Normally it is recommended that you only expose properties in the header file when they need to be accessed from outside the class. In order to assist reader focus, the code in this book goes against this recommendation and keeps the implementation files as empty as possible. Note also that it is possible to adopt a protocol privately within the interface directive of an implementation file. Again, Grocery Dude will instead place such code in the header file for clarity.

There should now be a `scrollView`, `nameTextField`, and `quantityTextField` property in `ItemVC.h`.

`ItemVC` Implementation

The `ItemVC` implementation file is categorized into sections similar to the way `PrepareTVC` and `ShopTVC` are. `ItemVC` will initially have the following sections:

- **INTERACTION** will contain methods responsible for hiding the keyboard when the background is tapped. It will also have methods that return the user to the `PrepareTVC` table view whenever a new Done button is tapped.

- **DELEGATE: UITextField** will contain methods available to classes adopting the `UITextFieldDelegate` protocol. They will be leveraged to set an item name according to the contents of the text field and to ensure zero-length names aren't accepted.

- **VIEW** will contain methods responsible for ensuring each interface element is refreshed with appropriate data from the persistent store.

- **DATA** will contain methods responsible for ensuring items always have a home location and shop location object set, even when the location is unknown.

Interaction

The code from the `INTERACTION` section will be used in all view controllers in Grocery Dude. There are three methods in this section. The `done` method will be linked to a new Done button. When tapped, this button will pop the `ItemVC` view controller, which returns the user to the previous table view. The `hideKeyboardWhenBackgroundIsTapped` method configures a `UITapGestureRecognizer` ready to respond to the view background being tapped. Whenever the view background is tapped, the `hideKeyboard` method ends view editing, which hides the keyboard. Listing 6.3 shows the code involved.

Listing 6.3   **ItemVC.m: INTERACTION**

```objc
#import "ItemVC.h"
@implementation ItemVC
#define debug 1

#pragma mark - INTERACTION
- (IBAction)done:(id)sender {
if (debug==1) {
    NSLog(@"Running %@ '%@'", self.class, NSStringFromSelector(_cmd));
}
    [self hideKeyboard];
    [self.navigationController popViewControllerAnimated:YES];
}
- (void)hideKeyboardWhenBackgroundIsTapped {
if (debug==1) {
NSLog(@"Running %@ '%@'", self.class, NSStringFromSelector(_cmd));
}
    UITapGestureRecognizer *tgr =
    [[UITapGestureRecognizer alloc] initWithTarget:self
                                        action:@selector(hideKeyboard)];
    [tgr setCancelsTouchesInView:NO];
    [self.view addGestureRecognizer:tgr];
}
- (void)hideKeyboard {
if (debug==1) {
NSLog(@"Running %@ '%@'", self.class, NSStringFromSelector(_cmd));
}
    [self.view endEditing:YES];
}
@end
```

Update Grocery Dude as follows to configure the INTERACTION section:

1. Show the **Standard Editor** (⌘+**Return**).

2. Replace all existing code in `ItemVC.m` with the code from Listing 6.3 and then save the class file (⌘+**S**).

3. Select **Main.storyboard**.

4. Drag a **Bar Button Item** onto the top-right corner of the **Item** view.

5. Set the Bar Button Item **Identifier** to **Done** using **Attributes Inspector** (Option+⌘+**4**). The expected result is shown in Figure 6.8.

Figure 6.8   A new Done button

6. Hold down **Control** and drag a line from the new **Done** button to the yellow circle at the bottom of the **Item** view and then select **Sent Actions > done**.

DELEGATE: UITextField

The code for the DELEGATE: UITextField section will implement the textFieldDidBegin-Editing and textFieldDidEndEditing methods, which are optional UITextFieldDelegate protocol methods. These methods will be called whenever a text field gains or loses focus. When a text field gains focus, new items have their name set to a zero-length string. When a text field loses focus, it is an opportune time to update the selected managed object with the contents of the text field that just lost focus. Listing 6.4 shows the code involved.

Listing 6.4   **ItemVC.m: DELEGATE: UITextField**

```
#pragma mark - DELEGATE: UITextField
- (void)textFieldDidBeginEditing:(UITextField *)textField {
if (debug==1) {
    NSLog(@"Running %@ '%@'", self.class, NSStringFromSelector(_cmd));
}
    if (textField == self.nameTextField) {

        if ([self.nameTextField.text isEqualToString:@"New Item"]) {
            self.nameTextField.text = @"";
        }
    }
}
```

```
- (void)textFieldDidEndEditing:(UITextField *)textField {
if (debug==1) {
    NSLog(@"Running %@ '%@'", self.class, NSStringFromSelector(_cmd));
}

    CoreDataHelper *cdh =
    [(AppDelegate *)[[UIApplication sharedApplication] delegate] cdh];
    Item *item =
    (Item*)[cdh.context existingObjectWithID:self.selectedItemID error:nil];

    if (textField == self.nameTextField) {
        if ([self.nameTextField.text isEqualToString:@""]) {
            self.nameTextField.text = @"New Item";
        }
        item.name = self.nameTextField.text;
    }
    else if (textField == self.quantityTextField) {
        item.quantity =
        [NSNumber numberWithFloat:self.quantityTextField.text.floatValue];
    }
}
```

Update Grocery Dude as follows to implement the DELEGATE: UITextField section:

1. Add #import "AppDelegate.h" and #import "Item.h" to the top of ItemVC.m.

2. Add the code from Listing 6.4 to the bottom of ItemVC.m before @end.

View

The VIEW section will have four methods:

- The **refreshInterface** method refreshes the interface using the values of the selected managed object, provided there is one.

- The **viewDidLoad** method configures the view as a text field delegate. It also calls a method from the INTERACTION section responsible for hiding the keyboard when the view background is tapped.

- The **viewWillAppear** method calls refreshInterface whenever the view is about to appear, which ensures fresh data is visible. It also shows the keyboard immediately when a new item is being created.

- The **viewDidDisappear** method saves the context whenever the view disappears. Although it's not strictly necessary to save the context every time a view disappears, it's a good idea to persist data regularly in case the device loses power. When iCloud and Web Service integration is introduced, saving also becomes more important because it ensures changes are updated outside of the application.

Listing 6.5 shows the code involved.

Listing 6.5 **ItemVC.m: VIEW**

```objc
#pragma mark - VIEW
- (void)refreshInterface {
if (debug==1) {
    NSLog(@"Running %@ '%@'", self.class, NSStringFromSelector(_cmd));
}
    if (self.selectedItemID) {
        CoreDataHelper *cdh =
        [(AppDelegate *)[[UIApplication sharedApplication] delegate] cdh];
        Item *item =
        (Item*)[cdh.context existingObjectWithID:self.selectedItemID
                                           error:nil];
        self.nameTextField.text = item.name;
        self.quantityTextField.text = item.quantity.stringValue;
    }
}
- (void)viewDidLoad {
if (debug==1) {
    NSLog(@"Running %@ '%@'", self.class, NSStringFromSelector(_cmd));
}
    [super viewDidLoad];
    [self hideKeyboardWhenBackgroundIsTapped];
    self.nameTextField.delegate = self;
    self.quantityTextField.delegate = self;
}
- (void)viewWillAppear:(BOOL)animated {
if (debug==1) {
    NSLog(@"Running %@ '%@'", self.class, NSStringFromSelector(_cmd));
}
    [self refreshInterface];
    if ([self.nameTextField.text isEqual:@"New Item"]) {
        self.nameTextField.text = @"";
        [self.nameTextField becomeFirstResponder];
    }
}
- (void)viewDidDisappear:(BOOL)animated {
if (debug==1) {
    NSLog(@"Running %@ '%@'", self.class, NSStringFromSelector(_cmd));
}
    CoreDataHelper *cdh =
    [(AppDelegate *)[[UIApplication sharedApplication] delegate] cdh];
    [cdh saveContext];
}
```

Update Grocery Dude as follows to implement the VIEW section:

1. Add the code from Listing 6.5 to the bottom of ItemVC.m before @end.

2. Ensure the persistent store is empty by deleting the application from the device (or simulator).

3. Click **Product > Clean**.

4. Run the application and then click **+** on the **Prepare** tab to create a new item.

5. Set the item **Name** to **Coffee** and the **Quantity** to **2** and then press **Done**.

As you're returned to the Items table view, you won't be able to see the new item. This is because it isn't in an appropriate table view section. If you could see the item and then tapped it, it would disappear. This issue occurs because there's no home location set. This issue also occurs on the Shop tab, in this case because there's no shop location set. These locations are critical to the section layout of each table view. As a safeguard against this issue, two new methods will be added to a new DATA section in ItemVC.

Data

The DATA section will have two methods that rely on different fetch request templates. Each fetch request template will be configured to look for a home or shop location with the exact name ..**Unknown Location**... The leading dots will ensure that this location is located at the top of the table view, due to the sort descriptor of the fetch.

Update Grocery Dude as follows to configure the new fetch request templates:

1. Select **Model 6.xcdatamodel**.

2. Add a fetch request called **UnknownLocationAtHome**.

3. Add a fetch request called **UnknownLocationAtShop**.

4. Configure the **UnknownLocationAtHome** fetch request template to fetch all **LocationAtHome** objects where **storedIn** is ..**Unknown Location**.., as shown in Figure 6.9. You'll need to click the **+** to add fetch criteria.

5. Similarly, configure the **UnknownLocationAtShop** fetch request template to fetch all **LocationAtShop** objects where **aisle** is ..**Unknown Location**...

Here are the DATA section methods that will use these fetch request templates:

- The **ensureItemHomeLocationIsNotNull** method is responsible for setting an item's home location to ..**Unknown Location**.. whenever item.locationAtHome is nil.

- The **ensureItemShopLocationIsNotNull** method is responsible for setting an item's shop location to ..**Unknown Location**.. whenever item.locationAtShop is nil.

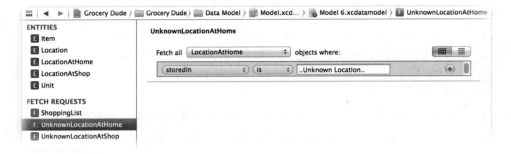

Figure 6.9   ..Unknown Location.. fetch request templates

Listing 6.6 shows the code involved.

Listing 6.6   **ItemVC.m: DATA**

```
#pragma mark - DATA
- (void)ensureItemHomeLocationIsNotNull {
if (debug==1) {
    NSLog(@"Running %@ '%@'", self.class, NSStringFromSelector(_cmd));
}
    if (self.selectedItemID) {
        CoreDataHelper *cdh =
        [(AppDelegate *)[[UIApplication sharedApplication] delegate] cdh];
        Item *item =
        (Item*)[cdh.context existingObjectWithID:self.selectedItemID
                                    error:nil];
    if (!item.locationAtHome) {
            NSFetchRequest *request =
            [[cdh model]
                fetchRequestTemplateForName:@"UnknownLocationAtHome"];
            NSArray *fetchedObjects =
            [cdh.context executeFetchRequest:request error:nil];

            if ([fetchedObjects count] > 0) {
                item.locationAtHome = [fetchedObjects objectAtIndex:0];
            }
            else {
                LocationAtHome *locationAtHome =
                [NSEntityDescription
                 insertNewObjectForEntityForName:@"LocationAtHome"
                        inManagedObjectContext:cdh.context];
                NSError *error = nil;
                if (![cdh.context obtainPermanentIDsForObjects:
                 [NSArray arrayWithObject:locationAtHome] error:&error]) {
                    NSLog(@"Couldn't obtain a permanent ID for object %@",
```

```
                                                            error);
            }
            locationAtHome.storedIn = @"..Unknown Location..";
            item.locationAtHome = locationAtHome;
        }
    }
}
}
- (void)ensureItemShopLocationIsNotNull {
if (debug==1) {
    NSLog(@"Running %@ '%@'", self.class, NSStringFromSelector(_cmd));
}
    if (self.selectedItemID) {
        CoreDataHelper *cdh =
        [(AppDelegate *)[[UIApplication sharedApplication] delegate] cdh];
        Item *item =
        (Item*)[cdh.context existingObjectWithID:self.selectedItemID
                                           error:nil];
    if (!item.locationAtShop) {
            NSFetchRequest *request =
            [[cdh model]
                fetchRequestTemplateForName:@"UnknownLocationAtShop"];
            NSArray *fetchedObjects =
            [cdh.context executeFetchRequest:request error:nil];

            if ([fetchedObjects count] > 0) {
                item.locationAtShop = [fetchedObjects objectAtIndex:0];
            }
            else {
                LocationAtShop *locationAtShop =
                [NSEntityDescription
                 insertNewObjectForEntityForName:@"LocationAtShop"
                        inManagedObjectContext:cdh.context];
                NSError *error = nil;
                if (![cdh.context obtainPermanentIDsForObjects:
                 [NSArray arrayWithObject:locationAtShop] error:&error]) {
                    NSLog(@"Couldn't obtain a permanent ID for object %@",
                                                            error);

                }
                locationAtShop.aisle = @"..Unknown Location..";
                item.locationAtShop = locationAtShop;
        }
    }
    }
}
```

The first thing the two new methods do is check that the selected managed object isn't nil. If it's not, a cdh pointer to the application delegate's CoreDataHelper instance is established.

The cdh pointer is then used to create an item pointer to the managed object using its objectID. If the relevant shop or home location object already exists, nothing else happens. If it doesn't exist, an appropriate ..**Unknown Location**.. object is set as its home or shop location. If the ..**Unknown Location**.. object itself doesn't exist, it is created for the first time and assigned to the item.

Update Grocery Dude as follows to implement the DATA section:

1. Add #import "LocationAtHome.h" to the top of ItemVC.m.

2. Add #import "LocationAtShop.h" to the top of ItemVC.m.

3. Add the code from Listing 6.6 to the bottom of ItemVC.m before @end.

4. Add the following code to the viewWillAppear method of ItemVC.m before [self refreshInterface]:

   ```
   [self ensureItemHomeLocationIsNotNull];
   [self ensureItemShopLocationIsNotNull];
   ```

5. Add the following code to the viewDidDisappear method of ItemVC.m before cdh is declared:

   ```
   [self ensureItemHomeLocationIsNotNull];
   [self ensureItemShopLocationIsNotNull];
   ```

6. Run the application again, tap the **accessory detail button** next to the **Coffee** item, and then tap **Done**. The expected result is shown in Figure 6.10. If you miss the disclosure indicator and tap the item before its location can be set, it may disappear. If this happens, just run the application again.

Figure 6.10   ..Unknown Location.. has its own section.

Units, Home Locations, and Shop Locations

Users must be able to add and edit units, home locations, and shop locations. The technique to achieve this goal will be similar to the technique used to add and edit items. This means there will be a table view with a custom `CoreDataTVC` subclass and an additional view for editing each of these object types.

Update Grocery Dude as follows to add the generic table view and view:

1. Select **Main.storyboard**.

2. Drag a new **Table View Controller** onto the storyboard to the right of the existing **Item** view.

3. Select the **Prototype Cell** of the new **Table View Controller** and set its **Reuse Identifier** to `Cell` using **Attributes Inspector (Option+⌘+4)**.

4. With the new **Table View Controller** selected, click **Editor > Embed In > Navigation Controller**.

5. Drag a **Bar Button Item** on to the top left of the new **Table View Controller**.

6. Set the new **Bar Button Item Identifier** to **Done**.

7. Drag a **Bar Button Item** onto the top right of the new **Table View Controller**.

8. Set the new **Bar Button Item Identifier** to **Add**.

9. Drag a new **View Controller** onto the storyboard to the right of the new **Table View Controller**.

10. Hold down **Control** and drag a line from the **Prototype Cell** of the new **Table View Controller** to the new **View Controller** and then select **Selection Segue > push**.

11. Set the **Storyboard Segue Identifier** of the new segue to `Edit Object Segue`.

12. Hold down **Control** and drag a line from the new **Table View Controller's Add** (+) button to the new **View Controller** and then select **Action Segue > push**.

13. Set the **Storyboard Segue Identifier** of the new segue to `Add Object Segue`.

14. Drag a **Bar Button Item** onto the top right of the new **View Controller**.

15. Set the new **Bar Button Item Identifier** to **Done**.

16. Drag a **Text Field** anywhere onto the new **View Controller** and then configure it as follows using **Attributes Inspector (Option+⌘+4)**:

    - Set **Font** to **System Bold 17.0**.

    - Set **Text Alignment** to **Center**.

    - Set **Placeholder Text** to **Name**.

    - Set **Border Style** to the **Line** (represented by a rectangle).

    - Set **Background** to **Other > Crayons > Mercury** (the second lightest gray crayon).

17. Configure the **Height** of the text field to **48** using **Size Inspector (Option+⌘+5)**.

18. Widen and position the **Name** text field to the edge guides, as shown on the right of Figure 6.11.

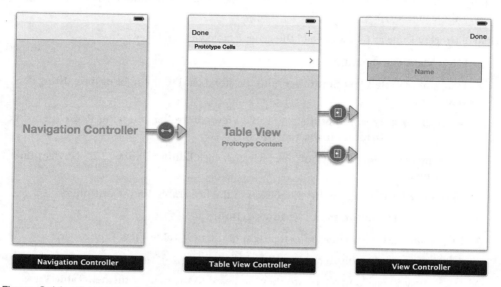

Figure 6.11   Generic controllers

The generic controllers are ready, so it's time to use them as the basis of the add/edit controllers for units, home locations, and shop locations.

Update Grocery Dude as follows to replicate the generic controllers:

1. Select together the generic **Navigation Controller**, **Table View Controller**, and **View Controller** built in the previous steps and then click **Edit > Duplicate**.

2. Drag the duplicated controllers above the original controllers.

3. Repeat the duplication procedure and arrange the controllers as shown in Figure 6.12.

You should have nine new controllers, as shown in Figure 6.12. The top three will be for units, the middle three for home locations, and the bottom three for shop locations. The controllers will be reached via three new buttons positioned on the Item view. Until the buttons are implemented, there may be a warning in Xcode regarding how these new controllers are unreachable, which you can safely ignore for the time being.

Figure 6.12   Generic controllers, in triplicate

Adding and Editing Units

To reach the new controllers, new buttons are required in the Item view. The first button required is the **Add Units** button. This button will segue to a Units table view, which is embedded in a Navigation Controller. The Units table view will behave like the Items table view in that it will have an associated view for editing the selected object (in this case, a unit).

Update Grocery Dude as follows to add the button icons:

1. Download and extract the button icons from http://www.timroadley.com/ LearningCoreData/Icons_ItemVC.zip.

2. Select the **Images.xcassets** asset catalog.

3. Drag the new icons into the asset catalog, as shown in Figure 6.13.

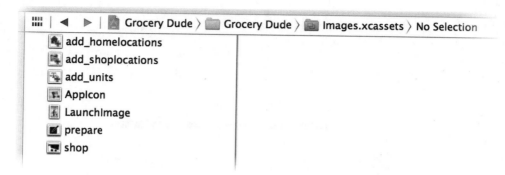

Figure 6.13   New button icons

Update Grocery Dude as follows to add the **Add Unit** button:

1. Select **Main.storyboard**.

2. Drag a **Button** anywhere onto the existing **Scroll View** of the **Item** view and then configure it as follows using **Attributes Inspector (Option+⌘+4)**:

   - Set the **Type** to **Custom**.

   - Delete the text that reads "Button."

   - Set the **Image** to **add_units**.

3. Configure the **Button** as follows using **Size Inspector (Option+⌘+5)**:

   - Ensure **Width** is **48**.

   - Ensure **Height** is **48**.

4. Hold down **Control** and drag a line from the new button to the **Navigation Controller** that leads to the top generic table view controller built in the previous steps and then select **Action Segue > modal**.

5. Set the **Navigation Item Title** of the table view controller that the new modal segue leads to as **Units**.

6. Select the **Prototype Cell** of the **Units** table view controller and set the **Reuse Identifier** to Unit Cell using **Attributes Inspector (Option+⌘+4)**.

7. Set the **Navigation Item Title** of the **View Controller** that the **Units** table view controller leads to as **Unit**.

8. Drag, center, and widen to fit a new **Text View** beneath the existing **Name** text field on the **Unit** view controller, configuring it as follows:

   - Set **Text** content to **Enter a unit of measurement, E.g. 'ml', 'pkt' or 'items'.**

   - Set **Color** to **Light Grey Color.**

- Set **Font** to **System Bold 16.0.**

- Set **Alignment** to **Centered.**

- Untick **Editable** and **Selectable.**

9. With the **Name Text Field** and **Text View** selected, click **Editor > Resolve Auto Layout Issues > Reset to Suggested Constraints.**

If you run the application and make your way to the Item view, you can test out the new Add Unit button. There's no code behind any of these views yet, so it's time to create a `CoreDataTVC` subclass so these views function correctly. Without this code, editing the unit name has no effect, nor does pressing the Done button. This means you'll currently get stuck in the modal popover.

Implementing `UnitsTVC`

The Units table view will display a list of available units. When the view loads, the table should be populated with all unit objects found in the persistent store, sorted by name. When a unit is swiped, it should be deleted. When the Done button is pressed, the units view should be dismissed. `UnitsTVC` will be a `CoreDataTVC` subclass and will implement this required functionality, as shown in Listing 6.7. All code found in this listing should be familiar because it has been similarly implemented previously.

Listing 6.7   **UnitsTVC.m**

```
#import "UnitsTVC.h"
#import "CoreDataHelper.h"
#import "AppDelegate.h"
#import "Unit.h"
@implementation UnitsTVC
#define debug 1
#pragma mark - DATA
- (void)configureFetch {
if (debug==1) {
    NSLog(@"Running %@ '%@'", self.class, NSStringFromSelector(_cmd));
}
    CoreDataHelper *cdh =
    [(AppDelegate *)[[UIApplication sharedApplication] delegate] cdh];
    NSFetchRequest *request =
    [NSFetchRequest fetchRequestWithEntityName:@"Unit"];
    request.sortDescriptors = [NSArray arrayWithObjects:
     [NSSortDescriptor sortDescriptorWithKey:@"name" ascending:YES],nil];
    [request setFetchBatchSize:50];
    self.frc =
```

```
        [[NSFetchedResultsController alloc] initWithFetchRequest:request
                                        managedObjectContext:cdh.context
                                          sectionNameKeyPath:nil
                                                   cacheName:nil];
    self.frc.delegate = self;
}

#pragma mark - VIEW
- (void)viewDidLoad {
if (debug==1) {
    NSLog(@"Running %@ '%@'", self.class, NSStringFromSelector(_cmd));
}
    [super viewDidLoad];
    [self configureFetch];
    [self performFetch];
    // Respond to changes in underlying store
    [[NSNotificationCenter defaultCenter] addObserver:self
                                    selector:@selector(performFetch)
                                        name:@"SomethingChanged"
                                      object:nil];
}
- (UITableViewCell*)tableView:(UITableView *)tableView
        cellForRowAtIndexPath:(NSIndexPath *)indexPath {
if (debug==1) {
    NSLog(@"Running %@ '%@'", self.class, NSStringFromSelector(_cmd));
}
    static NSString *cellIdentifier = @"Unit Cell";
    UITableViewCell *cell =
    [tableView dequeueReusableCellWithIdentifier:cellIdentifier
                                    forIndexPath:indexPath];
    Unit *unit = [self.frc objectAtIndexPath:indexPath];
    cell.textLabel.text = unit.name;
    return cell;
}
- (void)tableView:(UITableView *)tableView
 commitEditingStyle:(UITableViewCellEditingStyle)editingStyle
  forRowAtIndexPath:(NSIndexPath *)indexPath {
if (debug==1) {
    NSLog(@"Running %@ '%@'", self.class, NSStringFromSelector(_cmd));
}
    if (editingStyle == UITableViewCellEditingStyleDelete) {
        Unit *deleteTarget = [self.frc objectAtIndexPath:indexPath];
        [self.frc.managedObjectContext deleteObject:deleteTarget];
        [self.tableView reloadRowsAtIndexPaths:
                    [NSArray arrayWithObject:indexPath]
```

```
                                   withRowAnimation:UITableViewRowAnimationFade];
    }
}

#pragma mark - INTERACTION
- (IBAction)done:(id)sender {
if (debug==1) {
    NSLog(@"Running %@ '%@'", self.class, NSStringFromSelector(_cmd));
}
    [self.parentViewController
            dismissViewControllerAnimated:YES completion:nil];
}
@end
```

Update Grocery Dude as follows to implement `UnitsTVC`:

1. Select the **Grocery Dude Table View Controllers** group.

2. Click **File > New > File...**.

3. Create a new **iOS > Cocoa Touch > Objective-C class** and then click **Next**.

4. Set **Subclass of** to `CoreDataTVC` and **Class** name to `UnitsTVC` and then click **Next**.

5. Ensure the Grocery Dude target is ticked and then click **Create** to create the class in the Grocery Dude project directory.

6. Replace all code in `UnitsTVC.m` with the code from Listing 6.7 and then save the class file (press ⌘+**S**).

7. Select **Main.storyboard**.

8. Set the **Custom Class** of the **Units** table view controller to `UnitsTVC` using **Identity Inspector (Option+⌘+3)**.

9. Hold down **Control** and drag a line from the **Done** button on the **Units** table view controller to the yellow circle at the bottom of the same view and then select **Sent Actions > done**.

The Units table view is now ready. The next step is to implement the code required for the Unit view controller, including the relevant segue to get to it.

Implementing `UnitVC`

The Unit view will allow editing of a unit's name using a text field. When the view loads, the text field will be populated with the name of the unit that was selected on the table view. When the Done button is pressed, the view should be dismissed. `UnitVC` will be a `UIViewController` subclass and will implement this required functionality. The relevant header file is shown in Listing 6.8.

Listing 6.8   **UnitVC.h**

```
#import <UIKit/UIKit.h>
#import "CoreDataHelper.h"
@interface UnitVC : UIViewController <UITextFieldDelegate>
@property (strong, nonatomic) NSManagedObjectID *selectedObjectID;
@property (strong, nonatomic) IBOutlet UITextField *nameTextField;
@end
```

Update Grocery Dude as follows to add the `UnitVC` class:

1. Select the **Grocery Dude View Controllers** group.

2. Click **File > New > File...**.

3. Create a new **iOS > Cocoa Touch > Objective-C class** and then click **Next**.

4. Set **Subclass of** to `UIViewController` and **Class** name to `UnitVC` and then click **Next**.

5. Ensure the Grocery Dude target is ticked and then click **Create** to create the class in the Grocery Dude project directory.

6. Replace all code in `UnitVC.h` with the code from Listing 6.8.

Three sections will be implemented in `UnitVC.m`:

- The **VIEW** section will have three methods. The **viewDidLoad** method implements the standard keyboard-hiding techniques used previously in this book. The `viewWillAppear` method refreshes the interface and makes the only text field in the view the first responder so the keyboard is shown. The `refreshInterface` method populates the `nameTextField` with the name of the selected unit.

- The **TEXTFIELD** section implements an optional `UITextFieldDelegate` protocol method in order to update the `unit.name` value whenever editing finishes.

- The **INTERACTION** section matches the one used in `ItemVC`, so it will have methods responsible for hiding the keyboard when the background is tapped. It will also have methods that return the user to the `UnitsTVC` table view when a new Done button is tapped.

Listing 6.9 shows the code involved.

Listing 6.9   **UnitVC.m**

```
#import "UnitVC.h"
#import "Unit.h"
#import "AppDelegate.h"
@implementation UnitVC
#define debug 1
#pragma mark - VIEW
- (void)refreshInterface {
```

```
if (debug==1) {
    NSLog(@"Running %@ '%@'", self.class, NSStringFromSelector(_cmd));
}
    if (self.selectedObjectID) {
        CoreDataHelper *cdh =
        [(AppDelegate *)[[UIApplication sharedApplication] delegate] cdh];
        Unit *unit =
        (Unit*)[cdh.context existingObjectWithID:self.selectedObjectID
                                           error:nil];
        self.nameTextField.text = unit.name;
    }
}
- (void)viewDidLoad {
if (debug==1) {
    NSLog(@"Running %@ '%@'", self.class, NSStringFromSelector(_cmd));
}
    [super viewDidLoad];
    [self hideKeyboardWhenBackgroundIsTapped];
    self.nameTextField.delegate = self;
}
- (void)viewWillAppear:(BOOL)animated {
if (debug==1) {
    NSLog(@"Running %@ '%@'", self.class, NSStringFromSelector(_cmd));
}
    [self refreshInterface];
    [self.nameTextField becomeFirstResponder];
}

#pragma mark - TEXTFIELD
- (void)textFieldDidEndEditing:(UITextField *)textField {
if (debug==1) {
    NSLog(@"Running %@ '%@'", self.class, NSStringFromSelector(_cmd));
}
    CoreDataHelper *cdh =
    [(AppDelegate *)[[UIApplication sharedApplication] delegate] cdh];
    Unit *unit =
    (Unit*)[cdh.context existingObjectWithID:self.selectedObjectID
                                       error:nil];
    if (textField == self.nameTextField) {
        unit.name = self.nameTextField.text;
        [[NSNotificationCenter defaultCenter]
                        postNotificationName:@"SomethingChanged"
                                      object:nil];
    }
}
```

```objc
#pragma mark - INTERACTION
- (IBAction)done:(id)sender {
if (debug==1) {
    NSLog(@"Running %@ '%@'", self.class, NSStringFromSelector(_cmd));
}

    [self hideKeyboard];
    [self.navigationController popViewControllerAnimated:YES];
}
- (void)hideKeyboardWhenBackgroundIsTapped {
if (debug==1) {
    NSLog(@"Running %@ '%@'", self.class, NSStringFromSelector(_cmd));
}

    UITapGestureRecognizer *tgr =
    [[UITapGestureRecognizer alloc] initWithTarget:self
                                    action:@selector(hideKeyboard)];
    [tgr setCancelsTouchesInView:NO];
    [self.view addGestureRecognizer:tgr];
}
- (void)hideKeyboard {
if (debug==1) {
    NSLog(@"Running %@ '%@'", self.class, NSStringFromSelector(_cmd));
}

    [self.view endEditing:YES];
}
@end
```

Update Grocery Dude as follows to update the `UnitVC` implementation:

1. Replace all code in `UnitVC.m` with the code from Listing 6.9 and then save the class file (press ⌘+S).

2. Select **Main.storyboard**.

3. Set the **Custom Class** of the **Unit** view controller to `UnitVC` using **Identity Inspector** (**Option+⌘+3**).

4. Hold down **Control** and drag a line from the **Done** button on the **Unit** view controller to the yellow circle at the bottom of the same view. Then select **Sent Actions > done**.

5. Show the **Assistant Editor** (**Option+⌘+Return**).

6. Set the **Assistant Editor** to **Automatic > UnitVC.h**, as shown at the top of Figure 6.14.

7. Hold down **Control** and drag a line from the unit **Name** text field to the existing `nameTextField` property found in `UnitVC.h`, as shown in Figure 6.14.

Figure 6.14   Connecting the unit name text field to code

Segue from `UnitsTVC` to `UnitVC`

To reach `UnitVC`, a segue is required from `UnitsTVC`, as shown in Listing 6.10. This segue will pass the `objectID` of the selected unit to `UnitVC`. `UnitVC` will use this `objectID` to determine the selected unit before refreshing itself with the unit's data.

Listing 6.10   **`UnitsTVC.m: prepareForSegue`**

```
#pragma mark - SEGUE
- (void)prepareForSegue:(UIStoryboardSegue *)segue sender:(id)sender {
if (debug==1) {
    NSLog(@"Running %@ '%@'", self.class, NSStringFromSelector(_cmd));
}
    UnitVC *unitVC = segue.destinationViewController;
    if ([segue.identifier isEqualToString:@"Add Object Segue"])
    {
        CoreDataHelper *cdh =
        [(AppDelegate *)[[UIApplication sharedApplication] delegate] cdh];
        Unit *newUnit =
        [NSEntityDescription insertNewObjectForEntityForName:@"Unit"
                                    inManagedObjectContext:cdh.context];
        NSError *error = nil;
        if (![cdh.context obtainPermanentIDsForObjects:
            [NSArray arrayWithObject:newUnit] error:&error]) {
            NSLog(@"Couldn't obtain a permanent ID for object %@", error);
        }
        unitVC.selectedObjectID = newUnit.objectID;
    }
    else if ([segue.identifier isEqualToString:@"Edit Object Segue"])
```

```
    {
        NSIndexPath *indexPath = [self.tableView indexPathForSelectedRow];
        unitVC.selectedObjectID =
        [[self.frc objectAtIndexPath:indexPath] objectID];
    }
    else {
        NSLog(@"Unidentified Segue Attempted!");
    }
}
```

Update Grocery Dude as follows to implement the segue from `UnitsTVC` to `UnitVC`:

1. Show the **Standard Editor** (⌘+**Return**).

2. Add `#import "UnitVC.h"` to the top of `UnitsTVC.m`.

3. Add the code from Listing 6.10 to the bottom of `UnitsTVC.m` before `@end`.

Run the application and try adding some units via the new unit views. You won't be able to assign a unit to an item yet—that's a goal of the next chapter.

Adding and Editing Home or Shop Locations

The home and shop location table views and views will be a near match to `UnitsTVC` and `UnitVC`. The only difference is they will support home or shop location objects instead of unit objects. To avoid a large exercise in copy and paste, premade location class files are available for download.

Update Grocery Dude as follows to add the premade location class files:

1. Download and extract the location classes from http://www.timroadley.com/LearningCoreData/LocationClasses.zip.

2. Drag the `LocationsAtHomeTVC` and `LocationsAtShopTVC` class files into the **Grocery Dude Table View Controllers** group. Ensure **Copy items into destination group's folder** and the Grocery Dude target are ticked before clicking **Finish**.

3. Drag the `LocationAtHomeVC` and `LocationAtShopVC` class files into the **Grocery Dude View Controllers** group. Ensure **Copy items into destination group's folder** and the Grocery Dude target are ticked before clicking **Finish**.

Configuring the Home Location Views

To use these new classes, a similar exercise to the one used to configure the unit views is now required. These steps will configure buttons, connections, and text fields associated to the home location views.

Update Grocery Dude as follows:

1. Select **Main.storyboard**.

2. Drag a **Button** anywhere into the existing **Scroll View** of the **Item** view, and then configure it as follows using **Attributes Inspector (Option+⌘+4)**:

    - Set the **Type** to **Custom**.
    - Delete the text that reads "Button."
    - Set the **Image** to **add_homelocations**.

3. Configure the button as follows using **Size Inspector (Option+⌘+5)**:

    - Ensure **Width** is **48**.
    - Ensure **Height** is **48**.

4. Hold down **Control** and drag a line from the new button to the Navigation Controller beneath the Units Navigation Controller, which leads to the middle three generic controllers from previous steps. Then select **Action Segue > modal**.

5. Set the **Navigation Item Title** of the **Table View Controller** that the new modal segue leads to as **Home Locations**.

6. Select the **Prototype Cell** of the **Home Locations** table view controller and set the **Reuse Identifier** to `LocationAtHome Cell` using **Attributes Inspector (Option+⌘+4)**.

7. Set the **Navigation Item Title** of the **View Controller** that the Home Locations table view controller leads to as **Home Location**.

8. Copy the **Text View** from the **Unit** view to the same position in the **Home Location** view and then change the text content to **Enter the location an item is expected to be found at home. E.g. 'Pantry' or 'Bathroom'.**

9. With the **Name Text Field** and **Text View** selected on the **Home Location** view, click **Editor > Resolve Auto Layout Issues > Reset to Suggested Constraints**.

10. Set the **Custom Class** of the **Home Location** view controller to `LocationAtHomeVC` using **Identity Inspector (Option+⌘+3)**.

11. Set the **Custom Class** of the **Home Locations** table view controller to `LocationsAtHomeTVC` using **Identity Inspector (Option+⌘+3)**.

12. Hold down **Control** and drag a line from the **Done** button on the **Home Locations** table view controller to the yellow circle at the bottom of the same view, and then select **Sent Actions > done**.

13. Hold down **Control** and drag a line from the **Done** button on the **Home Location** view controller to the yellow circle at the bottom of the same view, and then select **Sent Actions > done**.

14. Show the **Assistant Editor (Option+⌘+Return)**.

15. Set the Assistant Editor to **Automatic > LocationAtHomeVC.h** using the approach demonstrated previously in Figure 6.14.

16. Hold down **Control** and drag a line from the **Home Location Name** text field to the existing `nameTextField` property found in `LocationAtHomeVC.h`. Use the approach demonstrated previously in Figure 6.14.

Configuring the Shop Location Views

To use the new shop location classes, another similar exercise is now required. These steps will configure the buttons, connections, and text fields associated to the shop location views.

Update Grocery Dude as follows:

1. Select **Main.storyboard** and show the **Standard Editor** (⌘+Return).

2. Drag a **Button** anywhere into the existing **Scroll View** of the **Item** view, and then configure it as follows using **Attributes Inspector** (Option+⌘+4):

   - Set the **Type** to **Custom**.
   - Delete the text that reads "Button."
   - Set the **Image** to **add_shoplocations**.

3. Configure the button as follows using **Size Inspector** (Option+⌘+5):

   - Ensure **Width** is **48**.
   - Ensure **Height** is **48**.

4. Hold down **Control** and drag a line from the new button to the **Navigation Controller** beneath the **Home Locations** Navigation Controller, which leads to the bottom three generic controllers from previous steps. Then select **Action Segue > modal**.

5. Set the **Navigation Item Title** of the table view controller that the new modal segue leads to as **Shop Locations**.

6. Select the **Prototype Cell** of the **Shop Locations** table view controller and set the **Reuse Identifier** to `LocationAtShop Cell` using **Attributes Inspector** (Option+⌘+4).

7. Set the **Navigation Item Title** of the view controller that the **Shop Locations** table view controller leads to as **Shop Location**.

8. Copy the **Text View** from the **Home Location** view to the same position in the **Shop Location** view and then change the text content to **Enter the location an item is expected to be found at the shop. E.g. 'Produce Section' or 'Deli'.**

9. With the **Name Text Field** and **Text View** selected on the **Shop Location** view, click **Editor > Resolve Auto Layout Issues > Reset to Suggested Constraints**.

10. Set the **Custom Class** of the **Shop Location** view controller to `LocationAtShopVC` using **Identity Inspector** (Option+⌘+3).

11. Set the **Custom Class** of the **Shop Locations** table view controller to
    `LocationsAtShopTVC` using **Identity Inspector (Option+⌘+3)**.

12. Hold down **Control** and drag a line from the **Done** button found on the **Shop Locations**
    table view controller to the yellow circle at the bottom of the same view, and then select
    Sent Actions > done.

13. Hold down **Control** and drag a line from the **Done** button found on the **Shop Location**
    view controller to the yellow circle at the bottom of the same view, and then select **Sent
    Actions > done**.

14. Show the **Assistant Editor (Option+⌘+Return)**.

15. Set the Assistant Editor to **Automatic > LocationAtShopVC.h** using the approach
    demonstrated previously in Figure 6.14.

16. Hold down **Control** and drag a line from the **Shop Location Name** text field to the
    existing `nameTextField` property found in `LocationAtShopVC.h`. Use the approach
    demonstrated previously in Figure 6.14.

17. Show the **Standard Editor (⌘+Return)**.

The means to edit units, home locations, and shop locations is now in place. Run the application
to examine your handiwork!

The expected view hierarchy is shown in Figure 6.15. Arrange the new buttons down the right
side of the item view to match.

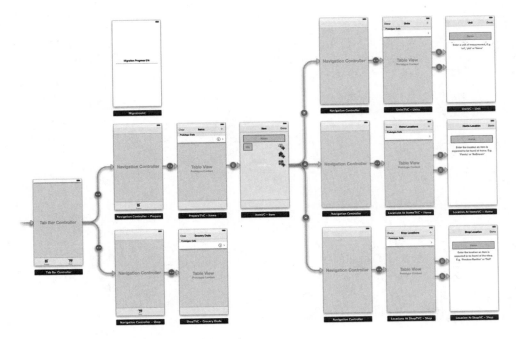

Figure 6.15   The Grocery Dude view hierarchy

Summary

The application is really starting to take shape, as the ability to edit items, units, home locations, and shop locations has been implemented. You've been shown how to pass an object between views and how to ensure the user interface is refreshed with the latest information available. In addition, you've also been shown how to perform a data-integrity check as a part of transitioning from a view, as demonstrated with the `ensureItemHomeLocationIsNotNull` and `ensureItemShopLocationIsNotNull` methods. Note that nothing prevents the user from inputting objects with the same name. De-duplication will be covered as a part of Chapter 15, "Taming iCloud."

Exercises

Why not build on what you've learned by experimenting?

1. Manually add some new items with new sections and then run the application again. (Hint: Copy the code from Listing 5.11, found in the previous chapter, to the `demo` method of `AppDelegate.m`.)

2. Select some items on the Prepare tab so they go orange. Change to the Shop tab and examine the section they're placed in. This feature is the crux of Grocery Dude—all you have to do is tap an item and it's already organized by its location in the Shop tab.

3. Test out the Clear feature on the Prepare and Shop tabs.

7

Picker Views

In the middle of difficulty lies opportunity.

Albert Einstein

In Chapter 6, "Views," you started building the Item view as the concept of passing managed objects around the application was demonstrated. Its primary focus introduced text fields as a means to edit managed objects. This chapter will explain how to create special text fields that have a Core Data–driven `UIPickerView` *as the input view. The purpose of a picker text field is to make selecting from predefined values, such as a shop aisle, as easy and fast as possible.*

Overview

Picker views make it easy for a user to relate managed objects. The item relationship properties `unit.name`, `locationAtHome.storedIn`, and `locationAtShop.aisle` are ideal candidates for setting with a picker view. The reason for this is that their potential values are relevant to many items. For example, a picker view can be used to define an item's aisle, as shown in Figure 7.1. To make the picker view appear, a special `UITextField` subclass will be created. This subclass will present the picker view as an input view, which is the same type of view that the keyboard is usually shown in.

> **Note**
>
> To continue building the sample application, you'll need to have added the previous chapter's code to Grocery Dude. Alternatively, you may download, unzip, and use the project up to this point from http://www.timroadley.com/LearningCoreData/GroceryDude-AfterChapter06.zip. Any time you start using an Xcode project from a ZIP file, it's good practice to click **Product** > **Clean**. This practice ensures there's no residual cache from previous projects using the same name.

Figure 7.1   A picker view

Introducing `CoreDataPickerTF`

To provide a picker view as an input view, a `UITextField` subclass called `CoreDataPickerTF`
will be created. This new class will adopt the `UIKeyInput`, `UIPickerViewDelegate`, and
`UIPickerViewDataSource` protocols. Just as `CoreDataTVC` underpins `PrepareTVC` and
`ShopTVC`, so too will `CoreDataPickerTF` underpin other custom subclasses. These custom
subclasses will be assigned to new text fields used to set an item's unit, home location, or shop
location.

When something is selected on the picker, the selected value needs to be reflected back to
the relevant text field. For example, once you've selected a shop location from the picker,
the name of the shop location should show up in the text field. For this to happen, the
`CoreDataPickerTF` class will define a `CoreDataPickerTFDelegate` protocol. Any text
fields that use a subclass of `CoreDataPickerTF` will need to adopt this protocol to be able to
receive the updated string value from the picker. Listing 7.1 shows the `selectedObjectID:`
`changedForPickerTF` method defined as a part of this new protocol in addition to some new
properties.

Listing 7.1   **`CoreDataPickerTF.h`**

```
#import <UIKit/UIKit.h>
#import "CoreDataHelper.h"
@class CoreDataPickerTF;
```

```
@protocol CoreDataPickerTFDelegate <NSObject>
- (void)selectedObjectID:(NSManagedObjectID*)objectID
      changedForPickerTF:(CoreDataPickerTF*)pickerTF;
@optional
- (void)selectedObjectClearedForPickerTF:(CoreDataPickerTF*)pickerTF;
@end

@interface CoreDataPickerTF : UITextField
<UIKeyInput, UIPickerViewDelegate, UIPickerViewDataSource>
@property (nonatomic, weak) id <CoreDataPickerTFDelegate> pickerDelegate;
@property (nonatomic, strong) UIPickerView *picker;
@property (nonatomic, strong) NSArray *pickerData;
@property (nonatomic, strong) UIToolbar *toolbar;
@property (nonatomic) BOOL showToolbar;
@property (nonatomic, strong) NSManagedObjectID *selectedObjectID;
@end
```

There are six properties in CoreDataPickerTF, as shown in Listing 7.1:

- **pickerDelegate** is a reference to anything that's set as a delegate of the CoreDataPickerTFDelegate protocol. Messages will be sent to delegates when a row is selected on the picker, telling them what was selected.

- **picker** is a reference to the picker view.

- **pickerData** is a reference to the array that'll be populated with Core Data fetch results.

- **toolbar** is a reference to the toolbar found directly above the picker view. The toolbar will have a Clear button and a Done button. The Clear button will clear the current selection, and the Done button will close the picker view.

- **showToolbar** is a flag used to indicate whether the toolbar should be hidden. This property exists only to make it easy for you to hide the toolbar in your own applications, should you choose to reuse CoreDataPickerTF. Grocery Dude will always show the toolbar.

- **selectedObjectID** is a reference to the objectID of the selected managed object associated to an item. When the selection on the picker changes, this property will change to reflect the new selection.

Update Grocery Dude as follows to configure CoreDataPickerTF:

1. Select the **Generic Core Data Classes** group.

2. Click **File > New > File....**

3. Create a new **iOS > Cocoa Touch > Objective-C class** and then click **Next**.

4. Set **Subclass of** to UITextField and **Class** name to CoreDataPickerTF and then click **Next**.

5. Ensure the Grocery Dude target is ticked and then click **Create** to create the class in the Grocery Dude project directory.

6. Replace all code in `CoreDataPickerTF.h` with the code from Listing 7.1.

The `CoreDataPickerTF` implementation has four sections:

- The **DELEGATE+DATASOURCE: UIPickerView** section will implement the protocol methods associated with populating the `UIPickerView`. It will also handle returning values to the `pickerDelegate` when an object is selected on the picker.

- The **INTERACTION** section will implement methods that handle new buttons available on the input accessory view, which clears the selection or hides the picker.

- The **DATA** section will implement methods that populate the `NSArray` with the data that drives the picker. It will also handle selecting an appropriate default row.

- The **VIEW** section will implement methods that create the picker view in an input view and the toolbar in the input accessory view. Redrawing due to device rotation will also be handled in this section.

DELEGATE+DATASOURCE: `UIPickerView`

This section has five methods that implement the required `UIPickerViewDataSource` protocol methods and some optional `UIPickerViewDelegate` protocol methods:

- The **numberOfComponentsInPickerView** method is used to specify how many columns the picker view has. In a picker view, a column is known as a component. Grocery Dude only needs one component so this method will be hard coded to return `1`. You may wish to implement multicomponent core data picker views in your own projects, so this is where you would specify how many components you want. If you do that then please note you'll need an array for each component.

- The **numberOfRowsInComponent** method is used to specify the total number of rows the picker view has. This value will vary depending on how many objects are in the `pickerData` array. The best way to provide this value is to return `[pickerData count]`, which indicates how many objects are in the `pickerData` array.

- The **widthForComponent** method is used to specify how wide each component is and will be hard coded to return `280`.

- The **titleForRow** method is used to specify what's displayed in each row of each component. This method is similar to the `cellForRowAtIndexPath` method a table-view uses to populate each row.

- The **didSelectRow** method is used to handle what happens when a row is selected. The `CoreDataPickerTF` will by default send a message to any delegates, notifying them that the string value has changed. The `CoreDataPickerTF` subclasses should override this method.

Listing 7.2 shows the code involved.

Listing 7.2 **CoreDataPickerTF.m: DELEGATE+DATASOURCE: UIPickerView**

```objc
#import "CoreDataPickerTF.h"
@implementation CoreDataPickerTF
#define debug 1

#pragma mark - DELEGATE & DATASOURCE: UIPickerView
- (NSInteger)numberOfComponentsInPickerView:(UIPickerView *)pickerView {
if (debug==1) {
    NSLog(@"Running %@ '%@'", self.class, NSStringFromSelector(_cmd));
}
    return 1;
}
- (NSInteger)pickerView:(UIPickerView *)pickerView
numberOfRowsInComponent:(NSInteger)component {
if (debug==1) {
    NSLog(@"Running %@ '%@'", self.class, NSStringFromSelector(_cmd));
}
    return [self.pickerData count];
}
- (CGFloat)pickerView:(UIPickerView *)pickerView
rowHeightForComponent:(NSInteger)component {
if (debug==1) {
    NSLog(@"Running %@ '%@'", self.class, NSStringFromSelector(_cmd));
}
    return 44.0f;
}
- (CGFloat)pickerView:(UIPickerView *)pickerView
    widthForComponent:(NSInteger)component {
if (debug==1) {
    NSLog(@"Running %@ '%@'", self.class, NSStringFromSelector(_cmd));
}
    return 280.0f;
}
- (NSString *)pickerView:(UIPickerView *)pickerView
           titleForRow:(NSInteger)row
         forComponent:(NSInteger)component {
if (debug==1) {
    NSLog(@"Running %@ '%@'", self.class, NSStringFromSelector(_cmd));
}
    return [self.pickerData objectAtIndex:row];
}
- (void)pickerView:(UIPickerView *)pickerView
      didSelectRow:(NSInteger)row
       inComponent:(NSInteger)component {
```

```
    if (debug==1) {
        NSLog(@"Running %@ '%@'", self.class, NSStringFromSelector(_cmd));
    }

        NSManagedObject *object = [self.pickerData objectAtIndex:row];
        [self.pickerDelegate selectedObjectID:object.objectID
                        changedForPickerTF:self];
    }
@end
```

Update Grocery Dude as follows to implement the DELEGATE+DATASOURCE: UIPickerView
section:

1. Replace all code in CoreDataPickerTF.m with the code from Listing 7.2.

Interaction

This section has two simple methods:

- The **done** method will be called when the Done button on the picker's toolbar is tapped. It dismisses the picker.

- The **clear** method will be called when the Clear button on the picker's toolbar is tapped. It sends a message to the picker delegate, telling it that the current selection should been cleared.

Listing 7.3 shows the code involved.

Listing 7.3   **CoreDataPickerTF.m: INTERACTION**

```
#pragma mark - INTERACTION
- (void)done {
if (debug==1) {
NSLog(@"Running %@ '%@'", self.class, NSStringFromSelector(_cmd));
}
    [self resignFirstResponder];
}
- (void)clear {
if (debug==1) {
    NSLog(@"Running %@ '%@'", self.class, NSStringFromSelector(_cmd));
}
    [self.pickerDelegate selectedObjectClearedForPickerTF:self];
    [self resignFirstResponder];
}
```

Update Grocery Dude as follows to implement the INTERACTION section:

1. Add the code from Listing 7.3 to the bottom of CoreDataPickerTF.m before @end.

Data

This section contains two methods, both of which are initially empty:

- The **fetch** method should be overridden in a CoreDataPickerTF subclass in order to populate self.pickerData with objects that the picker will display.

- The **selectDefaultRow** method should be overridden in a CoreDataPickerTF subclass. The overriding method should be configured to select a default row on the picker. Any existing association an item has to objects available on the picker will determine this default row selection. For example, if a "Milk" item object is already associated with the "Fridge" home location object, then the default picker selection will be Fridge.

Listing 7.4 shows the code involved. Because both methods must be overridden, these methods raise an exception if they're called.

Listing 7.4   **CoreDataPickerTF.m: DATA**

```
#pragma mark - DATA
- (void)fetch {
    [NSException raise:NSInternalInconsistencyException format:
    @"You must override the '%@' method to provide data to the picker",
    NSStringFromSelector(_cmd)];
}
- (void)selectDefaultRow {
    [NSException raise:NSInternalInconsistencyException format:
    @"You must override the '%@' method to set the default picker row",
    NSStringFromSelector(_cmd)];
}
```

Update Grocery Dude as follows to implement the DATA section:

1. Add the code from Listing 7.4 to the bottom of CoreDataPickerTF.m before @end.

View

This section contains five methods:

- The **createInputView** method returns a UIView containing a picker.

- The **createInputAccessoryView** method returns a UIView containing a toolbar with Clear and Done buttons.

- The **initWithFrame** and **initWithCoder** methods set the inputView and
  inputAccessoryView properties inherited from UITextField using createInputView
  and createInputAccessoryView.

- The **deviceDidRotate** method is used to ensure the picker view is redrawn whenever
  the device is rotated.

Listing 7.5 shows the code involved.

Listing 7.5 **CoreDataPickerTF.m: VIEW**

```
#pragma mark - VIEW
- (UIView *)createInputView {
if (debug==1) {
    NSLog(@"Running %@ '%@'", self.class, NSStringFromSelector(_cmd));
}
    self.picker = [[UIPickerView alloc] initWithFrame:CGRectZero];
    self.picker.showsSelectionIndicator = YES;
    self.picker.autoresizingMask = UIViewAutoresizingFlexibleHeight;
    self.picker.dataSource = self;
    self.picker.delegate = self;
    [self fetch];
    return self.picker;
}
- (UIView *)createInputAccessoryView {
if (debug==1) {
    NSLog(@"Running %@ '%@'", self.class, NSStringFromSelector(_cmd));
}
    self.showToolbar = YES;
    if (!self.toolbar && self.showToolbar) {
        self.toolbar = [[UIToolbar alloc] init];
        self.toolbar.barStyle = UIBarStyleBlackTranslucent;
        self.toolbar.autoresizingMask = UIViewAutoresizingFlexibleHeight;
        [self.toolbar sizeToFit];
        CGRect frame = self.toolbar.frame;
        frame.size.height = 44.0f;
        self.toolbar.frame = frame;

        UIBarButtonItem *clearBtn = [[UIBarButtonItem alloc]
                                initWithTitle:@"Clear"
                                style:UIBarButtonItemStyleBordered
                                target:self
                                action:@selector(clear)];
        UIBarButtonItem *spacer = [[UIBarButtonItem alloc]
        initWithBarButtonSystemItem:UIBarButtonSystemItemFlexibleSpace
                            target:nil
                            action:nil];
```

```
            UIBarButtonItem *doneBtn =[[UIBarButtonItem alloc]
            initWithBarButtonSystemItem:UIBarButtonSystemItemDone
                               target:self
                               action:@selector(done)];
        NSArray *array =
        [NSArray arrayWithObjects:clearBtn, spacer, doneBtn, nil];
        [self.toolbar setItems:array];
    }
    return self.toolbar;
}
-  (id)initWithFrame:(CGRect)aRect {
if (debug==1) {
    NSLog(@"Running %@ '%@'", self.class, NSStringFromSelector(_cmd));
}
    if (self = [super initWithFrame:aRect]) {

        self.inputView = [self createInputView];
        self.inputAccessoryView = [self createInputAccessoryView];
    }
    return self;
}
- (id)initWithCoder:(NSCoder*)aDecoder {
if (debug==1) {
    NSLog(@"Running %@ '%@'", self.class, NSStringFromSelector(_cmd));
}
    if (self = [super initWithCoder:aDecoder]) {
        self.inputView = [self createInputView];
        self.inputAccessoryView = [self createInputAccessoryView];
    }
    return self;
}
- (void)deviceDidRotate:(NSNotification*)notification {
if (debug==1) {
    NSLog(@"Running %@ '%@'", self.class, NSStringFromSelector(_cmd));
}
    [self.picker setNeedsLayout];
}
```

Update Grocery Dude as follows to implement the VIEW section:

1. Add the code from Listing 7.5 to the bottom of `CoreDataPickerTF.m` before `@end`.

CoreDataPickerTF is now ready to be subclassed to provide relevant picker views populated with data from Core Data. Three subclasses are required that will generate six new files in Grocery Dude. This calls for additional organization of the Xcode project.

Update Grocery Dude as follows to introduce a new group:

1. Right-click the existing **Grocery Dude** group and then select **New Group**.

2. Set the new group name to **Grocery Dude Picker Text Fields**.

Introducing `UnitPickerTF`

To choose an existing unit of measurement for an item, a picker is required. To present a picker, a text field with a custom `CoreDataPickerTF` subclass is required. A `CoreDataPickerTF` subclass implements three methods:

- The **fetch** method is responsible for constructing a Core Data fetch request and populating the `self.pickerData` array with Unit objects.

- The **selectDefaultRow** method will be configured to select a default row on the picker. Any existing association an item may have to the objects available on the picker will determine this default row selection. For example if a Bananas item object is already associated with a Kg unit object, then the default picker selection will be Kg. The `selectedObjectID` property is used to determine what object is currently selected by iterating through the `self.pickerData` array while looking for a `name` match. Note that currently it is possible for a unit to have the same name. This won't be possible by the end of the book once de-duplication is introduced in Chapter 15, "Taming iCloud."

- The **titleForRow** method will customize each row of the picker to show the name of the unit that the row represents.

Listing 7.6 shows the code involved.

Listing 7.6   **UnitPickerTF.m**

```
#import "UnitPickerTF.h"
#import "CoreDataHelper.h"
#import "AppDelegate.h"
#import "Unit.h"
@implementation UnitPickerTF
 #define debug 1
- (void)fetch {
if (debug==1) {
    NSLog(@"Running %@ '%@'", self.class, NSStringFromSelector(_cmd));
}
    CoreDataHelper *cdh =
    [(AppDelegate *)[[UIApplication sharedApplication] delegate] cdh];
    NSFetchRequest *request =
    [NSFetchRequest fetchRequestWithEntityName:@"Unit"];
    NSSortDescriptor *sort =
    [NSSortDescriptor sortDescriptorWithKey:@"name" ascending:YES];
```

```
        [request setSortDescriptors:[NSArray arrayWithObject:sort]];
        [request setFetchBatchSize:50];
        NSError *error;
        self.pickerData = [cdh.context executeFetchRequest:request
                                             error:&error];

        if (error) {
            NSLog(@"Error populating picker: %@, %@"
            , error, error.localizedDescription);}
        [self selectDefaultRow];
}
- (void)selectDefaultRow {
if (debug==1) {
    NSLog(@"Running %@ '%@'", self.class, NSStringFromSelector(_cmd));
}

    if (self.selectedObjectID && [self.pickerData count] > 0) {
        CoreDataHelper *cdh =
        [(AppDelegate *)[[UIApplication sharedApplication] delegate] cdh];
        Unit *selectedObject =
        (Unit*)[cdh.context existingObjectWithID:self.selectedObjectID
                                       error:nil];
        [self.pickerData enumerateObjectsUsingBlock:^(
         Unit *unit, NSUInteger idx, BOOL *stop) {
            if ([unit.name compare:selectedObject.name] == NSOrderedSame) {
                [self.picker selectRow:idx inComponent:0 animated:NO];
                [self.pickerDelegate selectedObjectID:self.selectedObjectID
                                  changedForPickerTF:self];

                *stop = YES;
            }
        }];
    }
}
- (NSString *)pickerView:(UIPickerView *)pickerView
            titleForRow:(NSInteger)row
          forComponent:(NSInteger)component {
if (debug==1) {
    NSLog(@"Running %@ '%@'", self.class, NSStringFromSelector(_cmd));
}
    Unit *unit = [self.pickerData objectAtIndex:row];
    return unit.name;
}
@end
```

Update Grocery Dude as follows to create the `UnitPickerTF` class:

1. Select the **Grocery Dude Picker Text Fields** group.

2. Click **File > New > File....**

3. Create a new **iOS > Cocoa Touch > Objective-C class** and then click **Next**.

4. Set **Subclass of** to `CoreDataPickerTF` and **Class** name to `UnitPickerTF` and then click **Next**.

5. Ensure the Grocery Dude target is ticked and then click **Create** to create the class in the Grocery Dude project directory.

6. Replace all code in `UnitPickerTF.m` with the code from Listing 7.6.

Creating the Unit Picker

The `UnitPickerTF` class is ready to use, so a new text field is required on `ItemVC`.

Update Grocery Dude as follows to create the unit picker text field:

1. Select **Main.storyboard**.

2. Drag a **Text Field** anywhere onto the **Scroll View** of the **Item** view and configure it as follows using **Attributes Inspector (Option+⌘+4)**:

   - Set the **Font** to **System Bold 17.0**.
   - Set the **Text Alignment** to **Center**.
   - Set the **Placeholder Text** to **Unit**.
   - Set the **Border Style** to the **Line** (represented by a rectangle).
   - Set **Background** to **Other > Crayons > Mercury** (the second lightest gray crayon).

3. Configure the **Height** of the **Text Field** to **48** using **Size Inspector (Option+⌘+5)**.

4. Arrange the **Unit** text field to the guides as shown in Figure 7.2, and then set its **Custom Class** to `UnitPickerTF` using **Identity Inspector (Option+⌘+3)**.

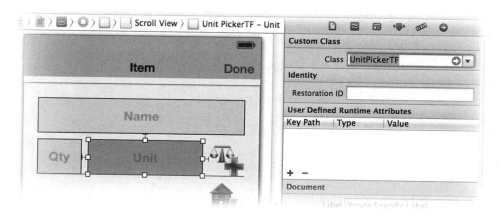

Figure 7.2   The unit picker text field

Connecting the Unit Picker

To reference the new picker text field in code, the outlets need to be connected. The Assistant Editor is used to achieve this.

Update Grocery Dude as follows to connect the unit picker text field to `ItemVC.h`:

1. Add `#import "UnitPickerTF.h"` to the top of `ItemVC.h`.

2. Select **Main.storyboard**.

3. Ensure the **Item** View Controller is selected and then show the **Assistant Editor** (**Option+⌘+Return**).

4. Set the Assistant Editor to **Automatic > ItemVC.h** if it isn't set to this already.

5. Hold down **Control** and drag a line from the **Unit Text Field** to the bottom of `ItemVC.h` before `@end`. Set the **Name** of the new property to `unitPickerTextField`, as shown in Figure 7.3. Double-check that the **Type** is `UnitPickerTF` and the **Storage** is **Strong**.

6. Show the Standard Editor (⌘+**Return**).

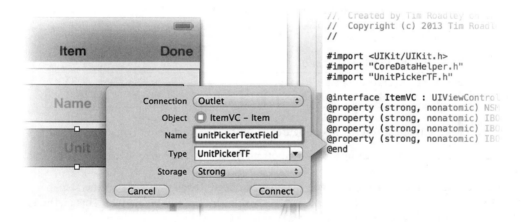

Figure 7.3   Connecting the unit picker text field

Configuring `ItemVC` for the Unit Picker

The Assistant Editor was used to create a reference to the unit picker text field through a new `unitPickerTextField` property. For picker text fields to send selected values back to the text field, the `ItemVC` needs to adopt the `CoreDataPickerTFDelegate` protocol.

Update Grocery Dude as follows:

1. Update `ItemVC.h` to adopt the `CoreDataPickerTFDelegate` protocol. For convenience, Listing 7.7 shows what `ItemVC.h` should look like once this update has been made.

Listing 7.7   `ItemVC.h`

```
#import <UIKit/UIKit.h>
#import "CoreDataHelper.h"
#import "UnitPickerTF.h"
@interface ItemVC : UIViewController
<UITextFieldDelegate,CoreDataPickerTFDelegate>
@property (strong, nonatomic) NSManagedObjectID *selectedItemID;
@property (strong, nonatomic) IBOutlet UIScrollView *scrollView;
@property (strong, nonatomic) IBOutlet UITextField *nameTextField;
@property (strong, nonatomic) IBOutlet UITextField *quantityTextField;
@property (strong, nonatomic) IBOutlet UnitPickerTF *unitPickerTextField;
@end
```

Because the `ItemVC` class now adopts both the `CoreDataPickerTFDelegate` and `UITextFieldDelegate` protocols, it needs to be set as a delegate of each for the picker text field. Being a delegate of the former will ensure selected values on the unit picker can be reflected in the unit text field. Being a delegate of the latter will ensure the unit text field moves into view when obscured by the unit picker. To achieve this functionality, the `UITextFieldDelegate` methods will set the selected text field as the `activeField` later in the chapter. Listing 7.8 shows the code involved in setting the delegates.

Listing 7.8   `ItemVC.m: viewDidLoad`

```
self.unitPickerTextField.delegate = self;
self.unitPickerTextField.pickerDelegate = self;
```

Update Grocery Dude as follows to configure the unit picker text field delegates:

1. Add the code from Listing 7.8 to the bottom of the `viewDidLoad` method of `ItemVC.m`.

As these updates are implemented, you may have noticed Xcode warning that the `selectedObjectID:changedForPickerTF` method hasn't been implemented. This method is required of the `CoreDataPickerTFDelegate` protocol. It will be updated for each of the picker text fields that are implemented. This will all be done in a new PICKERS section in `ItemVC.m`.

The PICKERS section will have two methods:

- The **`selectedObjectID:changedForPickerTF`** method will be called whenever the picker sends this message to its delegates. This method will set the selected item unit value and update the `unitPickerTextField.text` value to reflect the unit name. This approach will also be used for the upcoming `homeLocationPickerTextField` and `shopLocationPickerTextField`.

- The **`selectedObjectClearedForPickerTF`** method will be called whenever the picker sends this message to its delegates. This method will clear the selected item unit value and any text in `unitPickerTextField.text`. This approach will also be used for the upcoming `homeLocationPickerTextField` and `shopLocationPickerTextField`.

Listing 7.9 shows the code involved.

Listing 7.9 **`ItemVC.m`: PICKERS**
_____

```
#pragma mark - PICKERS
- (void)selectedObjectID:(NSManagedObjectID *)objectID
      changedForPickerTF:(CoreDataPickerTF *)pickerTF {
if (debug==1) {
    NSLog(@"Running %@ '%@'", self.class, NSStringFromSelector(_cmd));
}
    if (self.selectedItemID) {
        CoreDataHelper *cdh =
        [(AppDelegate *)[[UIApplication sharedApplication] delegate] cdh];

        Item *item =
        (Item*)[cdh.context existingObjectWithID:self.selectedItemID
                                    error:nil];;

        NSError *error;
        if (pickerTF == self.unitPickerTextField) {
            Unit *unit = (Unit*)[cdh.context existingObjectWithID:objectID
                                                    error:&error];

            item.unit = unit;
            self.unitPickerTextField.text = item.unit.name;
        }
        [self refreshInterface];
        if (error) {
            NSLog(@"Error selecting object on picker: %@, %@",
            error, error.localizedDescription);}
    }
}
- (void)selectedObjectClearedForPickerTF:(CoreDataPickerTF *)pickerTF {
if (debug==1) {
    NSLog(@"Running %@ '%@'", self.class, NSStringFromSelector(_cmd));
}
    if (self.selectedItemID) {
        CoreDataHelper *cdh =
        [(AppDelegate *)[[UIApplication sharedApplication] delegate] cdh];
        Item *item =
        (Item*)[cdh.context existingObjectWithID:self.selectedItemID
                                    error:nil];

        if (pickerTF == self.unitPickerTextField) {
            item.unit = nil;
            self.unitPickerTextField.text = @"";
```

```
        }
        [self refreshInterface];
    }
}
```

Update Grocery Dude as follows to implement the `PICKERS` section:

1. Add `#import "Unit.h"` to the top of `ItemVC.m`.

2. Add the code from Listing 7.9 to the bottom of `ItemVC.m` before `@end`.

To ensure that the unit picker can be refreshed with the latest data each time it is shown, the `fetch` method in `UnitPickerTF.m` needs to be exposed. This will allow it to be called from the `textFieldDidBeginEditing` method of `ItemVC.m`. In addition, the picker will need to reload after `fetch` is called. Listing 7.10 shows the code involved.

Listing 7.10   **ItemVC.m: textFieldDidBeginEditing**

```
if (textField == _unitPickerTextField && _unitPickerTextField.picker) {
    [_unitPickerTextField fetch];
    [_unitPickerTextField.picker reloadAllComponents];
}
```

Update Grocery Dude as follows to ensure the unit picker always has the latest data:

1. Add the following code to `UnitPickerTF.h` before `@end`:

   `- (void)fetch;`

2. Add the code from Listing 7.10 to the bottom of the `textFieldDidBeginEditing` method of `ItemVC.m`.

The final touch required to the unit picker text field is to ensure that its text value is populated with the current unit name whenever the view appears. The `viewWillAppear` method already has a call to `refreshInterface`, so this is an ideal place to set the unit picker text field text value. In addition, the item's associated unit should be set as the selected unit on the picker using its `objectID`. Listing 7.11 shows the code involved.

Listing 7.11   **ItemVC.m: refreshInterface**

```
- (void)refreshInterface {
if (debug==1) {
    NSLog(@"Running %@ '%@'", self.class, NSStringFromSelector(_cmd));
}
    if (self.selectedItemID) {
        CoreDataHelper *cdh =
        [(AppDelegate *)[[UIApplication sharedApplication] delegate] cdh];
```

```
        Item *item =
        (Item*)[cdh.context existingObjectWithID:self.selectedItemID
                                         error:nil];
        self.nameTextField.text = item.name;
        self.quantityTextField.text = item.quantity.stringValue;
        self.unitPickerTextField.text = item.unit.name;
        self.unitPickerTextField.selectedObjectID = item.unit.objectID;
    }
}
```

Update Grocery Dude as follows to ensure the `unitPickerTextField` displays the appropriate unit name:

1. Replace the **refreshInterface** method of `ItemVC.m` with the method from Listing 7.11.

2. Run the application. If there are no items or units in the persistent store, create some using the add/edit views created in the previous chapter. Once there are items and units in the persistent store, test setting an item's unit using the picker. The expected result is shown in Figure 7.4.

Figure 7.4   The unit picker text field in action

The unit picker is now completely operational, so it's time to perform a similar process to implement the home and shop location pickers.

Introducing `LocationAtHomePickerTF`

A picker is required to set the location an item is stored in at home. The same technique used to create the unit picker will be applied to create the home location picker. Again, the `fetch`, `selectDefaultRow`, and `titleForRow` methods will be implemented in a `CoreDataPickerTF` subclass.

Listing 7.12 shows the code involved.

Listing 7.12   `LocationAtHomePickerTF.m`

```
#import "LocationAtHomePickerTF.h"
#import "CoreDataHelper.h"
#import "AppDelegate.h"
#import "LocationAtHome.h"
@implementation LocationAtHomePickerTF
#define debug 1
- (void)fetch {
if (debug==1) {
    NSLog(@"Running %@ '%@'", self.class, NSStringFromSelector(_cmd));
}
    CoreDataHelper *cdh =
    [(AppDelegate *)[[UIApplication sharedApplication] delegate] cdh];
    NSFetchRequest *request =
    [NSFetchRequest fetchRequestWithEntityName:@"LocationAtHome"];
    NSSortDescriptor *sort =
    [NSSortDescriptor sortDescriptorWithKey:@"storedIn" ascending:YES];
    [request setSortDescriptors:[NSArray arrayWithObject:sort]];
    [request setFetchBatchSize:50];
    NSError *error;
    self.pickerData = [cdh.context executeFetchRequest:request
                                                 error:&error];
    if (error) {
        NSLog(@"Error populating picker: %@, %@",
        error, error.localizedDescription);
    }
    [self selectDefaultRow];
}
- (void)selectDefaultRow {
if (debug==1) {
    NSLog(@"Running %@ '%@'", self.class, NSStringFromSelector(_cmd));
}
    if (self.selectedObjectID && [self.pickerData count] > 0) {
```

```
            CoreDataHelper *cdh =
            [(AppDelegate *)[[UIApplication sharedApplication] delegate] cdh];
            LocationAtHome *selectedObject = (LocationAtHome*)[cdh.context
                            existingObjectWithID:self.selectedObjectID
                                            error:nil];
        [self.pickerData enumerateObjectsUsingBlock:^(
            LocationAtHome *locationAtHome, NSUInteger idx, BOOL *stop) {
            if ([locationAtHome.storedIn compare:selectedObject.storedIn]
                == NSOrderedSame) {
                [self.picker selectRow:idx inComponent:0 animated:NO];
                [self.pickerDelegate selectedObjectID:self.selectedObjectID
                                changedForPickerTF:self];
                *stop = YES;
            }
        }];
    }
}
- (NSString *)pickerView:(UIPickerView *)pickerView
            titleForRow:(NSInteger)row
        forComponent:(NSInteger)component {
if (debug==1) {
    NSLog(@"Running %@ '%@'", self.class, NSStringFromSelector(_cmd));
}
    LocationAtHome *locationAtHome = [self.pickerData objectAtIndex:row];
    return locationAtHome.storedIn;
}
@end
```

Update Grocery Dude as follows to create the `LocationAtHomePickerTF` class:

1. Select the **Grocery Dude Picker Text Fields** group.

2. Click **File > New > File...**.

3. Create a new **iOS > Cocoa Touch > Objective-C class** and then click **Next**.

4. Set **Subclass of** to `CoreDataPickerTF` and **Class** name to `LocationAtHomePickerTF` and then click **Next**.

5. Ensure the Grocery Dude target is ticked and then click **Create** to create the class in the Grocery Dude project directory.

6. Replace all code in `LocationAtHomePickerTF.m` with the code from Listing 7.12.

Because the code structure is so similar, it makes sense to create the equivalent code for the shop location picker now, too.

Introducing `LocationAtShopPickerTF`

A picker is required to set the location where an item is stored in a shop. Again, the `fetch`, `selectDefaultRow`, and `titleForRow` methods will be implemented in a `CoreDataPickerTF` subclass.

Listing 7.13 shows the code involved.

Listing 7.13 **`LocationAtShopPickerTF.m`**

```objc
#import "LocationAtShopPickerTF.h"
#import "CoreDataHelper.h"
#import "AppDelegate.h"
#import "LocationAtShop.h"
@implementation LocationAtShopPickerTF
#define debug 1
- (void)fetch {
if (debug==1) {
    NSLog(@"Running %@ '%@'", self.class, NSStringFromSelector(_cmd));
}
    CoreDataHelper *cdh =
    [(AppDelegate *)[[UIApplication sharedApplication] delegate] cdh];
    NSFetchRequest *request =
    [NSFetchRequest fetchRequestWithEntityName:@"LocationAtShop"];
    NSSortDescriptor *sort =
    [NSSortDescriptor sortDescriptorWithKey:@"aisle" ascending:YES];
    [request setSortDescriptors:[NSArray arrayWithObject:sort]];
    [request setFetchBatchSize:50];
    NSError *error;
    self.pickerData = [cdh.context executeFetchRequest:request
                                                 error:&error];
    if (error) {
        NSLog(@"Error populating picker: %@, %@",
        error, error.localizedDescription);
    }
    [self selectDefaultRow];
}
- (void)selectDefaultRow {
if (debug==1) {
    NSLog(@"Running %@ '%@'", self.class, NSStringFromSelector(_cmd));
}
    if (self.selectedObjectID && [self.pickerData count] > 0) {
        CoreDataHelper *cdh =
        [(AppDelegate *)[[UIApplication sharedApplication] delegate] cdh];
        LocationAtShop *selectedObject = (LocationAtShop*)[cdh.context
                            existingObjectWithID:self.selectedObjectID
                                           error:nil];
```

```
        [self.pickerData enumerateObjectsUsingBlock:^(
            LocationAtShop *locationAtShop, NSUInteger idx, BOOL *stop) {
            if ([locationAtShop.aisle compare:selectedObject.aisle]
                == NSOrderedSame) {
                [self.picker selectRow:idx inComponent:0 animated:NO];
                [self.pickerDelegate selectedObjectID:self.selectedObjectID
                            changedForPickerTF:self];
                *stop = YES;
            }
        }];
    }
}
- (NSString *)pickerView:(UIPickerView *)pickerView
            titleForRow:(NSInteger)row
            forComponent:(NSInteger)component {
if (debug==1) {
    NSLog(@"Running %@ '%@'", self.class, NSStringFromSelector(_cmd));
}

    LocationAtShop *locationAtShop = [self.pickerData objectAtIndex:row];
    return locationAtShop.aisle;
}
@end
```

Update Grocery Dude as follows to create the `LocationAtShopPickerTF` class:

1. Select the **Grocery Dude Picker Text Fields** group.

2. Click **File > New > File...**.

3. Create a new **iOS > Cocoa Touch > Objective-C class** and then click **Next**.

4. Set **Subclass of** to `CoreDataPickerTF` and **Class** name to `LocationAtShopPickerTF` and then click **Next**.

5. Ensure the Grocery Dude target is ticked and then click **Create** to create the class in the Grocery Dude project directory.

6. Replace all code in `LocationAtShopPickerTF.m` with the code from Listing 7.13.

Creating the Location Pickers

The `LocationAtHomePickerTF` and `LocationAtShopPickerTF` classes are ready to use, so two new text fields are required on `ItemVC`.

Update Grocery Dude as follows to create the home and shop location picker text fields:

1. Select **Main.storyboard**.

2. Drag two **Text Fields** anywhere onto the **Scroll View** of the **Item** view and configure them as follows using **Attributes Inspector (Option+⌘+4)**:

- Set the **Font** of both new text fields to **System Bold 17.0.**

- Set the **Text Alignment** of both new text fields to **Center.**

- Set the **Border Style** of both new text fields to **Line** (represented by a rectangle).

- Set **Background** to **Other > Crayons > Mercury** (the second lightest gray crayon).

- Set the **Placeholder Text** of one of the text fields to **Location at Home** and the other to **Location at Shop.**

3. Set the **Custom Class** of the **Location at Home** text field to `LocationAtHomePickerTF` and the **Custom Class** of the **Location at Shop** text field to `LocationAtShopPickerTF` using **Identity Inspector (Option+⌘+3).**

4. Configure the **Height** of both new text fields to **48** using **Size Inspector (Option+⌘+5).**

5. Arrange the text fields to the guides as shown in Figure 7.5. Then click **Editor > Resolve Auto Layout Issues > Reset to Suggested Constraints in ItemVC.**

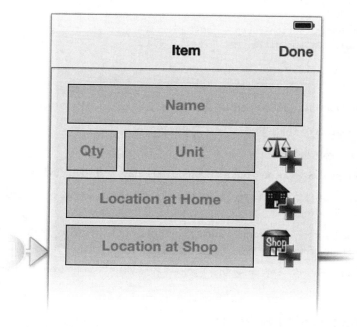

Figure 7.5   The home location and shop location picker text fields

Connecting the Location Pickers

To reference the new picker text fields in code, the outlets need to be connected. The Assistant Editor is used to achieve this.

Update Grocery Dude as follows to connect the home and shop location picker text fields to `ItemVC.h`:

1. Add `#import "LocationAtHomePickerTF.h"` to the top of `ItemVC.h`.

2. Add `#import "LocationAtShopPickerTF.h"` to the top of `ItemVC.h`.

3. Select **Main.storyboard**.

4. Ensure the **Item** View Controller is selected.

5. Show the **Assistant Editor** (**Option+⌘+Return**).

6. Set the Assistant Editor to **Automatic > ItemVC.h** if it isn't set to this already.

7. Hold down **Control** and drag a line from the **Location at Home** text field to `ItemVC.h` before `@end`. Set the **Name** of the new property to `homeLocationPickerTextField`. Double-check the **Type** is `LocationAtHomePickerTF` and the **Storage** is **Strong**.

8. Hold down **Control** and drag a line from the **Location at Shop** text field to `ItemVC.h` before `@end`. Set the **Name** of the new property to `shopLocationPickerTextField`. Double-check the **Type** is `LocationAtShopPickerTF` and the **Storage** is **Strong**.

9. Show the **Standard Editor** (**⌘+Return**).

When you examine `ItemVC.h`, there should now be filled-in circles next to each of the connected picker text fields. The expected result is shown in Figure 7.6.

```
#import <UIKit/UIKit.h>
#import "CoreDataHelper.h"
#import "UnitPickerTF.h"
#import "LocationAtHomePickerTF.h"
#import "LocationAtShopPickerTF.h"

@interface ItemVC : UIViewController <UITextFieldDelegate,CoreDataPickerTFDelegate>
@property (strong, nonatomic) NSManagedObjectID *selectedItemID;
@property (strong, nonatomic) IBOutlet UIScrollView *scrollView;
@property (strong, nonatomic) IBOutlet UITextField *nameTextField;
@property (strong, nonatomic) IBOutlet UITextField *quantityTextField;
@property (strong, nonatomic) IBOutlet UnitPickerTF *unitPickerTextField;
@property (strong, nonatomic) IBOutlet LocationAtHomePickerTF *homeLocationPickerTextField;
@property (strong, nonatomic) IBOutlet LocationAtShopPickerTF *shopLocationPickerTextField;
@end
```

Figure 7.6 Connected picker text fields

Configuring `ItemVC` for the Location Pickers

To ensure the home and shop location pickers are refreshed with the latest data like the unit picker, the respective `fetch` methods need to be exposed. Likewise, the `fetch` and `reloadAllComponents` call will need to be implemented, too. Listing 7.14 shows the new code involved in bold.

Listing 7.14 **ItemVC.m: textFieldDidBeginEditing**

```
- (void)textFieldDidBeginEditing:(UITextField *)textField {
if (debug==1) {
    NSLog(@"Running %@ '%@'", self.class, NSStringFromSelector(_cmd));
}
    if (textField == self.nameTextField) {

        if ([self.nameTextField.text isEqualToString:@"New Item"]) {
            self.nameTextField.text = @"";
        }
    }
    if (textField == _unitPickerTextField && _unitPickerTextField.picker) {
        [_unitPickerTextField fetch];
        [_unitPickerTextField.picker reloadAllComponents];
    } else if (textField == _homeLocationPickerTextField &&
               _homeLocationPickerTextField.picker) {
        [_homeLocationPickerTextField fetch];
        [_homeLocationPickerTextField.picker reloadAllComponents];
    } else if (textField == _shopLocationPickerTextField &&
               _shopLocationPickerTextField.picker) {
        [_shopLocationPickerTextField fetch];
        [_shopLocationPickerTextField.picker reloadAllComponents];
    }
}
```

Update Grocery Dude as follows to ensure the home and show location pickers always have the latest data:

1. Add the following code to the bottom of LocationAtHomePickerTF.h and LocationAtShopPickerTF.h before @end:

   ```
   - (void)fetch;
   ```

2. Replace the existing textFieldDidBeginEditing method in ItemVC.m with the code from Listing 7.14.

The ItemVC also needs to be set as a delegate of homeLocationPickerTextField and shopLocationPickerTextField in the same way as with unitPickerTextField. Listing 7.15 shows the code involved in configuring these delegates.

Listing 7.15 **ItemVC.m: viewDidLoad**

```
self.homeLocationPickerTextField.delegate = self;
self.homeLocationPickerTextField.pickerDelegate = self;
self.shopLocationPickerTextField.delegate = self;
self.shopLocationPickerTextField.pickerDelegate = self;
```

Update Grocery Dude as follows to configure the home and shop location picker and text field delegates:

1. Add the code from Listing 7.15 to the bottom of the `viewDidLoad` method of `ItemVC.m`.

In addition, the `refreshInterface` method needs to be updated to cater for the home and shop location picker text fields. Listing 7.16 shows the code involved.

Listing 7.16   **`ItemVC.m: refreshInterface`**

```
- (void)refreshInterface {
if (debug==1) {
    NSLog(@"Running %@ '%@'", self.class, NSStringFromSelector(_cmd));
}
    if (self.selectedItemID) {
        CoreDataHelper *cdh =
        [(AppDelegate *)[[UIApplication sharedApplication] delegate] cdh];
        Item *item =
        (Item*)[cdh.context existingObjectWithID:self.selectedItemID
                                error:nil];
        self.nameTextField.text = item.name;
        self.quantityTextField.text = item.quantity.stringValue;
        self.unitPickerTextField.text = item.unit.name;
        self.unitPickerTextField.selectedObjectID = item.unit.objectID;
        self.homeLocationPickerTextField.text =
            item.locationAtHome.storedIn;
        self.homeLocationPickerTextField.selectedObjectID =
            item.locationAtHome.objectID;
        self.shopLocationPickerTextField.text =
            item.locationAtShop.aisle;
        self.shopLocationPickerTextField.selectedObjectID =
            item.locationAtShop.objectID;
    }
}
```

Update Grocery Dude as follows to ensure the home and shop location text fields display the appropriate information:

1. Replace the **`refreshInterface`** method of `ItemVC.m` with the method from Listing 7.16.

The final touches involve updating the `PICKERS` section methods in `ItemVC.m` to cater for the home and shop location pickers. The `selectedObjectID:changedForPickerTF` method in `ItemVC.m` has an existing `if/else` statement used to react to the appropriate picker when a delegate method is called. Listing 7.17 shows the new code in bold.

Listing 7.17   **ItemVC.m: selectedObjectID:changedForPickerTF**

```
- (void)selectedObjectID:(NSManagedObjectID *)objectID
      changedForPickerTF:(CoresDataPickerTF *)pickerTF {
if (debug==1) {
    NSLog(@"Running %@ '%@'", self.class, NSStringFromSelector(_cmd));
}
    if (self.selectedItemID) {
        CoreDataHelper *cdh =
        [(AppDelegate *)[[UIApplication sharedApplication] delegate] cdh];

        Item *item =
        (Item*)[cdh.context existingObjectWithID:self.selectedItemID
                                     error:nil];;
        NSError *error;
        if (pickerTF == self.unitPickerTextField) {
            Unit *unit = (Unit*)[cdh.context existingObjectWithID:objectID
                                                      error:&error];
            item.unit = unit;
            self.unitPickerTextField.text = item.unit.name;
        }
        else if (pickerTF == self.homeLocationPickerTextField) {
            LocationAtHome *locationAtHome =
            (LocationAtHome*)[cdh.context existingObjectWithID:objectID
                                                   error:&error];
            item.locationAtHome = locationAtHome;
            self.homeLocationPickerTextField.text =
            item.locationAtHome.storedIn;
        }
        else if (pickerTF == self.shopLocationPickerTextField) {
            LocationAtShop *locationAtShop =
            (LocationAtShop*)[cdh.context existingObjectWithID:objectID
                                                   error:&error];
            item.locationAtShop = locationAtShop;
            self.shopLocationPickerTextField.text =
            item.locationAtShop.aisle;
        }
        [self refreshInterface];
        if (error) {
            NSLog(@"Error selecting object on picker: %@, %@",
            error, error.localizedDescription);
        }
    }
}
```

Update Grocery Dude as follows to update the first PICKER section method:

1. Replace the `selectedObjectID:changedForPickerTF` method in `ItemVC.m` with the code from Listing 7.17.

The same approach will be used to update `selectedObjectClearedForPickerTF` in `ItemVC.m`. This method nils out an item's home or shop locations, which will force the "..Unknown.." object to be used instead. Listing 7.18 shows the new code in bold.

Listing 7.18   `ItemVC.m`: `selectedObjectClearedForPickerTF`

```
- (void)selectedObjectClearedForPickerTF:(CoreDataPickerTF *)pickerTF {
if (debug==1) {
    NSLog(@"Running %@ '%@'", self.class, NSStringFromSelector(_cmd));
}
    if (self.selectedItemID) {
        CoreDataHelper *cdh =
        [(AppDelegate *)[[UIApplication sharedApplication] delegate] cdh];
        Item *item =
        (Item*)[cdh.context existingObjectWithID:self.selectedItemID
                                    error:nil];

        if (pickerTF == self.unitPickerTextField) {
            item.unit = nil;
            self.unitPickerTextField.text = @"";
        }
        else if (pickerTF == self.homeLocationPickerTextField) {
            item.LocationAtHome = nil;
            self.homeLocationPickerTextField.text = @"";
        }
        else if (pickerTF == self.shopLocationPickerTextField) {
            item.LocationAtShop = nil;
            self.shopLocationPickerTextField.text = @"";
        }
        [self refreshInterface];
    }
}
```

Update Grocery Dude as follows to update the second PICKER section method:

1. Replace the `selectedObjectClearedForPickerTF` method in `ItemVC.m` with the code from Listing 7.18.

All picker views are now completely configured. Run the application and create some units, home locations, and shop locations.

Picker-Avoiding Text Field

When a picker is shown, there's less room to display its related text field. This means it's likely that the related text field (referred to as the active text field) will become hidden behind its picker. To keep the active text field visible on the Item view, the scroll view needs to be resized in response to the keyboard being shown or hidden. Once the scroll view is resized, the active text field can be made visible using the `scrollRectToVisible` method of `UIScrollView`. The following two methods will be implemented in preparation for this functionality:

- The **keyboardDidShow** method finds the top of the keyboard input view where the picker will be located and resizes the `scrollView`. The offset will differ depending on the current orientation. Once the `scrollView` frame size matches the remaining visible area, the active text field can be brought into view.

- The **keyboardWillHide** method does the same thing as keyboardWillShow; it just makes the `scrollView` bigger instead of smaller.

Listing 7.19 shows the code involved.

Listing 7.19   **ItemVC.m: INTERACTION**

```
- (void)keyboardDidShow:(NSNotification *)n {

    // Find top of keyboard input view (i.e. picker)
    CGRect keyboardRect =
    [[[n userInfo] objectForKey:UIKeyboardFrameEndUserInfoKey] CGRectValue];
    keyboardRect = [self.view convertRect:keyboardRect fromView:nil];
    CGFloat keyboardTop = keyboardRect.origin.y;

    // Resize scroll view
    CGRect newScrollViewFrame =
    CGRectMake(0, 0, self.view.bounds.size.width, keyboardTop);
    newScrollViewFrame.size.height = keyboardTop - self.view.bounds.origin.y;
    [self.scrollView setFrame:newScrollViewFrame];

    // Scroll to the active Text-Field
    [self.scrollView scrollRectToVisible:self.activeField.frame animated:YES];
}
- (void)keyboardWillHide:(NSNotification *)n {
if (debug==1) {
    NSLog(@"Running %@ '%@'", self.class, NSStringFromSelector(_cmd));
}
    CGRect defaultFrame =
    CGRectMake(self.scrollView.frame.origin.x,
               self.scrollView.frame.origin.y,
               self.view.frame.size.width,
               self.view.frame.size.height);
```

```
    // Reset Scrollview to the same size as the containing view
    [self.scrollView setFrame:defaultFrame];

    // Scroll to the top again
    [self.scrollView scrollRectToVisible:self.nameTextField.frame
                               animated:YES];
}
```

Update Grocery Dude as follows to add to the INTERACTION section:

1. Add the following property to `ItemVC.h` before `@end`. This property will be used to store a reference to the active text field:

   `@property (strong, nonatomic) IBOutlet UITextField *activeField;`

2. Add the code from Listing 7.19 to the bottom of the INTERACTION section of `ItemVC.m`.

3. Add `_activeField = textField;` to the bottom of the `textFieldDidBeginEditing` method of `ItemVC.m`.

4. Add `_activeField = nil;` to the bottom of the `textFieldDidEndEditing` method of `ItemVC.m`.

The next step is to ensure the methods from Listing 7.19 are called when the keyboard is shown or hidden. This is achieved by observing `UIKeyboardDidShowNotification` and `UIKeyboardWillHideNotification`. The code involved is shown in Listing 7.20.

Listing 7.20   **ItemVC.m: viewWillAppear**

```
// Register for keyboard notifications while the view is visible.
[[NSNotificationCenter defaultCenter] addObserver:self
                                selector:@selector(keyboardDidShow:)
                                    name:UIKeyboardDidShowNotification
                                  object:self.view.window];
[[NSNotificationCenter defaultCenter] addObserver:self
                                selector:@selector(keyboardWillHide:)
                                    name:UIKeyboardWillHideNotification
                                  object:self.view.window];
```

Update Grocery Dude as follows to observe and respond to keyboard notifications:

1. Add the code from Listing 7.20 to the top of the `viewWillAppear` method of `ItemVC.m`.

There's no need to continue observing keyboard notifications when the Item view is not onscreen. The `viewDidDisappear` method is an ideal place to remove these observers. Listing 7.21 shows the code involved.

Listing 7.21 **ItemVC.m: viewDidDisappear**

```
// Unregister for keyboard notifications while the view is not visible.
[[NSNotificationCenter defaultCenter] removeObserver:self
                                 name:UIKeyboardDidShowNotification
                               object:nil];
[[NSNotificationCenter defaultCenter] removeObserver:self
                                 name:UIKeyboardWillHideNotification
                               object:nil];
```

Update Grocery Dude as follows to stop observing keyboard notifications:

1. Add the code from Listing 7.21 to the bottom of the viewDidDisappear method of ItemVC.m.

Run the application again, and ensure that there are several shop locations in the persistent store. On the Item view, tap the Shop Location picker text field and change the shop location of an item. You should notice that the shop location picker text field comes into view automatically.

Summary

Throughout this chapter, you've seen how to bind Core Data fetched results to a picker, then present that picker in an inputView triggered from a custom text field. The picker text fields for Grocery Dude were fully implemented in the process, so configuring an item should now be very fast. This will become even more apparent once there are several units, home locations, and shop locations added to the persistent store.

Exercises

Why not build on what you've learned by experimenting?

1. Temporarily set self.showToolbar = NO; in the createInputAccessoryView method of CoreDataPickerTF.m and then run the application to prove the toolbar is hidden on all picker views. Note that you can override this method in specific subclasses if you only want to hide the toolbar on specific pickers.

2. Temporarily create a multicomponent picker by creating an additional array in one of the CoreDataPickerTF subclasses. Note that you'll have to override the numberOfComponentsInPickerView method to achieve this.

8

Preloading Data

Never memorize something you can look up.

Albert Einstein

In Chapter 7, "Picker Views," you focused on configuring user interface elements bound to Core Data objects. As a result, the main functionality of Grocery Dude is now in place. This chapter will dive back into the data model as preloading default data is explained and demonstrated. There are several approaches to providing default data with an application. In some cases, it makes sense to just import data directly in code, as you've experienced in previous chapters. A more advanced technique is to generate a persistent store from an XML file. The resulting persistent store can then be shipped with the application and inserted as the initial persistent store before Core Data is set up for the first time.

Default Data

When your Core Data application is released, you may wish to ship it with some default data. In some cases, default data only serves as an example of how to use an application. In other cases, the application would be useless without it. When no default data is included, it may not be immediately apparent how Grocery Dude is supposed to be used. This is especially true when the user is confronted with empty picker views on the Item view. If default data is included with an application, it becomes easier to learn to use. The easier a program is to use, the more likely it is that people will continue to use it. The longer people use an application, the more chance that word about the application will spread, thus increasing sales potential.

Before an application imports default data, it's prudent to check for the following:

- The import is required.
- The user wants the default data imported (optional).

The import source for default data can vary greatly from case to case. Whatever the source, it can help to dump the data raw into a spreadsheet, generate XML using the upcoming techniques, and then generate a persistent store to ship with the application. The key to remember is that you must let Core Data generate any persistent store that you want Core Data to use.

> **Note**
>
> To continue building the sample application, you'll need to have added the previous chapter's code to Grocery Dude. Alternatively, you may download, unzip, and use the project up to this point from http://www.timroadley.com/LearningCoreData/GroceryDude-AfterChapter07.zip. Any time you start using an Xcode project from a ZIP file, it's good practice to click **Product** > **Clean**. This practice ensures there's no residual cache from previous projects using the same name.

Is an Import Required?

To indicate that an import is not required, an appropriate value can be set in a persistent store's metadata. Each time the application runs, this value can be checked to verify whether an import is required. This technique acts as a safety switch against importing duplicate default data. The first time the application is launched, this value won't exist and the default data is free to import.

You may also wish to include an additional line of defense against duplicate data by asking the user whether he or she wants to import default data. Grocery Dude will use this approach to give the user control over whether the import occurs. A secondary effect of this extra check is that if an accidental import is triggered, perhaps due to a bug, then the user has a chance to cancel the import. A `UIAlertView` will be used to ask the user whether he or she wants to continue with the data import. A `UIAlertViewDelegate` will be used to receive and handle the user's decision.

Update Grocery Dude as follows to add the import alert view:

1. Adopt the `UIAlertViewDelegate` protocol by updating the interface declaration in `CoreDataHelper.h` as follows:

   ```
   @interface CoreDataHelper : NSObject <UIAlertViewDelegate>
   ```

2. Add the following property to `CoreDataHelper.h` below the existing property declarations:

   ```
   @property (nonatomic, retain) UIAlertView *importAlertView;
   ```

When Grocery Dude is launched and the stores have been set up, it's a good time to check whether a default data import is required. Listing 8.1 shows the first method in a new DATA IMPORT section.

Listing 8.1　**CoreDataHelper.m: isDefaultDataAlreadyImportedForStoreWithURL**

```objc
#pragma mark - DATA IMPORT
- (BOOL)isDefaultDataAlreadyImportedForStoreWithURL:(NSURL*)url
                                             ofType:(NSString*)type {
if (debug==1) {
    NSLog(@"Running %@ '%@'", self.class, NSStringFromSelector(_cmd));
}
    NSError *error;
    NSDictionary *dictionary =
    [NSPersistentStoreCoordinator metadataForPersistentStoreOfType:type
                                                    URL:url
                                                  error:&error];

    if (error) {
        NSLog(@"Error reading persistent store metadata: %@",
        error.localizedDescription);
    }
    else {
        NSNumber *defaultDataAlreadyImported =
        [dictionary valueForKey:@"DefaultDataImported"];
        if (![defaultDataAlreadyImported boolValue]) {
            NSLog(@"Default Data has NOT already been imported");
            return NO;
        }
    }
    if (debug==1) {NSLog(@"Default Data HAS already been imported");}
    return YES;
}
```

The isDefaultDataAlreadyImportedForStoreWithURL method has the job of returning YES or NO when asked if default data has already been imported for a particular store. It works this out by looking for an existing metadata value for the key @"DefaultDataImported". If this key doesn't exist or exists with a NO value, the default data import is assumed to be required.

> **Note**
>
> The key name @"DefaultDataImported" is an arbitrary (random) name. The key name itself is not important. What is important is that it matches the key name set in the upcoming setDefaultDataAsImportedForStoreWithURL method, which is responsible for marking a store as imported.

Update Grocery Dude to add the DATA IMPORT section:

1. Add the code from Listing 8.1 to the bottom of CoreDataHelper.m before @end.

The next method required is checkIfDefaultDataNeedsImporting. This method will call isDefaultDataAlreadyImportedForStoreWithURL as it checks whether an import is required. If an import is required, the importAlert view will be shown to the user in order to double-check that he or she wants the import to occur. If an import is not required, nothing will happen. Listing 8.2 shows the code involved.

Listing 8.2   **CoreDataHelper.m: checkIfDefaultDataNeedsImporting**

```
- (void)checkIfDefaultDataNeedsImporting {
if (debug==1) {
    NSLog(@"Running %@ '%@'", self.class, NSStringFromSelector(_cmd));
}
    if (![self isDefaultDataAlreadyImportedForStoreWithURL:[self storeURL]
                                         ofType:NSSQLiteStoreType]) {
        self.importAlertView =
        [[UIAlertView alloc] initWithTitle:@"Import Default Data?"
                                                    message:
@"If you've never used Grocery Dude before then some default data might
➥help you understand how to use it. Tap 'Import' to import default data.
➥Tap 'Cancel' to skip the import, especially if you've done this before on other
➥devices."
                                            delegate:self
                                    cancelButtonTitle:@"Cancel"
                                    otherButtonTitles:@"Import", nil];
        [self.importAlertView show];
    }
}
```

Update Grocery Dude as follows to implement code to check if an import is required:

1. Add the code from Listing 8.2 to the bottom of the DATA IMPORT section of CoreDataHelper.m before @end.

2. Add [self checkIfDefaultDataNeedsImporting]; to the bottom of the existing setupCoreData method of CoreDataHelper.m.

After you've made those changes, run the application. The expected result is shown in Figure 8.1. For the moment, this prompt will display every time the application is launched because the data import code hasn't been implemented yet.

Figure 8.1   Checking whether the user wants to load default data

Importing from XML

Importing data from XML is a technique you can use to generate a persistent store containing default data. Once you have a "default data" persistent store, you can then ship it with your application bundle without the XML file. The advantage with this approach is that the default data will be ready to go instantly because no XML import process is required.

Many good XML parsers are available that can be used to create the default data store. Although some of those parsers would give better performance, the NSXMLParser included in the iOS SDK is fit for this purpose. The process to create the default data store isn't something the user will have to sit through, so performance isn't an issue. NSXMLParser is a streaming event-driven parser. This means that once parse is called on an instance of NSXMLParser, its delegate will be informed of what was found in the XML file as it is found.

> **Note**
>
> XML isn't your only choice for an import source. For example, you could import data using a JSON file with NSJSONSerialization or you could use a property list instead.

Update Grocery Dude as follows to adopt the NSXMLParserDelegate protocol:

1. Adopt the NSXMLParserDelegate protocol by updating the interface declaration in CoreDataHelper.h as follows:

   ```
   @interface CoreDataHelper : NSObject <UIAlertViewDelegate,
   NSXMLParserDelegate>
   ```

The next step is to implement importFromXML. This method is responsible for configuring the CoreDataHelper instance as an NSXMLParser delegate and then triggering the XML file parse. Once the parse is complete, a notification is sent to ensure that the table views are refreshed with the latest data. There would be no need for this notification if context were a parent of an import context. Parent context hierarchies are discussed in Chapter 11, "Background Processing."

The required code is shown in Listing 8.3.

Listing 8.3   **CoreDataHelper.m: importFromXML**

```
- (void)importFromXML:(NSURL*)url {
if (debug==1) {
    NSLog(@"Running %@ '%@'", self.class, NSStringFromSelector(_cmd));
}
    self.parser = [[NSXMLParser alloc] initWithContentsOfURL:url];
    self.parser.delegate = self;

    NSLog(@"**** START PARSE OF %@", url.path);
    [self.parser parse];
    [[NSNotificationCenter defaultCenter]
                  postNotificationName:@"SomethingChanged" object:nil];
    NSLog(@"***** END PARSE OF %@", url.path);
}
```

Update Grocery Dude as follows to implement the XML Parser trigger code:

1. Add the following property to CoreDataHelper.h below the existing property declarations:

   ```
   @property (nonatomic, strong) NSXMLParser *parser;
   ```

2. Add the code from Listing 8.3 to the bottom of the DATA IMPORT section of CoreDataHelper.m before @end.

Before anything can be imported, you'll need an XML file to import. The XML format that you'll need for Grocery Dude is shown in Listing 8.4.

Listing 8.4   **Default Data XML Example Format**

```
<items>
<item name="" unit="" locationathome=""locationatshop="" ></item>
</items>
```

Creating an XML file in this format is easy using a spreadsheet application such as Numbers or Excel. After pasting existing data into a spreadsheet, you can then insert the appropriate part of the XML string you're trying to create between the columns, as shown in Figure 8.2. The advantage in using Numbers or Excel is that you can fill down the repeated XML tags. Alternatively, you can use any editor you're comfortable with to produce the XML file, so long as the format is consistent.

	A	B	C	D	E	F	G	H	I
3	\<item name="	After Shave	" unit="		" locationathome="	Ensuite	" locationatshop="	Aisle 6	\>\</item\>
4	\<item name="	Air Freshener	" unit="	can	" locationathome="	Ensuite	" locationatshop="	Aisle 7	\>\</item\>
5	\<item name="	Aluminum Foil	" unit="	roll	" locationathome="	Pantry	" locationatshop="	Aisle 2	\>\</item\>
6	\<item name="	Apple Sauce	" unit="	jar	" locationathome="	Fridge	" locationatshop="	Aisle 2	\>\</item\>
7	\<item name="	Apples	" unit="		" locationathome="	Fridge	" locationatshop="	Produce	\>\</item\>
8	\<item name="	Arborio Rice	" unit="	pk	" locationathome="	Pantry	" locationatshop="	Produce	\>\</item\>
9	\<item name="	Avocado	" unit="		" locationathome="	Fridge	" locationatshop="	Produce	\>\</item\>
10	\<item name="	Baby Clothes Washing Liquid - Purity	" unit="		" locationathome="	Laundry	" locationatshop="	Aisle 7	\>\</item\>
11	\<item name="	Baby Corn		" unit="		" locationathome="	Fridge	" locationatshop="	Produce	\>\</item\>

Figure 8.2   Creating an XML file using Excel or Numbers

The columns in Figure 8.2 have been shaded to indicate what is data and what is part of the XML elements. Once imported, each row will become a managed object based on the Item entity. When the spreadsheet is ready, it's just a matter of saving it as a plain text file with an XML extension. After you remove any stray tab stops or spaces that may come from converting a spreadsheet to text, the XML will then be ready to use. An XML file containing a big list of ~400 items has been premade for you so you can maintain focus on building Grocery Dude.

Update Grocery Dude as follows to add the Default Data XML file:

1. Extract the premade **DefaultData.xml** from http://www.timroadley.com/ LearningCoreData/DefaultData.xml.zip.

2. Drag **DefaultData.xml** into the **Data Model** group. Ensure **Copy items into destination group's folder** and the Grocery Dude target are ticked before clicking **Finish**. The expected result after you click the XML file is shown in Figure 8.3.

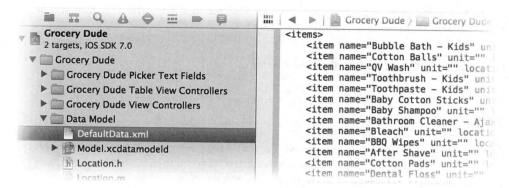

Figure 8.3   Default Data XML, ready for import

Creating an Import Context

When importing data, you should use a managed object context that does not run on the main thread. It is recommended that you use a context existing solely for importing data. This ensures there's no chance it will block the queue of another context—most importantly, the main queue context. An import context can use the same persistent store coordinator as another context. To reduce the resource requirements of the import context, it is recommended that you disable its undo manager by setting it to `nil`. On iOS, a context's undo manager is `nil` by default. Still, it's good practice to explicitly set the undo manager to `nil` just in case this default changes in the future.

Update Grocery Dude as follows to add the `importContext` property:

1. Add the following property to `CoreDataHelper.h` on the line after the existing `context` property is declared:

```
@property (nonatomic, readonly) NSManagedObjectContext
*importContext;
```

The import context is implemented in the same way as the foreground context; however, it will have a different concurrency type. You have three concurrency types to choose from when configuring an `NSManagedObjectContext`:

- The **NSMainQueueConcurrencyType** should be used when you want the context to operate on the main thread. Any heavy work performed in this queue may slow down or even freeze the user interface. You need at least one context working in the foreground to update user interface elements.

- The **NSPrivateQueueConcurrencyType** should be used when you don't want the context to operate on the main thread. This is an ideal concurrency type for potentially heavy work, such as saving or importing data.

- The **NSConfinementConcurrencyType** is the default legacy option, which you should typically avoid unless you need backward compatibility with pre–iOS 5.0 devices.

Any context with an NSPrivateQueueConcurrencyType should only be sent messages using performBlock or performBlockAndWait. Choose performBlock if you don't care when the block returns. Use performBlockAndWait if you need the block to return before continuing. If you call performBlockAndWait on a context running on the main thread, it will block the main thread. The code to configure the importContext to run on a private (background) queue is shown in Listing 8.5.

Listing 8.5   **CoreDataHelper.m: init**

```
_importContext = [[NSManagedObjectContext alloc]
                     initWithConcurrencyType:NSPrivateQueueConcurrencyType];
[_importContext performBlockAndWait:^{
    [_importContext setPersistentStoreCoordinator:_coordinator];
    [_importContext setUndoManager:nil]; // the default on iOS
}];
```

Update Grocery Dude as follows to implement the import context:

1. Add the code from Listing 8.5 to the bottom of the init method of CoreDataHelper.m before return self;.

Preventing Duplicate Default Data

To prevent default data from being imported more than once, a DefaultDataImported metadata key set to YES needs to be applied to the persistent store. To do this, a copy of the persistent store's existing metadata NSDictionary is needed. The DefaultDataImported key can then be added to the metadata dictionary copy, which can in turn be reapplied to the persistent store. This process occurs in the setDefaultDataAsImportedForStore method, as shown in Listing 8.6.

Listing 8.6   **CoreDataHelper.m: setDefaultDataAsImportedForStore**

```
- (void)setDefaultDataAsImportedForStore:(NSPersistentStore*)aStore {
if (debug==1) {
    NSLog(@"Running %@ '%@'", self.class, NSStringFromSelector(_cmd));
}
    // get metadata dictionary
    NSMutableDictionary *dictionary =
    [NSMutableDictionary dictionaryWithDictionary:[[aStore metadata] copy]];
```

```
    if (debug==1) {
        NSLog(@"__Store Metadata BEFORE changes__ \n %@", dictionary);
    }

    // edit metadata dictionary
    [dictionary setObject:@YES forKey:@"DefaultDataImported"];

    // set metadata dictionary
    [self.coordinator setMetadata:dictionary forPersistentStore:aStore];

    if (debug==1) {NSLog(@"__Store Metadata AFTER changes__ \n %@", dictionary);}
}
```

Update Grocery Dude as follows to implement code to set default data as imported:

1. Add the code from Listing 8.6 to the bottom of the DATA IMPORT section of CoreDataHelper.m before @end.

Triggering a Default Data Import

When the importAlertView is displayed, the user can tap Cancel to bypass the import or tap Import to proceed with loading default data. A new method called alertView: clickedButtonAtIndex will be added to a new DELEGATE: UIAlertView section of CoreDataHelper.m to handle the user's selection. Listing 8.7 shows the code involved.

Listing 8.7   **CoreDataHelper.m: alertView:clickedButtonAtIndex**

```
#pragma mark - DELEGATE: UIAlertView
- (void)alertView:(UIAlertView *)alertView
clickedButtonAtIndex:(NSInteger)buttonIndex {
if (debug==1) {
    NSLog(@"Running %@ '%@'", self.class, NSStringFromSelector(_cmd));
}
    if (alertView == self.importAlertView) {
        if (buttonIndex == 1) { // The 'Import' button on the importAlertView

            NSLog(@"Default Data Import Approved by User");
            [_importContext performBlock:^{
                // XML Import
                [self importFromXML:[[NSBundle mainBundle]
                        URLForResource:@"DefaultData" withExtension:@"xml"]];
            }];
        } else {
            NSLog(@"Default Data Import Cancelled by User");
        }
```

```
        // Set the data as imported regardless of the user's decision
        [self setDefaultDataAsImportedForStore:_store];
    }
}
```

When a button at index `1` is tapped, the previously implemented `importFromXML` method will be called. The Import button is at index `1`. Note that the import is performed using a `performBlock` without `AndWait`. This means the block of code will get back to the application whenever it is ready, without adversely impacting the user experience.

Regardless of what the user has chosen on the `importAlertView`, the method `setDefault-DataAsImportedForStore` is called to prevent the alert from harassing the user every time the application launches. If the user selects the wrong option, there is currently no recourse to reverse the decision. For brevity, this issue will remain out of scope in order to maintain focus on the primary objectives of this chapter. If you want to handle this situation in your own applications, examine Chapter 14, "iCloud," to see how iCloud is toggled with the Settings app. The same approach could be used to expose an **import default data** flag to the user, which could in turn be used to reverse the effect of the `setDefaultDataAsImportedForStore` method.

Update Grocery Dude as follows to implement code to trigger a default data import:

1. Add the code from Listing 8.7 to the bottom of `CoreDataHelper.m` before `@end`.

Run the application and tap Import to begin the data import. The expected result is shown in Figure 8.4. The lines in the console log may have a different order for you because the `parse` isn't executed on the main thread. Notice how after the method `setDefaultDataAsImportedForStoreWithURL` is run that the store metadata includes a line that reads `DefaultDataImported = 1;`.

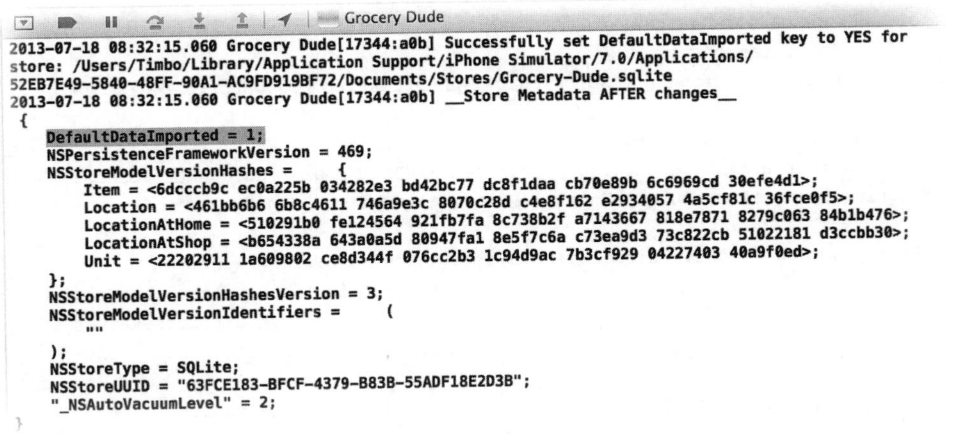

```
2013-07-18 08:32:15.060 Grocery Dude[17344:a0b] Successfully set DefaultDataImported key to YES for
store: /Users/Timbo/Library/Application Support/iPhone Simulator/7.0/Applications/
52EB7E49-5840-48FF-90A1-AC9FD919BF72/Documents/Stores/Grocery-Dude.sqlite
2013-07-18 08:32:15.060 Grocery Dude[17344:a0b] __Store Metadata AFTER changes__
 {
    DefaultDataImported = 1;
    NSPersistenceFrameworkVersion = 469;
    NSStoreModelVersionHashes =     {
        Item = <6dcccb9c ec0a225b 034282e3 bd42bc77 dc8f1daa cb70e89b 6c6969cd 30efe4d1>;
        Location = <461bb6b6 6b8c4611 746a9e3c 8070c28d c4e8f162 e2934057 4a5cf81c 36fce0f5>;
        LocationAtHome = <510291b0 fe124564 921fb7fa 8c738b2f a7143667 818e7871 8279c063 84b1b476>;
        LocationAtShop = <b654338a 643a0a5d 80947fa1 8e5f7c6a c73ea9d3 73c822cb 51022181 d3ccbb30>;
        Unit = <22202911 1a609802 ce8d344f 076cc2b3 1c94d9ac 7b3cf929 04227403 40a9f0ed>;
    };
    NSStoreModelVersionHashesVersion = 3;
    NSStoreModelVersionIdentifiers =     (
        ""
    );
    NSStoreType = SQLite;
    NSStoreUUID = "63FCE183-BFCF-4379-B83B-55ADF18E2D3B";
    "_NSAutoVacuumLevel" = 2;
}
```

Figure 8.4 `DefaultDataImported` metadata option

Although the parse is triggered as expected, no data is imported. This is because the NSXMLParser delegate methods have not yet been implemented.

Introducing CoreDataImporter

To create managed objects based on an XML file, you'll need to map what data goes where. This process requires intimate knowledge of the application source data and destination model. For Grocery Dude, this is a straightforward process because the data model is simple. The principles used for Grocery Dude can be applied to more complicated data models. To keep CoreDataHelper as clear as possible, a new class called CoreDataImporter will be created. CoreDataImporter will contain generic methods used to import unique managed objects. The methods are generic so they can be used with any data model.

Before inserting a new object into the target context, a check will be performed to ensure the proposed object doesn't already exist. Because the import is from XML, the only uniqueness indicator to match against is one of the target context entity attribute values. For Grocery Dude, this is an easy selection because item **name**, unit **name**, location at home **storedIn**, and location at shop **aisle** fit the bill nicely. In other applications, email addresses or phone numbers might be more appropriate. In some cases, you may end up needing to add a unique-ness ID to your source and target data.

An instance of CoreDataImporter relies on an NSDictionary with entity names keyed to a selected unique attribute. A new entitiesWithUniqueAttributes dictionary will store the unique attribute selection. To retrieve the name of the unique attribute for a given entity, a uniqueAttributeForEntity method will be implemented. The header file for CoreDataImporter, which contains these method headers, is shown in Listing 8.8.

Listing 8.8   **CoreDataImporter.h**

```
#import <Foundation/Foundation.h>
#import <CoreData/CoreData.h>
@interface CoreDataImporter : NSObject
@property (nonatomic, retain) NSDictionary *entitiesWithUniqueAttributes;

+ (void)saveContext:(NSManagedObjectContext*)context;
- (CoreDataImporter*)initWithUniqueAttributes:(NSDictionary*)uniqueAttributes;
- (NSString*)uniqueAttributeForEntity:(NSString*)entity;

- (NSManagedObject*)insertUniqueObjectInTargetEntity:(NSString*)entity
                        uniqueAttributeValue:(NSString*)uniqueAttributeValue
                             attributeValues:(NSDictionary*)attributeValues
                                   inContext:(NSManagedObjectContext*)context;

- (NSManagedObject*)insertBasicObjectInTargetEntity:(NSString*)entity
                        targetEntityAttribute:(NSString*)targetEntityAttribute
```

```
    sourceXMLAttribute:(NSString*)sourceXMLAttribute
        attributeDict:(NSDictionary*)attributeDict
              context:(NSManagedObjectContext*)context;
@end
```

Update Grocery Dude as follows to create the `CoreDataImporter` class:

1. Select the **Generic Core Data Classes** group.

2. Click **File** > **New** > **File**....

3. Create a new **iOS** > **Cocoa Touch** > **Objective-C class** and then click **Next**.

4. Set **Subclass of** to `NSObject` and **Class** name to `CoreDataImporter`. Click **Next**.

5. Ensure the Grocery Dude target is ticked and then click **Create** to create the class in the Grocery Dude project directory.

6. Replace all code in `CoreDataImporter.h` with the code from Listing 8.8.

When an instance of `CoreDataImporter` is created, it should be initialized using `initWithUniqueAttributes`. This will ensure there is a dictionary mapping for each target entity to a unique attribute name. As mentioned previously, the `uniqueAttributeForEntity` method is used to determine the unique attribute for the given entity. The code involved is shown in Listing 8.9.

Listing 8.9 `CoreDataImporter.m: saveContext, initWithUniqueAttributes, uniqueAttributeForEntity`

```
#import "CoreDataImporter.h"
@implementation CoreDataImporter
#define debug 1
+ (void)saveContext:(NSManagedObjectContext*)context {
if (debug==1) {
    NSLog(@"Running %@ '%@'", self.class, NSStringFromSelector(_cmd));
}
[context performBlockAndWait:^{
    if ([context hasChanges]) {
    NSError *error = nil;
        if ([context save:&error]) {NSLog(
@"CoreDataImporter SAVED changes from context to persistent store");
        } else {NSLog(
@"CoreDataImporter FAILED to save changes from context to persistent store: %@"
, error);
        }
    } else {NSLog(
@"CoreDataImporter SKIPPED saving context as there are no changes");
    }
}];
```

```
}
- (CoreDataImporter*)initWithUniqueAttributes:(NSDictionary*)uniqueAttributes {
if (debug==1) {
    NSLog(@"Running %@ '%@'", self.class, NSStringFromSelector(_cmd));
}
    if (self = [super init]) {

        self.entitiesWithUniqueAttributes = uniqueAttributes;

        if (self.entitiesWithUniqueAttributes) {
            return self;
        } else {NSLog(
@"FAILED to initialize CoreDataImporter: entitiesWithUniqueAttributes is nil");
            return nil;
        }
    }
    return nil;
}
- (NSString*)uniqueAttributeForEntity:(NSString*)entity {
if (debug==1) {
    NSLog(@"Running %@ '%@'", self.class, NSStringFromSelector(_cmd));
}
    return [self.entitiesWithUniqueAttributes valueForKey:entity];
}
@end
```

Notice that `CoreDataImporter` includes a `saveContext` method separate from the one found in `CoreDataHelper`. This improves `CoreDataImporter`'s portability to other applications.

Update Grocery Dude as follows to implement the first few `CoreDataImporter` methods:

1. Replace all existing code in `CoreDataImporter.m` with the code from Listing 8.9. There will still be an incomplete implementation warning after this change.

Before you insert a managed object, a check is needed against the target context to ensure that the proposed object does not already exist. To achieve this, a fetch is performed on the target context with a predicate specific to the unique attribute and unique attribute value. The code involved is shown in Listing 8.10.

Listing 8.10 **CoreDataImporter.m: existingObjectInContext**

```
- (NSManagedObject*)existingObjectInContext:(NSManagedObjectContext*)context
                            forEntity:(NSString*)entity
                withUniqueAttributeValue:(NSString*)uniqueAttributeValue {
if (debug==1) {
    NSLog(@"Running %@ '%@'", self.class, NSStringFromSelector(_cmd));
}
```

```
    NSString *uniqueAttribute = [self uniqueAttributeForEntity:entity];
    NSPredicate *predicate =
    [NSPredicate predicateWithFormat:@"%K==%@",
                                    uniqueAttribute, uniqueAttributeValue];
    NSFetchRequest *fetchRequest =
    [NSFetchRequest fetchRequestWithEntityName:entity];
    [fetchRequest setPredicate:predicate];
    [fetchRequest setFetchLimit:1];
    NSError *error;
    NSArray *fetchRequestResults =
    [context executeFetchRequest:fetchRequest error:&error];
    if (error) {NSLog(@"Error: %@", error.localizedDescription);}
    if (fetchRequestResults.count == 0) {return nil;}
    return fetchRequestResults.lastObject;
}
```

Update Grocery Dude as follows to implement the `existingObjectInContext` method:

1. Add the code from Listing 8.10 to the bottom of `CoreDataImporter.m` before `@end`. There will still be an incomplete implementation warning after this change.

If the `existingObjectInContext` method returns `nil`, the object does not exist in the target context. This result indicates that a new object with the given unique attribute value is required in the target context. To insert objects, a new method called `insertUniqueObjectInTarget-Entity` is required, which is shown in Listing 8.11.

Listing 8.11 `CoreDataImporter.m`: `insertUniqueObjectInTargetEntity`

```
- (NSManagedObject*)insertUniqueObjectInTargetEntity:(NSString*)entity
                  uniqueAttributeValue:(NSString*)uniqueAttributeValue
                     attributeValues:(NSDictionary*)attributeValues
                           inContext:(NSManagedObjectContext*)context {
if (debug==1) {
    NSLog(@"Running %@ '%@'", self.class, NSStringFromSelector(_cmd));
}
    NSString *uniqueAttribute = [self uniqueAttributeForEntity:entity];
    if (uniqueAttributeValue.length > 0) {
        NSManagedObject *existingObject =
        [self existingObjectInContext:context
                            forEntity:entity
             withUniqueAttributeValue:uniqueAttributeValue];
        if (existingObject) {
            NSLog(@"%@ object with %@ value '%@' already exists",
                        entity, uniqueAttribute, uniqueAttributeValue);
            return existingObject;
        } else {
```

```
        NSManagedObject *newObject =
        [NSEntityDescription insertNewObjectForEntityForName:entity
                                 inManagedObjectContext:context];
        [newObject setValuesForKeysWithDictionary:attributeValues];
        NSLog(@"Created %@ object with %@ '%@'",
                    entity, uniqueAttribute, uniqueAttributeValue);
        return newObject;
    }
  } else {
NSLog(@"Skipped %@ object creation: unique attribute value is 0 length",
entity);
  }
  return nil;
}
```

The `insertUniqueObjectInTargetEntity` method returns an `NSManagedObject` with its attributes populated from the dictionary of attribute values given to the method. If no unique attribute value is supplied, `nil` will be returned. Update Grocery Dude as follows to implement the `insertUniqueObjectInTargetEntity` method:

1. Add the code from Listing 8.11 to the bottom of `CoreDataImporter.m` before `@end`. There will still be an incomplete implementation warning after this change.

The final method required in `CoreDataImporter` is called `insertBasicObjectInTarget-Entity` and will leverage `insertUniqueObjectInTargetEntity`. Its purpose will be to insert a basic `NSManagedObject` with only one attribute populated (namely, the unique attribute). It exists solely to make the final import code easier to read. To use this method, you'll need to supply a target entity, target entity attribute, equivalent source XML attribute, the full `attributeDict` from the `XMLParser` delegate method, and a context. This method returns the resulting managed object, which can then be updated with the remaining attributes, if any. Listing 8.12 shows the code involved.

Listing 8.12 `CoreDataImporter.m: insertBasicObjectInTargetEntity`

```
- (NSManagedObject*)insertBasicObjectInTargetEntity:(NSString*)entity
                    targetEntityAttribute:(NSString*)targetEntityAttribute
                    sourceXMLAttribute:(NSString*)sourceXMLAttribute
                    attributeDict:(NSDictionary*)attributeDict
                    context:(NSManagedObjectContext*)context {

    NSArray *attributes = [NSArray arrayWithObject:targetEntityAttribute];
    NSArray *values =
    [NSArray arrayWithObject:[attributeDict valueForKey:sourceXMLAttribute]];

    NSDictionary *attributeValues =
    [NSDictionary dictionaryWithObjects:values forKeys:attributes];
```

```
    return [self insertUniqueObjectInTargetEntity:entity
          uniqueAttributeValue:[attributeDict valueForKey:sourceXMLAttribute]
              attributeValues:attributeValues
                    inContext:context];
}
```

Update Grocery Dude as follows to implement `insertBasicObjectInTargetEntity`:

1. Add the code from Listing 8.12 to the bottom of `CoreDataImporter.m` before `@end`. The incomplete implementation warning should disappear after this change.

> **Note**
>
> You may have noticed `CoreDataImporter` doesn't use `NSManagedObject` subclasses. Instead, key-value coding is used to access entity attributes. This is intentional because it provides the flexibility to remain data model agnostic at the cost of losing the convenient dot-notation syntax provided by `NSManagedObject` subclasses. When using this approach, note that `%K` is used as a substitution for a key path when specifying a predicate. An example of `%K` usage was shown previously in Listing 8.10.

Selecting Unique Attributes

A `CoreDataImporter` relies on a unique attribute being preselected for each entity before it can begin importing data. The mapping from entity to unique attribute will be configured in a new method called `selectedUniqueAttributes`. This method returns an `NSDictionary` with the unique attribute selection, as shown in Listing 8.13. Note that this code will go into `CoreDataHelper` and not `CoreDataImporter`. If you redeploy `CoreDataImporter` and `CoreDataHelper` to your own applications to import data, you will need to update this method with selected unique attributes specific to your own managed object model.

Listing 8.13 **CoreDataHelper.m: selectedUniqueAttributes**

```
#pragma mark - UNIQUE ATTRIBUTE SELECTION (This code is Grocery Dude data
➥specific and is used when instantiating CoreDataImporter)
- (NSDictionary*)selectedUniqueAttributes {
if (debug==1) {
    NSLog(@"Running %@ '%@'", self.class, NSStringFromSelector(_cmd));
}
    NSMutableArray *entities   = [NSMutableArray new];
    NSMutableArray *attributes = [NSMutableArray new];

    // Select an attribute in each entity for uniqueness
    [entities addObject:@"Item"];[attributes addObject:@"name"];
    [entities addObject:@"Unit"];[attributes addObject:@"name"];
```

```
[entities addObject:@"LocationAtHome"];[attributes addObject:@"storedIn"];
[entities addObject:@"LocationAtShop"];[attributes addObject:@"aisle"];

NSDictionary *dictionary = [NSDictionary dictionaryWithObjects:attributes
                                              forKeys:entities];

return dictionary;
}
```

Update Grocery Dude as follows to implement the UNIQUE ATTRIBUTE SELECTION section:

1. Add the code from Listing 8.13 to the bottom of CoreDataHelper.m before @end.

Mapping XML Data to Entity Attributes

The data import engine that CoreDataImporter provides can now be leveraged by the parse results of an NSXMLParser. All that's left to do is implement the appropriate delegate methods defined by the NSXMLParserDelegate protocol. There are two methods to be implemented in a new DELEGATE: NSXMLParser section:

- A **parseErrorOccurred** method will be used to log any errors that occur during the XML parse, usually from the NSXMLParserErrorDomain. If you receive errors, they'll probably be due to a formatting error or invalid character in the XML file.

- A **didStartElement** method will be called every time the parser finds a new element in the given XML file. In the case of Grocery Dude's default data XML file, this is the <item> element. Every attribute and associated value found within this element is passed to the delegate method as an NSDictionary. This dictionary is perfect for creating managed objects with. If you were to adapt this import technique to another application, the didStartElement method is where you would do the model-specific import customization.

The code involved is shown in Listing 8.14.

Listing 8.14   **CoreDataHelper.m: DELEGATE: NSXMLParser**

```
#pragma mark - DELEGATE: NSXMLParser (This code is Grocery Dude data
➥specific)
- (void)parser:(NSXMLParser *)parser
                        parseErrorOccurred:(NSError *)parseError {
if (debug==1) {
    NSLog(@"Parser Error: %@", parseError.localizedDescription);
}
}
```

```objc
- (void)parser:(NSXMLParser *)parser
                    didStartElement:(NSString *)elementName
                       namespaceURI:(NSString *)namespaceURI
                      qualifiedName:(NSString *)qName
                         attributes:(NSDictionary *)attributeDict {

[self.importContext performBlockAndWait:^{

    // STEP 1: Process only the 'item' element in the XML file
    if ([elementName isEqualToString:@"item"]) {

        // STEP 2: Prepare the Core Data Importer
        CoreDataImporter *importer =
        [[CoreDataImporter alloc] initWithUniqueAttributes:
        [self selectedUniqueAttributes]];

        // STEP 3a: Insert a unique 'Item' object
        NSManagedObject *item =
        [importer insertBasicObjectInTargetEntity:@"Item"
                      targetEntityAttribute:@"name"
                         sourceXMLAttribute:@"name"
                             attributeDict:attributeDict
                                   context:_importContext];

        // STEP 3b: Insert a unique 'Unit' object
        NSManagedObject *unit =
        [importer insertBasicObjectInTargetEntity:@"Unit"
                      targetEntityAttribute:@"name"
                         sourceXMLAttribute:@"unit"
                             attributeDict:attributeDict
                                   context:_importContext];

        // STEP 3c: Insert a unique 'LocationAtHome' object
        NSManagedObject *locationAtHome =
        [importer insertBasicObjectInTargetEntity:@"LocationAtHome"
                      targetEntityAttribute:@"storedIn"
                         sourceXMLAttribute:@"locationathome"
                             attributeDict:attributeDict
                                   context:_importContext];

        // STEP 3d: Insert a unique 'LocationAtShop' object
        NSManagedObject *locationAtShop =
        [importer insertBasicObjectInTargetEntity:@"LocationAtShop"
                      targetEntityAttribute:@"aisle"
                         sourceXMLAttribute:@"locationatshop"
```

```
                                   attributeDict:attributeDict
                                         context:_importContext];

        // STEP 4: Manually add extra attribute values.
        [item setValue:@NO forKey:@"listed"];

        // STEP 5: Create relationships
        [item setValue:unit forKey:@"unit"];
        [item setValue:locationAtHome forKey:@"locationAtHome"];
        [item setValue:locationAtShop forKey:@"locationAtShop"];

        // STEP 6: Save new objects to the persistent store.
        [CoreDataImporter saveContext:_importContext];

        // STEP 7: Turn objects into faults to save memory
        [_importContext refreshObject:item mergeChanges:NO];
        [_importContext refreshObject:unit mergeChanges:NO];
        [_importContext refreshObject:locationAtHome mergeChanges:NO];
        [_importContext refreshObject:locationAtShop mergeChanges:NO];
    }
  }];
}
```

The `didStartElement` delegate method is called every time the XML parser finds a new element in the XML file. If the XML element name is equal to "item," the import routine begins. First, a `CoreDataImporter` instance is created using the `selectedUniqueAttributes` method. Basic managed objects with one unique attribute value are then inserted using the `insertBasicObjectInTargetEntity` method. Once inserted, additional attributes and relationships can be set. Finally, the context is saved and objects turned into faults to save memory. This whole process is run within `performBlockAndWait` on the import context so that each item is completely processed before moving on to the next. The main thread is not blocked and the application remains usable during the import only because the `importContext` runs on a private queue.

Update Grocery Dude as follows to implement the DELEGATE: NSXMLParser section:

1. Add `#import "CoreDataImporter.h"` to the top of `CoreDataHelper.m`.

2. Add the code from Listing 8.14 to the bottom of `CoreDataHelper.m` before `@end`.

3. Delete Grocery Dude from the iOS Simulator so the persistent store does not have the `DefaultDataImported` key set to 1.

4. Click **Product** > **Clean** and run Grocery Dude on the iOS Simulator. Tap **Import** to begin the import. As the default data is imported, you can still use the application. The expected result is shown in Figure 8.5.

Figure 8.5   Preloaded default data

Importing from a Persistent Store

If you want to ship an application with default data from a persistent store, you have a couple of options. Which option you choose will depend on whether customer devices already have an existing persistent store:

- **Option 1: Use the default data persistent store as the initial persistent store.** This is achieved by copying the default data store onto the device before Core Data is set up for the first time. This is by far the easiest and most efficient option. This approach cannot be used when you have already shipped your application *without* default data. If that's the case, users will have already generated a persistent store with their own data, which you likely don't want to overwrite.

- **Option 2: Deep copy unique data from the default data persistent store to an existing persistent store.** This is achieved by copying the attribute values and relationships of each entity. The copy is referred to as "deep" because the relationships are all walked and objects are created as necessary. This find-or-create technique is a processor-intensive task that is best performed in the background. This option is a complicated topic and is discussed in Chapter 9, "Deep Copy." You should avoid this option when feasible. One alternative that is faster yet will potentially create duplicate objects is the `migratePersistentStore` instance method of `NSPersistentStore`.

Using the Default Data Store as the Initial Store

A persistent store full of default data has been created by Core Data as a part of the XML import. Core Data created the database so the format will be correct. To set a default store as the initial store, the database file needs to exist in the application bundle. When preparing a default database to ship with your application, you'll need to take into account the database journaling mode. Since iOS 7, a new default journaling mode called **Write-Ahead Logging** (**WAL**) has been set for SQLite databases. This new default increases performance and provides better concurrency support. As a side effect, there are now three files per database by default:

- The `sqlite` file is the database file, as per usual.

- The `sqlite-wal` file is the **Write-Ahead Log** file containing uncommitted database transactions. If you delete this file, you will lose data. If this file does not exist, there are no pending transactions waiting to be committed.

- The `sqlite-shm` file is the **Shared Memory** file containing an index of the WAL file. This file can be regenerated automatically so you don't need to worry about it.

Figure 8.6 shows an example of Grocery Dude SQLite WAL and SHM files.

Name	Date Modified
▼ 🗀 7.0	Today 8:12 AM
▶ 🗀 tmp	Today 8:12 AM
▼ 🗀 Applications	Today 8:12 AM
▼ 🗀 64EE080A-3A16-4977-AEAB-F7F897F30B03	Today 7:56 AM
🔖 Grocery Dude	Today 8:12 AM
▼ 🗀 Documents	Today 7:56 AM
▼ 🗀 Stores	Today 7:54 AM
🗋 Grocery-Dude.sqlite-shm	Today 8:12 AM
🗋 Grocery-Dude.sqlite-wal	Today 7:54 AM
🗋 Grocery-Dude.sqlite	Today 7:54 AM

Macintosh HD ▶ 🗀 Users ▶ 🏠 Timbo ▶ 🗀 Library ▶ 🗀 Application Support ▶ 🗀 iPhone Simulator ▶ 🗀 7.0 ▶

1 of 32 selected, 283.45 GB available

Figure 8.6   SQLite database files in WAL journaling mode

The `journal_mode` was intentionally set to DELETE in Chapter 2, "Managed Object Model Basics," to ensure that `-wal` and `-shm` files aren't present. This allows you to take a copy of the newly generated persistent store file without having to worry about extra files.

Extract the Grocery Dude persistent store as follows:

1. Right-click **Finder** and then select **Go to Folder**....

2. Enter **/Users/*Tim*/Library/Application Support/iPhone Simulator/** in the **Go to the Folder** dialog box. (Note: You'll need to substitute "Tim" with your own account name.)

3. Navigate the folder structure to find the `Grocery-Dude.sqlite` file, as shown in Figure 8.7. The application GUID will vary. If you have a lot of applications installed in the simulator and need help locating the appropriate GUID, search the console log for `Grocery-Dude.sqlite` and examine its containing path.

4. Ensure Grocery Dude isn't running.

5. Copy `Grocery-Dude.sqlite` to the desktop and rename it to `DefaultData.sqlite`.

Figure 8.7 shows an example of where the persistent store is located in the iOS Simulator application sandbox.

Name	Date Modified
▼ 📁 7.0	Today 5:45 PM
▶ 📁 tmp	Today 5:46 PM
▼ 📁 Applications	Today 5:45 PM
▼ 📁 CE0B157B-7B2C-44...35-C878C76ABD0E	Today 1:37 PM
📷 Grocery Dude	Today 5:45 PM
▼ 📁 Documents	Today 1:37 PM
▼ 📁 Stores	Today 5:50 PM
📄 Grocery-Dude.sqlite	Today 5:46 PM
▶ 📁 Library	Today 1:36 PM
▶ 📁 tmp	Today 1:36 PM

Macintosh HD ▶ 📁 Us ▶ ⌂ Ti ▶ 📁 Li ▶ 📁 Ap ▶ 📁 iP ▶ 📁 7.0 ▶ 📁 Media

Figure 8.7   SQLite database file in DELETE journaling mode

> **Note**
>
> If you are unable to find `Grocery-Dude.sqlite`, you may download a copy from http://www.timroadley.com/LearningCoreData/DefaultData.sqlite.zip.

Now that you have a `DefaultData.sqlite` store, you can include it in the application bundle and re-enable WAL mode.

Update Grocery Dude as follows:

1. Re-enable WAL journaling by commenting out the `NSSQLitePragmasOption` option in the `loadStore` method of `CoreDataHelper.m`.

2. Drag `DefaultData.sqlite` from your desktop into the **Data Model** group in Xcode. Ensure **Copy items into destination group's folder** and the Grocery Dude target are ticked before clicking **Finish**.

Now that the `DefaultData.sqlite` file exists in the application bundle, a new method called `setDefaultDataStoreAsInitialStore` can be implemented. This method will be called first by `setupCoreData`, so the default store can be put in place before it is required, as long as it doesn't already exist. There are a couple of ways to move the default store into place. You could use the `NSPersistentStoreCoordinator` method `migratePersistentStore`, which, it should be noted, can transparently handle store type conversions. The other option is the more basic `NSFileManager` method `copyItemAtURL`, which Grocery Dude will use. The code involved is shown in Listing 8.15.

Listing 8.15   **CoreDataHelper.m: setDefaultDataStoreAsInitialStore**

```
- (void)setDefaultDataStoreAsInitialStore {
if (debug==1) {
    NSLog(@"Running %@ '%@'", self.class, NSStringFromSelector(_cmd));
}
    NSFileManager *fileManager = [NSFileManager defaultManager];
    if (![fileManager fileExistsAtPath:self.storeURL.path]) {
        NSURL *defaultDataURL =
        [NSURL fileURLWithPath:[[NSBundle mainBundle]
             pathForResource:@"DefaultData" ofType:@"sqlite"]];
        NSError *error;
        if (![fileManager copyItemAtURL:defaultDataURL
                                  toURL:self.storeURL
                                  error:&error]) {
            NSLog(@"DefaultData.sqlite copy FAIL: %@",
            error.localizedDescription);
        }
        else {
NSLog(@"A copy of DefaultData.sqlite was set as the initial store for %@",
self.storeURL.path);
        }
    }
}
```

The `setDefaultDataStoreAsInitialStore` method first checks if there is already a persistent store at the target location. If there isn't, it proceeds to copy the default store into place from the main bundle using `copyItemAtURL`.

Update Grocery Dude as follows to implement `setDefaultDataStoreAsInitialStore`:

1. Add the code from Listing 8.15 to the bottom of the DATA IMPORT section of `CoreDataHelper.m`.

2. Add `[self setDefaultDataStoreAsInitialStore];` to the `setupCoreData` method of `CoreDataHelper.m` on the line before `[self loadStore];`.

3. Delete Grocery Dude from your device or simulator.

4. Click **Product > Clean** to clear any residual cache.

5. Run the application, which should open prepopulated with default data. The expected result is shown in Figure 8.8.

Figure 8.8   Preloaded default data

Summary

This chapter has shown how to configure multiple managed object contexts to allow a data import to occur in the background. Tips for preparing an XML file from raw data were given as the basic functionality of `CoreDataImporter` was implemented. This new class has enabled a model-agnostic creation of unique managed objects in a target context, based on an XML file. Don't forget that the size of any imported XML file should be kept to a minimum because the entire file needs to be stored in memory while the import occurs. This isn't too much of a problem when you're running an import on the iOS Simulator to create a default store. Where possible, it is recommended that you ship a prepopulated persistent store with your applications so it may be used as the initial store. If a persistent store already exists on customer devices then you may have to deep copy or migrate data from a preloaded persistent store. This topic is covered in the next chapter.

Exercises

Why not build on what you've learned by experimenting?

1. Add a **quantity** attribute with a random number to some of the items in the `DefaultData.XML` file.

2. Reactivate XML import by commenting out `[self setDefaultDataStoreAsInitialStore];` in the `setupCoreData` method of `CoreDataHelper.m`. Add the code shown in Listing 8.16 to the bottom of **STEP 4** in the `parser:didStartElement` method of `CoreDataHelper.m`. Delete and re-run the application to trigger the import. The quantities added to `DefaultData.XML` should have applied to the appropriate objects that were imported.

3. Turn off WAL journaling mode and re-run the application. Stop the application and edit the name of an item in the persistent store using **SQLite Database Browser**. Run the application again and see that the change appears in the iOS Simulator. Be careful not to have the SQLite file open by both the browser and simulator at the same time.

Listing 8.16   `CoreDataHelper.m: didStartElement (STEP 4)`

```
NSNumberFormatter *f = [NSNumberFormatter new];
if ([attributeDict valueForKey:@"quantity"]) {
[item setValue:[f numberFromString:[attributeDict valueForKey:@"quantity"]]
        forKey:@"quantity"];
}
```

Reverse any changes made during the exercises before moving to the next chapter.

Deep Copy

The only sure way to avoid making mistakes is to have no new ideas.

Albert Einstein

In Chapter 8, "Preloading Data," importing default data from an XML file was demonstrated. This import method is suitable only when the XML source file is small enough to fit into memory. Another option is to use a prepopulated persistent store as the initial persistent store. If customers already have existing data and you want to add a lot more to it, this option isn't suitable either. When you find yourself in this position, you may need to perform a "deep copy" of managed objects from a source persistent store to an existing persistent store. This option provides de-duplication and more granularity than the migratePersistentStore *instance method of* NSPersistentStore*, although it isn't as fast.*

Overview

A deep copy involves copying managed objects and their relationships from one persistent store to another. Once an object has been copied, the relationships from its source object are walked to find *related* source objects. Those related source objects are then copied to the target store as required. Relationships in the source store are then replicated in the target store between the copied objects. As this cycle continues for each object, every relationship in all directions is eventually copied into the target persistent store. Needless to say, this is a CPU-intensive task and should only be run in the background.

Depending on an application's data model, it may be more efficient to copy all objects in one pass and then reestablish the relationships later. In fact, this should be the preference. Unfortunately for Grocery Dude, this approach cannot be used. This is due to the items shown in the Prepare and Shop tabs having a reliance on a related object. If items are imported without a relationship to a home or shop location, the tables won't be divided into sections properly during the import process. This wouldn't look right to the user, who may get the impression that there is a bug in the application.

Deep copy will only work when the source and target stores have the same managed object model. That said, a separate coordinator and context is needed for the source and target stores, too. The contexts used for the source and target stores should also be separate from the main queue context. Figure 9.1 shows a high-level overview of the Core Data components that deep copy requires.

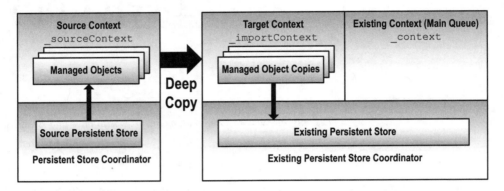

Figure 9.1   Deep copy

The existing _importContext will be reused as the target context for the deep copy demonstration. Copying an object to another context isn't as straightforward as a copy-and-paste command. To copy an object, you actually need to create a new object in the target context and then copy all the attribute values from a source object to the new object. That leaves the relationships, which can't be copied in the same way. If you were to copy a relationship the same way you copied an attribute value, you would end up with an illegal cross-store relationship between the copied object and object(s) in the source store. Instead of copying a relationship, a deep copy needs to identify *related copied objects* in the target context and then establish a relationship to them from the copied object. Figure 9.2 illustrates a To-One relationship copy.

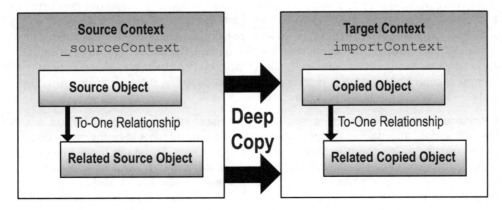

Figure 9.2   Copying a To-One relationship

Before a relationship can be copied, checks are needed to ensure that objects required as a part of a copied relationship already exist in the target context. Objects that are missing in the target context will be created on demand based on their equivalent source object.

To-Many relationships present an interesting challenge and are a big part of the reason that a deep copy is a CPU-intensive task. A deep copy needs to iteratively check every object and all of its relationships, so this process can take a long time. The other factor to account for is ordered and unordered relationships. An ordered relationship is, under the covers, an `NSMutableOrderedSet` of related objects. An unordered relationship is an `NSMutableSet` of related objects, so the deep copy code needs to reflect this. Figure 9.3 illustrates this more complicated relationship copy.

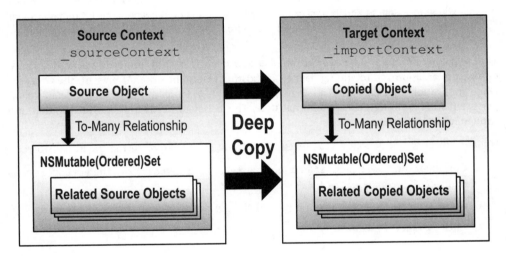

Figure 9.3   Copying a To-Many relationship

To deep copy objects, several methods from the previous chapter will be used. The deep copy process will rely on a unique attribute name being chosen for each entity upfront. This allows a uniqueness check to take place prior to an object being copied, which prevents duplicated data. The following shows the high-level process for performing a deep copy:

- An instance of `CoreDataImporter` is created with an `NSDictionary` of entity names mapped to a unique attribute per entity.

- An `NSArray` of entity names to copy is given to the `CoreDataImporter` instance, which it iterates through one by one, copying all objects for each entity as required. You only need to specify the entities you want copied. Related objects of entities earmarked for copy will be copied regardless, however.

- If equivalent objects from the source context don't already exist in the target context, new managed objects are inserted. New objects are given the attribute values of the source object.

- If a source object has a relationship, it is walked to find the related object(s). Related object(s) are copied to the target context as required.

- Once all objects involved in a relationship exist in the target context, the relationship itself is reformed from the copied object to the related copied object(s) as previously illustrated in Figure 9.2 and Figure 9.3.

> **Note**
>
> To continue building the sample application, you'll need to have added the previous chapter's code to Grocery Dude. Alternatively, you may download, unzip, and use the project up to this point from http://www.timroadley.com/LearningCoreData/GroceryDude-AfterChapter08.zip. Any time you start using an Xcode project from a ZIP file, it's good practice to click **Product** > **Clean**. This practice ensures there's no residual cache from previous projects using the same name.

The deep copy process will be demonstrated as another approach to importing default data, as opposed to an approach to adding data to an existing persistent store. At present, the Grocery Dude application checks to see if a persistent store exists at launch. If it doesn't, a default data persistent store is configured as the initial store. This behavior needs to be disabled so that deep copy may be demonstrated.

Update Grocery Dude as follows to prevent the default store from replacing the initial store:

1. Comment out `[self setDefaultDataStoreAsInitialStore];` in the `setupCoreData` method of `CoreDataHelper.m`.

2. Delete Grocery Dude from your device or the iOS simulator, whichever you're using.

3. Click **Product** > **Clean**.

Configuring a Source Stack

Core Data stack is a term referring to the combination of persistent store, persistent store coordinator, managed object model, and managed object context. To perform a deep copy from a source store, you'll need a separate Core Data stack from the one that already exists for the target store. This has the effect of providing a source and target context, which is where the copies will be performed. The only commonality between the two stacks is that they will use the same managed object model. Listing 9.1 shows new code required in the header of `CoreDataHelper` for this new stack.

Listing 9.1 **CoreDataHelper.h**

```
@property (nonatomic, readonly) NSManagedObjectContext      *sourceContext;
@property (nonatomic, readonly) NSPersistentStoreCoordinator
*sourceCoordinator;
@property (nonatomic, readonly) NSPersistentStore           *sourceStore;
```

Update Grocery Dude as follows to introduce a new stack for the source data:

1. Add the code from Listing 9.1 to `CoreDataHelper.h` after the existing declaration of `store`.

The next step is to use these new properties to initialize the new Core Data stack, ready for the source data. As well as initializing the `_sourceContext` the same way the `_importContext` has been, the `_sourceCoordinator` is also configured to use the same model as the existing `_coordinator`. The code involved is shown in Listing 9.2.

Listing 9.2 **`CoreDataHelper.m`: init**

```
_sourceCoordinator =
[[NSPersistentStoreCoordinator alloc] initWithManagedObjectModel:_model];
_sourceContext =
[[NSManagedObjectContext alloc]
initWithConcurrencyType:NSPrivateQueueConcurrencyType];
[_sourceContext performBlockAndWait:^{
    [_sourceContext setPersistentStoreCoordinator:_sourceCoordinator];
    [_sourceContext setUndoManager:nil]; // the default on iOS
}];
```

Update Grocery Dude as follows to include source stack support:

1. Add the code from Listing 9.2 to the bottom of the `init` method of `CoreDataHelper.m`, before `return self;`.

Configuring the Source Store

The same approach used to configure the existing store will be used to configure the source store. This means specifying the source store filename and a new method that returns the `NSURL` of the source store. Both of these will be used by a new `loadSourceStore` method, which will ultimately be responsible for loading the source store prior to a deep copy. Listing 9.3 shows the new line of code to be added to the `FILES` section, which specifies the source store filename. The existing `DefaultData.sqlite` store will be reused for this demonstration of deep copy.

Listing 9.3 **`CoreDataHelper.m`: FILES**

```
NSString *sourceStoreFilename = @"DefaultData.sqlite";
```

Update Grocery Dude as follows to configure the source store filename:

1. Add the code from Listing 9.3 to the bottom of the `FILES` section at the top of `CoreDataHelper.m`.

Just as the existing `storeURL` method returns the existing store URL, so too will a new `sourceStoreURL` return the source store URL. Listing 9.4 shows the code involved.

Listing 9.4   **CoreDataHelper.m: PATHS**

```
- (NSURL *)sourceStoreURL {
if (debug==1) {
    NSLog(@"Running %@ '%@'", self.class, NSStringFromSelector(_cmd));
}

return [NSURL fileURLWithPath:[[NSBundle mainBundle]
            pathForResource:[sourceStoreFilename stringByDeletingPathExtension]
                ofType:[sourceStoreFilename pathExtension]]];

}
```

Update Grocery Dude as follows to configure the `sourceStoreURL` method:

1. Add the code from Listing 9.4 to the bottom of the PATHS section of `CoreDataHelper.m`.

The next step is to implement the `loadSourceStore` method. This method is responsible for adding the source store to the source coordinator. Because the source store lives in the application bundle, it must be loaded as read-only. Note that this means that if the model is upgraded in the future, you'll need to ship a pre-upgraded version of `DefaultData.sqlite` with it. Listing 9.5 shows the code involved, which is similar to the existing code found in the `loadStore` method.

Listing 9.5   **CoreDataHelper.m: loadSourceStore**

```
- (void)loadSourceStore {
if (debug==1) {
    NSLog(@"Running %@ '%@'", self.class, NSStringFromSelector(_cmd));
}
    if (_sourceStore) {return;} // Don't load source store if it's already loaded

    NSDictionary *options =
    @{
      NSReadOnlyPersistentStoreOption:@YES
      };
    NSError *error = nil;
    _sourceStore =
    [_sourceCoordinator addPersistentStoreWithType:NSSQLiteStoreType
                                configuration:nil
                                        URL:[self sourceStoreURL]
                                    options:options
                                      error:&error];
```

```
    if (!_sourceStore) {
        NSLog(@"Failed to add source store. Error: %@",
        error);abort();
    } else {
        NSLog(@"Successfully added source store: %@", _sourceStore);
    }
}
```

Update Grocery Dude as follows to complete the configuration of the Core Data stack initialization code:

1. Add the `loadSourceStore` method from Listing 9.5 to the SETUP section of `CoreDataHelper.m` beneath the existing `loadStore` method.

If you ran the application now, it would still import default data from XML. The call to import from XML needs to be replaced with a call to import from a persistent store instead. Before that change can be made, the `CoreDataImporter` class needs updating to support deep copy from a persistent store.

Enhancing `CoreDataImporter`

To enable deep copy, the `CoreDataImporter` class will be enhanced to allow the complicated procedure of copying a managed object. There will be eight new methods, ranging from a few lines to around 20 lines each. The complexity comes from relationship copies, as each relationship must be walked to find related objects. The three relationship types (To-One, To-Many, and Ordered To-Many) must also be supported. As complicated as this process can be, by breaking it down into understandable chunks, it should become easier to understand. This breakdown is the reason there are so many methods required to perform a deep copy.

Object Info

The first of the eight methods required is the most simple. A new `objectInfo` method will be used to cut down repetitive code otherwise required in most of the other deep copy methods. By passing a managed object to this method, you get back an `NSString` containing the object's entity name, unique attribute, and unique attribute value information. Listing 9.6 shows the code involved.

Listing 9.6 **`CoreDataImporter.m: objectInfo`**

```
#pragma mark - DEEP COPY
- (NSString*)objectInfo:(NSManagedObject*)object {

    if (!object) {return nil;}
```

```
    NSString *entity = object.entity.name;
    NSString *uniqueAttribute = [self uniqueAttributeForEntity:entity];
    NSString *uniqueAttributeValue = [object valueForKey:uniqueAttribute];

    return [NSString stringWithFormat:@"%@ '%@'",
    entity, uniqueAttributeValue];
}
```

Update Grocery Dude to implement the `objectInfo` method:

  1. Add the code from Listing 9.6 to the bottom of `CoreDataImporter.m` before `@end`.

Array For Entity

The next method required is `arrayForEntity`. This method is responsible for returning an array of managed objects for the specified entity, with respect to the given context and predicate. This is another helper method that exists to reduce the amount of code required for a deep copy. Listing 9.7 shows the code involved, which should look familiar from previous chapters.

Listing 9.7   **`CoreDataImporter.m: arrayForEntity`**

```
- (NSArray*)arrayForEntity:(NSString*)entity
                 inContext:(NSManagedObjectContext*)context
             withPredicate:(NSPredicate*)predicate {
if (debug==1) {
    NSLog(@"Running %@ '%@'", self.class, NSStringFromSelector(_cmd));
}
    NSFetchRequest *request =
    [NSFetchRequest fetchRequestWithEntityName:entity];
    [request setFetchBatchSize:50];
    [request setPredicate:predicate];
    NSError *error;
    NSArray *array = [context executeFetchRequest:request error:&error];
    if (error) {
        NSLog(@"ERROR fetching objects: %@", error.localizedDescription);
    }
    return array;
}
```

Update Grocery Dude as follows to implement the `arrayForEntity` method:

  1. Add the code from Listing 9.7 to the bottom of `CoreDataImporter.m` before `@end`.

Copy Unique Object

The next method required is copyUniqueObject. This method is responsible for ensuring a unique copy of an object exists in the specified context. If a nil object or context is given to this method, it will return nil. Technically, this method does not copy a managed object. Instead, it creates a new object in the target context and then copies the attribute values from the source object to the new object. As discussed in the previous chapter, the method insertUniqueObjectInTargetEntity is used to ensure only unique objects are inserted. If the object already exists, this method just returns the existing object. Note that relationships are not copied in this method because they need to be copied in another way. Listing 9.8 shows the code involved.

Listing 9.8   **CoreDataImporter.m: copyUniqueObject**

```
- (NSManagedObject*)copyUniqueObject:(NSManagedObject*)object
                         toContext:(NSManagedObjectContext*)targetContext {
if (debug==1) {
    NSLog(@"Running %@ '%@'", self.class, NSStringFromSelector(_cmd));
}
    // SKIP copying object with missing info
    if (!object || !targetContext) {
        NSLog(@"FAILED to copy %@ to context %@",
        [self objectInfo:object], targetContext);
        return nil;
    }

    // PREPARE variables
    NSString *entity = object.entity.name;
    NSString *uniqueAttribute = [self uniqueAttributeForEntity:entity];
    NSString *uniqueAttributeValue = [object valueForKey:uniqueAttribute];

    if (uniqueAttributeValue.length > 0) {

        // PREPARE attributes to copy
        NSMutableDictionary *attributeValuesToCopy =
        [NSMutableDictionary new];
        for (NSString *attribute in object.entity.attributesByName) {
        [attributeValuesToCopy setValue:[[object valueForKey:attribute] copy]
                            forKey:attribute];
        }

        // COPY object
        NSManagedObject *copiedObject =
        [self insertUniqueObjectInTargetEntity:entity
                    uniqueAttributeValue:uniqueAttributeValue
                        attributeValues:attributeValuesToCopy
                            inContext:targetContext];
```

```
        return copiedObject;
    }
    return nil;
}
```

Update Grocery Dude as follows to implement the `copyUniqueObject` method:

1. Add the code from Listing 9.8 to the bottom of `CoreDataImporter.m` before `@end`.

Establish To-One Relationship

The next method required is `establishToOneRelationship`. This method is responsible for establishing a To-One relationship by name, from one object to another. The majority of this method exists to validate the proposed relationship. The relationship creation is skipped whenever the following are true:

- The given source object, target object, or the relationship name is `nil`.

- The relationship already exists.

- The object that would be related is of the wrong entity type for the specified relationship name.

Establishing a To-One relationship is a single line of code. It is established by setting the value of the relationship's key-value pair on an object. The relationship name is the key and the related object is the value.

The final part of the `establishToOneRelationship` method is the important cleanup task that removes references to the specified objects from each context. By calling `refreshObject` for each object after a context save, the managed objects are *faulted*. This removes the objects from memory, thus breaking strong reference cycles that would otherwise keep unneeded objects around wasting resources. Without this step, importing from a persistent store would be no better than importing from XML, as all of the source data would be loaded in memory. Although it can be expensive to call `save` so frequently, it keeps the memory overhead low. In addition, the process occurs in the background, so it won't impact the user interface. The general overview of this concept was shown previously in Figure 9.2, and is demonstrated in code in Listing 9.9.

Listing 9.9 **CoreDataImporter.m: establishToOneRelationship**

```
- (void)establishToOneRelationship:(NSString*)relationshipName
                        fromObject:(NSManagedObject*)object
                          toObject:(NSManagedObject*)relatedObject {
if (debug==1) {
    NSLog(@"Running %@ '%@'", self.class, NSStringFromSelector(_cmd));
}
// SKIP establishing a relationship with missing info
```

```
if (!relationshipName || !object || !relatedObject) {
    NSLog(@"SKIPPED establishing To-One relationship '%@' between %@ and %@",
    relationshipName,
    [self objectInfo:object],
    [self objectInfo:relatedObject]);
    NSLog(@"Due to missing Info!");
    return;
}

// SKIP establishing an existing relationship
NSManagedObject *existingRelatedObject =
[object valueForKey:relationshipName];
if (existingRelatedObject) {
    return;
}

// SKIP establishing a relationship to the wrong entity
NSDictionary *relationships = [object.entity relationshipsByName];
NSRelationshipDescription *relationship =
[relationships objectForKey:relationshipName];
if (![relatedObject.entity isEqual:relationship.destinationEntity]) {
    NSLog(@"%@ is the of wrong entity type to relate to %@",
    [self objectInfo:object], [self objectInfo:relatedObject]);
    return;
}

// ESTABLISH the relationship
[object setValue:relatedObject forKey:relationshipName];
NSLog(@"ESTABLISHED %@ relationship from %@ to %@",
relationshipName,
[self objectInfo:object],
[self objectInfo:relatedObject]);

// REMOVE the relationship from memory after it is committed to disk
[CoreDataImporter saveContext:relatedObject.managedObjectContext];
[CoreDataImporter saveContext:object.managedObjectContext];
[object.managedObjectContext refreshObject:object mergeChanges:NO];
[relatedObject.managedObjectContext refreshObject:relatedObject
                                    mergeChanges:NO];
}
```

Update Grocery Dude as follows to implement the establishToOneRelationship method:

1. Add the code from Listing 9.9 to the bottom of CoreDataImporter.m before @end.

Establish To-Many Relationship

The next method required is `establishToManyRelationship`, which is responsible for establishing a To-Many relationship from an object. It is expected that the object passed to this method will be from the deep copy target context. The given `NSMutableSet` should contain objects from the source context. The method will create missing objects required as a part of the new relationship in the target context.

A To-Many relationship is established by adding an object to another object's `NSMutableSet` that represents a particular relationship. The `NSMutableSet` is accessed through the object's key-value pair. The relationship name is the key, and the `NSMutableSet` is the value. An `NSMutableSet` can only contain distinct objects, so there is no chance of accidentally duplicating a relationship from the same object. The general overview of this concept was shown previously in Figure 9.3, and is demonstrated in code in Listing 9.10.

Listing 9.10   **CoreDataImporter.m: establishToManyRelationship**

```
- (void)establishToManyRelationship:(NSString*)relationshipName
                      fromObject:(NSManagedObject*)object
                   withSourceSet:(NSMutableSet*)sourceSet {

if (!object || !sourceSet || !relationshipName) {
NSLog(@"SKIPPED establishing a To-Many relationship from %@",
[self objectInfo:object]);
NSLog(@"Due to missing Info!");
return;
}

NSMutableSet *copiedSet =
[object mutableSetValueForKey:relationshipName];

for (NSManagedObject *relatedObject in sourceSet) {

    NSManagedObject *copiedRelatedObject =
    [self copyUniqueObject:relatedObject
            toContext:object.managedObjectContext];

    if (copiedRelatedObject) {
        [copiedSet addObject:copiedRelatedObject];
NSLog(@"A copy of %@ is now related via To-Many '%@' relationship to %@",
[self objectInfo:object],
relationshipName,
[self objectInfo:copiedRelatedObject]);
    }
}
```

```
// REMOVE the relationship from memory after it is committed to disk
[CoreDataImporter saveContext:object.managedObjectContext];
[object.managedObjectContext refreshObject:object mergeChanges:NO];
}
```

Update Grocery Dude as follows to implement the `establishToManyRelationship` method:

1. Add the code from Listing 9.10 to the bottom of `CoreDataImporter.m` before `@end`.

Establish Ordered To-Many Relationship

The next method required is `establishOrderedToManyRelationship`, which is responsible for establishing an Ordered To-Many relationship from an object. It is expected that the object passed to this method will be from the deep copy target context. The given `NSMutableOrderedSet` should contain objects from the source context. The method will create missing objects required as a part of the new relationship in the target context.

An Ordered To-Many relationship is established by adding one object to another object's `NSMutableOrderedSet` that represents a particular relationship. The `NSMutableOrderedSet` is accessed through the object's key-value pair. The relationship name is the key, and the `NSMutableOrderedSet` is the value. An `NSMutableOrderedSet` can only contain distinct objects, so there is no chance of accidentally duplicating a relationship from the same object. The order of the set in the target context needs to match the order of the set from the source context. The order of the source set is maintained as the equivalent objects are added to the target object's ordered set in the order they are found. The general overview of this concept was shown previously in Figure 9.3, and is demonstrated in code in Listing 9.11.

Listing 9.11 **CoreDataImporter.m: establishOrderedToManyRelationship**

```
- (void)establishOrderedToManyRelationship:(NSString*)relationshipName
                    fromObject:(NSManagedObject*)object
                 withSourceSet:(NSMutableOrderedSet*)sourceSet {

if (!object || !sourceSet || !relationshipName) {
NSLog(@"SKIPPED establishment of an Ordered To-Many relationship from %@",
[self objectInfo:object]);
NSLog(@"Due to missing Info!");
return;
}

NSMutableOrderedSet *copiedSet =
[object mutableOrderedSetValueForKey:relationshipName];

for (NSManagedObject *relatedObject in sourceSet) {
```

```
        NSManagedObject *copiedRelatedObject =
        [self copyUniqueObject:relatedObject
                    toContext:object.managedObjectContext];

        if (copiedRelatedObject) {
            [copiedSet addObject:copiedRelatedObject];
NSLog(@"A copy of %@ is related via Ordered To-Many '%@' relationship to %@",
[self objectInfo:object],
relationshipName,
[self objectInfo:copiedRelatedObject]);
        }
    }

// REMOVE the relationship from memory after it is committed to disk
[CoreDataImporter saveContext:object.managedObjectContext];
[object.managedObjectContext refreshObject:object mergeChanges:NO];
}
```

Update Grocery Dude as follows to implement the establishOrderedToManyRelationship method:

1. Add the code from Listing 9.11 to the bottom of CoreDataImporter.m before @end.

There are no ordered relationships in Grocery Dude; however, this method is included in case you would like to use CoreDataImporter in your own projects.

Copy Relationships

The next method required is copyRelationshipsFromObject, which is responsible for copying all relationships from an object in the source context to an equivalent object in the target context. This method is what the other methods implemented so far have been building up to.

The first task this method performs, after ensuring the given object and context aren't nil, is to ensure there is an equivalent object in the target context. Referred to as the copiedObject, this object is created as required using the previously implemented copyUniqueObject method. If it still doesn't exist after a copy is attempted, this method returns prematurely.

To copy relationships, the method works out what relationships exist on the source object using [sourceObject.entity relationshipsByName]. This dictionary is then iterated through to find valid relationships. Provided the relationship exists, the equivalent relationship is re-created from the copiedObject. Before copying a relationship, its type is first determined. For To-Many or Ordered To-Many relationships, the appropriate source set is passed to the appropriate "copy To-Many" method. For a To-One relationship, the object to be related is copied to the target context before the appropriate method is called to establish the relationship. Listing 9.12 shows the code involved.

Listing 9.12   **CoreDataImporter.m: copyRelationshipsFromObject**

```objc
- (void)copyRelationshipsFromObject:(NSManagedObject*)sourceObject
                        toContext:(NSManagedObjectContext*)targetContext {
if (debug==1) {
    NSLog(@"Running %@ '%@'", self.class, NSStringFromSelector(_cmd));
}
// SKIP establishing relationships with missing info
if (!sourceObject || !targetContext) {
    NSLog(@"FAILED to copy relationships from '%@' to context '%@'",
    [self objectInfo:sourceObject], targetContext);
    return;
}

// SKIP establishing relationships from nil objects
NSManagedObject *copiedObject =
[self copyUniqueObject:sourceObject toContext:targetContext];
if (!copiedObject) {
    return;
}

// COPY relationships
NSDictionary *relationships = [sourceObject.entity relationshipsByName];
for (NSString *relationshipName in relationships) {

    NSRelationshipDescription *relationship =
    [relationships objectForKey:relationshipName];
    if ([sourceObject valueForKey:relationshipName]) {

        if (relationship.isToMany && relationship.isOrdered) {

            // COPY To-Many Ordered
            NSMutableOrderedSet *sourceSet =
            [sourceObject mutableOrderedSetValueForKey:relationshipName];
            [self establishOrderedToManyRelationship:relationshipName
                              fromObject:copiedObject
                           withSourceSet:sourceSet];

        } else if (relationship.isToMany && !relationship.isOrdered) {

            // COPY To-Many
            NSMutableSet *sourceSet =
            [sourceObject mutableSetValueForKey:relationshipName];
            [self establishToManyRelationship:relationshipName
                          fromObject:copiedObject
                       withSourceSet:sourceSet];
```

```
        } else {

            // COPY To-One
            NSManagedObject *relatedSourceObject =
            [sourceObject valueForKey:relationshipName];
            NSManagedObject *relatedCopiedObject =
            [self copyUniqueObject:relatedSourceObject
                          toContext:targetContext];
            [self establishToOneRelationship:relationshipName
                                  fromObject:copiedObject
                                    toObject:relatedCopiedObject];

        }
    }
  }
}
```

Update Grocery Dude as follows to implement the `copyRelationshipsFromObject` method:

1. Add the code from Listing 9.12 to the bottom of `CoreDataImporter.m` before `@end`.

Deep Copy Entities

The final method required is `deepCopyEntities`, which is responsible for copying all objects from the specified entities in one context to another context. There are several ways this method could have been implemented, and the user experience would have differed with each option. If you search the Internet for **core data programming guide: efficiently importing data**, you should find an Apple guide that discusses techniques for importing data. It says that *when possible* it is more efficient to copy all the objects in a single pass and then fix up relationships later. Depending on the application, this may not be feasible. An import can take a long time, and if the relationships are missing even for a few seconds, the user might assume the application has a bug. The options open to you to combat this issue are as follows (your selection will vary depending on the nature of your application):

- **Prevent the user from using the application, partially or wholly.** During the import, you could display a progress indicator, such as `MBProgressHUD`. If the import takes a long time, this may annoy the user. Depending on the application, you may instead only be able to disable partial functionality, until the data is ready.

- **Import all objects first and then establish relationships.** The user might see half-imported data with little or no established relationships. Depending on the data model, this may or may not be acceptable.

- **Import objects and relationships together.** Although this is certainly not as efficient as the other options, the entire deep copy process is run in the background so the user impact is minimal to non-existent. You will use more battery power than the alternative; however, the application will remain usable.

CoreDataImporter will be configured to import objects and relationships together. The deep copy of each object will be wrapped in an autorelease pool so that memory is freed up regularly during the import process. Listing 9.13 shows the code involved.

Listing 9.13 **CoreDataImporter.m: deepCopyEntities**

```
- (void)deepCopyEntities:(NSArray*)entities
            fromContext:(NSManagedObjectContext*)sourceContext
              toContext:(NSManagedObjectContext*)targetContext {
if (debug==1) {
    NSLog(@"Running %@ '%@'", self.class, NSStringFromSelector(_cmd));
}
    for (NSString *entity in entities) {

        NSLog(@"COPYING %@ objects to target context...", entity);
        NSArray *sourceObjects =
        [self arrayForEntity:entity
                   inContext:sourceContext
               withPredicate:nil];

        for (NSManagedObject *sourceObject in sourceObjects) {

            if (sourceObject) {
                @autoreleasepool {
                    [self copyUniqueObject:sourceObject
                                 toContext:targetContext];
                    [self copyRelationshipsFromObject:sourceObject
                                            toContext:targetContext];
                }
            }
        }
    }
}
```

Update Grocery Dude as follows to implement the deepCopyEntities method:

1. Add the code from Listing 9.13 to the bottom of CoreDataImporter.m before @end.

The required code is now in place to support a deep copy. The only thing left to do is to trigger it from CoreDataHelper.m. For that to happen, the deepCopyEntities method header needs to be in CoreDataImporter.h. Listing 9.14 shows the code involved.

Listing 9.14 **CoreDataHelper.h: deepCopyEntities**

```
- (void)deepCopyEntities:(NSArray*)entities
            fromContext:(NSManagedObjectContext*)sourceContext
              toContext:(NSManagedObjectContext*)targetContext;
```

Update Grocery Dude as follows to add `deepCopyEntities` to the `CoreDataImporter` header:

1. Add the code from Listing 9.14 to the bottom of `CoreDataImporter.h` before `@end`.

Triggering a Deep Copy

As mentioned at the beginning of this chapter, a deep copy will be demonstrated using the existing default data store. The default data store `DefaultData.sqlite` was previously configured as the initial store during `setupCoreData` via `setDefaultDataStoreAsInitialStore`. This method call has since been commented out, so on new installations an import from XML would be triggered instead. This is due to the call to `checkIfDefaultDataNeedsImporting` in the `setupCoreData` method that triggers an alert view giving the option to `importFromXML`. To trigger a deep copy from a persistent store instead, a new method called `deepCopyFrom-PersistentStore` is required in `CoreDataHelper.m`. Once an instance of `CoreDataImporter` has been created, the deep copy will be triggered using the new `deepCopyEntities` method of `CoreDataImporter`. Once the copy process has finished, the interface will perform a final refresh in response to a `SomethingChanged` notification. Listing 9.15 shows the code involved.

Listing 9.15   **CoreDataHelper.m: deepCopyFromPersistentStore**

```
- (void)deepCopyFromPersistentStore:(NSURL*)url {
if (debug==1) {
    NSLog(@"Running %@ '%@' %@", self.class,
    NSStringFromSelector(_cmd),url.path);
}
    [_sourceContext performBlock:^{

    NSLog(@"*** STARTED DEEP COPY FROM DEFAULT DATA PERSISTENT STORE ***");

        NSArray *entitiesToCopy = [NSArray arrayWithObjects:
                @"LocationAtHome",@"LocationAtShop",@"Unit",@"Item", nil];

        CoreDataImporter *importer = [[CoreDataImporter alloc]
                initWithUniqueAttributes:[self selectedUniqueAttributes]];

        [importer deepCopyEntities:entitiesToCopy
                    fromContext:_sourceContext
                      toContext:_importContext];

        [_context performBlock:^{
            // Tell the interface to refresh once import completes
[[NSNotificationCenter defaultCenter]
                    postNotificationName:@"SomethingChanged" object:nil];
        }];
```

```
    NSLog(@"*** FINISHED DEEP COPY FROM DEFAULT DATA PERSISTENT STORE ***");
    }];
}
```

Update Grocery Dude as follows to implement the `deepCopyFromPersistentStore` method:

1. Add the code from Listing 9.15 to the bottom of the DATA IMPORT section of
   `CoreDataHelper.m`.

Finally, the `deepCopyFromPersistentStore` method needs to be called in response to user
interaction, instead of `importFromXML`. This means the `UIAlertView` delegate method needs
updating, as shown in Listing 9.16.

Listing 9.16 **CoreDataHelper.m: alertView:clickedButtonAtIndex**

```
- (void)alertView:(UIAlertView *)alertView
clickedButtonAtIndex:(NSInteger)buttonIndex {
if (debug==1) {
    NSLog(@"Running %@ '%@'", self.class, NSStringFromSelector(_cmd));
}
    if (alertView == self.importAlertView) {
        if (buttonIndex == 1) { // The 'Import' button on the importAlertView

            NSLog(@"Default Data Import Approved by User");
            /*
            // XML Import
            [_importContext performBlock:^{
                [self importFromXML:[[NSBundle mainBundle]
                    URLForResource:@"DefaultData"
                     withExtension:@"xml"]];
            }];
            */

            // Deep Copy Import From Persistent Store
            [self loadSourceStore];
            [self deepCopyFromPersistentStore:[self sourceStoreURL]];

        } else {
            NSLog(@"Default Data Import Cancelled by User");
        }
        // Set the data as imported regardless of the user's decision
        [self setDefaultDataAsImportedForStore:_store];
    }
}
```

Update Grocery Dude as follows to revise the `UIAlertView` delegate method:

1. Replace the existing `alertView:clickedButtonAtIndex` method found in `CoreDataHelper.m` with the method from Listing 9.16.

2. Delete Grocery Dude from your device or the iOS Simulator and click **Product** > **Clean**.

3. Run the application and tap **Import** to import default data.

As the import occurs, notice that you can still use the application. Figure 9.4 shows the expected result after the import has completed.

Figure 9.4   Data imported from a persistent store via deep copy

The import process can take a while, particularly on older phones. It's a nice touch to update the user interface periodically during the import process, to show new data as it is imported. In preparation, a new method will be added to `CoreDataHelper.m` that sends a `SomethingChanged` notification. Listing 9.17 shows the code involved.

Listing 9.17   **CoreDataHelper.m: somethingChanged**

```
#pragma mark - UNDERLYING DATA CHANGE NOTIFICATION
- (void)somethingChanged {
if (debug==1) {
    NSLog(@"Running %@ '%@'", self.class, NSStringFromSelector(_cmd));
}
    // Send a notification that tells observing interfaces to refresh their data
 [[NSNotificationCenter defaultCenter]
                      postNotificationName:@"SomethingChanged" object:nil];
}
```

Update Grocery Dude as follows to implement a change notification method:

1. Add the code from Listing 9.17 to the bottom of `CoreDataHelper.m` before `@end`.

An `NSTimer` will be used to trigger periodic calls to the `somethingChanged` method during an import. Listing 9.18 shows the code involved in an updated `deepCopyFromPersistentStore` method in bold.

Listing 9.18 **CoreDataHelper.m: deepCopyFromPersistentStore**

```
- (void)deepCopyFromPersistentStore:(NSURL*)url {
if (debug==1) {
    NSLog(@"Running %@ '%@' %@", self.class,
    NSStringFromSelector(_cmd),url.path);
}
// Periodically refresh the interface during the import
_importTimer =
[NSTimer scheduledTimerWithTimeInterval:2.0
                                  target:self
                                selector:@selector(somethingChanged)
                                userInfo:nil
                                 repeats:YES];

[_sourceContext performBlock:^{

    NSLog(@"*** STARTED DEEP COPY FROM DEFAULT DATA PERSISTENT STORE ***");

    NSArray *entitiesToCopy = [NSArray arrayWithObjects:
                @"LocationAtHome",@"LocationAtShop",@"Unit",@"Item", nil];

    CoreDataImporter *importer = [[CoreDataImporter alloc]
                initWithUniqueAttributes:[self selectedUniqueAttributes]];

    [importer deepCopyEntities:entitiesToCopy
                   fromContext:_sourceContext
                     toContext:_importContext];

    [_context performBlock:^{
        // Stop periodically refreshing the interface
        [_importTimer invalidate];

        // Tell the interface to refresh once import completes
        [self somethingChanged];
    }];

    NSLog(@"*** FINISHED DEEP COPY FROM DEFAULT DATA PERSISTENT STORE ***");
}];
}
```

Update Grocery Dude as follows so the import process periodically updates the user interface:

1. Add the following property to `CoreDataHelper.h` beneath the existing properties:

   `@property (nonatomic, strong) NSTimer *importTimer;`

2. Replace the existing `deepCopyFromPersistentStore` method in `CoreDataHelper.m` with the code from Listing 9.18.

3. Delete Grocery Dude from your device or the iOS Simulator.

4. Click **Product > Clean**.

5. Run Grocery Dude and then tap Import to import the default data.

The interface should be updated with imported data seconds after it is imported, without noticeable impact to the user experience.

Summary

You've now experienced the complicated topic of deep copy. If you do find yourself in a position where you need to populate unique data into an existing persistent store, then this option is now open to you. The `CoreDataImporter` classes are model agnostic, so you may use them freely in your own applications. Remember that to prevent unnecessary imports, you will need to set a metadata key-value on the existing persistent store. This technique was demonstrated in the previous chapter, so there was no need to repeat it here.

When deciding on how you'll migrate data from one store to another, ensure you evaluate the `migratePersistentStore` method of `NSPersistentStoreCoordinator`. This method allows you to migrate the *entire* contents of a persistent store into another persistent store. Unfortunately, there are no de-duplication options, nor is there the ability to be selective about what entities you migrate. That said, `migratePersistentStore` is much faster than deep copy.

Exercises

Why not build on what you've learned by experimenting?

1. Set `#define debug 0` in the following implementation files and then trigger the import process again. You should notice an increased import speed without the heavy logging.

   - `CoreDataImporter.m`

   - `CoreDataTVC.m`

   - `LocationsAtHomeTVC.m`

   - `LocationsAtShopTVC.m`

   - `PrepareTVC.m`

   - `ShopTVC.m`

   - `UnitsTVC.m`

2. Delete the Grocery Dude from the device and then quickly press the home button (**Shift+⌘+H**) during another import. Notice how the import process is paused and restarts when you return to the application. If the application is terminated, the import process will not be triggered again and the imported data may not be complete.

3. Test the `migratePersistentStore` method of `NSPersistentStoreCoordinator` by adding the code shown in Listing 9.19 to the bottom of the `setupCoreData` method of `CoreDataHelper.m`. Run the application again, and you will notice that duplicate data is inserted.

Uncomment `[self setDefaultDataStoreAsInitialStore]`; in the `setupCoreData` method of `CoreDataHelper.m` before continuing on to the next chapter. Also comment out the code added in Exercise 3.

Listing 9.19 **CoreDataHelper.m: setupCoreData**

```
// The code below demonstrates how to migrate one persistent store to another.
[self loadSourceStore];
[_sourceContext performBlock:^{

    NSLog(@"*** Attempting to migrate '%@' into '%@' .. Please Wait ***",
    sourceStoreFilename, storeFilename);

    NSError *error = nil;
    if (![_sourceCoordinator migratePersistentStore:_sourceStore
                                        toURL:[self storeURL]
                                      options:nil
                                     withType:NSSQLiteStoreType
                                        error:&error]) {

        NSLog(@"FAILED to migrate: %@", error);
    } else {
    NSLog(@"The source store '%@' has been migrated to the target store '%@'",
                                    sourceStoreFilename, storeFilename);

        [_context performBlock:^{

            // Tell the interface to refresh once import completes
            [self somethingChanged];
        }];
    }
}];
```

10

Performance

Insanity is doing the same thing, over and over again, but expecting different results.

Albert Einstein

In Chapter 9, "Deep Copy," techniques were demonstrated that populate a persistent store with data. As persistent stores grow, it's important to ensure that the application remains responsive. The fetched results controllers in Grocery Dude have already been configured for improved performance using batched fetch requests. What may not be apparent, however, is that the managed object model design plays a key role in producing better performance. This chapter will take you through the process of identifying and eliminating performance issues.

Identifying Performance Issues

As an application nears the end of its development cycle, it's important to iron out performance issues. Without suitable performance testing, it may not be apparent that an application has a performance issue until it's too late. The worst-case scenario is that customers use an application for some time and the application slows as their data grows. To prevent this, it's recommended that you test on the slowest possible device with a data set that's larger than you would expect any customer to have.

Depending on the nature of an application, performance issues will reveal themselves in different ways. That said, there are some common things to look for in all iOS applications that indicate good or bad performance:

- The application should load quickly.
- Table views should scroll smoothly.
- Views should transition quickly.
- The user interface should remain responsive at all times.

With a large test data set, performance issues should become more obvious. The more obvious performance issues are, the easier it will be to track down the root cause. In addition to a large data set, using large objects such as photos is a common cause of application performance issues. The camera functionality will now be added to Grocery Dude, which opens the door to large objects making their way into the application. Later in this chapter, tips will be given on how the model can be optimized for large objects such as photos.

> **Note**
>
> To continue building the sample application, you'll need to have added the previous chapter's code to Grocery Dude. Alternatively, you may download, unzip, and use the project up to this point from http://www.timroadley.com/LearningCoreData/GroceryDude-AfterChapter09.zip. Any time you start using an Xcode project from a ZIP file, it's good practice to click **Product > Clean**. This practice ensures there's no residual cache from previous projects using the same name. Before you begin, also remove any existing copies of Grocery Dude from your device to ensure default data is loaded.

Implementing the Camera

When you're preparing a shopping list, it would be great if you could take a photo of that obscure brand of coffee you love so much. When you're at the store and can't remember what it is called, you could then simply refer to the photo. The ability to take a photo will be added to the existing Item view. When an item has a photo, it will be shown both on the Item view and in the table views of the Prepare and Shop tabs. To take a photo, a new button is required on the Item view, and an Image view is needed to display it.

Update Grocery Dude as follows to implement the camera button and Image view:

1. Download and extract add_photo icons from the following URL: http://www.timroadley. com/LearningCoreData/Icons_add_photo.zip.

2. Select the **Images.xcassets** asset catalog, and then drag the new **add_photo** icons into it.

3. Select **Main.storyboard**.

4. Drag an **Image View** into the existing **Scroll View** of the Item view.

5. Ensure **Attributes Inspector** is visible (**Option+⌘+4**).

6. Set the **Background** color of the **Image View** to **Other > Crayons > Mercury** (the second lightest gray crayon).

7. Drag a **Button** into the existing Scroll view of the Item view and configure it as follows using **Attributes Inspector** (**Option+⌘+4**):

   - Set **Type** to **Custom**.

   - Delete the "Button" title text.

   - Set **Image** to **add_photo**.

8. Ensure both the **Height** and **Width** of the new button are **48** using **Size Inspector** (**Option+⌘+5**).

9. Resize the **Image View** to have an equal width and height and then align it with the new button, as shown in Figure 10.1.

10. Select the Scroll view of the Item view and click **Editor > Resolve Auto Layout Issues > Reset to Suggested Constraints in ItemVC**.

Figure 10.1   Add_photo button and Image view

The outlets to the new objects must now be connected so they can be referenced in code. The **Assistant Editor** is used to achieve this.

Update Grocery Dude as follows to connect the camera button and Image view to ItemVC.h:

1. Ensure **Main.storyboard** is selected.

2. Ensure the **Item View Controller** is selected.

3. Show the **Assistant Editor** (**Option+⌘+Return**).

4. Set the Assistant Editor to **Automatic > ItemVC.h** if it isn't set to this already, as shown at the top of Figure 10.2.

5. Hold **Control** and drag a line from the new **Image View** to the bottom of ItemVC.h before @end. Set the name of the new property to photoImageView. Double-check that **Type** is UIImageView and that **Storage** is **Strong**.

6. Hold **Control** and drag a line from the camera button to the bottom of ItemVC.h before @end. Set the name of the new property to cameraButton. Double-check that **Type** is UIButton and that **Storage** is **Strong**. Once it's connected, if you mouse over the circle to the left of the cameraButton property, you should see the camera button highlighted, as shown in Figure 10.2.

7. Show the **Standard Editor** (**⌘+Return**).

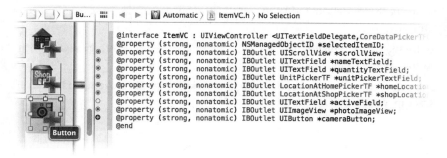

Figure 10.2 Connected camera properties

So that photos can be taken, the next step is to configure the appropriate protocol and delegate. The ItemVC class will adopt the UIImagePickerControllerDelegate protocol so it receives messages containing the captured photo data. In addition, the ItemVC class will adopt the UINavigationControllerDelegate protocol so it can present the camera interface. Finally, a new property is required to hold the UIImagePickerController instance, known as the camera property.

Update Grocery Dude as follows to configure the ItemVC header for the camera:

1. Add two protocol adoptions (shown in bold) to ItemVC.h as follows:

   ```
   <UITextFieldDelegate,CoreDataPickerTFDelegate,
   UIImagePickerControllerDelegate,UINavigationControllerDelegate>
   ```

2. Add the following property to the bottom of ItemVC.h before @end:

   ```
   @property (strong, nonatomic) UIImagePickerController *camera;
   ```

To implement the camera, which in reality is a UIImagePickerController, four new methods are required:

- The **checkCamera** method ensures the camera is available and toggles the camera button appropriately. This method will be called each time the Item view appears.

- The **showCamera** method is connected to the cameraButton. When this button is pressed, the camera will show.

- The **imagePickerController:didFinishPickingMediaWithInfo** method is an image picker delegate method. This delegate method will be called when a photo has been taken. In this method, the photo data will be saved into the photoData attribute value for the currently selected item. The photo is saved as a 640-by-640 JPG image at 50% quality.

- The **imagePickerControllerDidCancel** method is another image picker delegate method. It is called when Camera view is cancelled. The code in this method will dismiss the Camera view.

Listing 10.1 shows the code involved.

Listing 10.1 `ItemVC.m: CAMERA`

```
#pragma mark - CAMERA
- (void)checkCamera {
if (debug==1) {
    NSLog(@"Running %@ '%@'", self.class, NSStringFromSelector(_cmd));
}
    self.cameraButton.enabled =
    [UIImagePickerController
                isSourceTypeAvailable:UIImagePickerControllerSourceTypeCamera];
}
- (IBAction)showCamera:(id)sender {
if (debug==1) {
    NSLog(@"Running %@ '%@'", self.class, NSStringFromSelector(_cmd));
}
    if ([UIImagePickerController
        isSourceTypeAvailable:UIImagePickerControllerSourceTypeCamera])
    {
        NSLog(@"Camera is available");
        _camera = [[UIImagePickerController alloc] init];
        _camera.sourceType = UIImagePickerControllerSourceTypeCamera;
        _camera.mediaTypes =
        [UIImagePickerController
         availableMediaTypesForSourceType:UIImagePickerControllerSourceTypeCamera];
        _camera.allowsEditing = YES;
        _camera.delegate = self;
        [self.navigationController presentViewController:_camera
                                        animated:YES
                                       completion:nil];
    }
    else
    {
        NSLog(@"Camera not available");
    }
}

- (void)imagePickerController:(UIImagePickerController *)picker
didFinishPickingMediaWithInfo:(NSDictionary *)info {
if (debug==1) {
    NSLog(@"Running %@ '%@'", self.class, NSStringFromSelector(_cmd));
}
    CoreDataHelper *cdh =
    [(AppDelegate *)[[UIApplication sharedApplication] delegate] cdh];
```

```
    Item *item =
    (Item*)[cdh.context existingObjectWithID:self.selectedItemID error:nil];

    UIImage *photo =
    (UIImage *)[info objectForKey:UIImagePickerControllerEditedImage];

    NSLog(@"Captured %f x %f photo",photo.size.height, photo.size.width);

    item.photoData = UIImageJPEGRepresentation(photo, 0.5);

    self.photoImageView.image = photo;

    [picker dismissViewControllerAnimated:YES completion:nil];
}
- (void)imagePickerControllerDidCancel:(UIImagePickerController *)picker {
if (debug==1) {
    NSLog(@"Running %@ '%@'", self.class, NSStringFromSelector(_cmd));
}
    [picker dismissViewControllerAnimated:YES completion:nil];
}
```

Update Grocery Dude to implement the camera:

1. Add the code from Listing 10.1 to the bottom of ItemVC.m before @end.

2. Add the following code to the bottom of the refreshInterface method of ItemVC.m within the if statement:

   ```
   self.photoImageView.image = [UIImage imageWithData:item.photoData];
   [self checkCamera];
   ```

3. Select **Main.storyboard**.

4. Hold down **Control** and drag a line from the camera button to the yellow circle at the bottom of the Item view; then select **Sent Events > showCamera:**. If you cannot see the **Sent Events > showCamera:** option, you may need to save ItemVC.m and try again.

5. Test the new camera functionality on a physical device. You should be able to take photos of items. Note that the camera does not work on the iOS Simulator.

Now that photos can be taken, the table views on the Prepare and Shop tabs will be updated to display photos.

Update Grocery Dude as follows to prepare the table view cells to display photos:

1. Ensure **Main.storyboard** is selected.

2. Select the **Prototype Cell** in the table view titled **Grocery Dude**.

3. Set the **Style** of the **Prototype Cell** to **Right Detail** using **Attributes Inspector** (**Option+⌘+4**).

4. Delete the text "Detail" from within the Prototype Cell.

5. Select the **Prototype Cell** in the table view titled Items.

6. Set the **Style** of the Prototype Cell to **Right Detail**.

7. Delete the text "Detail" from within the Prototype Cell.

8. Add the following code to the bottom of the `cellForRowAtIndexPath` methods of `PrepareTVC.m` and `ShopTVC.m` before `return cell;`:

```
cell.imageView.image = [UIImage imageWithData:item.photoData];
```

Run the application again. Photos you've taken should now appear in the table views. Figure 10.3 shows the expected results.

Figure 10.3   The 'Prepare' table view with smaller font and photo support

Generating Test Data

Creating a large test data set is easy with some `for` loops and a little patience. If you need more data, just keep looping through object creation until you have enough for your needs. Techniques to generate test data were touched on early in the book and will be used again, this time with the inclusion of a large image. A copy of the image will intentionally be used separately for each test item. This will simulate the effect of having a unique photo for each test item. The test image will be 2000×2000, which is big enough to emulate a sizable photo taken from the camera. Listing 10.2 shows the code involved in generating test data. Note that for demonstration purposes this method has no reliance on NSManagedObject subclass files. Instead, it uses key-value coding that is Grocery Dude model specific.

Listing 10.2   **CoreDataHelper.m: TEST DATA IMPORT**

```
#pragma mark - TEST DATA IMPORT (This code is Grocery Dude data specific)
- (void)importGroceryDudeTestData {
if (debug==1) {
    NSLog(@"Running %@ '%@'", self.class, NSStringFromSelector(_cmd));
}

    NSNumber *imported =
    [[NSUserDefaults standardUserDefaults] objectForKey:@"TestDataImport"];

    if (!imported.boolValue) {
        NSLog(@"Importing test data...");
        [_importContext performBlock:^{

            NSManagedObject *locationAtHome =
            [NSEntityDescription insertNewObjectForEntityForName:@"LocationAtHome"
                                        inManagedObjectContext:_importContext];
            NSManagedObject *locationAtShop =
            [NSEntityDescription insertNewObjectForEntityForName:@"LocationAtShop"
                                        inManagedObjectContext:_importContext];
            [locationAtHome setValue:@"Test Home Location" forKey:@"storedIn"];
            [locationAtShop setValue:@"Test Shop Location" forKey:@"aisle"];

            for (int a = 1; a < 101; a++) {

                @autoreleasepool {

                    NSManagedObject *item =
                    [NSEntityDescription insertNewObjectForEntityForName:@"Item"
                                        inManagedObjectContext:_importContext];
                    [item setValue:[NSString stringWithFormat:
                                        @"Test Item %i",a] forKey:@"name"];
                    [item setValue:locationAtHome forKey:@"locationAtHome"];
                    [item setValue:locationAtShop forKey:@"locationAtShop"];
                    [item setValue:UIImagePNGRepresentation(
                        [UIImage imageNamed:@"GroceryHead.png"])
                            forKey:@"photoData"];
                    NSLog(@"Inserting %@", [item valueForKey:@"name"]);
                    [CoreDataImporter saveContext:_importContext];
                    [_importContext refreshObject:item mergeChanges:NO];
```

```
            }
        }
        // force table view refresh
        [self somethingChanged];

        // ensure import was a one off
        [[NSUserDefaults standardUserDefaults]
                    setObject:[NSNumber numberWithBool:YES]
                        forKey:@"TestDataImport"];
        [[NSUserDefaults standardUserDefaults] synchronize];
    }];
    }
    else {
        NSLog(@"Skipped test data import");
    }
}
```

Update Grocery Dude as follows to add test data import functionality:

1. Add the code from Listing 10.2 to `CoreDataHelper.m` after the existing DATA IMPORT section.

2. Download, extract, and add the following large image to **Images.xcassets**: http://www.timroadley.com/LearningCoreData/GroceryHead.zip.

The `importGroceryDudeTestData` method will be called from the `setupCoreData` method and the existing import methods commented out. The updated code is shown in Listing 10.3.

Listing 10.3   **CoreDataHelper.m: setupCoreData**

```
- (void)setupCoreData {
if (debug==1) {
    NSLog(@"Running %@ '%@'", self.class, NSStringFromSelector(_cmd));
}
    //[self setDefaultDataStoreAsInitialStore];
    [self loadStore];
    [self importGroceryDudeTestData];
    //[self checkIfDefaultDataNeedsImporting];
}
```

If the user modifies items during the import process, there is the potential that the same object could be modified in two contexts at the same time. When one of those contexts is then saved, a merge conflict could result. To handle merge conflicts, a merge policy will be configured in advance. The merge policy decides who wins when these conflicts arise. There are five options:

- **NSErrorMergePolicy** is the default policy. Merge conflicts prevent the context from being saved.

- **NSMergeByPropertyObjectTrumpMergePolicy** resolves merge conflicts using object property values from the context to overwrite those in the persistent store.

- **NSMergeByPropertyStoreTrumpMergePolicy** resolves merge conflicts using object property values from the persistent store to overwrite those in the context.

- **NSOverwriteMergePolicy** resolves merge conflicts using entire objects from the context to overwrite those in the persistent store.

- **NSRollbackMergePolicy** resolves merge conflicts using entire objects from the persistent store to overwrite those in the context.

The merge policies boil down to a decision on whether the context or persistent store should win, at either an object or property level.

Update Grocery Dude as follows to enable a merge policy and trigger a test data import:

1. Update the `setupCoreData` method in `CoreDataHelper.m` to match the code from Listing 10.3.

2. Replace the `init` method in `CoreDataHelper.m` with the one shown in Listing 10.4. The updated code introduces merge policies to each context and is shown in bold.

Listing 10.4 **CoreDataHelper.m: init**

```
- (id)init {
if (debug==1) {
    NSLog(@"Running %@ '%@'", self.class, NSStringFromSelector(_cmd));
}
    self = [super init];
    if (!self) {return nil;}

    _model = [NSManagedObjectModel mergedModelFromBundles:nil];
    _coordinator = [[NSPersistentStoreCoordinator alloc]
                                            initWithManagedObjectModel:_model];
    _context = [[NSManagedObjectContext alloc]
                        initWithConcurrencyType:NSMainQueueConcurrencyType];
    [_context setPersistentStoreCoordinator:_coordinator];
    [_context setMergePolicy:NSMergeByPropertyObjectTrumpMergePolicy];

    _importContext = [[NSManagedObjectContext alloc]
                        initWithConcurrencyType:NSPrivateQueueConcurrencyType];
    [_importContext performBlockAndWait:^{
        [_importContext setPersistentStoreCoordinator:_coordinator];
        [_importContext setMergePolicy:NSMergeByPropertyObjectTrumpMergePolicy];
        [_importContext setUndoManager:nil]; // the default on iOS
    }];
```

```
    _sourceCoordinator = [[NSPersistentStoreCoordinator alloc]
                                    initWithManagedObjectModel:_model];
    _sourceContext = [[NSManagedObjectContext alloc]
                        initWithConcurrencyType:NSPrivateQueueConcurrencyType];
    [_sourceContext performBlockAndWait:^{
        [_sourceContext setMergePolicy:NSMergeByPropertyObjectTrumpMergePolicy];
        [_sourceContext setPersistentStoreCoordinator:_sourceCoordinator];
        [_sourceContext setUndoManager:nil]; // the default on iOS
    }];
    return self;
}
```

Delete Grocery Dude from the iOS Simulator and run it to install it again. The expected result once the import has completed is shown in Figure 10.4.

Figure 10.4   Test data

Once the test data has been imported, try scrolling through the items. You should notice scrolling isn't smooth, unless you have a fast Mac. If you were to run Grocery Dude on a device, you would receive memory warnings and most likely experience a crash.

Measuring Performance with SQLDebug

Assuming the underlying persistent store is SQLite, one technique for troubleshooting Core Data performance is to use SQLDebug. You can use SQLDebug to gain visibility of how long the automatically generated SQL queries are taking to execute. Debug level 1 is enough to show query execution time. As discussed in Chapter 2, "Managed Object Model Basics," SQLDebug is enabled by editing the scheme of the application.

Update Grocery Dude as follows to enable SQL Debug level 1:

1. Click **Product > Scheme > Edit Scheme....**

2. Ensure **Run Grocery Dude...** and the **Arguments** tab are selected.

3. Add a new argument by clicking + in the **Arguments Passed On Launch** section.

4. Enter `-com.apple.CoreData.SQLDebug 1` as a new argument and then click **OK**.

5. Run Grocery Dude on the iOS Simulator again and examine the console log. The expected result is shown in Figure 10.5.

```
2013-07-26 18:26:21.798 Grocery Dude[4658:a0b] CoreData: annotation: sql connection fetch time: 0.0005s
2013-07-26 18:26:21.799 Grocery Dude[4658:a0b] CoreData: annotation: total fetch execution time: 0.0008s for 1 rows.
2013-07-26 18:26:21.802 Grocery Dude[4658:a0b] CoreData: sql: SELECT 0, t0.Z_PK, t0.Z_OPT, t0.ZCOLLECTED, t0.ZLISTED,
t0.ZNAME, t0.ZPHOTODATA, t0.ZQUANTITY, t0.ZLOCATIONATHOME, t0.ZLOCATIONATSHOP, t0.ZUNIT FROM ZITEM t0 LEFT OUTER JOIN
ZLOCATION t1 ON t0.ZLOCATIONATHOME = t1.Z_PK WHERE  t0.Z_PK IN
(?,?,?,?,?,?,?,?,?,?,?,?,?,?,?,?,?,?,?,?,?,?,?,?,?,?,?,?,?,?,?,?,?,?,?,?,?,?,?,?,?,?,?,?,?,?,?,?,?,?)  ORDER BY
t1.ZSTOREDIN, t0.ZNAME LIMIT 50
2013-07-26 18:26:21.854 Grocery Dude[4658:a0b] CoreData: annotation: sql connection fetch time: 0.0462s
2013-07-26 18:26:21.854 Grocery Dude[4658:a0b] CoreData: annotation: total fetch execution time: 0.0526s for 50 rows.
2013-07-26 18:26:21.867 Grocery Dude[4658:a0b] Running AppDelegate 'applicationDidBecomeActive:'
2013-07-26 18:26:21.867 Grocery Dude[4658:a0b] Running AppDelegate 'cdh'
```

Figure 10.5   Measuring query execution time

Figure 10.5 shows the automatically generated SQL query that fetches items for the prepare table view. Although 100 test items exist in the persistent store, only 50 rows have been retrieved due to `setFetchBatchSize:50` configured in the `configureFetch` method of `PrepareTVC.m`. Even if there were thousands of items in the persistent store, this code would still protect the application from loading them all into memory at once. A good rule of thumb when choosing a batch fetch size is to think about how many objects you need displayed at the same time. A table view using the default row height on a 4-inch Retina display shows around 10 rows at once. This means a fetch batch size of 50 is excessive. If only 10 rows are visible at once, there's no point having 40 extra rows loaded and wasting resources. The batch size should be just slightly bigger than the amount of rows that need to be visible at once, so 15 is a more conservative batch size for standard table views. For the picker views, a batch size of around the same amount is good enough.

Update Grocery Dude as follows to alter the fetch request batch sizes:

1. Search the Xcode project for `setFetchBatchSize:50`.

2. Replace `setFetchBatchSize:50` with `setFetchBatchSize:15` for every class in the project. If prompted, don't worry about enabling snapshots.

3. Run Grocery Dude on the iOS Simulator and examine the console log again. The expected result is shown in Figure 10.6.

```
            Grocery Dude
2013-07-28 11:18:05.676 Grocery Dude[8903:a0b] CoreData: sql: SELECT  t1.ZSTOREDIN, COUNT (DISTINCT  t0.Z_PK) FROM
ZITEM t0 LEFT OUTER JOIN ZLOCATION t1 ON t0.ZLOCATIONATHOME = t1.Z_PK GROUP BY  t1.ZSTOREDIN ORDER BY t1.ZSTOREDIN
2013-07-28 11:18:05.677 Grocery Dude[8903:a0b] CoreData: annotation: sql connection fetch time: 0.0008s
2013-07-28 11:18:05.677 Grocery Dude[8903:a0b] CoreData: annotation: total fetch execution time: 0.0011s for 1 rows.
2013-07-28 11:18:05.681 Grocery Dude[8903:a0b] CoreData: sql: SELECT 0, t0.Z_PK, t0.Z_OPT, t0.ZCOLLECTED, t0.ZLISTED,
t0.ZNAME, t0.ZPHOTODATA, t0.ZQUANTITY, t0.ZLOCATIONATHOME, t0.ZLOCATIONATSHOP, t0.ZUNIT FROM ZITEM t0 LEFT OUTER JOIN
ZLOCATION t1 ON t0.ZLOCATIONATHOME = t1.Z_PK WHERE  t0.Z_PK IN  (?,?,?,?,?,?,?,?,?,?,?,?,?,?,?)  ORDER BY
t1.ZSTOREDIN, t0.ZNAME LIMIT 15
2013-07-28 11:18:05.694 Grocery Dude[8903:a0b] CoreData: annotation: sql connection fetch time: 0.0121s
2013-07-28 11:18:05.695 Grocery Dude[8903:a0b] CoreData: annotation: total fetch execution time: 0.0141s for 15 rows.
2013-07-28 11:18:05.707 Grocery Dude[8903:a0b] Running AppDelegate 'applicationDidBecomeActive:'
2013-07-28 11:18:05.708 Grocery Dude[8903:a0b] Running AppDelegate 'cdh'
```

Figure 10.6   Improved query execution time

The query execution time is faster because fewer rows are fetched. Although setting an appropriate batch size is a good starting point, the scrolling still isn't smooth, so more investigation is required.

Measuring Performance with Instruments

To measure an application's performance, profile it with Instruments. Unfortunately, the option to profile Core Data is not available for physical iOS devices. This means you must profile Core Data on the iOS Simulator instead. Although this is not ideal, it still provides good insight into key Core Data–specific metrics such as fetches, cache misses, and saves.

To profile an application using Instruments, you simply run the application in a different way. Instead of just pressing the Run button, press and hold the Run button to select Profile instead. Try this now and notice how the button changes as Instruments loads. The expected result is shown in Figure 10.7.

Figure 10.7   Profiling an application

Once Instruments loads, you'll be prompted to select a Trace Template, as shown in Figure 10.8. Core Data is found in the File System category.

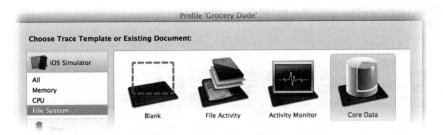

Figure 10.8   Profiling an application using the Core Data template

Select the Core Data template and click Profile. This will start recording the performance profile of Grocery Dude. It is recommended that Time Profiler and Allocations be used in conjunction with the Core Data template, so stop recording so they can be added.

Configure Instruments as follows to add Time Profiler and Allocations:

1. Press ⌘+L to make the Library visible if it isn't already.

2. Drag **Time Profiler** and **Allocations** from the Library onto the main Instruments window.

3. (Optional) Save this template by clicking **File > Save As Template...** and then fill in the appropriate information. This will ensure you don't have to repeat this setup each time you begin profiling.

4. Press **Record** to begin profiling again and test the scrolling speed of the Prepare table view. Figure 10.9 shows the expected result.

As the application launches, you should see a flurry of activity in Time Profiler. You should also see the Allocations increase as the table view scrolls, with Core Data fetches lining up with these increases. If you click either Time Profiler or Allocations and use the Call Tree options, shown in Figure 10.10, you'll reveal the methods responsible for the heaviest resource utilization.

Clearly the `cellForRowAtIndexPath` method of `PrepareTVC` is responsible for the majority of the memory footprint. This is no surprise because the table view cell was configured to display a test image, which happens to be 2000×2000. To see how long the fetches took, select Core Data Fetches and examine the Event List, as shown in Figure 10.11.

Fetch durations are displayed in microseconds, and depending on the type of Mac you're using, your fetch duration may vary from the screenshot. If you need to know what class and method made these calls, click Event List and change to Call Tree. Of course, you'll want to set the appropriate options to show only Obj-C and hide system libraries. The same technique applies for viewing Core Data saves and Core Data cache misses. A *cache miss* is a trip to the persistent store, required because an object was not already in memory.

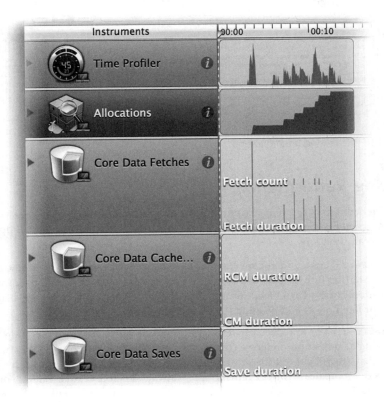

Figure 10.9   Profiling Grocery Dude

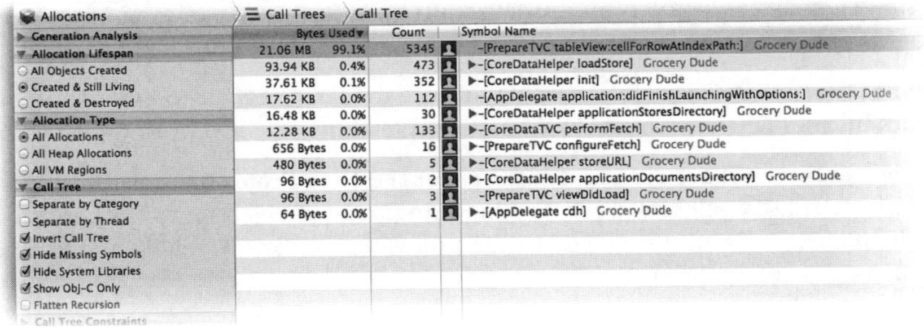

Figure 10.10   Grocery Dude resource utilization

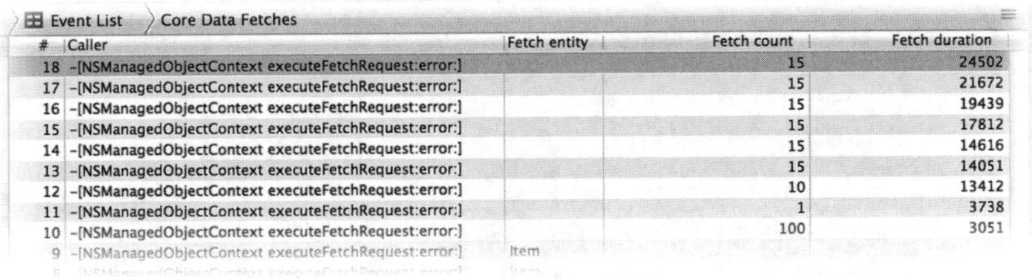

Event List > Core Data Fetches

#	Caller	Fetch entity	Fetch count	Fetch duration
18	-[NSManagedObjectContext executeFetchRequest:error:]		15	24502
17	-[NSManagedObjectContext executeFetchRequest:error:]		15	21672
16	-[NSManagedObjectContext executeFetchRequest:error:]		15	19439
15	-[NSManagedObjectContext executeFetchRequest:error:]		15	17812
14	-[NSManagedObjectContext executeFetchRequest:error:]		15	14616
13	-[NSManagedObjectContext executeFetchRequest:error:]		15	14051
12	-[NSManagedObjectContext executeFetchRequest:error:]		10	13412
11	-[NSManagedObjectContext executeFetchRequest:error:]		1	3738
10	-[NSManagedObjectContext executeFetchRequest:error:]		100	3051
9	-[NSManagedObjectContext executeFetchRequest:error:]	Item		

Figure 10.11 Measuring fetch duration

Improving Performance

A reduced fetched results size helps improve performance. Beyond `setFetchBatchSize`, there are other `NSFetchRequest` options you can use to minimize the result set. Not all options are appropriate to all situations:

- Use **`setFetchLimit`** and **`setFetchOffset`** to reduce fetch results to a specific number of rows starting from a specific point. This may, for example, be appropriate for an application using a Page View Controller to display information. Each page could have a different fetch offset and possibly the same fetch limit.

- Use **`setPredicate`** to reduce the result set according to the supplied predicate. If you're supplying a compound predicate (that is, two or more things to filter by), ensure the predicate that will cut out the most results is put first. Performance gains can also be achieved if a predicate filters against numerical values before textual values. For example, *`someNumber > 0 && someText LIKE 'whatever'`* is more efficient than *`someText LIKE 'whatever' && someNumber > 0`*.

- Use **`setPropertiesToGroupBy`** and **`setResultType`** together to emulate the `GROUP BY` operator otherwise available with raw SQL. When used in conjunction with `setHavingPredicate`, you can restrict results even further. As an example, you could use this option to produce a count of items in a particular home location.

- Use **`setIncludesPropertyValues:NO`** to force the fetch request to exclude property values in cases where you're only interested in fetching the `objectID` for each object.

- Use **`setRelationshipKeyPathsForPrefetching`** to indicate what relationships should be pre-fetched. Pre-fetching a relationship brings related objects into the context to avoid the inefficiency of fault firing. Use this option when you know you'll need to access those related objects soon.

None of the additional fetch request options are appropriate for Grocery Dude, and yet the performance is still bad. Once a fetch request has been fully optimized, the performance optimization does not stop there. Obviously showing such a large image on a table view is the main contributor to the performance issues given that `cellForRowAtIndexPath` is reported to be the busiest method. Perhaps using a pre-scaled thumbnail image would be a better idea.

Although thumbnail generation won't be added until the next chapter, the groundwork can be laid now.

Update Grocery Dude as follows to implement thumbnails:

1. Select **Model.xcdatamodeld**.

2. Click **Editor > Add Model Version...**.

3. Click **Finish** to accept the default model name of **Model 7**.

4. Ensure **Model 7.xcdatamodel** is selected.

5. Add a **Binary Data** attribute called **thumbnail** to the **Item** entity.

6. Select **Model.xcdatamodeld** and set the **Current Model Version** to **Model 7** using **File Inspector (Option+⌘+1)**.

7. Regenerate the `NSManagedObject` subclass files for the Item entity, overwriting the existing files by clicking **Editor > Create NSManagedObject Subclass...** and following the prompts. Ensure the Grocery Dude target is ticked before clicking **Create**.

8. Update the `cellForRowAtIndexPath` method in `PrepareTVC.m` and `ShopTVC.m` to set the row image to display a `thumbnail` instead of the full `photoData`, as follows:

   ```
   cell.imageView.image = [UIImage imageWithData:item.thumbnail];
   ```

Profile Grocery Dude as you scroll through the prepare table view again. No images are displayed because there's no data in the thumbnail attribute yet. Despite the lack of images, the memory footprint is still very large. Figure 10.12 shows the expected result.

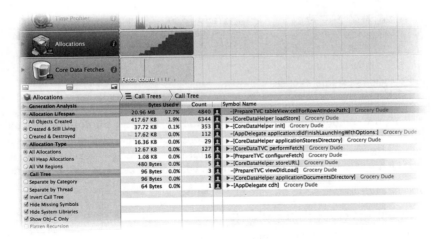

Figure 10.12   A large memory footprint

The key point here is that when an object is fetched from the persistent store, *all* of its attributes are fetched into memory, including the large image. To work around this model constraint, any attribute that is expected to hold a large value should be moved to another entity. A relationship can then be created to that entity so the data is still accessible via the original entity, as required. This *faulting* technique ensures that the large object is only loaded into memory when it is needed. Once you're finished with objects, remember to turn them back into a fault by calling refreshObject with the mergeChanges:NO option. If changes have been made to the object, you should save it before turning it into a fault.

In addition to faulting, it is recommended that large objects be allowed to reside outside the persistent store. An **Allows External Storage** option is available for Binary Data attributes underpinned by an SQLite persistent store. This option ensures objects larger than ~1MB are automatically stored outside the SQLite database. This approach is a more efficient way to store large objects. Figure 10.13 shows an example of large objects stored externally to the sqlite file within the application sandbox. Assuming an application with this setting has been run on a device already, the sandbox is viewable in Xcode by clicking **Window > Organizer** and selecting Applications of a connected device.

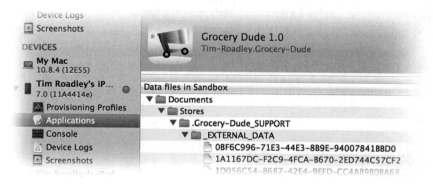

Figure 10.13   Allows External Storage

To apply the improved model design principles to Grocery Dude, the **photoData** attribute will be migrated to a new Item_Photo entity and renamed to **data**. The Item_Photo entity will be accessible via a new To-One relationship called **photo**. The inverse To-One relationship will be called **item**. What was once accessed via **photoData** will now be accessed via **photo.data**.

Update Grocery Dude as follows to migrate photoData:

1. Ensure **Model.xcdatamodeld** is selected.

2. Click **Editor > Add Model Version....**

3. Click **Finish** to accept the default model name of **Model 8**.

4. Ensure **Model 8.xcdatamodel** is selected.

5. Delete the **photoData** attribute from the **Item** entity.

6. Create a new entity called **Item_Photo**.

7. Create a new **Binary Data** attribute called **data** in the **Item_Photo** entity.

8. Configure the **data** attribute to enable the **Allows External Storage** option using **Data Model Inspector (Option+⌘+3)**.

9. Create a **To-One relationship** from the **Item** entity to the **Item_Photo** entity called **photo**. Also, set the inverse relationship name to **item**. It's easiest to change the editor style to **Graph** in order to create the relationship. To create a relationship, just hold **Control** and drag a line from one entity to another.

10. Set the **Delete Rule** of the **photo** relationship to **Cascade** using **Data Model Inspector (Option+⌘+3)**. This will ensure that when an item is deleted, its photo data is deleted, too.

11. Update the `selectedUniqueAttributes` method of `CoreDataHelper.m` to cater to the new **Item_Photo** entity by adding the following line of code on the line before the dictionary is created:

```
[entities addObject:@"Item_Photo"];[attributes addObject:@"data"];
```

The resulting data model is shown in Figure 10.14.

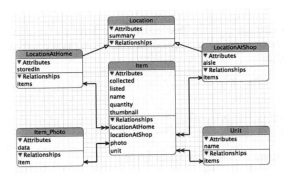

Figure 10.14   Grocery Dude Model 8

This type of model change cannot be completely inferred by Core Data unless you don't mind losing the existing values of **photoData**. In reality, you would not want to lose existing customer photos, so a model-mapping file is required. Whenever automatic store migration with an inferred mapping is triggered, Core Data checks for a model-mapping file prior to guessing what maps to where. The model-mapping file will need to do the following:

- Map the old **photoData** attribute from the **Item** entity to the new **data** attribute in the **Item_Photo** entity.

- Map the new **photo** relationship from the **Item** entity to the **Item_Photo** entity.

- Map the new **item** relationship from the **Item_Photo** entity to the **Item** entity.

Although it may have been obvious that the photoData attribute needed to be mapped to the data attribute, it is less obvious that a mapping is required for the new photo and item relationships. Without this relationship mapping, existing photos from photoData will not be correctly related to the new data attribute. This mapping will be created using a Value Expression similar to those inferred for other relationships in the model-mapping file.

Update Grocery Dude as follows to manually map Model 7 to Model 8:

1. Select the **Data Model** group and then click **File > New > File....**

2. Click **iOS > Core Data > Mapping Model > Next.**

3. Select **Model 7.xcdatamodel** as the source model and click **Next.**

4. Select **Model 8.xcdatamodel** as the target model and click **Next.**

5. Save the mapping model as **Model7toModel8**, ensure the Grocery Dude target is selected, and then click **Create.**

6. Select the **Item_Photo** entity mapping within **Model7toModel8.xcmappingmodel.**

7. Change the **Source** of the **Item_Photo** entity mapping to the **Item** using the **Mapping Model Inspector (Option+⌘+3).** This will automatically rename the entity mapping to **ItemToItem_Photo.**

8. Set the **Value Expression** of the **Destination Attribute** called **data** to $source. photoData, which ensures objects from the old **photoData** attribute are migrated to the new **data** attribute.

9. Likewise, set the **Value Expression** of the **Destination Relationship** called **item** to the following:
   ```
   FUNCTION($manager, "destinationInstancesForEntityMappingNamed:sourceInstances:"
   ,"ItemToItem", $source)
   ```

10. Select the **ItemToItem** entity mapping.

11. Set the **Value Expression** of the **Destination Relationship** called **photo** to the following:
    ```
    FUNCTION($manager, "destinationInstancesForEntityMappingNamed:sourceInstances:"
    ,"ItemToItem_Photo", $source)
    ```

12. Select **Model.xcdatamodeld** and set the **Current Model Version** to **Model 8** using **File Inspector (Option+⌘+1).**

13. Regenerate the NSManagedObject subclass files for all entities in Model 8, overwriting the existing files by clicking **Editor > Create NSManagedObject Subclass...** and following the prompts. Ensure the Grocery Dude target is ticked before clicking **Create.**

14. Repeat step 13 to ensure relationships are generated correctly within the NSManagedObject subclass files.

Once the model is upgraded, it is important to remember that the existing `sourceStore` used to populate default data will become incompatible with the data model. If you tried to load the existing `sourceStore`, the application would crash. For your convenience, a pre-upgraded source store has been created to include with the project bundle. In reality, you would have had to generate this source store again by first importing default data from Model 6 and then upgrading it to Model 7 and then Model 8. Attempt to run the application again, and you will be prompted to resolve references to the now non-existent `photoData` attribute.

Update Grocery Dude as follows to use the new attributes and an upgraded default store:

1. Add `#import "Item_Photo.h"` to the top of `ItemVC.m`.

2. Update the `refreshInterface` method of `ItemVC.m` to set the item image view as follows:

   ```
   self.photoImageView.image = [UIImage imageWithData:item.photo.data];
   ```

3. Update the `didFinishPickingMediaWithInfo` method of `ItemVC.m` to store captured photos using the new data attribute. The following code should replace the line of code that Xcode will be reporting as an issue.

   ```
   if (!item.photo) { // Create photo object it doesn't exist
       Item_Photo *newPhoto =
       [NSEntityDescription insertNewObjectForEntityForName:@"Item_Photo"
                                   inManagedObjectContext:cdh.context];
       [cdh.context obtainPermanentIDsForObjects:
                       [NSArray arrayWithObject:newPhoto] error:nil];
     item.photo = newPhoto;
   }
   item.photo.data = UIImageJPEGRepresentation(photo, 0.5);
   ```

4. Download the persistent store from the following URL and drag it into Grocery Dude: http://www.timroadley.com/LearningCoreData/Model_8_DefaultData.zip. Ensure **Copy items into destination group's folder** and the Grocery Dude target is ticked. This persistent store is the Model 8 version of `DefaultData.sqlite` and should replace the existing file.

Profile Grocery Dude again and scroll through the prepare table view. Compare the results shown previously in Figure 10.12 with those shown in Figure 10.15.

You should notice a significant difference in the memory usage, as ~20MB used by the `cellForRowAtIndexPath` method has been reduced to ~263KB. By your moving the large objects to the Item_Photo entity, the photo data remains a fault. This means the photo data is not drawn into memory whenever Item objects are fetched.

If you haven't run the application on the device since upgrading the model, the `importGroceryDudeTestData` method of `CoreDataHelper.m` will cause a crash because it is configured for the old model. Listing 10.5 shows an updated method that supports Model 8.

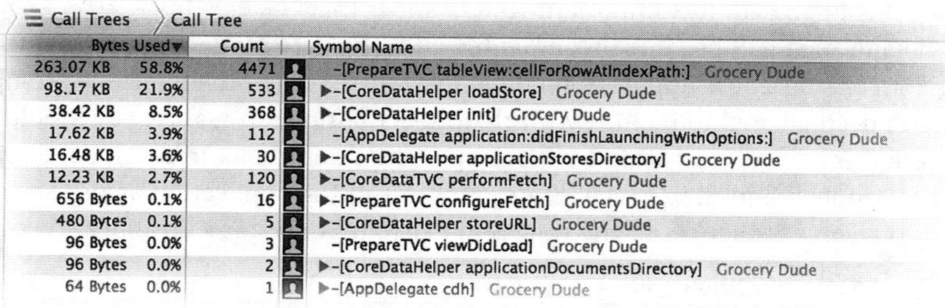

Call Trees > Call Tree

Bytes Used		Count	Symbol Name
263.07 KB	58.8%	4471	-[PrepareTVC tableView:cellForRowAtIndexPath:] Grocery Dude
98.17 KB	21.9%	533	▶-[CoreDataHelper loadStore] Grocery Dude
38.42 KB	8.5%	368	▶-[CoreDataHelper init] Grocery Dude
17.62 KB	3.9%	112	-[AppDelegate application:didFinishLaunchingWithOptions:] Grocery Dude
16.48 KB	3.6%	30	▶-[CoreDataHelper applicationStoresDirectory] Grocery Dude
12.23 KB	2.7%	120	▶-[CoreDataTVC performFetch] Grocery Dude
656 Bytes	0.1%	16	▶-[PrepareTVC configureFetch] Grocery Dude
480 Bytes	0.1%	5	▶-[CoreDataHelper storeURL] Grocery Dude
96 Bytes	0.0%	3	-[PrepareTVC viewDidLoad] Grocery Dude
96 Bytes	0.0%	2	▶-[CoreDataHelper applicationDocumentsDirectory] Grocery Dude
64 Bytes	0.0%	1	▶-[AppDelegate cdh] Grocery Dude

Figure 10.15 A minimized memory footprint

Listing 10.5 **CoreDataHelper.m: importGroceryDudeTestData**

```
#pragma mark - TEST DATA IMPORT (This code is Grocery Dude data specific)
- (void)importGroceryDudeTestData {
if (debug==1) {
    NSLog(@"Running %@ '%@'", self.class, NSStringFromSelector(_cmd));
}
    NSNumber *imported =
    [[NSUserDefaults standardUserDefaults] objectForKey:@"TestDataImport"];

    if (!imported.boolValue) {
        NSLog(@"Importing test data...");
        [_importContext performBlock:^{

            NSManagedObject *locationAtHome =
            [NSEntityDescription insertNewObjectForEntityForName:@"LocationAtHome"
                                          inManagedObjectContext:_importContext];
            NSManagedObject *locationAtShop =
            [NSEntityDescription insertNewObjectForEntityForName:@"LocationAtShop"
                                          inManagedObjectContext:_importContext];
            [locationAtHome setValue:@"Test Home Location" forKey:@"storedIn"];
            [locationAtShop setValue:@"Test Shop Location" forKey:@"aisle"];

            for (int a = 1; a < 101; a++) {

                @autoreleasepool {

                    // Insert Item
                    NSManagedObject *item =
                    [NSEntityDescription insertNewObjectForEntityForName:@"Item"
                                          inManagedObjectContext:_importContext];
                    [item setValue:[NSString stringWithFormat:@"Test Item %i",a]
                            forKey:@"name"];
```

```
                [item setValue:locationAtHome forKey:@"locationAtHome"];
                [item setValue:locationAtShop forKey:@"locationAtShop"];

                // Insert Photo
                NSManagedObject *photo =
                [NSEntityDescription insertNewObjectForEntityForName:@"Item_Photo"
                                        inManagedObjectContext:_importContext];
                [photo setValue:UIImagePNGRepresentation(
                        [UIImage imageNamed:@"GroceryHead.png"])
                        forKey:@"data"];

                // Relate Item and Photo
                [item setValue:photo forKey:@"photo"];

                NSLog(@"Inserting %@", [item valueForKey:@"name"]);
                [CoreDataImporter saveContext:_importContext];
                [_importContext refreshObject:item mergeChanges:NO];
                [_importContext refreshObject:photo mergeChanges:NO];
            }
        }
        // force table view refresh
        [self somethingChanged];

        // ensure import was a one off
        [[NSUserDefaults standardUserDefaults]
                        setObject:[NSNumber numberWithBool:YES]
                            forKey:@"TestDataImport"];
        [[NSUserDefaults standardUserDefaults] synchronize];
    }];
    }
    else {
        NSLog(@"Skipped test data import");
    }
}
```

Update Grocery Dude as follows to enable Model 8 support in the test import method:

1. Replace the `importGroceryDudeTestData` method in `CoreDataHelper.m` with the method from Listing 10.5.

Clean Up

When you're finished with managed objects, it's important to free up memory by removing them from the context. You can achieve this by turning them into a fault. Whenever the item view disappears, it's a good opportunity to turn the previously selected item and photo into a fault.

Update Grocery Dude as follows to turn previously selected items into a fault:

1. Add the code shown in Listing 10.6 to the bottom of the `viewDidDisappear` method of `ItemVC.m`.

Listing 10.6   **ItemVC.m: viewDidDisappear**

```
// Turn item & item photo into a fault
NSError *error;
Item *item =
(Item*)[cdh.context existingObjectWithID:self.selectedItemID error:&error];
if (error) {
    NSLog(@"ERROR!!! --> %@", error.localizedDescription);
} else {
    [cdh.context refreshObject:item.photo mergeChanges:NO];
    [cdh.context refreshObject:item mergeChanges:NO];
}
```

Summary

This chapter has shown what to look for when using Instruments to measure Core Data performance. The various options of `NSFetchRequest` have been explained and their merits demonstrated. It has also been shown how model design plays a key role in the performance of an application, particularly when large objects are involved. Remember that it is important to execute your testing on the slowest possible device with the largest data set your customers are likely to use. If an application works well on a slow device with a large data set, it will perform even better on the latest devices.

Exercises

Why not build on what you've learned by experimenting?

1. Comment out the code to set the request batch size in the `configureFetch` method of `PrepareTVC.m`. Check the query execution time and investigate the performance using Instruments.

2. Set the request fetch limit and offset in the `configureFetch` method of `PrepareTVC.m` using the code from Listing 10.7. Examine the query execution time and investigate the performance using Instruments. Notice the effect this change has had on the items shown in the Prepare table view.

Listing 10.7   **PrepareTVC.m: configureFetch**

```
[request setFetchLimit:20];
[request setFetchOffset:50];
```

Background Processing

Everything must be made as simple as possible, but not simpler.

Albert Einstein

Chapter 10, "Performance," gave recommendations on how to configure a managed object model for optimal performance. Measuring performance with Instruments was also demonstrated. Full-size photos were removed from the Prepare and Shop table view cells, and yet there are no thumbnails in their place. The process to create thumbnails from photos will be intensive, so it cannot be performed in the foreground. Thumbnail creation aside, even the simple act of saving a context has the potential to impact the user interface if there are many changes to commit. This chapter will use the example of thumbnail generation to demonstrate how to perform an intensive task using a private queue context. In addition, background save will be implemented by introducing a parent context between the persistent store and existing main queue context.

Background Save

Because the excessive memory usage issues were resolved in Chapter 10, the Prepare and Shop table views now display `nil` thumbnails. The process to create thumbnail images dynamically will be an intensive one, so it should be performed in the background to prevent impact on the user interface. To support the process of thumbnail creation, background save will be implemented first. The easiest way to achieve background save is to use two contexts in a parent and child hierarchy. The background context, referred to as the `_parentContext`, will be configured to use a private queue by setting its concurrency type to `NSPrivateQueueConcurrencyType`. The foreground context that underpins the user interface is referred to as `_context`. It is already configured to use the main queue, because its concurrency type is `NSMainQueueConcurrencyType`. Both contexts exist in memory, so intercommunication between them is very fast.

A child context has no persistent store. Instead, a parent context acts as the persistent store for its child context. When a child context is saved, changes go to its parent. For those changes to be persisted, a save must then be performed on the parent context, too. As the parent context runs on a private queue, the save will not impact the user interface. Figure 11.1 shows an overview of this process.

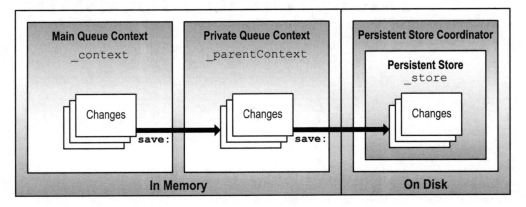

Figure 11.1   Background save with parent and child contexts

> **Note**
>
> To continue building the sample application, you'll need to have added the previous chapter's code to Grocery Dude. Alternatively, you may download, unzip, and use the project up to this point from http://www.timroadley.com/LearningCoreData/GroceryDude-AfterChapter10.zip. Any time you start using an Xcode project from a ZIP file, it's good practice to click **Product** > **Clean**. This practice ensures there's no residual cache from previous projects using the same name.

When the context hierarchy is configured, at least one context will be configured on a private queue. Private queue context configuration must be performed using blocks. Use `performBlockAndWait` when configuring a context on a private queue so that it is ready before it is needed. The `_context` configuration can be performed outside of a block because it already runs on the main queue. As discussed in Chapter 10, it's a good idea to configure all contexts with a non-default merge policy to settle conflicts, in case they arise. The updated code involved in configuring a context hierarchy is shown in Listing 11.1 in bold.

Listing 11.1   `CoreDataHelper.m: init`

```
- (id)init {
if (debug==1) {
    NSLog(@"Running %@ '%@'", self.class, NSStringFromSelector(_cmd));
}
    self = [super init];
```

```objc
if (!self) {return nil;}

_model = [NSManagedObjectModel mergedModelFromBundles:nil];
_coordinator =
[[NSPersistentStoreCoordinator alloc] initWithManagedObjectModel:_model];

_parentContext = [[NSManagedObjectContext alloc]
                    initWithConcurrencyType:NSPrivateQueueConcurrencyType];
[_parentContext performBlockAndWait:^{
    [_parentContext setPersistentStoreCoordinator:_coordinator];
    [_parentContext
            setMergePolicy:NSMergeByPropertyObjectTrumpMergePolicy];
}];

_context = [[NSManagedObjectContext alloc]
                        initWithConcurrencyType:NSMainQueueConcurrencyType];
[_context setParentContext:_parentContext];
[_context setMergePolicy:NSMergeByPropertyObjectTrumpMergePolicy];

_importContext = [[NSManagedObjectContext alloc]
                    initWithConcurrencyType:NSPrivateQueueConcurrencyType];
[_importContext performBlockAndWait:^{
    [_importContext setPersistentStoreCoordinator:_coordinator];
    [_importContext setMergePolicy:NSMergeByPropertyObjectTrumpMergePolicy];
    [_importContext setUndoManager:nil]; // the default on iOS
}];

_sourceCoordinator = [[NSPersistentStoreCoordinator alloc]
                                    initWithManagedObjectModel:_model];
_sourceContext = [[NSManagedObjectContext alloc]
                    initWithConcurrencyType:NSPrivateQueueConcurrencyType];
[_sourceContext performBlockAndWait:^{
    [_sourceContext setMergePolicy:NSMergeByPropertyObjectTrumpMergePolicy];
    [_sourceContext setPersistentStoreCoordinator:_sourceCoordinator];
    [_sourceContext setUndoManager:nil]; // the default on iOS
}];
    return self;
}
```

Update Grocery Dude as follows to implement a parent and child context hierarchy:

1. Add the following code to `CoreDataHelper.h` before any other properties are declared:

   ```objc
   @property (nonatomic, readonly) NSManagedObjectContext      *parentContext;
   ```

2. Replace the `init` method of `CoreDataHelper.m` with the code from Listing 11.1.

The next step is to implement a new method called backgroundSaveContext. This method will save the child context to the parent context and then the parent context to the persistent store. The save to the parent context will be fast because it is performed within memory. It doesn't matter if the save from the parent context to the persistent store takes a while because it occurs asynchronously on a private queue. The code involved is similar to the existing saveContext method and is shown in Listing 11.2.

Listing 11.2   **CoreDataHelper.m: backgroundSaveContext**

```
- (void)backgroundSaveContext {
if (debug==1) {
    NSLog(@"Running %@ '%@'", self.class, NSStringFromSelector(_cmd));
}
    // First, save the child context in the foreground (fast, all in memory)
    [self saveContext];

    // Then, save the parent context.
    [_parentContext performBlock:^{
        if ([_parentContext hasChanges]) {
            NSError *error = nil;
            if ([_parentContext save:&error]) {
                NSLog(@"_parentContext SAVED changes to persistent store");
            }
            else {
                NSLog(@"_parentContext FAILED to save: %@", error);
                [self showValidationError:error];
            }
        }
        else {
            NSLog(@"_parentContext SKIPPED saving as there are no changes");
        }
    }];
}
```

Update Grocery Dude as follows to implement background save:

1. Add the code from Listing 11.2 to the bottom of the SAVING section of CoreDataHelper.m.

2. Add the following code to CoreDataHelper.h before @end so that other classes may take advantage of background save:

   `- (void)backgroundSaveContext;`

3. Replace [cdh saveContext]; with [cdh backgroundSaveContext]; in the viewDidDisappear method of ItemVC.m.

4. Replace `[[self cdh] saveContext];` with `[[self cdh] backgroundSaveContext];` in the `applicationDidEnterBackground` and `applicationWillTerminate` methods of `AppDelegate.m`.

5. Add `[cdh backgroundSaveContext];` to the bottom of the `clear` and `clearList` methods of `PrepareTVC.m`.

6. Add the following code to the bottom of the `clear` method of `ShopTVC.m` and to the bottom of the `didSelectRowAtIndexPath` method of `ShopTVC.m` and `PrepareTVC.m`:

   ```
   CoreDataHelper *cdh = [(AppDelegate *)[[UIApplication
   sharedApplication] delegate] cdh];
       [cdh backgroundSaveContext];
   ```

7. Add the code from the previous step to the bottom of the `commitEditingStyle` method of `LocationsAtHomeTVC.m`, `LocationsAtShopTVC.m`, `PrepareTVC.m`, and `UnitsTVC.m`.

Background save has now been implemented. When an attribute value of an object *related* to an item changes, the Prepare and Shop table views must be refreshed manually. This is because a fetched results controller does not track changes to objects related to its fetched objects. In this case, the fetched results controllers for `PrepareTVC` and `ShopTVC` only track changes to Item objects. To work around this issue, a `viewDidDisappear` method needs to be added to `LocationAtHomeVC.m`, `LocationAtShopVC.m`, and `UnitVC.m`. As shown in Listing 11.3, this new method will post a notification that something has changed whenever the view in question disappears, which will be used to trigger a refresh.

Listing 11.3 **`LocationAtHomeVC.m`, `LocationAtShopVC.m`, and `UnitVC.m`: `viewDidDisappear`**

```
- (void)viewDidDisappear:(BOOL)animated {
if (debug==1) {
    NSLog(@"Running %@ '%@'", self.class, NSStringFromSelector(_cmd));
}
    CoreDataHelper *cdh =
    [(AppDelegate *)[[UIApplication sharedApplication] delegate] cdh];
    [cdh backgroundSaveContext];
 [[NSNotificationCenter defaultCenter] postNotificationName:@"SomethingChanged"
                                          object:nil
                                          userInfo:nil];

}
```

Update Grocery Dude as follows to configure object change notifications:

1. Add the method from Listing 11.3 to the bottom of the VIEW section of `LocationAtHomeVC.m`, `LocationAtShopVC.m`, and `UnitVC.m`.

The application is now ready to test background save:

1. Delete Grocery Dude from the iOS Simulator and click **Product > Clean** in Xcode.

2. Run Grocery Dude on the iOS Simulator and wait for the test data import process to finish. You can track progress in the console log, as the table view will remain blank until the import completes.

3. Create a new item by clicking + on the Prepare tab. Give the new item any name and press **Done**. A save will be triggered when the `ItemVC` view disappears.

Whenever a save triggers, you should see the main queue `_context` and private queue `_parentContext` log a SAVED result to the console, as shown in Figure 11.2.

```
2013-07-29 11:55:39.345 Grocery Dude[15239:a0b] Running CoreDataHelper 'backgroundSaveContext'
2013-07-29 11:55:39.346 Grocery Dude[15239:a0b] Running CoreDataHelper 'saveContext'
2013-07-29 11:55:39.346 Grocery Dude[15239:a0b] _context SAVED changes to persistent store
2013-07-29 11:55:39.346 Grocery Dude[15239:3b13] CoreData: sql: BEGIN EXCLUSIVE
2013-07-29 11:55:39.347 Grocery Dude[15239:3b13] CoreData: sql: COMMIT
2013-07-29 11:55:39.347 Grocery Dude[15239:3b13] CoreData: sql: BEGIN EXCLUSIVE
2013-07-29 11:55:39.347 Grocery Dude[15239:3b13] CoreData: sql: INSERT INTO ZITEM(Z_PK, Z_ENT, Z_OPT,
ZLOCATIONATHOME, ZLOCATIONATSHOP, ZPHOTO, ZUNIT, ZCOLLECTED, ZLISTED, ZNAME, ZQUANTITY, ZTHUMBNAIL)
VALUES(?, ?, ?, ?, ?, ?, ?, ?, ?, ?, ?, ?)
2013-07-29 11:55:39.347 Grocery Dude[15239:3b13] CoreData: sql: INSERT INTO ZLOCATION(Z_PK, Z_ENT,
Z_OPT, ZSUMMARY, ZSTOREDIN) VALUES(?, ?, ?, ?, ?)
2013-07-29 11:55:39.348 Grocery Dude[15239:3b13] CoreData: sql: INSERT INTO ZLOCATION(Z_PK, Z_ENT,
Z_OPT, ZSUMMARY, ZAISLE) VALUES(?, ?, ?, ?, ?)
2013-07-29 11:55:39.348 Grocery Dude[15239:3b13] CoreData: sql: COMMIT
2013-07-29 11:55:39.349 Grocery Dude[15239:3b13] _parentContext SAVED changes to persistent store
```

Figure 11.2   Background save

With background save now implemented, you may be wondering how much benefit it has really added. Saving in the foreground in Grocery Dude was fast to begin with, so the benefits are arguably small. The benefits of background save are more obvious when a larger amount of data needs to be saved. A scenario where background save is beneficial is during an import process.

Background Processing

With the introduction of a parent context, there are implications on the way data is imported. You have already seen how the imported test data was not reflected in the table views during the import. The problem is that the fetched results controller of the Items table view has no idea that the new data is available in the persistent store. Although you could set up notification observers to trigger a merge, there's no need to when you can instead configure `_context` as the parent of `_importContext`. Figure 11.3 illustrates this concept.

Update Grocery Dude as follows to configure `_importContext` with a parent:

1. Remove the following line of code from the init method of `CoreDataHelper.m`:

   ```
   [_importContext setPersistentStoreCoordinator:_coordinator];
   ```

2. Add the following code in its place:

```
[_importContext setParentContext:_context];
```

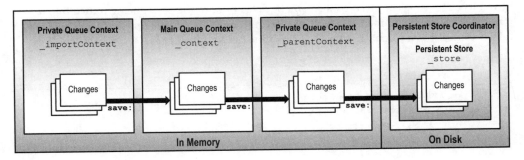

Figure 11.3   `_context` as a parent of `_importContext`

Although it won't be used in this chapter, the `_sourceContext` should also be updated with `_context` as its parent.

Update Grocery Dude as follows to configure `_sourceContext` with a parent:

1. Remove the following line of code from the `init` method of `CoreDataHelper.m`:

```
[_sourceContext setPersistentStoreCoordinator:_sourceCoordinator];
```

2. Add the following code in its place:

```
[_sourceContext setParentContext:_context];
```

3. Comment out the following code from the `init` method of `CoreDataHelper.m`:

```
_sourceCoordinator =
[[NSPersistentStoreCoordinator alloc] initWithManagedObjectModel:_model];
```

Now that `_importContext` is a child of `_context`, imported data will be immediately visible on table views watching `_context` after `_importContext` is saved. This is a benefit of using a fetched results controller–backed table view.

Introducing `Faulter`

The process of generating thumbnails will impact a potentially large number of objects. Any time a large number of objects are processed, care should be taken to ensure memory bloating and interface lag is avoided. As explained in Chapter 10, you should turn objects into faults once you're finished with them using `refreshObject:mergeChanges:NO` after saving the containing context. With a parent and child context hierarchy, you'll need to do this for every context in the hierarchy. That means for every object imported, a save and fault are required in all three contexts.

The process of saving a context and turning a particular object into a fault is a repeatable one. The code needed to perform this task can be reused regardless of the context involved. As such, a new class called `Faulter` will be implemented that can be used to turn an object into a fault given its `objectID`. The given context will be saved prior to the object being turned into a fault. `Faulter` will automatically fault the object through the parent context hierarchy if the given context has a parent. Listing 11.4 shows the header of `Faulter`.

Listing 11.4   **Faulter.h**

```
#import <Foundation/Foundation.h>
#import <CoreData/CoreData.h>

@interface Faulter : NSObject

+ (void)faultObjectWithID:(NSManagedObjectID*)objectID
                inContext:(NSManagedObjectContext*)context;

@end
```

Update Grocery Dude as follows to add the `Faulter` class:

1. Select the **Generic Core Data Classes** group.

2. Click **File > New > File...**.

3. Create a new **iOS > Cocoa Touch > Objective-C class** and then click **Next**.

4. Set **Subclass of** to `NSObject` and **Class name** to `Faulter` and then click **Next**.

5. Ensure the Grocery Dude target is ticked and then click **Create** to create the class in the Grocery Dude project directory.

6. Replace all code in `Faulter.h` with the code from Listing 11.4.

The `faultObjectWithID:inContext` method of the `Faulter` implementation will first of all save the given context if there are outstanding changes. If the object to be faulted isn't already a fault, it is turned into a fault using the `refreshObject` method of `NSManagedObjectContext`. Once the object is a fault in the given context, the process is repeated in the parent context, if there is one. The code involved is shown in Listing 11.5.

Listing 11.5   **Faulter.m**

```
#import "Faulter.h"
@implementation Faulter

+ (void)faultObjectWithID:(NSManagedObjectID*)objectID
                inContext:(NSManagedObjectContext*)context {
```

```
    if (!objectID || !context) {
        return;
    }

    [context performBlockAndWait:^{

        NSManagedObject *object = [context objectWithID:objectID];

        if (object.hasChanges) {
            NSError *error = nil;
            if (![context save:&error]) {
                NSLog(@"ERROR saving: %@", error);
            }
        }

        if (!object.isFault) {

            NSLog(@"Faulting object %@ in context %@", object.objectID, context);
            [context refreshObject:object mergeChanges:NO];
        } else {
            NSLog(@"Skipped faulting an object that is already a fault");
        }

        // Repeat the process if the context has a parent
        if (context.parentContext) {
            [self faultObjectWithID:objectID inContext:context.parentContext];
        }
    }];
}
@end
```

Update Grocery Dude as follows to implement the `Faulter` class:

1. Replace all code in `Faulter.m` with the code from Listing 11.5.

The `Faulter` class will first be used by the existing `importGroceryDudeTestData` method of `CoreDataHelper.m`. The test data import process currently only saves and faults objects in the `_importContext`. With the new context hierarchy in place, the import process now needs to save and fault new objects in `_context` and `_parentContext`, too. Without these additional saves, inserted data would never make its way to the persistent store. Listing 11.6 shows an updated test data import method.

Listing 11.6 **CoreDataHelper.m: importGroceryDudeTestData**

```objc
- (void)importGroceryDudeTestData {
if (debug==1) {
    NSLog(@"Running %@ '%@'", self.class, NSStringFromSelector(_cmd));
}
    NSNumber *imported =
    [[NSUserDefaults standardUserDefaults] objectForKey:@"TestDataImport"];

    if (!imported.boolValue) {
        NSLog(@"Importing test data...");
        [_importContext performBlock:^{

            NSManagedObject *locationAtHome =
            [NSEntityDescription insertNewObjectForEntityForName:@"LocationAtHome"
                                        inManagedObjectContext:_importContext];
            NSManagedObject *locationAtShop =
            [NSEntityDescription insertNewObjectForEntityForName:@"LocationAtShop"
                                        inManagedObjectContext:_importContext];
            [locationAtHome setValue:@"Test Home Location" forKey:@"storedIn"];
            [locationAtShop setValue:@"Test Shop Location" forKey:@"aisle"];

            for (int a = 1; a < 101; a++) {

                @autoreleasepool {

                    // Insert Item
                    NSManagedObject *item =
                    [NSEntityDescription insertNewObjectForEntityForName:@"Item"
                                        inManagedObjectContext:_importContext];
                    [item setValue:[NSString stringWithFormat:@"Test Item %i",a]
                            forKey:@"name"];
                    [item setValue:locationAtHome
                            forKey:@"locationAtHome"];
                    [item setValue:locationAtShop
                            forKey:@"locationAtShop"];

                    // Insert Photo
                    NSManagedObject *photo =
                    [NSEntityDescription insertNewObjectForEntityForName:@"Item_Photo"
                                        inManagedObjectContext:_importContext];
                    [photo setValue:UIImagePNGRepresentation(
                                        [UIImage imageNamed:@"GroceryHead.png"])
                            forKey:@"data"];

                    // Relate Item and Photo
                    [item setValue:photo forKey:@"photo"];
```

```
                    NSLog(@"Inserting %@", [item valueForKey:@"name"]);
                    [Faulter faultObjectWithID:photo.objectID
                                    inContext:_importContext];
                    [Faulter faultObjectWithID:item.objectID
                                    inContext:_importContext];
                }
            }
            [_importContext reset];

            // ensure import was a one off
            [[NSUserDefaults standardUserDefaults]
                                    setObject:[NSNumber numberWithBool:YES]
                                       forKey:@"TestDataImport"];
            [[NSUserDefaults standardUserDefaults] synchronize];
        }];
    }
    else {
        NSLog(@"Skipped test data import");
    }
}
```

Update Grocery Dude as follows to enhance the test data import method:

1. Add `#import "Faulter.h"` to the top of `CoreDataHelper.m`.

2. Replace the existing `importGroceryDudeTestData` method in `CoreDataHelper.m` with the method from Listing 11.6.

3. Delete Grocery Dude from the iOS Simulator and click **Product > Clean** in Xcode.

4. Run Grocery Dude on the iOS Simulator and wait for the test data import process to finish. You should see items appear immediately as they are imported; however, they still won't have thumbnails.

The `Faulter` class will now be used by a new class responsible for creating thumbnails.

Introducing `Thumbnailer`

`Thumbnailer` is the name of the new class that will be used to generate photo thumbnails in the background. This class assumes the context hierarchy is configured as per Figure 11.3. To remain generic enough for reuse in other applications, this class takes the following variables:

- **`entityName`** is the string name of the entity with a thumbnail attribute.

- **`thumbnailAttributeName`** is the string name of the binary data attribute where the proposed thumbnail should be created. This attribute is assumed to exist in the entity specified by `entityName`.

- **photoRelationshipName** is the string name of the relationship that starts from the entity specified by entityName and leads to another entity containing the photo data.

- **photoAttributeName** is the string name of the binary data attribute containing the photo. This attribute is assumed to exist at the destination of the relationship specified in photoRelationshipName.

- **sortDescriptors** is an optional variable used to sort the array of objects with missing thumbnails. The order of this array determines the order thumbnails are created in. It will look better to the user if thumbnails are generated in the same order as the table view where the thumbnails are displayed.

- **importContext** should be a context running on a private queue. The thumbnails will be created inside this context.

Listing 11.7 shows the header of the Thumbnailer class.

Listing 11.7   **Thumbnailer.h**

```
#import <Foundation/Foundation.h>
#import <CoreData/CoreData.h>

@interface Thumbnailer : NSObject

+ (void)createMissingThumbnailsForEntityName:(NSString*)entityName
                withThumbnailAttributeName:(NSString*)thumbnailAttributeName
                withPhotoRelationshipName:(NSString*)photoRelationshipName
                  withPhotoAttributeName:(NSString*)photoAttributeName
                     withSortDescriptors:(NSArray*)sortDescriptors
                       withImportContext:(NSManagedObjectContext*)importContext;
@end
```

Update Grocery Dude as follows to add the Thumbnailer class:

1. Select the **Generic Core Data Classes** group.

2. Click **File > New > File...**.

3. Create a new **iOS > Cocoa Touch > Objective-C class** and then click **Next**.

4. Set **Subclass of** to NSObject and **Class name** to Thumbnailer and then click **Next**.

5. Ensure the Grocery Dude target is ticked and then click **Create** to create the class in the Grocery Dude project directory.

6. Replace all code in Thumbnailer.h with the code from Listing 11.7.

The implementation code in Thumbnailer is wrapped in a block. It is expected that the given import context is running on a private background queue. When it is called, the first thing Thumbnailer does is to build an NSFetchRequest using the given variables. This results in an array of pointers to objects with a photo and without a thumbnail. A thumbnail is generated for each of these objects. Once the thumbnail has been created, the now unneeded objects are turned into a fault to save memory. The code involved is shown in Listing 11.8.

Listing 11.8 **Thumbnailer.m**

```objc
#import "Thumbnailer.h"
#import "Faulter.h"

@implementation Thumbnailer
#define debug 1

+ (void)createMissingThumbnailsForEntityName:(NSString*)entityName
                withThumbnailAttributeName:(NSString*)thumbnailAttributeName
                withPhotoRelationshipName:(NSString*)photoRelationshipName
                 withPhotoAttributeName:(NSString*)photoAttributeName
                   withSortDescriptors:(NSArray*)sortDescriptors
                    withImportContext:(NSManagedObjectContext*)importContext {
if (debug==1) {
    NSLog(@"Running %@ '%@'", self.class, NSStringFromSelector(_cmd));
}
    [importContext performBlock:^{

        NSFetchRequest *request =
        [NSFetchRequest fetchRequestWithEntityName:entityName];
        request.predicate =
        [NSPredicate predicateWithFormat:@"%K==nil && %K.%K!=nil",
            thumbnailAttributeName, photoRelationshipName, photoAttributeName];
        request.sortDescriptors = sortDescriptors;
        request.fetchBatchSize = 15;
        NSError *error;
        NSArray *missingThumbnails =
        [importContext executeFetchRequest:request error:&error];
        if (error) {NSLog(@"Error: %@", error.localizedDescription);}

        for (NSManagedObject *object in missingThumbnails) {

            NSManagedObject *photoObject =
            [object valueForKey:photoRelationshipName];

            if (![object valueForKey:thumbnailAttributeName] &&
                [photoObject valueForKey:photoAttributeName]) {

                // Create Thumbnail
                UIImage *photo =
            [UIImage imageWithData:[photoObject valueForKey:photoAttributeName]];
                CGSize size = CGSizeMake(66, 66);
```

```
            UIGraphicsBeginImageContextWithOptions(size, NO, 0.0);
            [photo drawInRect:CGRectMake(0, 0, size.width, size.height)];
            UIImage *thumbnail = UIGraphicsGetImageFromCurrentImageContext();
            UIGraphicsEndImageContext();
            [object setValue:UIImagePNGRepresentation(thumbnail)
                    forKey:thumbnailAttributeName];

            // Fault photo object out of memory
            [Faulter faultObjectWithID:photoObject.objectID
                          inContext:importContext];
            [Faulter faultObjectWithID:object.objectID
                          inContext:importContext];

            // Remove unused variables
            photo = nil;
            thumbnail = nil;
        }
      }
   }];
}
@end
```

Update Grocery Dude as follows to implement the `Thumbnailer` class:

1. Replace all code in `Thumbnailer.m` with the code from Listing 11.8.

As table views containing items appear, they should use the `Thumbnailer` class to generate missing thumbnails. This means a `viewDidAppear` method needs to be added to the `PrepareTVC` and `ShopTVC` classes. The call to the class method of `Thumbnailer` will need to be configured as shown in Listing 11.9.

Listing 11.9   **PrepareTVC.m and ShopTVC.m: viewDidAppear**

```
- (void)viewDidAppear:(BOOL)animated {
if (debug==1) {
    NSLog(@"Running %@ '%@'", self.class, NSStringFromSelector(_cmd));
}
    [super viewDidAppear:animated];

    // Create missing Thumbnails
    CoreDataHelper *cdh =
    [(AppDelegate *)[[UIApplication sharedApplication] delegate] cdh];
    NSArray *sortDescriptors =
     [NSArray arrayWithObjects:
     [NSSortDescriptor sortDescriptorWithKey:@"locationAtHome.storedIn"
                                    ascending:YES],
```

```
                [NSSortDescriptor sortDescriptorWithKey:@"name"
                                        ascending:YES],
                                        nil];

        [Thumbnailer createMissingThumbnailsForEntityName:@"Item"
                            withThumbnailAttributeName:@"thumbnail"
                            withPhotoRelationshipName:@"photo"
                                withPhotoAttributeName:@"data"
                                    withSortDescriptors:sortDescriptors
                                        withImportContext:cdh.importContext];
}
```

Update Grocery Dude as follows to ensure missing thumbnails are created:

1. Add #import "Thumbnailer.h" to the top of PrepareTVC.m and ShopTVC.m.

2. Add the viewDidAppear method from Listing 11.9 to the top of the VIEW section of PrepareTVC.m and ShopTVC.m.

Run the application again, and you should see thumbnails appear as they're automatically generated (see Figure 11.4). Scrolling should remain smooth at all times.

Figure 11.4   Photo thumbnails generated in the background

If a photo changes and a thumbnail already exists, it won't be updated. To resolve this, the associated thumbnail should be set to nil whenever a new photo is taken.

Update Grocery Dude as follows to ensure that new photos have appropriate thumbnails:

1. Update the `didFinishPickingMediaWithInfo` method of `ItemVC.m` by inserting `item.thumbnail = nil;` on the line after `item.photo.data` is set.

If you run the application on a slow device and navigate to the item view, you may notice slight lag as the item view loads. This is due to the large image being pulled from the store into memory. A `performBlock` can be used to offload intensive tasks such as this. Listing 11.10 shows in bold additional code used to lazily load a photo on the item view.

Listing 11.10   **ItemVC.m: refreshInterface**

```
- (void)refreshInterface {
if (debug==1) {
    NSLog(@"Running %@ '%@'", self.class, NSStringFromSelector(_cmd));
}
    if (self.selectedItemID) {
        CoreDataHelper *cdh =
        [(AppDelegate *)[[UIApplication sharedApplication] delegate] cdh];
        Item *item =
        (Item*)[cdh.context existingObjectWithID:self.selectedItemID error:nil];
        self.nameTextField.text = item.name;
        self.quantityTextField.text = item.quantity.stringValue;
        self.unitPickerTextField.text = item.unit.name;
        self.unitPickerTextField.selectedObjectID = item.unit.objectID;
        self.homeLocationPickerTextField.text = item.locationAtHome.storedIn;
        self.homeLocationPickerTextField.selectedObjectID =
        item.locationAtHome.objectID;
        self.shopLocationPickerTextField.text = item.locationAtShop.aisle;
        self.shopLocationPickerTextField.selectedObjectID =
        item.locationAtShop.objectID;

        [cdh.context performBlock:^{
            self.photoImageView.image =
            [UIImage imageWithData:item.photo.data];
        }];

        [self checkCamera];
    }
}
```

Update Grocery Dude as follows to lazily load the photo on the item view:

1. Replace the `refreshInterface` method of `ItemVC.m` with the one from Listing 11.10.

Run the application again and navigate to the item view. The photo will be loading slightly after the item view interface loads. This likely won't be noticeable on the iOS Simulator because it is has more resources than a physical iOS device.

Summary

This chapter has shown how to save and import in the background. These techniques ensure you don't impact the user interface during intensive operations. At the same time, a useful class, `Faulter`, has been introduced. This class helps reduce the additional code required to save and fault objects through a context hierarchy. You may wish to adopt `Faulter` in your own projects where a context hierarchy is in play. Likewise, another new class `Thumbnailer` can be adapted into your own projects to assist in generating thumbnail images.

Exercises

Why not build on what you've learned by experimenting?

1. If you have an iOS device, test that the import process and thumbnail creation do not impact the user interface.

2. Update the `parser:didStartElement` method of `CoreDataHelper.m` with `Faulter` support for the context hierarchy. This will allow you to test XML import with multiple contexts. To do this, replace the code in STEP 7 of the `parser:didStartElement` method of `CoreDataHelper.m` with the code shown in Listing 11.11.

Listing 11.11   **CoreDataHelper.m: parser:didStartElement**

```
[Faulter faultObjectWithID:item.objectID inContext:_importContext];
[Faulter faultObjectWithID:unit.objectID inContext:_importContext];
[Faulter faultObjectWithID:locationAtHome.objectID inContext:_importContext];
[Faulter faultObjectWithID:locationAtShop.objectID inContext:_importContext];
```

3. Test XML import with `Faulter` as follows:

   - Comment out `[self importGroceryDudeTestData];` from the `setupCoreData` method of `CoreDataHelper.m`.

   - Uncomment `[self checkIfDefaultDataNeedsImporting];` from the `setupCoreData` method of `CoreDataHelper.m`.

   - Replace the `alertView:clickedButtonAtIndex` method of `CoreDataHelper.m` with the one shown in Listing 11.12.

Listing 11.12   **CoreDataHelper.m: alertView:clickedButtonAtIndex**

```
- (void)alertView:(UIAlertView *)alertView
clickedButtonAtIndex:(NSInteger)buttonIndex {
if (debug==1) {
    NSLog(@"Running %@ '%@'", self.class, NSStringFromSelector(_cmd));
}
    if (alertView == self.importAlertView) {
        if (buttonIndex == 1) { // The 'Import' button on the importAlertView

            NSLog(@"Default Data Import Approved by User");
            // XML Import
            [_importContext performBlock:^{
              [self importFromXML:[[NSBundle mainBundle]
                    URLForResource:@"DefaultData"
                     withExtension:@"xml"]];
             }];
            // Deep Copy Import From Persistent Store
            //[self loadSourceStore];
            //[self deepCopyFromPersistentStore:[self sourceStoreURL]];

        } else {
            NSLog(@"Default Data Import Cancelled by User");
        }
        // Set the data as imported regardless of the user's decision
        [self setDefaultDataAsImportedForStore:_store];
    }
}
```

- Delete the application and run it again to test the XML import process with `Faulter`.
  The console log should show each object as it is faulted through the context
  hierarchy on the way to the persistent store. The `importContext`, `context`, and
  `parentContext` all have a different memory address logged to the console (for example,
  `<NSManagedObjectContext: 0x8e12345>`).

Prepare for the next chapter by commenting out everything in the `setupCoreData` method of
`CoreDataHelper.m` except for `[self setDefaultDataStoreAsInitialStore];` and `[self
loadStore];`.

12

Search

The measure of intelligence is the ability to change.

Albert Einstein

In Chapter 11, "Background Processing," the execution of background tasks such as save, import, and thumbnail creation was demonstrated. This chapter will implement search on the `PrepareTVC` *table view of the Prepare tab. Search results will have the same sectioning and sort order as the* `PrepareTVC` *table view so that it looks like search results are filtered in place. This functionality will be added in such a way that it will be easy to enable search on any table view, with only minor updates required. This flexibility will be achieved by implementing as much of the search functionality into the underlying* `CoreDataTVC` *as possible. The performance implications of the way search predicates are formed will also be discussed, along with recommendations for optimizing search for large data sets.*

To add search to a table view, you'll need to use a `UISearchDisplayController`*. This class contains a table view that is used to display search results. The* `UITableView` *data source methods implemented in* `CoreDataTVC` *will need to be updated to handle this additional table view. When a user taps in the search bar, the search display controller's table view will become visible. As the user types in search text, he or she will effectively be specifying the predicate that is used to filter the search fetch request. This fetch request will be given to a new fetched results controller put in place specifically for search results. The* `NSFetchedResultsController` *delegate methods in* `CoreDataTVC` *will also need to be updated to handle this additional fetched results controller.*

> **Note**
>
> To continue building the sample application, you'll need to have added the previous chapter's code to Grocery Dude. Alternatively, you may download, unzip, and use the project up to this point from http://www.timroadley.com/LearningCoreData/GroceryDude-AfterChapter11.zip. Any time you start using an Xcode project from a ZIP file, it's good practice to click **Product** > **Clean**. This practice ensures there's no residual cache from previous projects using the same name.

Updating `CoreDataTVC`

By updating `CoreDataTVC` to support search, all table views in Grocery Dude will inherit the ability to easily implement search. To add search support to `CoreDataTVC`, its header will need to be updated to adopt the `UISearchBarDelegate` and `UISearchDisplayDelegate` protocols. Listing 12.1 shows how the updated `CoreDataTVC` header will look once it adopts these search protocols.

Listing 12.1   **`CoreDataTVC.h`**

```
#import <UIKit/UIKit.h>
#import "CoreDataHelper.h"
@interface CoreDataTVC : UITableViewController
<NSFetchedResultsControllerDelegate, UISearchBarDelegate, UISearchDisplayDelegate>
@property (strong, nonatomic) NSFetchedResultsController *frc;
- (void)performFetch;
@end
```

Update Grocery Dude as follows to adopt the search protocols:

1. Update `CoreDataTVC.h` to adopt the `UISearchBarDelegate` and `UISearchDisplayDelegate` protocols by replacing all the code in `CoreDataTVC.h` with the code from Listing 12.1.

The next step will be to add two new properties to `CoreDataTVC`. The first property, `searchFRC`, will be a fetched results controller. It will efficiently manage search results. When a user types in search text, the `searchFRC` will be remade with a new predicate formed from the search text. The second property, `searchDC`, will be a search display controller for displaying search results. Listing 12.2 shows the two new properties.

Listing 12.2   **`CoreDataTVC.h`: `searchFRC` and `searchDC`**

```
@property (strong, nonatomic) NSFetchedResultsController *searchFRC;
@property (strong, nonatomic) UISearchDisplayController *searchDC;
```

Update Grocery Dude as follows to add two new properties for search:

1. Add the two properties from Listing 12.2 to `CoreDataTVC.h` beneath the existing `frc` property.

The `CoreDataTVC` now needs to be updated to support both `self.frc` and `self.searchFRC`. This means that the `UITableView` data source and `NSFetchedResultsController` delegate methods need updating. First, however, two new methods will be added to help determine what table view is used with what fetched results controller, and vice versa. Listing 12.3 shows the code involved, which uses a *ternary operator* to make these determinations.

Listing 12.3 **CoreDataTVC.m: GENERAL**

```
#pragma mark - GENERAL
- (NSFetchedResultsController*)frcFromTV:(UITableView*)tableView {
    /*
        If the given tableView is self.tableView return self.frc,
        otherwise self.searchFRC
    */
    return (tableView == self.tableView) ? self.frc : self.searchFRC;
}
- (UITableView*)TVFromFRC:(NSFetchedResultsController*)frc {
    /*
        If the given fetched results controller is self.frc return self.tableView,
        otherwise self.searchDC.searchResultsTableView
    */
    return (frc == self.frc) ? self.tableView : self.searchDC.searchResultsTableView;
}
```

Update Grocery Dude as follows to implement two new methods in a GENERAL section:

1. Add the code from Listing 12.3 to the bottom of CoreDataTVC.m before @end.

2. Add the following code to the bottom of CoreDataTVC.h before @end.

   - (NSFetchedResultsController*)frcFromTV:(UITableView*)tableView;
   - (UITableView*)TVFromFRC:(NSFetchedResultsController*)frc;

Listing 12.4 shows updated UITableView data source methods that leverage the new helper methods in the GENERAL section.

Listing 12.4 **CoreDataTVC.m: DATASOURCE: UITableView**

```
#pragma mark - DATASOURCE: UITableView
- (NSInteger)tableView:(UITableView *)tableView
 numberOfRowsInSection:(NSInteger)section {
if (debug==1) {
    NSLog(@"Running %@ '%@'", self.class, NSStringFromSelector(_cmd));
}
    return [[[[self frcFromTV:tableView]sections]
                                    objectAtIndex:section] numberOfObjects];
}
- (NSInteger)numberOfSectionsInTableView:(UITableView *)tableView {
if (debug==1) {
    NSLog(@"Running %@ '%@'", self.class, NSStringFromSelector(_cmd));
}
    return [[[self frcFromTV:tableView] sections] count];
}
- (NSInteger)tableView:(UITableView *)tableView
sectionForSectionIndexTitle:(NSString *)title
```

```
                       atIndex:(NSInteger)index {
if (debug==1) {
    NSLog(@"Running %@ '%@'", self.class, NSStringFromSelector(_cmd));
}
    return [[self frcFromTV:tableView]
                       sectionForSectionIndexTitle:title atIndex:index];
}
- (NSString *)tableView:(UITableView *)tableView
titleForHeaderInSection:(NSInteger)section {
if (debug==1) {
    NSLog(@"Running %@ '%@'", self.class, NSStringFromSelector(_cmd));
}
    return [[[[self frcFromTV:tableView] sections] objectAtIndex:section] name];
}
- (NSArray *)sectionIndexTitlesForTableView:(UITableView *)tableView {
if (debug==1) {
    NSLog(@"Running %@ '%@'", self.class, NSStringFromSelector(_cmd));
}
    return [[self frcFromTV:tableView] sectionIndexTitles];
}
```

Update Grocery Dude as follows to add support for the `searchFRC`:

1. Replace the entire DATASOURCE: UITableView section of `CoreDataTVC.m` with the code from Listing 12.4 (Tip: With the cursor inside `CoreDataTVC.m`, click **Editor** > **Code Folding** > **Fold Methods & Functions** to get a better view of class sections).

Search results will be displayed in a table view that is a property of `searchDC`. This property will be accessed via `searchDC.searchResultsTableView`. For it to be populated with search results, the fetched results controller delegate methods of `CoreDataTVC.m` need to be updated. The helper methods from the GENERAL section will be leveraged again. The code involved is shown in Listing 12.5.

Listing 12.5   `CoreDataTVC.m:` `DELEGATE: NSFetchedResultsController`

```
#pragma mark - DELEGATE: NSFetchedResultsController
- (void)controllerWillChangeContent:(NSFetchedResultsController *)controller {
if (debug==1) {
    NSLog(@"Running %@ '%@'", self.class, NSStringFromSelector(_cmd));
}
    [[self TVFromFRC:controller] beginUpdates];
}
- (void)controllerDidChangeContent:(NSFetchedResultsController *)controller {
if (debug==1) {
    NSLog(@"Running %@ '%@'", self.class, NSStringFromSelector(_cmd));
}
```

```objc
        [[self TVFromFRC:controller] endUpdates];
}
- (void)controller:(NSFetchedResultsController *)controller
   didChangeSection:(id <NSFetchedResultsSectionInfo>)sectionInfo
            atIndex:(NSUInteger)sectionIndex
      forChangeType:(NSFetchedResultsChangeType)type {
if (debug==1) {
    NSLog(@"Running %@ '%@'", self.class, NSStringFromSelector(_cmd));
}
    switch(type) {
        case NSFetchedResultsChangeInsert:
            [[self TVFromFRC:controller]
                insertSections:[NSIndexSet indexSetWithIndex:sectionIndex]
              withRowAnimation:UITableViewRowAnimationFade];
            break;

        case NSFetchedResultsChangeDelete:
            [[self TVFromFRC:controller]
              deleteSections:[NSIndexSet indexSetWithIndex:sectionIndex]
            withRowAnimation:UITableViewRowAnimationFade];
            break;
    }
}
- (void)controller:(NSFetchedResultsController *)controller
    didChangeObject:(id)anObject
        atIndexPath:(NSIndexPath *)indexPath
      forChangeType:(NSFetchedResultsChangeType)type
       newIndexPath:(NSIndexPath *)newIndexPath {
if (debug==1) {
    NSLog(@"Running %@ '%@'", self.class, NSStringFromSelector(_cmd));
}

    switch(type) {

        case NSFetchedResultsChangeInsert:
            [[self TVFromFRC:controller]
                    insertRowsAtIndexPaths:[NSArray arrayWithObject:newIndexPath]
                        withRowAnimation:UITableViewRowAnimationAutomatic];
            break;

        case NSFetchedResultsChangeDelete:
            [[self TVFromFRC:controller]
                    deleteRowsAtIndexPaths:[NSArray arrayWithObject:indexPath]
                        withRowAnimation:UITableViewRowAnimationAutomatic];
            break;

        case NSFetchedResultsChangeUpdate:
```

```
            if (!newIndexPath) {
                [[self TVFromFRC:controller]
                        reloadRowsAtIndexPaths:[NSArray arrayWithObject:indexPath]
                            withRowAnimation:UITableViewRowAnimationNone];
            }
            else {
                [[self TVFromFRC:controller]
                        deleteRowsAtIndexPaths:[NSArray arrayWithObject:indexPath]
                            withRowAnimation:UITableViewRowAnimationNone];
                [[self TVFromFRC:controller]
                        insertRowsAtIndexPaths:[NSArray arrayWithObject:newIndexPath]
                            withRowAnimation:UITableViewRowAnimationNone];
            }
            break;

        case NSFetchedResultsChangeMove:
            [[self TVFromFRC:controller]
                    deleteRowsAtIndexPaths:[NSArray arrayWithObject:indexPath]
                        withRowAnimation:UITableViewRowAnimationAutomatic];
            [[self TVFromFRC:controller]
                    insertRowsAtIndexPaths:[NSArray arrayWithObject:newIndexPath]
                        withRowAnimation:UITableViewRowAnimationAutomatic];
            break;
    }
}
```

Update Grocery Dude as follows to add support for the table view in `searchDC`:

1. Replace the `DELEGATE: NSFetchedResultsController` section of `CoreDataTVC.m` with the code from Listing 12.5.

The next step is to add a `UISearchDisplayController` delegate method to `CoreDataTVC.m`. This method will set the search fetched results controller and delegate to `nil` when the search ends. The code involved is shown in Listing 12.6.

Listing 12.6   **CoreDataTVC.m: DELEGATE: UISearchDisplayController**

```
#pragma mark - DELEGATE: UISearchDisplayController
- (void)searchDisplayControllerDidEndSearch:(UISearchDisplayController *)controller {
if (debug==1) {
    NSLog(@"Running %@ '%@'", self.class, NSStringFromSelector(_cmd));
}
    self.searchFRC.delegate = nil;
    self.searchFRC = nil;
}
```

Update Grocery Dude as follows to implement the `searchDisplayControllerDidEndSearch` method:

1. Add the code from Listing 12.6 to the bottom of `CoreDataTVC.m` before `@end`.

The next step is to update `CoreDataTVC` to enable it to reload the `searchFRC` each time the search text changes. A new method will be implemented that takes a predicate and uses it to fetch objects of a given entity in a given context. Sorting and sectioning information is also passed so the search results can be arranged appropriately. Listing 12.7 shows this new method header.

Listing 12.7 **CoreDataTVC.h: reloadSearchFRCForPredicate**

```
- (void)reloadSearchFRCForPredicate:(NSPredicate*)predicate
                         withEntity:(NSString*)entity
                          inContext:(NSManagedObjectContext*)context
                withSortDescriptors:(NSArray*)sortDescriptors
             withSectionNameKeyPath:(NSString*)sectionNameKeyPath;
```

Update Grocery Dude as follows to add the `reloadSearchFRCForPredicate` method header:

1. Add the code from Listing 12.7 to the bottom of `CoreDataTVC.h` before `@end`.

The implementation of the `reloadSearchFRCForPredicate` method should contain code that is quite familiar by now. All this method does is create a fetch request using the given variables and performs a fetch. The code involved is shown in Listing 12.8.

Listing 12.8 **CoreDataTVC.m: reloadSearchFRCForPredicate**

```
#pragma mark - SEARCH
- (void)reloadSearchFRCForPredicate:(NSPredicate*)predicate
                         withEntity:(NSString*)entity
                          inContext:(NSManagedObjectContext*)context
                withSortDescriptors:(NSArray*)sortDescriptors
             withSectionNameKeyPath:(NSString*)sectionNameKeyPath {
if (debug==1) {
    NSLog(@"Running %@ '%@'", self.class, NSStringFromSelector(_cmd));
}
    NSFetchRequest *request = [[NSFetchRequest alloc] initWithEntityName:entity];
    request.sortDescriptors = sortDescriptors;
    request.predicate = predicate;
    request.fetchBatchSize = 15;
```

```
    self.searchFRC =
    [[NSFetchedResultsController alloc] initWithFetchRequest:request
                                        managedObjectContext:context
                                         sectionNameKeyPath:sectionNameKeyPath
                                                  cacheName:nil];
    self.searchFRC.delegate = self;

    [self.searchFRC.managedObjectContext performBlockAndWait:^{
        NSError *error;
        if (![self.searchFRC performFetch:&error]) {
            NSLog(@"SEARCH FETCH ERROR: %@", error);
        }
    }];
}
```

Update Grocery Dude as follows to implement the `reloadSearchFRCForPredicate` method:

1. Add the code from Listing 12.8 to the bottom of `CoreDataTVC.m` before `@end`.

The final addition to `CoreDataTVC` is a new method called `configureSearch`, which will be used by its subclasses to enable search. This new method will programmatically add a `UISearchBar` to the header of the respective table view. In addition, appropriate search bar delegate and data source information will be configured. Listing 12.9 shows the code involved.

Listing 12.9   **CoreDataTVC.m: configureSearch**

```
- (void)configureSearch {
if (debug==1) {
    NSLog(@"Running %@ '%@'", self.class, NSStringFromSelector(_cmd));
}
    UISearchBar *searchBar =
    [[UISearchBar alloc] initWithFrame:
                         CGRectMake(0, 0, self.tableView.frame.size.width, 44.0)];
    searchBar.autocorrectionType = UITextAutocorrectionTypeNo;
    self.tableView.tableHeaderView = searchBar;

    self.searchDC =
    [[UISearchDisplayController alloc] initWithSearchBar:searchBar
                                     contentsController:self];
    self.searchDC.delegate = self;
    self.searchDC.searchResultsDataSource = self;
    self.searchDC.searchResultsDelegate = self;
}
```

Update Grocery Dude as follows to implement the `configureSearch` method:

1. Add the code from Listing 12.9 to the bottom of the SEARCH section of `CoreDataTVC.m` before `@end`.

2. Add the following code to the bottom of `CoreDataTVC.h` before `@end`:

    `- (void) configureSearch;`

The fundamental code is now in place to enable `CoreDataTVC` subclasses to implement search functionality.

Updating `PrepareTVC`

Being a `CoreDataTVC` subclass, most of the legwork in configuring `PrepareTVC` for search has already been done. The remaining configuration will be specific to the data the table view displays. A `UISearchDisplayController` delegate method will also be implemented in `PrepareTVC`. This method will be called every time the user types text into the search bar. Provided it has a length greater than zero, a predicate will be created from the given search string. This predicate will be given to the `reloadSearchFRCForPredicate` method so it can reload `searchFRC`. The section name key path and sort descriptors provided should match those used to populate the `PrepareTVC`. Listing 12.10 shows the code involved.

Listing 12.10   **PrepareTVC.m: SEARCH**

```
#pragma mark - SEARCH
- (BOOL)searchDisplayController:(UISearchDisplayController *)controller
shouldReloadTableForSearchString:(NSString *)searchString {
if (debug==1) {
    NSLog(@"Running %@ '%@'", self.class, NSStringFromSelector(_cmd));
}
    if (searchString.length > 0) {
        NSLog(@"--> Searching for '%@'", searchString);
        NSPredicate *predicate =
        [NSPredicate predicateWithFormat:@"name CONTAINS[cd] %@", searchString];

        NSArray *sortDescriptors =
        [NSArray arrayWithObjects:
         [NSSortDescriptor sortDescriptorWithKey:@"locationAtHome.storedIn"
                                       ascending:YES],
         [NSSortDescriptor sortDescriptorWithKey:@"name"
                                       ascending:YES], nil];

        CoreDataHelper *cdh =
        [(AppDelegate *)[[UIApplication sharedApplication] delegate] cdh];
```

```
            [self reloadSearchFRCForPredicate:predicate
                              withEntity:@"Item"
                               inContext:cdh.context
                       withSortDescriptors:sortDescriptors
                     withSectionNameKeyPath:@"locationAtHome.storedIn"];
        } else {
            return NO;
        }
        return YES;
    }
```

Update Grocery Dude as follows to configure search in `PrepareTVC`:

1. Add the code from Listing 12.10 to the bottom of `PrepareTVC.m` before `@end`.

2. Add `[self configureSearch];` to the bottom of the `viewDidLoad` method of `PrepareTVC.m`.

The predicates configured in `shouldReloadTableForSearchString` are the heart of search for a table view. This predicate configuration is where you will make the most changes when adapting search to your own applications. Here are some key pointers to keep in mind when configuring search:

- When using a compound predicate (two or more predicates together), put the predicate that filters out the most results first. The order in which the predicates are specified can have a big difference on query execution time.

- When using a compound predicate, put the predicate that filters out dates or numbers ahead of predicates filtering text. This is secondary to the previous point.

- When working with a large data set with thousands of rows, consider adding a pre-processed normalized string attribute for the entity being searched. A normalized string would be completely lowercase and contain no characters like "á." This allows you to avoid the need for a case- and diacritic-insensitive predicate, which will speed up the search results. Case and diacritic insensitivity is specified in a predicate using `[cd]`.

If you ran the application now and tried to search for items on the Prepare tab, it would crash because the `cellForRowAtIndexPath` is not configured to support the `searchFRC`. An updated method is shown in Listing 12.11. Updates are in bold.

Listing 12.11 `PrepareTVC.m: cellForRowAtIndexPath`

```
- (UITableViewCell*)tableView:(UITableView *)tableView
       cellForRowAtIndexPath:(NSIndexPath *)indexPath {
if (debug==1) {
    NSLog(@"Running %@ '%@'", self.class, NSStringFromSelector(_cmd));
}
    static NSString *cellIdentifier = @"Item Cell";
```

```
UITableViewCell *cell =
[tableView dequeueReusableCellWithIdentifier:cellIdentifier];
if (cell == nil) {
    cell = [[UITableViewCell alloc] initWithStyle:UITableViewCellStyleValue1
                                  reuseIdentifier:cellIdentifier];
}
cell.accessoryType = UITableViewCellAccessoryDetailButton;
Item *item = [[self frcFromTV:tableView] objectAtIndexPath:indexPath];

NSMutableString *title = [NSMutableString stringWithFormat:@"%@%@ %@",
                               item.quantity, item.unit.name, item.name];
[title replaceOccurrencesOfString:@"(null)"
                       withString:@""
                          options:0
                            range:NSMakeRange(0, [title length])];
cell.textLabel.text = title;

// make selected items orange
if ([item.listed boolValue]) {
    [cell.textLabel setFont:[UIFont fontWithName:@"Helvetica Neue" size:18]];
    [cell.textLabel setTextColor:[UIColor orangeColor]];
}
else {
    [cell.textLabel setFont:[UIFont fontWithName:@"Helvetica Neue" size:16]];
    [cell.textLabel setTextColor:[UIColor grayColor]];
}
cell.imageView.image = [UIImage imageWithData:item.thumbnail];
return cell;
}
```

The cellForRowAtIndexPath method has been updated to use dequeueReusableCellWith-Identifier instead of dequeueReusableCellWithIdentifier:forIndexPath because passing along the indexPath to the search results table view causes a crash. In addition, the item that's loaded in the cell will now be dependent on what table view this method is servicing.

Update Grocery Dude as follows to add searchFRC support to cellForRowAtIndexPath:

1. Replace the cellForRowAtIndexPath method of PrepareTVC.m with the code from Listing 12.11.

Delete and rerun the application, and then search for "baby." The expected result is shown in Figure 12.1.

Search is functioning yet the commitEditingStyle, didSelectRowAtIndexPath, and accessoryButtonTappedForRowWithIndexPath methods of PrepareTVC all need updating to support the searchFRC. An updated commitEditingStyle method is shown in Listing 12.12.

Figure 12.1   Search

Listing 12.12   PrepareTVC.m: commitEditingStyle

```
- (void)tableView:(UITableView *)tableView
commitEditingStyle:(UITableViewCellEditingStyle)editingStyle
 forRowAtIndexPath:(NSIndexPath *)indexPath {
if (debug==1) {
    NSLog(@"Running %@ '%@'", self.class, NSStringFromSelector(_cmd));
}
    if (editingStyle == UITableViewCellEditingStyleDelete) {

        NSFetchedResultsController *frc = [self frcFromTV:tableView];
        Item *deleteTarget = [frc objectAtIndexPath:indexPath];
        [frc.managedObjectContext deleteObject:deleteTarget];
        [tableView reloadRowsAtIndexPaths:[NSArray arrayWithObject:indexPath]
                    withRowAnimation:UITableViewRowAnimationFade];
    }
    CoreDataHelper *cdh =
    [(AppDelegate *)[[UIApplication sharedApplication] delegate] cdh];
    [cdh backgroundSaveContext];
}
```

Update Grocery Dude as follows to add further `searchFRC` support:

1. Replace the `commitEditingStyle` method of `PrepareTVC.m` with the code from Listing 12.12.

An updated `didSelectRowAtIndexPath` method is shown in Listing 12.13.

Listing 12.13 **PrepareTVC.m: `didSelectRowAtIndexPath`**

```
- (void)tableView:(UITableView *)tableView
didSelectRowAtIndexPath:(NSIndexPath *)indexPath  {
if (debug==1) {
    NSLog(@"Running %@ '%@'", self.class, NSStringFromSelector(_cmd));
}
    NSFetchedResultsController *frc = [self frcFromTV:tableView];
    NSManagedObjectID *itemid = [[frc objectAtIndexPath:indexPath] objectID];
    Item *item =
    (Item*)[frc.managedObjectContext existingObjectWithID:itemid error:nil];
    if ([item.listed boolValue]) {
        item.listed = [NSNumber numberWithBool:NO];
    }
    else {
        item.listed = [NSNumber numberWithBool:YES];
        item.collected = [NSNumber numberWithBool:NO];
    }
    CoreDataHelper *cdh =
    [(AppDelegate *)[[UIApplication sharedApplication] delegate] cdh];
    [cdh backgroundSaveContext];
}
```

Update Grocery Dude as follows to add further `searchFRC` support:

1. Replace the `didSelectRowAtIndexPath` method of `PrepareTVC.m` with the code from Listing 12.13.

An updated `accessoryButtonTappedForRowWithIndexPath` method is shown in Listing 12.14.

Listing 12.14 **PrepareTVC.m: `accessoryButtonTappedForRowWithIndexPath`**

```
- (void)tableView:(UITableView *)tableView
accessoryButtonTappedForRowWithIndexPath:(NSIndexPath *)indexPath {
if (debug==1) {
    NSLog(@"Running %@ '%@'", self.class, NSStringFromSelector(_cmd));
}
    ItemVC *itemVC =
    [self.storyboard instantiateViewControllerWithIdentifier:@"ItemVC"];
```

```
itemVC.selectedItemID =
[[[self frcFromTV:tableView] objectAtIndexPath:indexPath] objectID];
[self.navigationController pushViewController:itemVC animated:YES];
}
```

Update Grocery Dude as follows to add further `searchFRC` support:

1. Replace the `accessoryButtonTappedForRowWithIndexPath` method of `PrepareTVC.m`
    with the code from Listing 12.14.

Summary

You've now been shown how to add search to an application in such a way that it will be easy
to propagate it to any table view with ease. As a part of implementing search, ternary operators
were introduced as a technique for handling multiple table views and fetched result controllers
without bloating the code. Take care when you implement search in your own applications to
understand the expected size of the data sets where search will be required. When it is expected
that a large data set will be searched, consider adding special search attributes to your entities
with pre-processed normalized strings. This will ensure search is seamless and responsive for
your users. If you have advanced requirements for search, you may wish to investigate Apple's
Search Kit framework.

Exercises

Why not build on what you've learned by experimenting?

1. Alter the search predicate used in the `shouldReloadTableForSearchString` method
    of `PrepareTVC` with the following options. Search for the letter "j" as you compare the
    query execution times and search results between the different predicates:

    ```
    [NSPredicate predicateWithFormat:
    @"name beginswith[cd] %@ OR name endswith[cd]%@"
    , searchString, searchString];

    [NSPredicate predicateWithFormat:@"name contains %@", searchString];

    [NSPredicate predicateWithFormat:@"name like[cd] %@", [[[NSString
    stringWithFormat:@"*"] stringByAppendingString:searchString]
    stringByAppendingString:@"*"]];
    ```

2. Update `ShopTVC` to implement search using the same approach used to add search
    to `PrepareTVC`. Don't forget to update both the key path and sort descriptor to
    `locationAtShop.aisle` when adding the `shouldReloadTableForSearchString`

method to `ShopTVC.m`. To prevent crashes, you'll also need to update the `cellForRowAtIndexPath` method in the same way the same method in `PrepareTVC.m` has been updated.

3. Modify the search predicate in `ShopTVC.m` so that only listed items are searched.

Once you've completed the exercises, disable SQL debug mode. Also, disable debug in every class except `CoreDataHelper.m` and `AppDelegate.m`. To disable debug, search for `#define debug 1` and replace it with `#define debug 0`.

The code to enable search in `ShopTVC` is in the sample project and is commented out for reference.

13

Back Up and Restore
with Dropbox

Information is not knowledge.

Albert Einstein

In Chapter 12, "Search," the search functionality was added to Grocery Dude. The feature set will now be extended to include a data backup and restore capability. This capability will be achieved by integrating with Dropbox, which is a free web-service providing limited cloud-based storage. The Dropbox Sync API for iOS (www.dropbox.com/developers/sync) will be leveraged to provide a device-local Dropbox file system. Anything copied to this file system will be automatically synchronized with the user's Dropbox account. If Grocery Dude users don't have a Dropbox account, they will need to create one. This chapter will demonstrate the entire process of creating and restoring backup ZIP files, along with the transfer of those files to and from Dropbox. The restore process will include steps to reload the persistent store once a restore has been completed.

The intent of this chapter should not be confused with database synchronization. Rather, this chapter will demonstrate how to back up and restore a Core Data persistent store. If you instead need to synchronize a persistent store between a single user's iOS devices, the upcoming iCloud chapters are more appropriate. If you need to synchronize a persistent store between devices of multiple users, Chapter 16, "Web Service Integration," is more appropriate.

To back up Core Data, everything in the `applicationStoresDirectory` *needs to be preserved. When Grocery Dude launches, you can see in the console log that this is where* `Grocery-Dude.sqlite` *is located. When backing up a persistent store file, it is important to be aware that there are other critical files alongside it, including some hidden ones. These files need to be preserved in addition to the SQLite file. This is due to the WAL journaling mode and the **Allows External Storage** entity attribute setting. In addition, it may be possible that other stores will be added in the future; therefore, backing up the entire Stores directory is a good catchall for future enhancements.*

When a backup is taken, a ZIP file containing a copy of the entire Stores directory will be created. Creating a ZIP file is a great way to store a backup because it takes up less space than the original files and makes them more portable. Once created, the ZIP file will be moved to the local Dropbox cache, which automatically synchronizes with the Dropbox web service. Figure 13.1 shows an overview of this process.

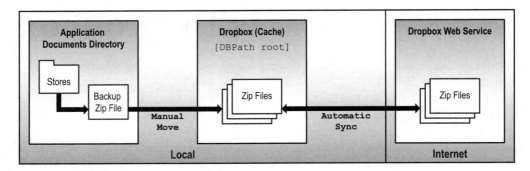

Figure 13.1   Data backup with Dropbox

Dropbox Integration

When an application is integrated with Dropbox, a local cache of the linked user's Dropbox file system will be accessible. Dropbox-integrated applications using the **Sync API** can be constrained to their own subfolder within the Dropbox Apps directory. For example, `Apps/Grocery Dude/` will be the root folder visible to Grocery Dude. Everything within this cached folder will be synchronized to the Dropbox web service automatically by the Dropbox framework. If you don't already have a Dropbox account, you'll need to create one at www.dropbox.com.

To integrate an application with Dropbox, you'll need to configure a new application on the Dropbox portal. The application name needs to be unique, and the name "Grocery Dude" is already taken. You'll need to use something along the lines of "Grocery Dude by *Your Name*" to ensure your own application is unique.

Create a new Dropbox API app as follows:

1. Access https://www.dropbox.com/developers/apps using your Dropbox account.

2. Create a new **Dropbox API app** with the **Files and datastores** setting and access only to files it creates (*also known as App Folder permission*).

3. Set **App name** to "Grocery Dude by *Your Name*," or something else unique.

The Dropbox website layout is subject to change in the future, so you may need to refer to their own tutorials on creating a new Sync API app. Generally, however, the expected result is shown in Figure 13.2.

Grocery Dude by Tim Roadley

Settings	Details

Status	Development	Apply for production
Development users	Only you	Enable additional users
Permission type	App folder	
App folder name	Grocery Dude by Tim Roadley	Change

Figure 13.2   Data backup with Dropbox

The Dropbox API app page should also show an **app key** and **app secret**. Write these both down because you'll need to substitute them into code shortly. For demonstration purposes, APP_KEY and APP_SECRET will be used in the sample code, yet should be replaced by your own key and secret.

> **Note**
>
> To continue building the sample application, you'll need to have added the previous chapter's code to Grocery Dude. Alternatively, you may download, unzip, and use the project up to this point from http://www.timroadley.com/LearningCoreData/GroceryDude-AfterChapter12.zip. Any time you start using an Xcode project from a ZIP file, it's good practice to click **Product > Clean**. This practice ensures there's no residual cache from previous projects using the same name.

Supporting Frameworks

To add Dropbox support to Grocery Dude, the first thing you'll need to do is download the Dropbox Sync API iOS SDK. At the time of writing the latest version is 1.1.3, and unfortunately it doesn't yet support the new iOS 64-bit architecture. The downloadable sample project will be updated once a new supporting release is available. In addition to the SDK, Grocery Dude will need to link to a number of supporting frameworks.

Update Grocery Dude as follows to add the required frameworks to support Dropbox:

1. Download and extract the latest **Sync API iOS SDK** from the Dropbox website (http://www.dropbox.com/developers/sync). At the time of writing, v1.1.3 was located at **Sync API > Install SDK > iOS**.

2. Drag the downloaded **Dropbox.framework** directory into the **Frameworks** folder of Grocery Dude, ensuring that "**Copy items into destination group's folder**" and the Grocery Dude target is ticked before clicking **Finish**.

3. Select the **Grocery Dude** target and scroll down to the **Linked Frameworks and Libraries** section of the **General** tab, as shown in Figure 13.3.

4. Add the **libc++.dylib**, **CFNetwork**, **Security**, **SystemConfiguration**, and **QuartzCore** frameworks, as shown in Figure 13.3.

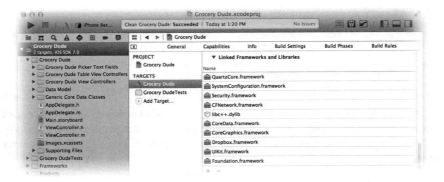

Figure 13.3   Additional frameworks required to support Dropbox

Linking to Dropbox

Integrating Grocery Dude with Dropbox requires a new `application:openURL` method in the `AppDelegate` and a `didFinishLaunchingWithOptions` update. This boilerplate code was provided in the Dropbox Sync API for iOS tutorial on the Dropbox website. Listing 13.1 shows the code involved.

Listing 13.1   **AppDelegate.m**

```
#pragma mark - DROPBOX
- (BOOL)application:(UIApplication *)app openURL:(NSURL *)url
  sourceApplication:(NSString *)source annotation:(id)annotation {

    DBAccount *account = [[DBAccountManager sharedManager] handleOpenURL:url];
    if (account) {
```

```objc
        DBFilesystem *filesystem = [[DBFilesystem alloc] initWithAccount:account];
        [DBFilesystem setSharedFilesystem:filesystem];
        NSLog(@"Linked to Dropbox!");
        return YES;
    }
    return NO;
}

- (BOOL)application:(UIApplication *)application
didFinishLaunchingWithOptions:(NSDictionary *)launchOptions {
if (debug==1) {
    NSLog(@"Running %@ '%@'", self.class, NSStringFromSelector(_cmd));
}

    DBAccountManager* accountMgr =
    [[DBAccountManager alloc] initWithAppKey:@"APP_KEY" secret:@"APP_SECRET"];
    [DBAccountManager setSharedManager:accountMgr];
    DBAccount *account = accountMgr.linkedAccount;
    if (account) {
        DBFilesystem *filesystem = [[DBFilesystem alloc] initWithAccount:account];
        [DBFilesystem setSharedFilesystem:filesystem];
    }
    return YES;
}
```

Update Grocery Dude as follows to enable Dropbox integration:

1. Add `#import <Dropbox/Dropbox.h>` to the top of `AppDelegate.m`.

2. Replace the existing `didFinishLaunchingWithOptions` method of `AppDelegate.m` with the code from Listing 13.1, including the new `application:openURL` method.

3. Update `APP_KEY` and `APP_SECRET` in `didFinishLaunchingWithOptions` with the key and secret you noted earlier.

The next step is to update Grocery Dude's information property list to register for a URL scheme, which is required for authentication to work. The URL scheme will be your `APP_KEY` prefixed with `db-`, as shown in Listing 13.2.

Listing 13.2 **Grocery Dude-Info.plist**

```xml
<key>CFBundleURLTypes</key>
<array>
    <dict>
        <key>CFBundleURLSchemes</key>
        <array>
            <string>db-APP_KEY</string>
```

```
        </array>
    </dict>
</array>
```

Update Grocery Dude as follows to register for the URL scheme required for authentication:

1. Right-click **Supporting Files/Grocery Dude-Info.plist** and then select **Open As > Source Code.**

2. Paste the code from Listing 13.2 on the line after the first `<dict>` tag in `Grocery Dude-Info.plist`.

3. Replace `APP_KEY` in `Grocery Dude-Info.plist` with the key you noted earlier, ensuring to leave the `db-` prefix in place.

Introducing `DropboxHelper`

To make it easy for you to add Dropbox support to your own applications, most of the integration code will be put into a class called `DropboxHelper`. This class will have convenience methods used to perform the following:

- Link to and unlink from a Dropbox account
- Manage files between the Dropbox cache and local file system
- Back up and restore from ZIP

The starting point header for `DropboxHelper` is shown in Listing 13.3. It begins with two methods: one used to link and another used to unlink an account. The method that links an account to Dropbox requires that a view controller be given so the user authentication screen can originate from it.

Listing 13.3 **DropboxHelper.h**

```objc
#import <Foundation/Foundation.h>
#import <Dropbox/Dropbox.h>
#import "CoreDataHelper.h"

@interface DropboxHelper : NSObject

#pragma mark - DROPBOX ACCOUNT
+ (void)linkToDropboxWithUI:(UIViewController*)controller;
+ (void)unlinkFromDropbox;
@end
```

Update Grocery Dude as follows to add the `DropboxHelper` class:

1. Select the **Grocery Dude** group.

2. Click **File > New > File...**.

3. Create a new **iOS > Cocoa Touch > Objective-C** class and then click **Next**.

4. Set **Subclass of** to `NSObject` and **Class name** to `DropboxHelper` and then click **Next**.

5. Ensure the Grocery Dude target is ticked and then click **Create** to create the class in the Grocery Dude project directory.

6. Replace all code in `DropboxHelper.h` with the code from Listing 13.3.

You need to be aware of several new Dropbox classes that are available since linking to the Dropbox framework. A description of each class is available from the class reference included with the SDK you've already downloaded. Using Finder, right-click the com.dropbox.Dropbox. docset file and select **Show Package Contents**. Next, open the documentation from Contents/ Resources/Documents/Index.html. You may recognize the classes from the new Dropbox code in `AppDelegate.m`.

The first two Dropbox classes to be used by `DropboxHelper` are `DBAccount` and `DBAccountManager`. The account manager is used to get reference to the linked account. The code to link and unlink an account is shown in Listing 13.4.

Listing 13.4 **DropboxHelper.m**

```
#import "DropboxHelper.h"
@implementation DropboxHelper

#pragma mark - DROPBOX ACCOUNT
+ (void)linkToDropboxWithUI:(UIViewController*)controller {
    DBAccount *account = [[DBAccountManager sharedManager] linkedAccount];
    if (!account.isLinked) {
        NSLog(@"Linking to Dropbox...");
        [[DBAccountManager sharedManager] linkFromController:controller];
    } else {
        NSLog(@"Already linked to Dropbox as %@", account.info.displayName);
    }
}
+ (void)unlinkFromDropbox {
    DBAccount *account = [[DBAccountManager sharedManager] linkedAccount];
    if (account.isLinked) {
        [account unlink];
        NSLog(@"Unlinked from Dropbox");
    }
}
@end
```

Update Grocery Dude as follows to link to Dropbox:

1. Replace all code in `DropboxHelper.m` with the code from Listing 13.4.

Introducing `DropboxTVC`

To create backups and perform restores, a new user interface is required. In addition, the user needs a way to link and unlink from Dropbox in case he or she needs to switch accounts. To support the new interface, a new tab called Backups will be added. This tab will contain a table view used to display a list of backups. This table view will be driven by a new `UITableViewController` subclass called `DropboxTVC`. This class will first be used to demonstrate linking to Dropbox and will then be expanded to provide the backup-and-restore capability.

The starting point header for `DropboxTVC` is shown in Listing 13.5. It begins with two properties, which will be set as the view loads. The `contents` property will store an array of `DBFileInfo` objects representing the contents of the Dropbox cache. This array will drive what's displayed in the table view. Another property called `loading` will be used to indicate that the table view contents are in the process of loading, to prevent an unnecessary reload of contents.

Listing 13.5 **`DropboxTVC.h`**

```
#import <UIKit/UIKit.h>
#import "AppDelegate.h"
#import "CoreDataHelper.h"
#import "DropboxHelper.h"

@interface DropboxTVC : UITableViewController
@property (strong, nonatomic) NSMutableArray *contents;
@property (assign, nonatomic) BOOL loading;
@end
```

Update Grocery Dude as follows to add the `DropboxTVC` class:

1. Select the **Grocery Dude Table View Controllers** group.

2. Click **File > New > File...**.

3. Create a new **iOS > Cocoa Touch > Objective-C** class and then click **Next**.

4. Set **Subclass of** to `UITableViewController` and **Class name** to `DropboxTVC` and then click **Next**.

5. Ensure the Grocery Dude target is ticked and then click **Create** to create the class in the Grocery Dude project directory.

6. Replace all code in `DropboxTVC.h` with the code from Listing 13.5.

To demonstrate linking to Dropbox, the `DropboxTVC` implementation will begin with just one method. The `viewDidLoad` method will set each of the previously mentioned properties and proceed to link with Dropbox. Listing 13.6 shows the code involved.

Listing 13.6 **DropboxTVC.m**

```
#import "DropboxTVC.h"
@implementation DropboxTVC

#pragma mark - VIEW
- (void)viewDidLoad {
    _contents = [NSMutableArray new];
    _loading = NO;
    DBAccount *account = [[DBAccountManager sharedManager] linkedAccount];
    if (!account.isLinked) {
        [DropboxHelper linkToDropboxWithUI:self];
    }
    [super viewDidLoad];
}
@end
```

Update Grocery Dude as follows to implement `DropboxTVC`:

1. Replace all code in `DropboxTVC.m` with the code from Listing 13.6.

The next step is to add the interface elements that will leverage the `DropboxTVC` class. This involves configuring a new Backups tab and `DropboxTVC` table view controller. The Backups tab will need an icon, as will the backup files that will be listed in the Dropbox table view.

Update Grocery Dude as follows to configure the Dropbox tab and table view:

1. Select **Images.xcassets**.

2. Download and extract the images from the following URL and then drag them to the inside of the **Images.xcassets** asset catalog: http://www.timroadley.com/ LearningCoreData/Icons_DataBackup.zip.

3. Select **Main.storyboard**.

4. Drag a new **Table View Controller** onto the storyboard and then align it beneath the existing **Navigation Controller – Shop**.

5. Ensure the new **Table View Controller** is selected and click **Editor > Embed In > Navigation Controller**.

6. Hold down **Control** and drag a line from the center of the **Tab Bar Controller** to the new **Navigation Controller** and then select **Relationship Segue > view controllers** from the popup menu.

7. Set the **Bar Item Title** of the new Navigation Controller to **Backups** using **Attributes Inspector (Option+⌘+4)**.

8. Set the **Bar Item Image** of the new Navigation Controller to **data**. The expected result is shown in Figure 13.4.

Figure 13.4   The new Backups tab

9. Set the **Navigation Item Title** of the new Table View Controller to **Backups**.

10. Set the **Identifier** of the Backups Table View Controller **Prototype Cell** to `Backup Cell` using **Attributes Inspector (Option+⌘+4)**.

11. Set the **Custom Class** of the Backups Table View Controller to `DropboxTVC` using **Identity Inspector (Option+⌘+3)**. Take care not to accidentally set the custom class of the `UITableViewCell`.

12. Delete the application from your device or the iOS Simulator so the persistent store has default data; then click **Product > Clean** in Xcode.

13. Run the application and select the **Backups** tab. You should be presented with a Dropbox authentication view such as the one shown in Figure 13.5.

Figure 13.5   Dropbox link

Once you've entered your Dropbox account credentials, the text "Linked to Dropbox!" should appear in the console log. If you get an error in the console log regarding the URL scheme, ensure the application key and secret have been set correctly.

Preparing `CoreDataHelper`

Before `DropboxHelper` can be further developed to facilitate backup and restore, `CoreDataHelper` needs to be enhanced to support reloading the `store`. When a restore occurs, the entire store's path will be replaced. When this happens, all contexts should be cleared and the old store files and underlying path removed. The Core Data stack should then be set up again as per usual with `setupCoreData`. New methods will now be added to `CoreDataHelper` to assist with this. The code involved is shown in Listing 13.7.

Listing 13.7   **CoreDataHelper.m: CORE DATA RESET**

```
#pragma mark - CORE DATA RESET
- (void)resetContext:(NSManagedObjectContext*)moc {
    [moc performBlockAndWait:^{
        [moc reset];
    }];
}
```

```
- (BOOL)reloadStore {
    BOOL success = NO;
    NSError *error = nil;
    if (![_coordinator removePersistentStore:_store error:&error]) {
        NSLog(@"Unable to remove persistent store : %@", error);
    }
    [self resetContext:_sourceContext];
    [self resetContext:_importContext];
    [self resetContext:_context];
    [self resetContext:_parentContext];
    _store = nil;
    [self setupCoreData];
    [self somethingChanged];
    if (_store) {success = YES;}
    return success;
}
```

Update Grocery Dude as follows to prepare `CoreDataHelper`:

1. Add the code from Listing 13.7 to the bottom of `CoreDataHelper.m` before `@end`.

2. Add `- (BOOL)reloadStore;` to the bottom of `CoreDataHelper.h` before `@end`.

Building `DropboxHelper`

Most of the legwork in creating backups and performing restores will involve file management. In particular, support for creating ZIP files and moving them between the local file system and Dropbox will be required. `DropboxHelper` will provide as many of these convenience methods as possible so the functionality can be ported to other applications easily. `DropboxHelper` will need three new sections to support the backup-and-restore capability.

Local File Management

The **LOCAL FILE MANAGEMENT** section will consist of three methods used during the backup-and-restore processes:

- `renameLastPathComponentOfURL` will be used to rename files at the given URL. In reality, a move will be executed to achieve the rename.

- `deleteFileAtURL` will delete the file at the given URL, provided the file exists.

- `createParentFolderForFile` will be used to ensure that the ZIP file extraction target folder exists before extraction occurs.

Listing 13.8 shows the code involved with this new section.

Listing 13.8 **DropboxHelper.m: LOCAL FILE MANAGEMENT**

```
#pragma mark - LOCAL FILE MANAGEMENT
+ (NSURL*)renameLastPathComponentOfURL:(NSURL*)url toName:(NSString*)name {

    NSURL *urlPath = [url URLByDeletingLastPathComponent];
    NSURL *newURL = [urlPath URLByAppendingPathComponent:name];
    NSError *error;
    [[NSFileManager defaultManager] moveItemAtPath:url.path
                                          toPath:newURL.path error:&error];
    if (error) {
        NSLog(@"ERROR renaming (i.e. moving) %@ to %@",
            url.lastPathComponent, newURL.lastPathComponent);
    } else {
        NSLog(@"Renamed %@ to %@", url.lastPathComponent, newURL.lastPathComponent);
    }
    return newURL;
}
+ (BOOL)deleteFileAtURL:(NSURL*)url {

    if ([[NSFileManager defaultManager] fileExistsAtPath:url.path]) {
        NSError *error;
        [[NSFileManager defaultManager] removeItemAtPath:url.path error:&error];
        if (error) {NSLog(@"Error deleting %@", url.lastPathComponent);}
        else {NSLog(@"Deleted '%@'", url.lastPathComponent);return YES;}
    }
    return NO;
}
+ (void)createParentFolderForFile:(NSURL*)url {

    NSURL *parent = [url URLByDeletingLastPathComponent];
    if (![[NSFileManager defaultManager] fileExistsAtPath:parent.path]) {
        NSError *error;
        [[NSFileManager defaultManager] createDirectoryAtURL:parent
                                  withIntermediateDirectories:YES
                                                   attributes:nil
                                                        error:&error];
        if (error) {NSLog(@"Error creating directory: %@", error);}
    }
}
```

Update Grocery Dude as follows to implement this new section:

   1. Copy the code from Listing 13.8 to the bottom of DropboxHelper.m before @end.

Dropbox File Management

The **DROPBOX FILE MANAGEMENT** section will consist of five methods used to manage files within the Dropbox cache:

- **fileExistsAtDropboxPath** will be used to check if a file exists in the Dropbox cache at the specified path.

- **listFilesAtDropboxPath** will be used to list the contents of the given Dropbox path in the console log. It runs on a background thread without fear of threading issues as the only method output is console logging.

- **deleteFileAtDropboxPath** will be used to delete a file at the specified Dropbox path.

- **copyFileAtDropboxPath:toURL** will be used to copy files from Dropbox to the local file system.

- **copyFileAtURL:toDropboxPath** will be used to copy files from the local file system to the Dropbox cache.

Listing 13.9 shows the code involved with this new section.

Listing 13.9 **DropboxHelper.m: DROPBOX FILE MANAGEMENT**

```
#pragma mark - DROPBOX FILE MANAGEMENT
+ (BOOL)fileExistsAtDropboxPath:(DBPath*)dropboxPath {

    DBFile *existingFile =
    [[DBFilesystem sharedFilesystem] openFile:dropboxPath error:nil];
    if (existingFile) {
        [existingFile close];
        return YES;
    }
    return NO;
}
+ (void)listFilesAtDropboxPath:(DBPath*)dropboxPath {

    dispatch_async(dispatch_get_global_queue(DISPATCH_QUEUE_PRIORITY_HIGH, 0), ^{
        NSError *error = nil;
        NSArray *contents =
        [[DBFilesystem sharedFilesystem] listFolder:dropboxPath error:&error];
        if (contents) {
            NSLog(@"****** Dropbox Directory Contents (path /%@)",
                                                dropboxPath.stringValue);
            for (DBFileInfo *info in contents) {
                float fileSize = info.size;
                NSLog(@" %@ (%.2fMB)", info.path, fileSize/1024/1024);
            }
```

```
            NSLog(@"*******************************************");
            if (error) {
                NSLog(@"ERROR listing Dropbox contents for %@ : %@",
                                              dropboxPath.stringValue, error);
            }
        } else {
            NSLog(@"Dropbox path '/%@' is empty", dropboxPath.stringValue);
        }
    });
}
+ (void)deleteFileAtDropboxPath:(DBPath*)dropboxPath {
    [[DBFilesystem sharedFilesystem] deletePath:dropboxPath error:nil];
}
+ (void)copyFileAtDropboxPath:(DBPath*)dropboxPath toURL:(NSURL*)url {

    DBError *openError = nil;
    DBFile *file = [[DBFilesystem sharedFilesystem] openFile:dropboxPath
                                                error:&openError];
    if (openError) {
        NSLog(@"Error opening file '%@': %@", dropboxPath.stringValue, openError);
    }
    DBError *readError = nil;
    NSData *fileData = [file readData:&readError];
    if (readError) {
        NSLog(@"Error reading file '%@': %@", dropboxPath.stringValue, readError);
}
    [self deleteFileAtURL:url];
    [[NSFileManager defaultManager] createFileAtPath:url.path
                                    contents:fileData
                                  attributes:nil];
}
+ (void)copyFileAtURL:(NSURL*)url toDropboxPath:(DBPath*)dropboxPath {

    NSLog(@"Copying %@ to Dropbox Path %@", url, dropboxPath);

    // Create File
    DBError *errorCreating;
    DBFile *file =
    [[DBFilesystem sharedFilesystem] createFile:dropboxPath error:&errorCreating];
    if (!file || errorCreating) {
        NSLog(@"Error creating file in Dropbox: %@", errorCreating);
    }

    // Write File
    DBError *errorWriting;
    if ([file writeContentsOfFile:url.path shouldSteal:NO error:&errorWriting]) {
```

```
            NSLog(@"Successfully copied %@ to Dropbox:%@",
                                url.lastPathComponent, dropboxPath.stringValue);
    } else {
        NSLog(@"Error writing file to Dropbox: %@", errorWriting);
    }
}
```

Update Grocery Dude as follows to implement this new section:

1. Copy the code vfrom Listing 13.9 to the bottom of `DropboxHelper.m` before `@end`.

Backup & Restore

The **BACKUP & RESTORE** section introduces three new methods used to orchestrate a backup or restore process. These methods will leverage those recently implemented.

- **zipFolderAtURL** will be used to create a ZIP file containing the contents of a given URL. If the ZIP file already exists, it will be overwritten. The ZIP compression will be provided by Objective-Zip, which is an Objective-C wrapper for MiniZip. MiniZip enables the creation and extraction of compressed .zip archive files.

- **unzipFileAtURL** will be used to extract the contents of a given ZIP file to the given URL. Objective-Zip will be used for decompression.

- **restoreFromDropboxStoresZip** will be used to restore the Stores folder from the contents of the given ZIP file. Measures will be taken to enable rollback in case the restore fails to leave the Core Data stack in a working state. This method will rely on knowledge of where the application stores directory is located. As such, the `applicationStoresDirectory` method of `CoreDataHelper` will have to be made public.

Listing 13.10 shows the code involved with this new section.

Listing 13.10   `DropboxHelper.m`: BACKUP / RESTORE

```
#pragma mark - BACKUP / RESTORE
+ (NSURL*)zipFolderAtURL:(NSURL*)url withZipfileName:(NSString*)zipFileName {

    NSURL *zipFileURL =
    [[url URLByDeletingLastPathComponent] URLByAppendingPathComponent:zipFileName];

    // Remove existing zip
    [self deleteFileAtURL:zipFileURL];

    // Create new zip
    ZipFile *zipFile =
    [[ZipFile alloc] initWithFileName:zipFileURL.path mode:ZipFileModeCreate];
```

```
    // Enumerate directory structure
    NSFileManager *fileManager = [[NSFileManager alloc] init];
    NSDirectoryEnumerator *directoryEnumerator =
    [fileManager enumeratorAtPath:url.path];

    // Write zip files for each file in the directory structure
    NSString *fileName;
    while (fileName = [directoryEnumerator nextObject]) {
        BOOL directory;
        NSString *filePath = [url.path stringByAppendingPathComponent:fileName];
        [fileManager fileExistsAtPath:filePath isDirectory:&directory];
        if (!directory) {

            // get file attributes
            NSError *error = nil;
            NSDictionary *attributes =
            [[NSFileManager defaultManager]attributesOfItemAtPath:filePath
                                                            error:&error];
            if (error) {
             NSLog(@"Failed to create zip, could not get file attributes. Error: %@",
                                                                         error);
                return nil;
            } else {
                NSDate *fileDate = [attributes objectForKey:NSFileCreationDate];
                ZipWriteStream *stream =
                [zipFile writeFileInZipWithName:fileName
                                       fileDate:fileDate
                              compressionLevel:ZipCompressionLevelBest];
                NSData *data = [NSData dataWithContentsOfFile:filePath];
                [stream writeData:data];
                [stream finishedWriting];
            }
        }
    }
    [zipFile close];

    return zipFileURL;
}
+ (void)unzipFileAtURL:(NSURL*)zipFileURL toURL:(NSURL*)unzipURL {

    @autoreleasepool {
        ZipFile *unzipFile = [[ZipFile alloc] initWithFileName:zipFileURL.path
                                                          mode:ZipFileModeUnzip];
        [unzipFile goToFirstFileInZip];
        for (int i = 0; i < [unzipFile numFilesInZip]; i++) {
            FileInZipInfo *info = [unzipFile getCurrentFileInZipInfo];
            [self createParentFolderForFile:
```

```objc
                                    [unzipURL URLByAppendingPathComponent:info.name]];
            NSLog(@"Unzipping '%@'...", info.name);
            ZipReadStream *read = [unzipFile readCurrentFileInZip];
            NSMutableData *data = [[NSMutableData alloc] initWithLength:info.length];
            [read readDataWithBuffer:data];
            [data writeToFile:[NSString stringWithFormat:@"%@/%@",
                                        unzipURL.path, info.name] atomically:YES];
            [read finishedReading];
            [unzipFile goToNextFileInZip];
        }
        [unzipFile close];
    }
}
+ (void)restoreFromDropboxStoresZip:(NSString*)fileName
              withCoreDataHelper:(CoreDataHelper*)cdh {

    [cdh.context performBlock:^{

        DBPath *zipFileInDropbox = [[DBPath alloc] initWithString:fileName];
        NSURL  *zipFileInSandbox =
        [[[cdh applicationStoresDirectory] URLByDeletingLastPathComponent]
                                    URLByAppendingPathComponent:fileName];
        NSURL  *unzipFolder =
        [[[cdh applicationStoresDirectory] URLByDeletingLastPathComponent]
                                    URLByAppendingPathComponent:@"Stores_New"];
        NSURL *oldBackupURL =
        [[[cdh applicationStoresDirectory] URLByDeletingLastPathComponent]
                                    URLByAppendingPathComponent:@"Stores_Old"];

        [DropboxHelper copyFileAtDropboxPath:zipFileInDropbox
                                        toURL:zipFileInSandbox];
        [DropboxHelper unzipFileAtURL:zipFileInSandbox toURL:unzipFolder];

        if ([[NSFileManager defaultManager] fileExistsAtPath:unzipFolder.path]) {
            [DropboxHelper deleteFileAtURL:oldBackupURL];
            [DropboxHelper renameLastPathComponentOfURL:[cdh applicationStoresDirectory]
                                        toName:@"Stores_Old"];
            [DropboxHelper renameLastPathComponentOfURL:unzipFolder
                                        toName:@"Stores"];
            if ([cdh reloadStore]) {
                [DropboxHelper deleteFileAtURL:oldBackupURL];
                UIAlertView *failAlert = [[UIAlertView alloc]
            initWithTitle:@"Restore Complete!"
                message:@"All data has been restored from the selected backup"
                delegate:nil
```

```
        cancelButtonTitle:nil
    otherButtonTitles:@"Ok", nil];
            [failAlert show];

        } else { // Attempt Recovery
    [DropboxHelper renameLastPathComponentOfURL:[cdh applicationStoresDirectory]
                                    toName:@"Stores_FailedRestore"];
    [DropboxHelper renameLastPathComponentOfURL:oldBackupURL
                                    toName:@"Stores"];
            [DropboxHelper deleteFileAtURL:oldBackupURL];
            if (![cdh reloadStore]) {
                UIAlertView *failAlert = [[UIAlertView alloc]
                    initWithTitle:@"Failed to Restore"
                        message:@"Please try to restore from another backup"
                        delegate:nil
                  cancelButtonTitle:nil
                  otherButtonTitles:@"Close", nil];
                [failAlert show];
            }
        }
    }
  }];
}
```

Update Grocery Dude as follows to implement this new section:

1. Download, extract, and drag the contents of the following ZIP file into the **Grocery Dude** group: www.timroadley.com/LearningCoreData/Objective-Zip.zip. Ensure that **"Copy items into destination group's folder"** and the Grocery Dude target is ticked before clicking **Finish**. This ZIP file contains the most recent version of Objective-Zip at the time of writing, and a header that imports each Objective-Zip class.

2. Add `#import "Objective-Zip.h"` to the top of `DropboxHelper.m`.

3. Add the following code to the bottom of `CoreDataHelper.h` before `@end`:
   ```
   - (NSURL *)applicationStoresDirectory;
   ```

4. Copy the code from Listing 13.10 to the bottom of `DropboxHelper.m` before `@end`.

So that the methods of `DropboxHelper` may be accessed outside the class, they need to be added to its header file. Listing 13.11 shows the code involved.

Listing 13.11   **DropboxHelper.h**

```
#pragma mark - LOCAL FILE MANAGEMENT
+ (NSURL*)renameLastPathComponentOfURL:(NSURL*)url toName:(NSString*)name;
+ (BOOL)deleteFileAtURL:(NSURL*)url;
+ (void)createParentFolderForFile:(NSURL*)url;

#pragma mark - DROPBOX FILE MANAGEMENT
+ (BOOL)fileExistsAtDropboxPath:(DBPath*)dropboxPath;
+ (void)listFilesAtDropboxPath:(DBPath*)dropboxPath;
+ (void)deleteFileAtDropboxPath:(DBPath*)dropboxPath;
+ (void)copyFileAtDropboxPath:(DBPath*)dropboxPath toURL:(NSURL*)url;
+ (void)copyFileAtURL:(NSURL*)url toDropboxPath:(DBPath*)dropboxPath;

#pragma mark - BACKUP / RESTORE
+ (NSURL*)zipFolderAtURL:(NSURL*)url withZipfileName:(NSString*)zipFileName;
+ (void)unzipFileAtURL:(NSURL*)zipFileURL toURL:(NSURL*)unzipURL;
+ (void)restoreFromDropboxStoresZip:(NSString*)fileName
                withCoreDataHelper:(CoreDataHelper*)cdh;
```

Update Grocery Dude as follows to make the new methods visible:

1. Add the code from Listing 13.11 to the bottom of `DropboxHelper.h` before `@end`.

Building `DropboxTVC`

With `DropboxHelper` in place, it's now time to use it to create, display, and restore backups. The `DropboxTVC` class will now be expanded to leverage its functionality. Three new properties and two protocol adoptions will be added to the `DropboxTVC` header:

- To link or unlink from Dropbox, an `options` action-sheet will be used. `DropboxTVC` will also become a `UIActionSheetDelegate` to receive user selections.

- To confirm that a user wants to restore, a `confirmRestore` alert view property will be added. `DropboxTVC` will also become a `UIAlertViewDelegate` to receive user selections from the alert view.

- To store the name of the ZIP file selected for restore, a string property called `selectedZipFileName` will be used.

Listing 13.12 shows the three new properties.

Listing 13.12   **DropboxTVC.h**

```
@property (strong, nonatomic) UIActionSheet *options;
@property (strong, nonatomic) UIAlertView *confirmRestore;
@property (strong, nonatomic) NSString *selectedZipFileName;
```

Update Grocery Dude as follows to add the three new properties and adopt the relevant protocols:

1. Add the properties from Listing 13.12 to the bottom of `DropboxTVC.h` before `@end`.

2. Configure `DropboxTVC.h` to adopt the alert view and action sheet protocols by replacing the `@interface` declaration with the following code:

```
@interface DropboxTVC : UITableViewController
<UIAlertViewDelegate, UIActionSheetDelegate>
```

The contents of the Backups table view driven by `DropboxTVC` will be determined by the contents of the local Dropbox cache. A `contents` array will be used to populate the table view and will need to be updated as the Dropbox cache changes. A new method called `reload` will be used to populate the `contents` array with the Dropbox cache listing. A new function called `sort` will be used to sort the array by modified date. As files are added and removed, the synchronization status will be shown in the navigation item title. A new method called `refreshStatus` will be used to update this information. The status is taken from the value of the `status` property of the shared `DBFilesystem`. Note that there will be no support for folder navigation. As such, folders will be removed from the `contents` array. Listing 13.13 shows the code involved.

Listing 13.13   **`DropboxTVC.m`: DATA**

```
#pragma mark - DATA
NSInteger sort(DBFileInfo *a, DBFileInfo *b, void *ctx) {
    return [[b modifiedTime] compare:[a modifiedTime]];
}
- (void)reload {
    [self refreshStatus];
    if (_loading) return;_loading = YES;
    dispatch_async(dispatch_get_global_queue(DISPATCH_QUEUE_PRIORITY_HIGH, 0), ^() {
        NSArray *actualContents =
        [[DBFilesystem sharedFilesystem] listFolder:[DBPath root] error:nil];
        NSMutableArray *updatedContents =
        [NSMutableArray arrayWithArray:actualContents];

        // Don't list folders
        NSMutableArray *folders = [NSMutableArray new];
        for (DBFileInfo *info in updatedContents) {
            if (info.isFolder) {[folders addObject:info];}
        }
        [updatedContents removeObjectsInArray:folders];

        // Don't list files that don't end with 'Stores.zip'
        NSMutableArray *notValid = [NSMutableArray new];
        for (DBFileInfo *info in updatedContents) {
            if (![[[info path] stringValue] hasSuffix:@"Stores.zip"]) {
```

```
                   NSLog(@"Not listing invalid file: %@", [[info path] stringValue]);
                   [notValid addObject:info];
               }
           }
           [updatedContents removeObjectsInArray:notValid];

           [updatedContents sortUsingFunction:sort context:NULL];
           dispatch_async(dispatch_get_main_queue(), ^() {
               self.contents = updatedContents;
               _loading = NO;
               [self.tableView reloadData];
               [self refreshStatus];
           });
       });
   }
- (void)refreshStatus {
       DBAccount *account = [[DBAccountManager sharedManager] linkedAccount];
       if (!account.isLinked) {
           self.navigationItem.title = @"Unlinked";
       } else if ([[DBFilesystem sharedFilesystem] status] > DBSyncStatusActive) {
           self.navigationItem.title = @"Syncing";
       } else {
           self.navigationItem.title = @"Backups";
       }
   }
```

Update Grocery Dude as follows to implement contents reloading code:

1. Add the code from Listing 13.13 to `DropboxTVC.m` just above the existing `VIEW` section.

The next step is to leverage the `reload` method at the appropriate times. Each time the view appears, the table should be reloaded to match an appropriate representation of the underlying Dropbox contents. In addition, an observer is needed to trigger a reload in case the Dropbox cache changes while the view is visible. To keep the sync status visible to the user, the sync status will be observed and refreshed whenever a change is detected, too. Listing 13.14 shows the code involved.

Listing 13.14   `DropboxTVC.m: VIEW`

```
- (void)viewWillAppear:(BOOL)animated {
       [super viewWillAppear:animated];
   __block DropboxTVC *DropboxTVC = self;
   [[DBFilesystem sharedFilesystem] addObserver:self block:^(){[self reload];}];
   [[DBFilesystem sharedFilesystem] addObserver:self
                       forPathAndChildren:[DBPath root] block:^() {
       [DropboxTVC reload];
```

```
        }];
        [DropboxTVC reload];
}
- (void)viewWillDisappear:(BOOL)animated {
        [super viewWillDisappear:animated];
        [[DBFilesystem sharedFilesystem] removeObserver:self];
}
```

Update Grocery Dude as follows to implement the code to trigger timely reloads:

1. Add the code from Listing 13.14 to the bottom of the existing VIEW section of
   DropboxTVC.m.

Creating Backups

Creating a backup is easy now that `DropboxHelper` is in place. Before a backup is taken, all
contexts should be saved to ensure that the latest data is persisted. The contexts will be saved
in an order appropriate to their hierarchy. In other words, the child contexts will be saved
before their parents to ensure changes are in the parent before the parent is saved. In your own
projects you may wish to introduce non-nil error handling for these saves as opposed to the
approach used in the upcoming code.

The procedure to create a backup involves setting an appropriate backup ZIP filename, creating
the backup ZIP, and then moving it to Dropbox. There will also be a small amount of logic to
deal with existing files. The process will only work if there is an account linked to Dropbox.
Depending on the result of the backup, an appropriate alert view will be shown. Listing 13.15
shows the code involved.

Listing 13.15 **DropboxTVC.m: BACKUP**

```
#pragma mark - BACKUP
- (IBAction)backup:(id)sender {
    [DropboxHelper linkToDropboxWithUI:self];
    DBAccount *account = [[DBAccountManager sharedManager] linkedAccount];
    if (account.isLinked) {
        CoreDataHelper *cdh =
        [(AppDelegate *)[[UIApplication sharedApplication] delegate] cdh];
        [cdh.context performBlock:^{
            // Save all contexts
            [cdh.sourceContext performBlockAndWait:^{[cdh.sourceContext save:nil];}];
            [cdh.importContext performBlockAndWait:^{[cdh.importContext save:nil];}];
            [cdh.context performBlockAndWait:^{[cdh.context save:nil];}];
            [cdh.parentContext performBlockAndWait:^{[cdh.parentContext save:nil];}];
```

```
            NSLog(@"Creating a dated backup of the Stores directory...");
            NSDateFormatter *formatter = [NSDateFormatter new];
            [formatter setDateFormat:@"[yyyy-MMM-dd] hh.mm a"];
            NSString *date = [formatter stringFromDate:[NSDate date]];
            NSString *zipFileName =
            [NSString stringWithFormat:@"%@ Stores.zip", date];
            NSURL *zipFile =
            [DropboxHelper zipFolderAtURL:[cdh applicationStoresDirectory]
                        withZipfileName:zipFileName];

            NSLog(@"Copying the backup zip to Dropbox...");
            DBPath *zipFileInDropbox =
            [[DBPath root] childPath:zipFile.lastPathComponent];
            if ([DropboxHelper fileExistsAtDropboxPath:zipFileInDropbox]) {
                NSLog(@"Removing existing backup with same name...");
                [DropboxHelper deleteFileAtDropboxPath:zipFileInDropbox];
            }
            [DropboxHelper copyFileAtURL:zipFile toDropboxPath:zipFileInDropbox];
            NSLog(@"Deleting the local backup zip...");
            [DropboxHelper deleteFileAtURL:zipFile];
            [DropboxHelper listFilesAtDropboxPath:[DBPath root]];
            [self alertSuccess:YES];
        }];
    } else {
        [self alertSuccess:NO];
    }
}
- (void)alertSuccess:(BOOL)success {
    NSString *title;
    NSString *message;
    if (success) {
        title = [NSString stringWithFormat:@"Success"];
        message = [NSString stringWithFormat:@"A backup has been created. It will
appear in the Apps/Grocery Dude directory of your Dropbox. Consider removing
old backups when you no longer require them"];
    } else {
        title = [NSString stringWithFormat:@"Fail"];
        message = @"You must be logged in to Dropbox to create backups";
    }
    UIAlertView *alert = [[UIAlertView alloc] initWithTitle:title
                                                    message:message
                                                   delegate:nil
                                          cancelButtonTitle:nil
                                          otherButtonTitles:@"Ok", nil];
    [alert show];
}
```

Update Grocery Dude as follows to implement the code to back up and link it to a new button:

1. Add the code from Listing 13.15 to the bottom of DropboxTVC.m before @end.

2. Select **Main.storyboard**.

3. Drag a **Bar Button Item** to the top left of the **Backups Table View Controller.**

4. Set the **Bar Item Title** of the new **Bar Button Item** to **Create** using **Attributes Inspector** (**Option+⌘+4**).

5. Set the **Bar Item Style** of the new **Bar Button Item** to **Done.**

6. Hold **Control** and drag a line from the Create button to the yellow circle at the bottom of the Backups Table View Controller; then select **Sent Actions > backup:.**

Run the application and create a backup by tapping Create on the Backups tab. The console log may warn you that you already have a linked account, and that *thedate_*stores.zip doesn't exist. These messages are normal checks performed as the account is verified and the backup file is created. Figure 13.6 shows the expected result: The table view will remain empty, as it hasn't yet been configured to display anything.

Figure 13.6   Successful backup

Displaying Backups

To display a list of available backups, the `DropboxTVC` needs to be updated with the appropriate `UITableView` data source methods. There will only be one section, and the number of rows will depend on the number of objects in the `contents` array. The table view cell will be configured to show a user-friendly version of the backup filename, without the stores or ZIP file extension. Invalid files, identified as not ending with `Stores.zip`, won't be displayed. For the remaining files, the file size and upload or download progress will be shown where relevant. For convenience, swipe-to-delete will also be added. Listing 13.16 shows the code involved.

Listing 13.16   **DropboxTVC.m: DATASOURCE: UITableView**

```
#pragma mark - DATASOURCE: UITableView
- (NSInteger)numberOfSectionsInTableView:(UITableView *)tableView {
    return 1;
}
- (NSInteger)tableView:(UITableView *)tableView
 numberOfRowsInSection:(NSInteger)section {
    return [_contents count];
}
- (UITableViewCell *)tableView:(UITableView *)tableView
        cellForRowAtIndexPath:(NSIndexPath *)indexPath {
    static NSString *CellIdentifier = @"Backup Cell";
    UITableViewCell *cell =
    [tableView dequeueReusableCellWithIdentifier:CellIdentifier
                                 forIndexPath:indexPath];
    DBFileInfo *info = [_contents objectAtIndex:[indexPath row]];
    NSString *string = info.path.name;
    cell.textLabel.text =
    [string stringByReplacingOccurrencesOfString:@" Stores.zip" withString:@""];
    float fileSize = info.size;

    NSMutableString *subtitle = [NSMutableString new];

    // Show transfer progress
    DBError *openError = nil;
    DBFile *file = [[DBFilesystem sharedFilesystem] openFile:info.path
                                                error:&openError];
    if (!file) {
        NSLog(@"Error opening file '%@': %@", info.path.stringValue, openError);
    }
    int progress = [[file status] progress] * 100;
    if (progress != 100) {
        if ([[file status] state] == DBFileStateDownloading) {
```

```
            [subtitle appendString:
                    [NSString stringWithFormat:@"Downloaded %i%% of ",progress]];
        } else if ([[file status] state] == DBFileStateUploading) {
            [subtitle appendString:
                    [NSString stringWithFormat:@"Uploaded %i%% of ",progress]];
        }
    }

    // Show File Size
    [subtitle appendString:
            [NSString stringWithFormat:@"%.2f Megabytes", fileSize/1024/1024]];
    cell.detailTextLabel.text = subtitle;

    return cell;
}
- (void)tableView:(UITableView *)tableView
commitEditingStyle:(UITableViewCellEditingStyle)editingStyle
 forRowAtIndexPath:(NSIndexPath *)indexPath {
    if (tableView == self.tableView &&
        editingStyle == UITableViewCellEditingStyleDelete) {
        DBFileInfo *deleteTarget = [_contents objectAtIndex:indexPath.row];
        [DropboxHelper deleteFileAtDropboxPath:deleteTarget.path];
        [_contents removeObjectAtIndex:indexPath.row];

        [self.tableView deleteRowsAtIndexPaths:[NSArray arrayWithObject:indexPath]
                            withRowAnimation:UITableViewRowAnimationFade];
    }
}
```

Update Grocery Dude as follows to make backups visible to the user:

1. Add the code from Listing 13.16 to the bottom of DropboxTVC.m before @end.

2. Select **Main.storyboard**.

3. Set the **Style** of the **Backups Table View Prototype Cell** to **Subtitle** using **Attributes Inspector (Option+⌘+4)**.

4. Set the **Image** of the Backups Table View Prototype Cell to **backup**.

Run Grocery Dude again, and you should see a backup listed on the Backups table view. Note that the population of this table view is asynchronous, so it may take a little while to update, particularly if this is the first time you've authenticated to Dropbox. Figure 13.7 shows the expected result.

Figure 13.7   Backups

Restore

The restore process will require four new methods in DropboxTVC. Due to the destructive nature of a restore, the process will require the user to tap several buttons in order to initiate a restore. First, the user will need to select a file to restore. Second, the user will need to tap an options button and then tap restore. Finally, the user will need to confirm the restore action. This is a safeguard against an accidental restore. The new DropboxTVC methods are as follows:

- **restore** will be used to set the selected ZIP filename and show the restore confirmation alert view. If a file is still downloading, isn't cached locally, or has a "newer" status, the restore will be skipped and the user notified.

- **options** will be tied to a new button that displays an action sheet allowing the user to choose to link/unlink from Dropbox, or to restore.

- **actionSheet:clickedButtonAtIndex** will be used to handle either linking/unlinking from Dropbox or to initiate a restore.

- **alertView:clickedButtonAtIndex** will be used to begin the restore process as long as the user has confirmed he or she would like this to occur.

The code involved is shown in Listing 13.17.

Listing 13.17   **DropboxTVC.m: RESTORE**

```
#pragma mark - RESTORE
- (void)restore {
    DBAccount *account = [[DBAccountManager sharedManager] linkedAccount];
    if (!account.isLinked) {[DropboxHelper linkToDropboxWithUI:self];}
    if (account) {
        NSIndexPath *indexPath = [self.tableView indexPathForSelectedRow];
        if (indexPath) {
            DBFileInfo *info = [_contents objectAtIndex:indexPath.row];

            // Don't restore partially downloaded files
            if (![[[[DBFilesystem sharedFilesystem] openFile:info.path
                                                 error:nil] status] cached] ||
                [[[DBFilesystem sharedFilesystem] openFile:info.path
                                                 error:nil] newerStatus]

                ) {

                UIAlertView *failAlert = [[UIAlertView alloc]
                                    initWithTitle:@"Failed to Restore"
                                          message:@"The file is not ready"
                                         delegate:nil
                                cancelButtonTitle:nil
                                otherButtonTitles:@"Close", nil];
                [failAlert show];
                return;
            }
            _selectedZipFileName = info.path.name;
            NSLog(@"Selected '%@' for restore", _selectedZipFileName);
            NSString *restorePoint =
            [_selectedZipFileName stringByReplacingOccurrencesOfString:@" Stores.zip"
                                                            withString:@""];

            NSString *message = [NSString stringWithFormat:@"Are you sure want to
➥restore from %@ backup? Existing data will be lost. The application may pause
➥for the duration of the restore.", restorePoint];

            _confirmRestore = [[UIAlertView alloc] initWithTitle:nil
                                                message:message
                                               delegate:self
                                      cancelButtonTitle:@"Cancel"
                                      otherButtonTitles:@"Restore", nil];
            [_confirmRestore show];
```

```objc
        } else {
            UIAlertView *alert =
             [[UIAlertView alloc] initWithTitle:nil
                                        message:@"Please select a backup to restore"
                                       delegate:self
                              cancelButtonTitle:@"Ok"
                              otherButtonTitles:nil];
            [alert show];
        }
    }
}
- (IBAction)options:(id)sender {
    NSString *title, *toggleLink, *restore;
    DBAccount *account = [[DBAccountManager sharedManager] linkedAccount];
    if (account.isLinked) {
        restore = [NSString stringWithFormat:@"Restore Selected Backup"];
        toggleLink = [NSString stringWithFormat:@"Unlink from Dropbox"];
        if (account.info.displayName) {
            title = [NSString stringWithFormat:@"Dropbox: %@",
                                                     account.info.displayName];
        } else {
            title = [NSString stringWithFormat:@"Dropbox: Linked"];
        }
    } else {
        toggleLink = [NSString stringWithFormat:@"Link to Dropbox"];
        title = [NSString stringWithFormat:@"Dropbox: Not Linked"];
    }
    _options = [[UIActionSheet alloc] initWithTitle:title
                                           delegate:self
                                  cancelButtonTitle:@"Cancel"
                             destructiveButtonTitle:nil
                                  otherButtonTitles:toggleLink,restore, nil];
    [_options showFromTabBar:self.navigationController.tabBarController.tabBar];
}
- (void)actionSheet:(UIActionSheet *)actionSheet
clickedButtonAtIndex:(NSInteger)buttonIndex {
    DBAccount *account = [[DBAccountManager sharedManager] linkedAccount];
    if (actionSheet == _options) {
        switch (buttonIndex) {
            case 0:
                if (account.isLinked) {
                    [DropboxHelper unlinkFromDropbox];
                    [self reload];
                } else {
```

```
                [DropboxHelper linkToDropboxWithUI:self];
                [self reload];
            }
            break;
        case 1:
            [self restore];
            break;
        default:
            break;
        }
    }
}
- (void)alertView:(UIAlertView *)alertView
clickedButtonAtIndex:(NSInteger)buttonIndex {
    if (alertView == _confirmRestore && buttonIndex == 1) {
        CoreDataHelper *cdh =
        [(AppDelegate *)[[UIApplication sharedApplication] delegate] cdh];
        [DropboxHelper restoreFromDropboxStoresZip:_selectedZipFileName
                            withCoreDataHelper:cdh];
    }
}
```

Update Grocery Dude as follows to implement a restore:

1. Add the code from Listing 13.17 to the bottom of `DropboxTVC.m` before `@end`.

2. Select **Main.storyboard**.

3. Drag a **Bar Button Item** to the top right of the **Backups Table View Controller**.

4. Set the **Bar Item Title** of the new **Bar Button Item** to **Options**.

5. Hold down **Control** and drag a line from the Options button to the yellow circle at the bottom of the **Backups Table View Controller**; then select **Sent Actions > options:**. If `options:` is not an option on the popup menu, you may need to save `DropboxTVC.m` and try again.

Run Grocery Dude again, and you should be able to restore from a backup. Remember to first select a backup and then tap **Options > Restore Selected Backup > Restore**. Figure 13.8 shows the expected result.

Note that the backup-and-restore processes run on the main thread, which will freeze the application for the duration of each. Unless the store is big, this will only be for a few seconds and the user is warned ahead of time. In reality, you should block user interaction the same way the `MigrationVC` view does in Chapter 3, "Managed Object Model Migration." Using that approach, these processes could be performed in the background while an activity or progress indicator is displayed. These steps have been omitted from this chapter for brevity.

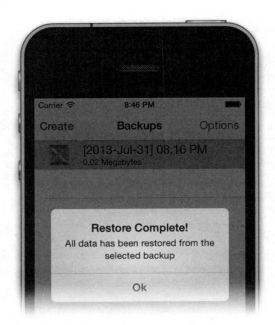

Figure 13.8   Restore

Summary

You've now been shown how to integrate an application with Dropbox for the purpose of backup and restore. The process of creating a backup ZIP file has also been demonstrated as the entire Stores directory was preserved within a ZIP file. Having a backup-and-restore option available to your users can make them feel that their data is safer. This should make them more comfortable with storing important data on their device. Even if their device were stolen, they would not lose any data provided they had created a backup. The backup-and-restore option is a great (if rudimentary) option for transferring data between devices with the same application.

Exercises

Why not build on what you've learned by experimenting?

1. Try unlinking and relinking to Dropbox using the Options menu on the Data tab. Note that this will clear the local Dropbox cache so it may take some time to resynchronize, depending on how many backups have been taken.

2. Modify the `setupCoreData` method of `CoreDataHelper.m` to import test data instead of setting the default store as the initial store. Delete the application from the device and allow the test data to import. Once the import is complete and the thumbnails have been automatically generated, link to Dropbox and take a backup. This will create a ~19MB ZIP file that may take a while to upload to Dropbox.

> **Note**
> Bit length overflow messages in the console log are a normal part of the image compression.

3. Log on to the Dropbox website and download the ~19MB backup ZIP file from your `Apps/Grocery Dude` directory. Extract and examine the contents of the ZIP file. You will likely only see the `Grocery-Dude.sqlite` and associated WAL and SHM files. The externally stored images are hidden.

4. Examine the contents of the extracted backup files by temporarily enabling hidden file visibility in Finder as follows:

   - Open **Terminal** on your Mac from **Applications > Utilities.**

   - In **Terminal**, execute `defaults write com.apple.Finder AppleShowAllFiles YES`

   - In **Terminal**, execute `killall Finder`

   - Examine the contents of the extracted ZIP file from step 3. The expected result is shown in Figure 13.9. The _EXTERNAL_DATA directory is the Core Data managed folder of images, stored externally from the SQLite store. If you add a .png file extension for a file, you will be able to view the file!

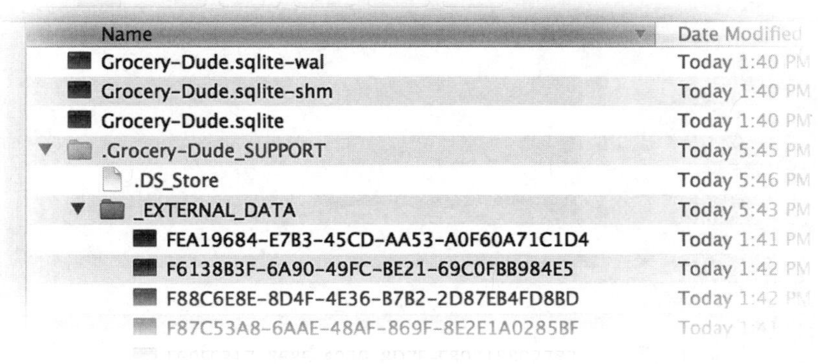

Figure 13.9 Backup ZIP contents include _EXTERNAL_DATA structure

   - In **Terminal**, execute `defaults write com.apple.Finder AppleShowAllFiles NO`

   - In **Terminal**, execute `killall Finder`

Reverse the changes from step 2 of the exercises before moving to the next chapter.

14

iCloud

You never fail until you stop trying.

Albert Einstein

In Chapter 13, "Back Up and Restore with Dropbox," a manual approach to storing data files "in the Cloud" was demonstrated using Dropbox. In this chapter, automatic data synchronization between user devices will be achieved using iCloud. Once Core Data is integrated with iCloud, changes made to application data on one user device will automatically be reflected on their other devices. At the time of writing, neither Dropbox nor iCloud allows data to be synchronized between accounts. If an application requires the ability for multiple accounts to synchronize with the same data, custom web service integration will be more appropriate than Dropbox or iCloud. Likewise, if an application requires ordered relationships, or needs a mapping model for migration in future releases, be aware that neither are supported with iCloud at this time.

This chapter covers the basics of Core Data integration with iCloud. You'll first be shown how to enable the iCloud capability and then you'll be shown just how easy it has become to integrate Core Data with iCloud since Xcode 5 and iOS 7. Once these are integrated, the new iCloud debugging features will be introduced, alongside tips for working with iCloud during the development phase. Finally, you'll be shown how to allow users to opt out of using iCloud, even though they may be using an authenticated iCloud account.

Overview

iCloud is used to synchronize documents and data between devices belonging to one user. When Core Data is integrated with iCloud, its data is ubiquitous. The term *ubiquitous* means "available everywhere," which is the fundamental intention of iCloud. For changes on one device to be reflected on another, each device needs to be signed in as the same iCloud user. The first device to use the application with iCloud will form a ubiquitous Core Data baseline for that application in iCloud. This baseline is the starting point used by other devices to build their own local copy of the application's data from iCloud. This local copy of the application data is known as the iCloud Store. The iCloud Store is updated automatically according to change logs in the ubiquity container, which is maintained by Apple's iCloud servers.

Three key components are involved when integrating Core Data with iCloud:

- The **Application Stores Directory**, also known as the application sandbox, is a local directory that currently holds the original `Grocery-Dude.sqlite` store. An `iCloud.sqlite` store will be added to this folder in a subfolder specific to each iCloud user. The per-user subfolders are managed transparently by Core Data. The folder structure is shown at the end of the chapter in the "Exercises" section.

- The **Ubiquity Container** is where iCloud documents and data specific to the authenticated iCloud user are found. Everything in this folder is synchronized automatically with the iCloud servers. If a directory with a `.nosync` suffix is stored in the ubiquity container, its contents will not be synchronized. You may have seen implementations of iCloud where the iCloud Store was placed in a `.nosync` folder of the ubiquity container. This approach is no longer recommended since iOS 7 because it prevents Core Data from transparently managing a **Fallback Store**. A Fallback Store is used to provide seamless transitions between iCloud accounts and reduce the time it takes for the iCloud Store to become usable for the first time. The Fallback Store is also used when the user is logged out of iCloud, or has disabled iCloud Documents & Data.

- **iCloud** is the name of the service allowing a user's data to be synchronized across all of his or her devices. It is possible to see the contents of your iCloud container for debugging purposes at https://developer.icloud.com. You can also perform metadata queries to inspect the contents of iCloud or use the iCloud Debug Navigator introduced in Xcode 5, which will be shown later in the chapter. Each application using iCloud has its own directory at the root of iCloud, and applications from the same developer can be configured to share a ubiquity container within it. This is useful if you need to maintain separate free and paid versions of an application that need to access the same data.

Figure 14.1 shows an overview of the key components involved in Core Data and iCloud integration, along with the placement of stores and change logs.

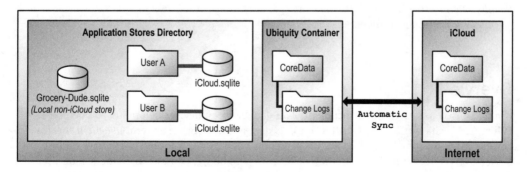

Figure 14.1   iCloud overview

> **Note**
>
> To continue building the sample application, you'll need to have added the previous chapter's code to Grocery Dude. Alternatively, you may download, unzip, and use the project up to this point from http://www.timroadley.com/LearningCoreData/GroceryDude-AfterChapter13.zip. Any time you start using an Xcode project from a ZIP file, it's good practice to click **Product > Clean**. This practice ensures there's no residual cache from previous projects using the same name.
>
> You will also need to ensure that a valid developer profile has been selected as the Code Signing Identity for iCloud to work. You can set this in the **Identity** section of the **General** tab that is available when the Grocery Dude application target is selected.

Enabling iCloud

Prior to iOS 7, enabling iCloud required you to configure an App ID and provisioning profile entitled to use iCloud. Although this is still a requirement, it is handled for you automatically when you toggle the iCloud switch. This switch to enable iCloud is available on the **Capabilities** tab of the application target.

Update Grocery Dude as follows to enable the iCloud Capability:

1. Select the **Capabilities** tab of the Grocery Dude target, as shown in Figure 14.2.

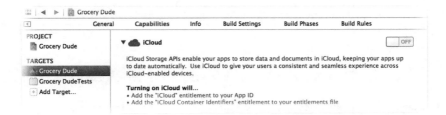

Figure 14.2   iCloud is off.

2. Ensure you're connected to the Internet and turn on iCloud, as shown in Figure 14.3.

In the process of enabling iCloud, you'll need to choose an appropriate Development Team. Once iCloud has been enabled, you should see an automatically generated ubiquity container name. You can set this container name to whatever you like, as long as you don't change it once customers have data at this location. If you need data between free and paid versions of an application to remain consistent, you should ensure that the ubiquity container name in each application matches.

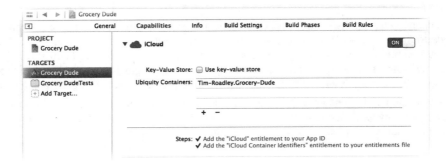

Figure 14.3   iCloud is now on.

Updating `CoreDataHelper` for iCloud

To make it easy to reuse the sample code in your own projects, `CoreDataHelper` will be updated to include iCloud support. The first new method required is called `iCloudAccountIsSignedIn` and is used to check the iCloud account status. Only when an iCloud account has been authenticated will this method return YES. Listing 14.1 shows the code involved.

Listing 14.1   **`CoreDataHelper.m: iCloudAccountIsSignedIn`**

```
#pragma mark - ICLOUD
- (BOOL)iCloudAccountIsSignedIn {
if (debug==1) {
    NSLog(@"Running %@ '%@'", self.class, NSStringFromSelector(_cmd));
}
    id token = [[NSFileManager defaultManager] ubiquityIdentityToken];
    if (token) {
        NSLog(@"** iCloud is SIGNED IN with token '%@' **", token);
        return YES;
    }
    NSLog(@"** iCloud is NOT SIGNED IN **");
    NSLog(@"--> Is iCloud Documents and Data enabled for a valid iCloud account on
➥your Mac & iOS Device or iOS Simulator?");
    NSLog(@"--> Have you enabled the iCloud Capability in the Application Target?");
    NSLog(@"--> Is there a CODE_SIGN_ENTITLEMENTS Xcode warning that needs fixing?
➥You may need to specifically choose a developer instead of using Automatic
➥selection");
    NSLog(@"--> Are you using a Pre-iOS7 Simulator?");
    return NO;
}
```

Update Grocery Dude as follows to enable iCloud account status checks:

1. Add the following code to the bottom of `CoreDataHelper.h` before `@end`:

   ```
   - (BOOL)iCloudAccountIsSignedIn;
   ```

2. Add the code from Listing 14.1 to the bottom of `CoreDataHelper.m` before `@end`.

3. Add the following code to the bottom of the `didFinishLaunchingWithOptions` method of `AppDelegate.m` before `return YES;`:

   ```
   [[self cdh] iCloudAccountIsSignedIn];
   ```

4. Ensure your test iOS device or iOS Simulator is signed in to iCloud. The only mandatory iCloud setting you need to ensure is enabled is **Documents & Data**. You can check this via **Settings > iCloud**.

5. Run Grocery Dude on your test device and examine the top of the console log. Figure 14.4 shows the expected results; the token will vary.

```
    Grocery Dude.app
y Dude[59157:a0b]  Running CoreDataHelper 'applicationStoresDirectory'
y Dude[59157:a0b]  Running CoreDataHelper 'applicationDocumentsDirectory'
y Dude[59157:a0b]  Successfully added store: <NSSQLCore: 0x8a49ce0> (URL: file:///Users/Timbo/Library/
 Simulator/7.0/Applications/EC5D9802-BB60-4BDB-A913-4A51C17AF9FF/Documents/Stores/Grocery-Dude.sqlite)
y Dude[59157:a0b]  Running CoreDataHelper 'iCloudAccountIsSignedIn'
y Dude[59157:a0b]  ** iCloud is SIGNED IN with token '<f16a91e0 44f43933 c5d7dd34 a27467db 80850c20>' **
y Dude[59157:a0b]  Running AppDelegate 'cdh'
y Dude[59157:a0b]  Running AppDelegate 'applicationDidBecomeActive:'
  Dude[59157:a0b]  Running AppDelegate 'cdh'
  Dude[59157:a0b]  Running AppDelegate 'cdh'
```

Figure 14.4   Signed in to iCloud

The iCloud Store

To hold a reference to the iCloud Store, a new property called `iCloudStore` will be added to the header of `CoreDataHelper`. Listing 14.2 shows the code involved.

Listing 14.2   **CoreDataHelper.h**

```
@property (nonatomic, readonly) NSPersistentStore *iCloudStore;
```

Update Grocery Dude as follows to add the `iCloudStore` property:

1. Add the property from Listing 14.2 to `CoreDataHelper.h` on the line after the existing `sourceStore` property is declared.

The iCloud Store content will be generated automatically based on change logs found in the ubiquity container of the authenticated iCloud user. The iCloud Store filename will be set to `iCloud.sqlite`; however, feel free to use any store name you think is appropriate in your own projects.

Update Grocery Dude as follows to configure the iCloud Store filename:

1. Add the following code to the bottom of the FILES section of `CoreDataHelper.m`:

   ```
   NSString *iCloudStoreFilename = @"iCloud.sqlite";
   ```

The iCloud Store will be placed in a Stores directory within the application sandbox. For convenience, a new method will be added to the PATHS section of `CoreDataHelper.m` that returns the URL to the iCloud Store. Listing 14.3 shows the code involved.

Listing 14.3   **CoreDataHelper.m: iCloudStoreURL**

```
- (NSURL *)iCloudStoreURL {
if (debug==1) {
    NSLog(@"Running %@ '%@'", self.class, NSStringFromSelector(_cmd));
}
    return [[self applicationStoresDirectory]
            URLByAppendingPathComponent:iCloudStoreFilename];
}
```

Update Grocery Dude as follows to implement the `iCloudStoreURL` method:

1. Add the code from Listing 14.3 to the bottom of the PATHS section of `CoreDataHelper.m`.

The next step is to implement the method that will load the iCloud Store. Listing 14.4 shows the code involved.

Listing 14.4   **CoreDataHelper.m: loadiCloudStore**

```
- (BOOL)loadiCloudStore {
if (debug==1) {
    NSLog(@"Running %@ '%@'", self.class, NSStringFromSelector(_cmd));
}
    if (_iCloudStore) {return YES;} // Don't load iCloud store if it's already loaded

    NSDictionary *options =
    @{
      NSMigratePersistentStoresAutomaticallyOption:@YES
      ,NSInferMappingModelAutomaticallyOption:@YES
      ,NSPersistentStoreUbiquitousContentNameKey:@"Grocery-Dude"
    //,NSPersistentStoreUbiquitousContentURLKey:@"ChangeLogs" // Optional since iOS7
      };
    NSError *error;
```

```
    _iCloudStore = [_coordinator addPersistentStoreWithType:NSSQLiteStoreType
                                        configuration:nil
                                                 URL:[self iCloudStoreURL]
                                             options:options
                                               error:&error];
    if (_iCloudStore) {
        NSLog(@"** The iCloud Store has been successfully configured at '%@' **",
                                                    _iCloudStore.URL.path);
        return YES;
    }
    NSLog(@"** FAILED to configure the iCloud Store : %@ **", error);
    return NO;
}
```

Loading an iCloud Store has been greatly simplified since iOS 7 and the entire process can now be performed on the main thread. You still add a persistent store to the coordinator, similar to the approach used in the `loadStore` method. To use iCloud you pass an additional option key called `NSPersistentStoreUbiquitousContentNameKey`. This key is a mandatory part of configuring Core Data integration with iCloud. Its value can be any string you would like to represent the ubiquitous store. Once Core Data has been integrated with iCloud, examining the contents of https://developer.icloud.com/ will reveal this key's usage as a directory name within the change logs.

Since iOS 7, what was a mandatory key for specifying the location of the change logs is now optional. This key, called `NSPersistentStoreUbiquitousContentURLKey`, should only be used when you need to manually control where the ubiquitous change logs are located—for example, in cases where your users have existing iCloud application data created on iOS 6.

Once all the persistent store options are set, they are given to the `addPersistentStore` method. This method returns immediately with a store the application can use. The store returned is actually the Fallback Store, which will be used transparently in lieu of the real iCloud Store until it is ready.

Update Grocery Dude as follows to implement `loadiCloudStore`:

1. Add the method from Listing 14.4 to the bottom of the ICLOUD section of `CoreDataHelper.m`.

iCloud Notifications

Once the iCloud Store is ready, a notification called `NSPersistentStoreCoordinatorStores-WillChangeNotification` will be sent to indicate that the store is about to change. Once it is changed, another notification called `NSPersistentStoreCoordinatorStoresDidChange-Notification` will be sent. Additionally, when a store imports ubiquitous content, a notification called `NSPersistentStoreDidImportUbiquitousContentChangesNotification` is sent.

All of these notifications must be observed in order to trigger an appropriate response. Listing 14.5 shows the code involved in a new method called `listenForStoreChanges`, which is used to configure the application to observe these critical notifications.

Listing 14.5   **CoreDataHelper.m: listenForStoreChanges**

```
- (void)listenForStoreChanges {
if (debug==1) {
    NSLog(@"Running %@ '%@'", self.class, NSStringFromSelector(_cmd));
}
    NSNotificationCenter *dc = [NSNotificationCenter defaultCenter];
    [dc addObserver:self
          selector:@selector(storesWillChange:)
              name:NSPersistentStoreCoordinatorStoresWillChangeNotification
            object:_coordinator];

    [dc addObserver:self
          selector:@selector(storesDidChange:)
              name:NSPersistentStoreCoordinatorStoresDidChangeNotification
            object:_coordinator];

    [dc addObserver:self
          selector:@selector(persistentStoreDidImportUbiquitousContentChanges:)
              name:NSPersistentStoreDidImportUbiquitousContentChangesNotification
            object:_coordinator];
}
```

Update Grocery Dude as follows to listen for store changes:

1. Add the code from Listing 14.5 to the bottom of the ICLOUD section of `CoreDataHelper.m`. Xcode will now warn that the selectors that these notifications trigger are undeclared, which will be resolved shortly.

2. Add `[self listenForStoreChanges];` to the bottom of the `init` method of `CoreDataHelper.m` before `return self;`.

The next step is to implement each of the methods that will be called when the store change notifications mentioned in Listing 14.5 are received. The code involved is shown in Listing 14.6.

Listing 14.6   **CoreDataHelper.m: ICLOUD**

```
- (void)storesWillChange:(NSNotification *)n {
if (debug==1) {
    NSLog(@"Running %@ '%@'", self.class, NSStringFromSelector(_cmd));
}
    [_importContext performBlockAndWait:^{
```

```
        [_importContext save:nil];
        [self resetContext:_importContext];
    }];
    [_context performBlockAndWait:^{
        [_context save:nil];
        [self resetContext:_context];
    }];
    [_parentContext performBlockAndWait:^{
        [_parentContext save:nil];
        [self resetContext:_parentContext];
    }];

    // Refresh UI
    [[NSNotificationCenter defaultCenter] postNotificationName:@"SomethingChanged"
                                                        object:nil
                                                      userInfo:nil];
}
- (void)storesDidChange:(NSNotification *)n {
if (debug==1) {
    NSLog(@"Running %@ '%@'", self.class, NSStringFromSelector(_cmd));
}
    // Refresh UI
    [[NSNotificationCenter defaultCenter] postNotificationName:@"SomethingChanged"
                                                        object:nil
                                                      userInfo:nil];
}
- (void)persistentStoreDidImportUbiquitiousContentChanges:(NSNotification*)n {
if (debug==1) {
    NSLog(@"Running %@ '%@'", self.class, NSStringFromSelector(_cmd));
}
    [_context performBlock:^{
        [_context mergeChangesFromContextDidSaveNotification:n];
        [[NSNotificationCenter defaultCenter] postNotificationName:@"SomethingChanged"
                                                            object:nil];
    }];
}
```

As shown in Listing 14.6, there are three methods positioned to react to the three store change notifications previously shown in Listing 14.5:

- The `storesWillChange` method will be called just before the underlying persistent store is about to change. One scenario leading to this could be that the current iCloud account has changed. When this happens, the underlying store must change to another store containing the new user's data. Because the old user might start using his or her account again in the future, this is an opportune time to save their data and reset each context. Because Grocery Dude has a context hierarchy, each context is synchronously saved and reset in order of child to parent. The calls in this method need to be synchronous because the old store is detached once the method returns.

- The `storesDidChange` method will be called once the underlying store has changed. This is an opportune time to refresh the user interface. This is achieved by sending the `SomethingChanged` notification that views in Grocery Dude already observe.

- The `persistentStoreDidImportUbiquitiousContentChanges` method is used to bring the managed object context up to speed with changes from iCloud. Whenever the underlying iCloud Store is updated, the notification that triggers this method is used to update the context driving the user interface.

Update Grocery Dude as follows to implement the methods used to respond to iCloud notifications:

1. Add the code from Listing 14.6 to the bottom of the ICLOUD section of `CoreDataHelper.m`.

The `setupCoreData` method of `CoreDataHelper` now needs to be updated to orchestrate the loading of an appropriate store. If the iCloud Store fails to load, the local store will be loaded instead. Listing 14.7 shows the code involved.

Listing 14.7   **CoreDataHelper.m: loadiCloudStore**

```
if (![self loadiCloudStore]) {
    [self setDefaultDataStoreAsInitialStore];
    [self loadStore];
}
```

Update Grocery Dude as follows to ensure an appropriate store is loaded:

1. Replace the existing code in the `setupCoreData` method of `CoreDataHelper.m` with the code from Listing 14.7.

2. Run the application and examine the console log. Figure 14.5 shows the expected results.

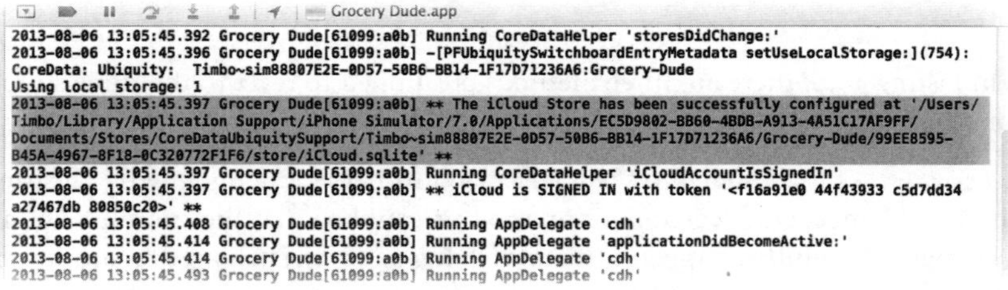

Figure 14.5   Core Data and iCloud integration successfully configured

Since iOS 7, Core Data has taken on the responsibility of maintaining a **Fallback Store**. The Fallback Store allows the user to instantly begin using the application with iCloud, even if the network is unavailable. You can now expect to see two new entries in the console log, as follows:

- `Using Local Storage 1` means that the Fallback Store is in use, so the user's data won't be available on other devices until the initial sync has completed.

- `Using Local Storage 0` means that the transition to the iCloud Store is complete and the Fallback Store isn't being used anymore. This is the message to look for that indicates iCloud synchronization is up and running. At this point, you should start seeing changes reflected on other devices using the same application with iCloud enabled.

You might not see the `Using Local Storage 0` message immediately; however, provided you have seen `Using Local Storage 1`, then the persistent store is ready to work with. Later, when the background process responsible for completely bringing up the iCloud Store has completed, you should see `Using Local Storage 0` in the console log.

The Debug Navigator

Since Xcode 5, greater visibility of iCloud activity has become possible. Using the **Debug Navigator** with a running iCloud application will reveal capacity, uploads, downloads, and individual document-level statuses. This lets you track the progress of the change logs and gives a better sense of what is going on under the hood. Figure 14.6 shows the Debug Navigator focused on iCloud.

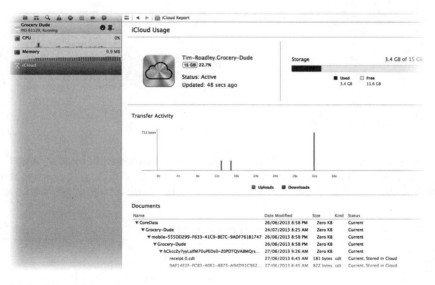

Figure 14.6   iCloud debugging

If the Debug Navigator informs you that iCloud is not configured, try enabling **Documents & Data** on your Mac in **System Preferences > iCloud**.

Disabling iCloud

Even though Grocery Dude now supports iCloud, it doesn't mean that the user necessarily *wants* to use it. The user may wish to selectively disable iCloud for Grocery Dude yet still use iCloud with his or her other applications. To add this flexibility, a settings bundle with an `iCloudEnabled` key will be added to allow the user to change his or her preference on using iCloud with Grocery Dude.

Update Grocery Dude as follows to implement the `iCloudEnabled` setting:

1. Select the **Grocery Dude** group and click **File > New > File...**.

2. Click **iOS > Resource > Settings Bundle** and then click **Next**.

3. Ensure the Grocery Dude target and an appropriate directory have been selected, and then click **Create**.

4. Expand **Settings.bundle** and select **Root.plist**.

5. Configure the Root.plist as shown in Figure 14.7.

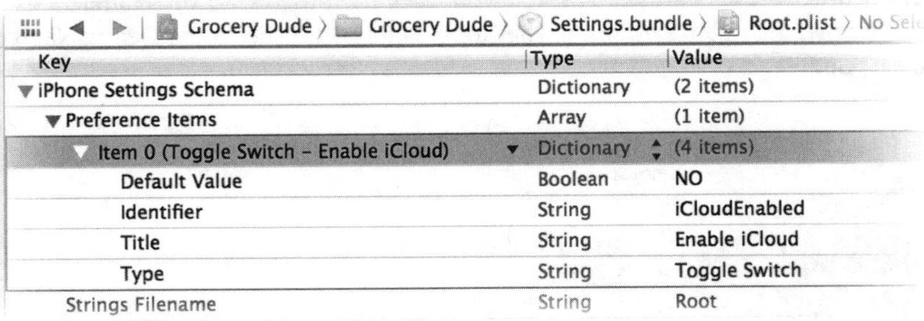

Key	Type	Value
▶ Grocery Dude ⟩ 📁 Grocery Dude ⟩ ⬡ Settings.bundle ⟩ 📄 Root.plist ⟩ No Sel		
▼ iPhone Settings Schema	Dictionary	(2 items)
▼ Preference Items	Array	(1 item)
▼ Item 0 (Toggle Switch – Enable iCloud) ▼	Dictionary ↕	(4 items)
Default Value	Boolean	NO
Identifier	String	iCloudEnabled
Title	String	Enable iCloud
Type	String	Toggle Switch
Strings Filename	String	Root

Figure 14.7   Settings bundle

To get the current value of the `iCloudEnabled` key, a new method will be added to `CoreDataHelper.m` called `iCloudEnabledByUser`. As shown in Listing 14.8, this method retrieves the current value of the `iCloudEnabled` key and returns an equivalent `BOOL` value.

Listing 14.8   **CoreDataHelper.m: iCloudEnabledByUser**

```
- (BOOL)iCloudEnabledByUser {
if (debug==1) {
    NSLog(@"Running %@ '%@'", self.class, NSStringFromSelector(_cmd));
}
```

```
    [[NSUserDefaults standardUserDefaults] synchronize]; // Ensure current value
    if ([[[NSUserDefaults standardUserDefaults]
                        objectForKey:@"iCloudEnabled"] boolValue]) {
        NSLog(@"** iCloud is ENABLED in Settings **");
        return YES;
    }
    NSLog(@"** iCloud is DISABLED in Settings **");
    return NO;
}
```

Update Grocery Dude with code to check the user's iCloud preference as follows:

1. Add the code from Listing 14.8 to the bottom of the ICLOUD section of CoreDataHelper.m.

In your own applications, you may wish to present the user with an alert view asking whether he or she would like to use iCloud. To keep this chapter as succinct as possible, users of Grocery Dude will need to use the Settings App to enable iCloud. Because this setting can only change when the application enters the background, the user's preference on using iCloud will be checked each time the application enters the foreground. If an authenticated iCloud user has opted to disable iCloud support in Grocery Dude, the Core Data stack will need to be reset and the non-iCloud store loaded instead. Listing 14.9 shows the code involved in resetting the Core Data stack.

Listing 14.9 **CoreDataHelper.m: CORE DATA RESET**

```
- (void)removeAllStoresFromCoordinator:(NSPersistentStoreCoordinator*)psc {
if (debug==1) {
    NSLog(@"Running %@ '%@'", self.class, NSStringFromSelector(_cmd));
}
    for (NSPersistentStore *s in psc.persistentStores) {
        NSError *error = nil;
        if (![psc removePersistentStore:s error:&error]) {
            NSLog(@"Error removing persistent store: %@", error);
        }
    }
}
- (void)resetCoreData {
if (debug==1) {
    NSLog(@"Running %@ '%@'", self.class, NSStringFromSelector(_cmd));
}
    [_importContext performBlockAndWait:^{
        [_importContext save:nil];
        [self resetContext:_importContext];
    }];
    [_context performBlockAndWait:^{
```

```
        [_context save:nil];
        [self resetContext:_context];
    }];
    [_parentContext performBlockAndWait:^{
        [_parentContext save:nil];
        [self resetContext:_parentContext];
    }];
    [self removeAllStoresFromCoordinator:_coordinator];
    _store = nil;
    _iCloudStore = nil;
}
```

The `removeAllStoresFromCoordinator` method removes each store found in the given coordinator. The `resetCoreData` method saves and resets each context and then uses `removeAllStoresFromCoordinator` to remove all stores from the _coordinator. The final step involves setting each store to `nil` so the Core Data stack is ready to be set up again.

Update Grocery Dude as follows to implement the remainder of the CORE DATA RESET section:

1. Add the code from Listing 14.9 to the bottom of the existing CORE DATA RESET section of CoreDataHelper.m.

As the application becomes active, a check needs to be performed to ensure that the appropriate store is loaded. Listing 14.10 shows the code involved in a new method called `ensureAppropriateStoreIsLoaded` that will perform this task.

Listing 14.10   CoreDataHelper.m: ensureAppropriateStoreIsLoaded

```
- (void)ensureAppropriateStoreIsLoaded {
if (debug==1) {
    NSLog(@"Running %@ '%@'", self.class, NSStringFromSelector(_cmd));
}
    if (!_store && !_iCloudStore) {
        return; // If neither store is loaded, skip (usually first launch)
    }
    if (![self iCloudEnabledByUser] && _store) {
        NSLog(@"The Non-iCloud Store is loaded as it should be");
        return;
    }
    if ([self iCloudEnabledByUser] && _iCloudStore) {
        NSLog(@"The iCloud Store is loaded as it should be");
        return;
    }
    NSLog(@"** The user preference on using iCloud with this application appears to
have changed. Core Data will now be reset. **");
```

```
[self resetCoreData];
[self setupCoreData];

[[NSNotificationCenter defaultCenter] postNotificationName:@"SomethingChanged"
                                      object:nil];

UIAlertView *alert = [[UIAlertView alloc] initWithTitle:
@"Your preference on using iCloud with this application appears to have changed"
                                      message:
@"Content has been updated accordingly"
                              delegate:nil
                      cancelButtonTitle:nil
                      otherButtonTitles:@"Ok", nil];
[alert show];
}
```

The `ensureAppropriateStoreIsLoaded` method is quite straightforward. If neither store is loaded, the method returns early. This will happen when the application is launching for the first time. If iCloud has been disabled and the non-iCloud `_store` is loaded, or iCloud is enabled and `_iCloudStore` is loaded, the method will also return early. Anything else is considered a discrepancy and Core Data is consequently reset, set up, and the views and user notified.

Update Grocery Dude as follows to ensure the appropriate store is loaded each time the application becomes active:

1. Add the code from Listing 14.10 to the bottom of the ICLOUD section of `CoreDataHelper.m`.

2. Add the following code to the bottom of `CoreDataHelper.h` before `@end`:

   `- (void)ensureAppropriateStoreIsLoaded;`

3. Add the following code to the bottom of the `applicationWillEnterForeground` method of `AppDelegate.m`:

   `[[self cdh] ensureAppropriateStoreIsLoaded];`

Even though a check is now in place to ensure that an appropriate store is loaded when the application enters the foreground, the `setupCoreData` method needs to be updated to ensure that an appropriate store is loaded during setup. This determination is made based on the user's `iCloudEnabled` preference. Listing 14.11 shows the code involved in an updated `setupCoreData` method.

Listing 14.11   **CoreDataHelper.m: setupCoreData**

```
- (void)setupCoreData {
if (debug==1) {
    NSLog(@"Running %@ '%@'", self.class, NSStringFromSelector(_cmd));
}
    if (!_store && !_iCloudStore) {
        if ([self iCloudEnabledByUser]) {
            NSLog(@"** Attempting to load the iCloud Store **");
            if ([self loadiCloudStore]) {
                return;
            }
        }
        NSLog(@"** Attempting to load the Local, Non-iCloud Store **");
        [self setDefaultDataStoreAsInitialStore];
        [self loadStore];
    } else {
        NSLog(@"SKIPPED setupCoreData, there's an existing Store:\n ** _store(%@)\n **
➥_iCloudStore(%@)", _store, _iCloudStore);
    }
}
```

The updated setupCoreData method begins by checking whether there's an existing _store or _iCloudStore. If there is, the method returns early; otherwise, it checks the user's preference on using iCloud and loads an appropriate store in response. If the iCloud Store load fails, the non-iCloud store is loaded instead.

Update Grocery Dude as follows to implement the modified setupCoreData method:

1. Replace the existing setupCoreData method in CoreDataHelper.m with the method from Listing 14.11.

2. Run the application on a test device. The local, non-iCloud store should load and be populated with default data.

3. Press the **Home** button and open the **Settings App.**

4. Scroll down and select Grocery Dude; then enable iCloud as shown in Figure 14.8.

5. Return to the Grocery Dude app and you should see the data set change, as shown in Figure 14.9.

It is important to realize that there are now two ways to disable iCloud, each having a different result:

- If iCloud is disabled by turning **Settings > Grocery Dude > Enable iCloud** off, then the local, non-iCloud Store will be used.

- If iCloud is disabled by turning **iCloud > Documents & Data > Grocery Dude** off, then the Fallback Store will be used transparently.

Figure 14.8   Enable iCloud for Grocery Dude

Figure 14.9   iCloud Preference Change

If an app isn't already on the App Store, or there's no need to cater for existing customer persistent stores, then you don't need the Settings.bundle or the [self iCloudEnabledBy User] check in the setupCoreData method of CoreDataHelper.m. Removing this check will prevent the non-iCloud store from ever being used, and will always provide the user with either an iCloud store or Fallback Store. Regardless of whether the user enables or disables iCloud

Documents & Data, his or her data will always be available. If you use this approach, features such as Dropbox backup shouldn't be used and will need to be disabled, which is discussed in the next chapter.

Summary

Core Data has now been integrated with iCloud and yet there's still work to do to ensure it behaves in a production-like manner. You may find that the initial sync time will vary, depending on the state of the change logs that have to be replayed and the speed of the network connection. Because iCloud provides background synchronization, changes made on one device may take a while to show up on other devices. One key point to remember is that unsaved changes in a context won't appear on other devices. Frequent saves will ensure that changes show up on other devices as fast as possible. The following chapter demonstrates techniques such as de-duplication and seeding, which will ensure that the user experience is a good one. It is recommended that you complete the next chapter prior to performing any further rigorous testing with iCloud.

Exercises

Why not build on what you've learned by experimenting?

1. Examine your iCloud contents by logging in to https://developer.icloud.com with your developer account.

2. Test iCloud debug logging as follows:

> **Warning**
>
> This is incredibly verbose, so disable it when you're finished testing it.

   a. Click **Product > Scheme > Edit Scheme....**

   b. Ensure **Run Grocery Dude...** and the **Arguments** tab are selected.

   c. Click the + in the **Arguments Passed On Launch** section.

   d. Type in **-com.apple.coredata.ubiquity.logLevel 3** and then click **OK**.

   e. Run the application again and examine the console log.

3. iCloud integration will now maintain a file structure in the application sandbox to cater to multiple iCloud accounts. Examine the contents of the Grocery Dude sandbox as follows:

   a. Ensure your iOS device is connected and has run Grocery Dude previously with iCloud enabled and signed in.

   b. Click **Window > Organizer** in Xcode.

c. Select the **Applications** subfolder beneath your device.

d. Select the **Grocery Dude** application and then click **Download** and save the
`filename`.xcappdata file to your **Documents** folder.

e. Navigate to the downloaded file in Finder and then right-click it and select **Show
Package Contents**.

f. Expand the folder structure as shown in Figure 14.10.

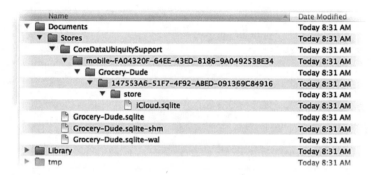

Figure 14.10   Core Data's application sandbox structure

As shown in Figure 14.10, the folder structure leading to `iCloud.sqlite` is different from
the one you've specified in the `iCloudStoreURL` method. The additional structure has been
inserted by Core Data to allow seamless support for multiple iCloud accounts. The structure
varies depending on whether or not you're using local storage. If you have an additional
iCloud account, try using it with Grocery Dude to see the additional store and folders that are
generated.

Taming iCloud

Only those who attempt the absurd can achieve the impossible.

Albert Einstein

In Chapter 14, "iCloud," the basic steps to integrate Core Data with iCloud were demonstrated. Still, several areas need to be addressed to ensure that the user's iCloud experience is as seamless as possible. For example, when multiple iCloud-enabled devices are in play, there's a risk that some data may be duplicated. Techniques for handling data duplication will be discussed as they are implemented in Grocery Dude. You'll also be shown how to seed iCloud from data found in a local "Non-iCloud" persistent store. This approach ensures that users don't lose data when they start using iCloud for the first time, even if they had existing data on separate devices.

De-Duplication

When iCloud is used across multiple devices, there's a risk that duplicate items may be created by the user or seeded to iCloud. In particular, when an item is created on an offline device, it won't appear on other devices until Internet connectivity is restored. In the meantime, if an item with the same name is created on another device, then duplicate items will result. To deal with this scenario, a new `Deduplicator` class will be used to selectively delete the oldest of the duplicate items. In your own applications, you may wish to add other logic to determine the most appropriate duplicate to delete. For example, you may wish to compare attribute values such as a `NSUUID` or even take into account relationships before choosing which duplicate to delete. Beyond that, you could even merge values with custom logic, if that makes sense for your application.

> **Note**
>
> To continue building the sample application, you'll need to have added the previous chapter's code to Grocery Dude. Alternatively, you may download, unzip, and use the project up to this point from http://www.timroadley.com/LearningCoreData/GroceryDude-AfterChapter14.zip. Any time you start using an Xcode project from a ZIP file, it's good practice to click **Product > Clean**. This practice ensures there's no residual cache from previous projects using the same name.
>
> You will also need to ensure that an appropriate profile has been selected as the **Code Signing Identity** in the **Code Signing** section of the **Build Settings** tab of the **Grocery Dude target**.
>
> If you are using the provided sample code, toggle the iCloud Capability off and then on again to ensure that your own development team is used.

Update Grocery Dude as follows to add the `Deduplicator` class:

1. Select the **Generic Core Data Classes** group.

2. Click **File > New > File...**.

3. Create a new **iOS > Cocoa Touch > Objective-C class** and then click **Next**.

4. Set **Subclass of** to `NSObject` and **Class name** to `Deduplicator` and then click **Next**.

5. Ensure the Grocery Dude target is ticked and then create the class by clicking **Create** in the Grocery Dude project directory.

Before objects can be de-duplicated, they must first be identified as duplicates. To identify an object as a duplicate, you'll need to choose an attribute that can be used to determine uniqueness. In other words, choose an attribute whose value should always be unique. In the case of Grocery Dude, the unique attributes for each entity where de-duplication will be enabled are shown in Table 15.1.

Table 15.1   Unique Attribute Names

Entity	Unique Attribute Name
Item	`name`
Unit	`name`
LocationAtHome	`storedIn`
LocationAtShop	`aisle`

Once a unique attribute has been chosen, it can be used to create a list showing how many objects have the unique value. Ideally, only one object should have the same unique attribute value. If more than one object has the same unique attribute value, it is considered a duplicate. Listing 15.1 shows the code involved in retrieving an array of duplicate attribute values for a given entity.

Listing 15.1 **Deduplicator.m: duplicatesForEntityWithName**

```
+ (NSArray*)duplicatesForEntityWithName:(NSString*)entityName
                withUniqueAttributeName:(NSString*)uniqueAttributeName
                            withContext:(NSManagedObjectContext*)context {

    // GET UNIQUE ATTRIBUTE
    NSDictionary *allEntities =
    [[context.persistentStoreCoordinator managedObjectModel] entitiesByName];
    NSAttributeDescription *uniqueAttribute =
    [[[allEntities objectForKey:entityName] propertiesByName]
                                    objectForKey:uniqueAttributeName];

    // CREATE COUNT EXPRESSION
    NSExpressionDescription *countExpression = [NSExpressionDescription new];
    [countExpression setName:@"count"];
    [countExpression setExpression:
    [NSExpression expressionWithFormat:@"count:(%K)",uniqueAttributeName]];
    [countExpression setExpressionResultType:NSInteger64AttributeType];

    // CREATE AN ARRAY OF _UNIQUE_ ATTRIBUTE VALUES
    NSFetchRequest *fetchRequest =
    [[NSFetchRequest alloc] initWithEntityName:entityName];
    [fetchRequest setIncludesPendingChanges:NO];
    [fetchRequest setFetchBatchSize:100];
    [fetchRequest setPropertiesToFetch:
    [NSArray arrayWithObjects:uniqueAttribute, countExpression, nil]];
    [fetchRequest setPropertiesToGroupBy:[NSArray arrayWithObject:uniqueAttribute]];
    [fetchRequest setResultType:NSDictionaryResultType];

    NSError *error;

    NSArray *instances = [context executeFetchRequest:fetchRequest error:&error];
    if (error) {NSLog(@"Fetch Error: %@", error);}

    // RETURN AN ARRAY OF _DUPLICATE_ ATTRIBUTE VALUES
    NSArray *duplicates = [instances filteredArrayUsingPredicate:
                        [NSPredicate predicateWithFormat:@"count > 1"]];
    return duplicates;
}
```

The duplicatesForEntityWithName method returns an array of attribute values that have
been identified as duplicates. This method requires that an entity name, unique attribute name,
and context be given. To provide the duplicates array, a fetch request is created that returns
each unique attribute value alongside a count of how many objects have these unique values.
Any unique attribute value that is seen more than once is considered a duplicate. Duplicate
attribute values are added to a predicate filtered array, which is then returned from the method.

Update Grocery Dude as follows to implement `duplicatesForEntityWithName`:

1. Add `#import <CoreData/CoreData.h>` to the top of `Deduplicator.h`.

2. Add the code from Listing 15.1 to the bottom of `Deduplicator.m` before `@end`.

The next step is to add a new method called `deDuplicateEntityWithName` to `Deduplicator`. This new method will be used to de-duplicate duplicated objects. The de-duplication process will be performed in the import context, which runs in the background. This ensures the user interface isn't impacted when a substantial amount of duplicates are being processed. The other benefit of using the import context is that the changes are immediately reflected in the main context once the import context is saved. This is due to the context hierarchy, which has been in place since Chapter 11, "Background Processing."

The first thing that the `deDuplicateEntityWithName` method will do is to use the existing `duplicatesForEntityWithName` method to obtain an array of duplicate attribute values. Those values are then used when creating a fetch request configured with an `IN` predicate. An `IN` predicate constrains the fetch request to return only objects that have a unique attribute value matching any value in the list of given duplicate values.

Once the fetch is performed, an array of all duplicate objects is returned that will be used to remove duplicate objects. Cleanup involves saving the context hierarchy and turning each object back into a fault using the existing `Faulter` class. Listing 15.2 shows the code involved.

Listing 15.2 **Deduplicator.m: deDuplicateEntityWithName**

```
+ (void)deDuplicateEntityWithName:(NSString*)entityName
          withUniqueAttributeName:(NSString*)uniqueAttributeName
               withImportContext:(NSManagedObjectContext*)importContext {

    [importContext performBlock:^{

        NSArray *duplicates =
        [Deduplicator duplicatesForEntityWithName:entityName
                       withUniqueAttributeName:uniqueAttributeName
                                   withContext:importContext];
        // FETCH DUPLICATE OBJECTS
        NSFetchRequest *fetchRequest =
        [[NSFetchRequest alloc] initWithEntityName:entityName];
        NSArray *sortDescriptors =
        [NSArray arrayWithObjects:
           [NSSortDescriptor sortDescriptorWithKey:uniqueAttributeName
                                        ascending:YES],nil];
        [fetchRequest setSortDescriptors:sortDescriptors];
        [fetchRequest setPredicate:[NSPredicate predicateWithFormat:@"%K IN (%@.%K)",
                           uniqueAttributeName, duplicates, uniqueAttributeName]];
        [fetchRequest setFetchBatchSize:100];
        [fetchRequest setIncludesPendingChanges:NO];
```

```
        NSError *error;
        NSArray *duplicateObjects =
        [importContext executeFetchRequest:fetchRequest error:&error];
        if (error) {NSLog(@"Fetch Error: %@", error);}

        // DELETE DUPLICATES
        NSManagedObject *lastObject;
        for (NSManagedObject *object in duplicateObjects) {
            if (lastObject) {
                if ([[object valueForKey:uniqueAttributeName]
                            isEqual:[lastObject valueForKey:uniqueAttributeName]]) {

                    // Add deletion logic here

                    // Save & fault objects
                    [Faulter faultObjectWithID:object.objectID
                                    inContext:importContext];
                    [Faulter faultObjectWithID:lastObject.objectID
                                    inContext:importContext];
                }
            }
            lastObject = object;
        }
    }];
}
```

Update Grocery Dude as follows to implement deDuplicateEntityWithName:

1. Add #import "Faulter.h" to the top of Deduplicator.m.

2. Add the code from Listing 15.2 to the bottom of Deduplicator.m before @end.

3. Add the code shown in Listing 15.3 to Deduplicator.h before @end. This code ensures that deDuplicateEntityWithName can be called from other classes.

Listing 15.3 **Deduplicator.h: deDuplicateEntityWithName**

```
+ (void)deDuplicateEntityWithName:(NSString*)entityName
        withUniqueAttributeName:(NSString*)uniqueAttributeName
            withImportContext:(NSManagedObjectContext*)importContext;
```

When deciding which duplicate object to delete, it's important to ensure that any device presented with the same duplicates will delete the same objects. To this end, the Deduplicator class will be updated to compare a new Date attribute called **modified**. This attribute will indicate which object is the oldest and therefore should be deleted. As a second line of defense against duplicates, objects with the least non-nil attribute values will be deleted if the modified dates match. Failing that, de-duplication will be skipped.

To add the modified attribute without causing existing installations to crash with incompatible models, a new model called **Model 9** will be added.

> **Note**
>
> If a user runs multiple versions of an iCloud application with different data models, synchronization of this data between his or her devices will not work. The users will need to upgrade all of their devices to the latest version in order for synchronization to resume. Be aware of this constraint during your testing, too.

Update Grocery Dude to implement the modified attribute:

1. Select **Model.xcdatamodeld**.

2. Click **Editor > Add Model Version....**

3. Click **Finish** to accept **Model 9** as the version name.

4. Ensure **Model 9.xcdatamodel** is selected.

5. Add an attribute called **modified** to the **Item** entity and then set its type to **Date**.

6. With the new **modified** attribute selected, un-tick **Optional** using the **Data Model Inspector (Option+⌘+3)**.

7. Set the **Default Value** of the **modified** attribute to `1970-01-01 12:00:00 +0000`.

8. Copy the **modified** attribute from the **Item** entity to the **Unit** entity and the **Location** entity. There's no need to create the **modified** attribute in the LocationAtHome and LocationAtShop entities because they inherit from the Location entity. You may need to switch the **Editor Style** to **Table** so you can copy and paste attributes, depending on your version of Xcode.

9. Select all entities in **Model 9** and then regenerate the `NSManagedObject` subclasses, replacing the existing files (via **Editor > Create NSManagedObject Subclass...**). Don't forget to ensure that the Grocery Dude target is selected before replacing the existing files.

10. Select **Model.xcdatamodeld** and then set the current model to **Model 9** using **File Inspector (Option+⌘+1)**, as shown on the right of Figure 15.1.

With the new model in place, the editing views need to be configured to update the modified date whenever an object is accessed. The existing `refreshInterface` method found in each view is a reasonable enough place for this new code because it already has a pointer to the object being edited. The code will differ slightly for each editing view, as shown in Table 15.2.

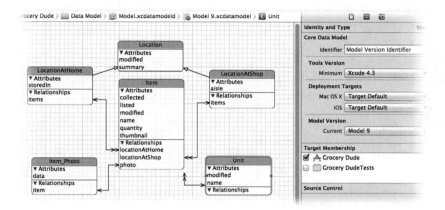

Figure 15.1   Model 9 is now the current model.

Table 15.2   **Code to Update Object Modified**

Class File	Code
ItemVC.m	item.modified = [NSDate date];
UnitVC.m	unit.modified = [NSDate date];
LocationAtHomeVC.m	locationAtHome.modified = [NSDate date];
LocationAtShopVC.m	locationAtShop.modified = [NSDate date];

Update Grocery Dude as follows to ensure the modified attribute value is updated to the current date and time when objects are edited:

1. Add item.modified = [NSDate date]; to the refreshInterface method of ItemVC.m on the line after the item object has been created.

2. Add unit.modified = [NSDate date]; to the refreshInterface method of UnitVC.m on the line after the unit object has been created.

3. Add locationAtHome.modified = [NSDate date]; to the refreshInterface method of LocationAtHomeVC.m on the line after the locationAtHome object has been created.

4. Add locationAtShop.modified = [NSDate date]; to the refreshInterface method of LocationAtShopVC.m on the line after the locationAtShop object has been created.

The deletion logic to be added to the deDuplicateEntityWithName method of Deduplicator will require the ability to save the full context hierarchy. To facilitate this, a new method called saveContextHierarchy will be added to Deduplicator. This method walks the context hierarchy all the way up through the parents, processing pending changes and saving each context as required. Listing 15.4 shows the code involved.

Listing 15.4   **Deduplicator.m: saveContextHierarchy**

```
#pragma mark - SAVING
+ (void)saveContextHierarchy:(NSManagedObjectContext*)moc {
    [moc performBlockAndWait:^{
        if ([moc hasChanges]) {
            [moc processPendingChanges];
            NSError *error;
            if (![moc save:&error]) {
                NSLog(@"ERROR Saving: %@",error);
            }
        }
        // Save the parent context, if any.
        if ([moc parentContext]) {
            [self saveContextHierarchy:moc.parentContext];
        }
    }];
}
```

Update Grocery Dude as follows to implement context hierarchy saving:

1. Add the code from Listing 15.4 to the bottom of Deduplicator.m before @end.

With the appropriate code in place to ensure objects have a modified date, the code to delete duplicated objects based on this attribute can now be implemented. Listing 15.5 shows the code involved.

Listing 15.5   **Deduplicator.m: deDuplicateEntityWithName (Cont.)**

```
NSLog(@"*** Deleting Duplicate %@ with %@ '%@' ***",

  entityName, uniqueAttributeName, [object valueForKey:uniqueAttributeName]);

// DELETE OLDEST DUPLICATE...
NSDate *date1 = [object valueForKey:@"modified"];
NSDate *date2 = [lastObject valueForKey:@"modified"];

if ([date1 compare:date2] == NSOrderedAscending) {
    [importContext deleteObject:object];
} else if ([date1 compare:date2] == NSOrderedDescending) {
    [importContext deleteObject:lastObject];
}
```

```
// ..or.. DELETE DUPLICATE WITH LESS ATTRIBUTE VALUES (if dates match)
else if ([[object committedValuesForKeys:nil] count] >
           [[lastObject committedValuesForKeys:nil] count]) {
    [importContext deleteObject:lastObject];
} else {
    NSLog(@"Skipped De-duplication, dates and value counts match");
}
[self saveContextHierarchy:importContext];
```

The logic to blindly delete the oldest object is a primitive way to achieve de-duplication. In some cases, the results of this hardline logic may annoy the users. For example, if a user created a new "apples" object not realizing that one already existed with a lovely photo of apples, that photo would be lost. In your own projects, consider adding further logic to merge old attribute values where a newer object has a `nil` value. For brevity, there is little value in adding this to Grocery Dude. However you choose to handle your de-duplication strategy, the fundamentals are now in place to support your desired logic.

Update Grocery Dude as follows to implement duplicate object deletion logic:

1. Add the code from Listing 15.5 to the `deDuplicateEntityWithName` method of `Deduplicator.m` by replacing the comment `//Add deletion logic here`.

The final step in implementing de-duplication is to call `deDuplicateEntityWithName` at an appropriate time. Listing 15.6 shows the code involved.

Listing 15.6 PrepareTVC.m: viewDidAppear

```
[cdh.context performBlock:^{
    [Deduplicator deDuplicateEntityWithName:@"Item"
                    withUniqueAttributeName:@"name"
                         withImportContext:cdh.context];

    [Deduplicator deDuplicateEntityWithName:@"Unit"
                    withUniqueAttributeName:@"name"
                         withImportContext:cdh.context];

    [Deduplicator deDuplicateEntityWithName:@"LocationAtHome"
                    withUniqueAttributeName:@"storedIn"
                         withImportContext:cdh.context];

    [Deduplicator deDuplicateEntityWithName:@"LocationAtShop"
                    withUniqueAttributeName:@"aisle"
                         withImportContext:cdh.context];
}];
```

Update Grocery Dude as follows to enable de-duplication:

1. Add #import "Deduplicator.h" to the top of PrepareTVC.m.

2. Add the code from Listing 15.6 to the bottom of the viewDidAppear method of PrepareTVC.m.

Run the application and create a new item with the same name as another item. One item should be deleted automatically. The expected result is shown in Figure 15.2.

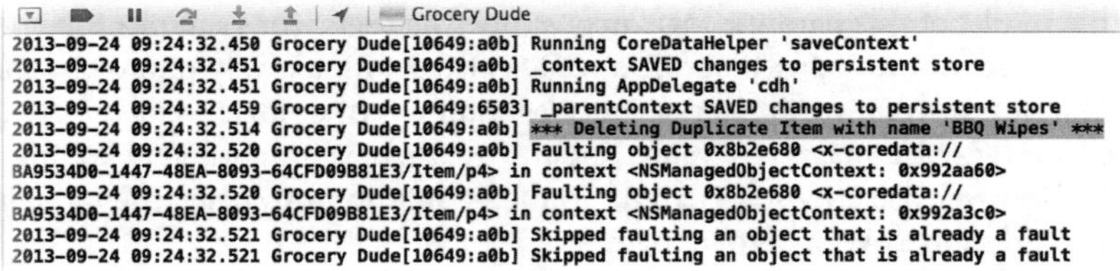

```
▣  ▶  II  ⟲  ⬇  ⬆  ◀ | ▭ Grocery Dude
2013-09-24 09:24:32.450 Grocery Dude[10649:a0b] Running CoreDataHelper 'saveContext'
2013-09-24 09:24:32.451 Grocery Dude[10649:a0b] _context SAVED changes to persistent store
2013-09-24 09:24:32.451 Grocery Dude[10649:a0b] Running AppDelegate 'cdh'
2013-09-24 09:24:32.459 Grocery Dude[10649:6503] _parentContext SAVED changes to persistent store
2013-09-24 09:24:32.514 Grocery Dude[10649:a0b] *** Deleting Duplicate Item with name 'BBQ Wipes' ***
2013-09-24 09:24:32.520 Grocery Dude[10649:a0b] Faulting object 0x8b2e680 <x-coredata://
BA9534D0-1447-48EA-8093-64CFD09B81E3/Item/p4> in context <NSManagedObjectContext: 0x992aa60>
2013-09-24 09:24:32.520 Grocery Dude[10649:a0b] Faulting object 0x8b2e680 <x-coredata://
BA9534D0-1447-48EA-8093-64CFD09B81E3/Item/p4> in context <NSManagedObjectContext: 0x992a3c0>
2013-09-24 09:24:32.521 Grocery Dude[10649:a0b] Skipped faulting an object that is already a fault
2013-09-24 09:24:32.521 Grocery Dude[10649:a0b] Skipped faulting an object that is already a fault
```

Figure 15.2   De-duplication

Seeding

When users enable iCloud support in an application they already use, chances are they have data that needs to be migrated to iCloud. The technique that will be used to migrate non-iCloud data to iCloud in Grocery Dude is deep copy, which was implemented in Chapter 9, "Deep Copy." Although more CPU intensive than migratePersistentStore, this approach provides the granularity of per-entity migration and allows object values to be updated as they are migrated. With the ability to update attribute values as they are migrated, the modified attribute can be set to today's date. This ensures that the de-duplication process is more effective when default data with the same date on multiple devices is migrated. Listing 15.7 shows new CoreDataImporter code required to update objects with a modified attribute of today's date as they're copied.

Listing 15.7   **CoreDataImporter.m: copyUniqueObject:toContext**

```
// Update modified date as appropriate
if ([[[copiedObject entity] attributesByName] objectForKey:@"modified"]) {
    [copiedObject setValue:[NSDate date] forKey:@"modified"];
}
```

Update Grocery Dude as follows to ensure deep copy updates the modified date:

1. Add the code from Listing 15.7 to the copyUniqueObject:toContext method of CoreDataImporter.m on the line before return copiedObject;.

The seeding process requires a context that is not a child of parentContext, so the existing sourceContext cannot be used for this purpose. Instead, a new seedContext and seedCoordinator will be added to CoreDataHelper. In addition, a new seedStore will be added so the Non-iCloud store can be loaded as read-only, ready to be seeded to iCloud. Listing 15.8 shows the new properties required, along with a new UIAlertView intended to confirm that the user wants the seed to take place, and a BOOL property that prevents migration from being triggered twice.

Listing 15.8   **CoreDataHelper.h**

```
@property (nonatomic, readonly) NSManagedObjectContext        *seedContext;
@property (nonatomic, readonly) NSPersistentStoreCoordinator *seedCoordinator;
@property (nonatomic, readonly) NSPersistentStore            *seedStore;
@property (nonatomic, retain)   UIAlertView                  *seedAlertView;
@property (nonatomic)           BOOL                          seedInProgress;
```

Update Grocery Dude as follows to implement the new properties required for seeding:

1. Add the properties from Listing 15.8 to CoreDataHelper.h.

The seed context will be configured in the same way as the other contexts; however, it will have its own coordinator instead of a parent context. The code involved is shown in Listing 15.9.

Listing 15.9   **CoreDataHelper.m: init**

```
_seedCoordinator =
[[NSPersistentStoreCoordinator alloc] initWithManagedObjectModel:_model];
_seedContext = [[NSManagedObjectContext alloc]
                 initWithConcurrencyType:NSPrivateQueueConcurrencyType];
[_seedContext performBlockAndWait:^{
    [_seedContext setPersistentStoreCoordinator:_seedCoordinator];
    [_seedContext setMergePolicy:NSMergeByPropertyObjectTrumpMergePolicy];
    [_seedContext setUndoManager:nil]; // the default on iOS
}];
_seedInProgress = NO;
```

Update Grocery Dude as follows to configure the seed properties:

1. Add the code from Listing 15.9 to the bottom of the init method of CoreDataHelper.m before [self listenForStoreChanges];.

The seeding process will rely on two new helper methods that will be added to the existing CORE DATA RESET section of CoreDataHelper.m. The first method, unloadStore, will be used to ensure that the given store does not exist. It does this by first removing the given store from its coordinator and then setting the store to nil.

The second method, `removeFileAtURL`, will be used to delete the old Non-iCloud store once seeding is finished. For brevity, there will be no check performed to ensure that seeding was successful before deleting the Non-iCloud data. In your own applications, you may wish to prompt the user prior to deleting the old store or implement code to detect seeding status prior to deletion.

The code involved with the new methods is shown in Listing 15.10.

Listing 15.10   **CoreDataHelper.m: CORE DATA RESET**

```
- (BOOL)unloadStore:(NSPersistentStore*)ps {
if (debug==1) {
    NSLog(@"Running %@ '%@'", self.class, NSStringFromSelector(_cmd));
}
    if (ps) {
        NSPersistentStoreCoordinator *psc = ps.persistentStoreCoordinator;
        NSError *error = nil;
        if (![psc removePersistentStore:ps error:&error]) {
            NSLog(@"ERROR removing store from the coordinator: %@",error);
            return NO; // Fail
        } else {
            ps = nil;
            return YES; // Reset complete
        }
    }
    return YES; // No need to reset, store is nil
}
- (void)removeFileAtURL:(NSURL*)url {

    NSError *error = nil;
    if (![[NSFileManager defaultManager] removeItemAtURL:url error:&error]) {
        NSLog(@"Failed to delete '%@' from '%@'",
        [url lastPathComponent], [url URLByDeletingLastPathComponent]);
    } else {
        NSLog(@"Deleted '%@' from '%@'",
        [url lastPathComponent], [url URLByDeletingLastPathComponent]);
    }
}
```

Update Grocery Dude as follows to add the two new methods:

1. Add the code from Listing 15.10 to the bottom of the existing CORE DATA RESET section of `CoreDataHelper.m`.

The next step is to add a new method called `loadNoniCloudStoreAsSeedStore`. As its name suggests, this method is responsible for loading the Non-iCloud store as the source store used to seed existing data to iCloud. This method is similar to the `loadStore` method already in place within `CoreDataHelper.m`. Listing 15.11 shows the code involved.

Listing 15.11   CoreDataHelper.m: loadNoniCloudStoreAsSeedStore

```
#pragma mark - ICLOUD SEEDING
- (BOOL)loadNoniCloudStoreAsSeedStore {
if (debug==1) {
    NSLog(@"Running %@ '%@'", self.class, NSStringFromSelector(_cmd));
}
    if (_seedInProgress) {
        NSLog(@"Seed already in progress ...");
        return NO;
    }

    if (![self unloadStore:_seedStore]) {
        NSLog(@"Failed to ensure _seedStore was removed prior to migration.");
        return NO;
    }

    if (![self unloadStore:_store]) {
        NSLog(@"Failed to ensure _store was removed prior to migration.");
        return NO;
    }

    NSDictionary *options =
    @{
      NSReadOnlyPersistentStoreOption:@YES
      };
    NSError *error = nil;
    _seedStore = [_seedCoordinator addPersistentStoreWithType:NSSQLiteStoreType
                                    configuration:nil
                                        URL:[self storeURL]
                                    options:options error:&error];
    if (!_seedStore) {
        NSLog(@"Failed to load Non-iCloud Store as Seed Store. Error: %@", error);
        return NO;
    }
    NSLog(@"Successfully loaded Non-iCloud Store as Seed Store: %@", _seedStore);
    return YES;
}
```

Update Grocery Dude as follows to implement the new method to load a seed store:

1. Add the code from Listing 15.11 to the bottom of `CoreDataHelper.m` before `@end`.

The next step is to implement a method responsible for the migration of the Non-iCloud seed store to iCloud. The mergeNoniCloudDataWithiCloud method begins by scheduling a timer that will periodically refresh the table views. Next, the seedContext that runs in the background loads the Non-iCloud store as the seedStore. Provided this is successful, the entities to copy are specified by name and given to an instance of CoreDataImporter. A deep copy is then triggered, and once it completes the old store is removed. Listing 15.12 shows the code involved.

Listing 15.12   **CoreDataHelper.m: mergeNoniCloudDataWithiCloud**

```
- (void)mergeNoniCloudDataWithiCloud {
if (debug==1) {
    NSLog(@"Running %@ '%@'", self.class, NSStringFromSelector(_cmd));
}
    _importTimer = [NSTimer scheduledTimerWithTimeInterval:5.0
                                                    target:self
                                                  selector:@selector(somethingChanged)
                                                  userInfo:nil
                                                   repeats:YES];
    [_seedContext performBlock:^{

        if ([self loadNoniCloudStoreAsSeedStore]) {

            NSLog(@"*** STARTED DEEP COPY FROM NON-ICLOUD STORE TO ICLOUD STORE ***");
            NSArray *entitiesToCopy = [NSArray arrayWithObjects:
                    @"LocationAtHome",@"LocationAtShop",@"Unit",@"Item", nil];
            CoreDataImporter *importer = [[CoreDataImporter alloc]
                        initWithUniqueAttributes:[self selectedUniqueAttributes]];
            [importer deepCopyEntities:entitiesToCopy fromContext:_seedContext
                                                        toContext:_importContext];

            [_context performBlock:^{
                // Tell the interface to refresh once import completes
                [[NSNotificationCenter defaultCenter]
                            postNotificationName:@"SomethingChanged" object:nil];
            }];
            NSLog(@"*** FINISHED DEEP COPY FROM NON-ICLOUD STORE TO ICLOUD STORE ***");
            NSLog(@"*** REMOVING OLD NON-ICLOUD STORE ***");
            if ([self unloadStore:_seedStore]) {

                [_context performBlock:^{
                    // Tell the interface to refresh once import completes
                    [[NSNotificationCenter defaultCenter]
                                postNotificationName:@"SomethingChanged"
                                            object:nil];
```

```
                        // Remove migrated store
                        NSString *wal = [storeFilename stringByAppendingString:@"-wal"];
                        NSString *shm = [storeFilename stringByAppendingString:@"-shm"];
                        [self removeFileAtURL:[self storeURL]];
                        [self removeFileAtURL:[[self applicationStoresDirectory]
                                                URLByAppendingPathComponent:wal]];
                        [self removeFileAtURL:[[self applicationStoresDirectory]
                                                URLByAppendingPathComponent:shm]];
                    }];
                }
            }
        [_context performBlock:^{
            // Stop periodically refreshing the interface
            [_importTimer invalidate];
        }];
    }];
}
```

After the store is migrated, it is removed along with all of its accompanying `wal` and `shm` files that exist because WAL journaling is being used.

Update Grocery Dude as follows to implement the code to seed data to iCloud:

1. Add the code from Listing 15.12 to the bottom of the ICLOUD SEEDING section of `CoreDataHelper.m`.

Whenever the iCloud store is loaded, a check will be performed to see if there's local data that needs to be migrated to iCloud. If there is, the user will be asked if he or she would like to merge it with iCloud. This requires a new method, `confirmMergeWithiCloud`, which will be used to show the `seedAlertView`. Listing 15.13 shows the code involved.

Listing 15.13 **CoreDataHelper.m: confirmMergeWithiCloud**

```
- (void)confirmMergeWithiCloud {
if (debug==1) {
    NSLog(@"Running %@ '%@'", self.class, NSStringFromSelector(_cmd));
}
    if (![[NSFileManager defaultManager] fileExistsAtPath:[[self storeURL] path]]) {
    NSLog(@"Skipped unnecessary migration of Non-iCloud store to iCloud (there's no
➥store file).");
        return;
    }
    _seedAlertView = [[UIAlertView alloc] initWithTitle:@"Merge with iCloud?"
                                                message:@"This will move your
➥existing data into iCloud. If you don't merge now, you can merge later by
➥toggling iCloud for this application in Settings."
```

```
                                       delegate:self
                          cancelButtonTitle:@"Don't Merge"
                          otherButtonTitles:@"Merge", nil];

    [_seedAlertView show];
}
```

Update Grocery Dude as follows to implement the code to confirm a merge with iCloud:

1. Add the code from Listing 15.13 to the bottom of the ICLOUD SEEDING section of
   CoreDataHelper.m.

2. Add the following code to the bottom of the alertView:clickedButtonAtIndex
   method of CoreDataHelper.m:

   ```
   if (alertView == self.seedAlertView) {
       if (buttonIndex == alertView.firstOtherButtonIndex) {
           [self mergeNoniCloudDataWithiCloud];
       }
   }
   ```

3. Add the following code to the loadiCloudStore method of CoreDataHelper.m on the
   line before return YES;:

   ```
   [self confirmMergeWithiCloud];
   ```

All code required to test seeding is now in place. Test seeding as follows:

1. Click **Product > Clean**.

2. Run **Grocery Dude** on a device or the iOS Simulator.

3. Press **Home (Option+⌘+H)** and enter the **Settings App**.

4. Scroll down, tap **Grocery Dude**, and ensure **Enable iCloud** is switched off.

5. Return to **Grocery Dude** and create an item called **LOCAL ITEM**.

6. Return to **Settings > Grocery Dude** and ensure **Enable iCloud** is switched on.

7. Ensure an account is signed in iCloud.

8. Return to Grocery Dude and click **Ok**. Then **Merge** as shown in Figure 15.3.

The local data should be migrated into iCloud and the Non-iCloud store removed once the migration completes. If you have additional devices, create some recognizable local data on them and seed it to iCloud. Upon initial import, there will be a lot of seeding activity and then subsequent de-duplication work. Once a second device seeds to iCloud, it's normal for many "Skipped faulting an object that is already a fault" messages to appear in the console log until de-duplication completes. Search the console log for "Using local storage: 0," which should appear within a few minutes of enabling iCloud, so long as your device has Internet connectivity and has a consistent ubiquity container.

Figure 15.3   Merging non-iCloud data with iCloud

Developing with a Clean Slate

Throughout testing, you may wish to revert iCloud to a clean slate. Usually this is so you can observe application behavior as if a user had just installed the application for the first time. Instead of deleting an application's iCloud directory contents each time you want to clear iCloud, you can now use the NSPersistentStoreCoordinator class method removeUbiquitousContentAndPersistentStoreAtURL. This method synchronously deletes everything in iCloud specific to the given persistent store, so it can take a little while. It then propagates this deletion to all participating devices when they come online. When you call this method, you'll need to provide an options dictionary to help locate the files associated to the given persistent store, just as you would when adding a persistent store normally. It is important to ensure that there are no active persistent store coordinators in use when this method is called. Listing 15.14 shows the code involved in a new ICLOUD RESET section.

Listing 15.14   **CoreDataHelper.m: ICLOUD RESET**

```
#pragma mark - ICLOUD RESET
- (void)destroyAlliCloudDataForThisApplication {

if (![[NSFileManager defaultManager] fileExistsAtPath:[[_iCloudStore URL] path]]) {
    NSLog(@"Skipped destroying iCloud content, _iCloudStore.URL is %@",
    [[_iCloudStore URL] path]);
    return;
}

    NSLog(@"\n\n\n\n\n **** Destroying ALL iCloud content for this application, this
➥could take a while...  **** \n\n\n\n\n\n");
```

```
[self removeAllStoresFromCoordinator:_coordinator];
[self removeAllStoresFromCoordinator:_seedCoordinator];
_coordinator = nil;
_seedCoordinator = nil;

NSDictionary *options =
@{
  NSPersistentStoreUbiquitousContentNameKey:@"Grocery-Dude"
 //,NSPersistentStoreUbiquitousContentURLKey:@"ChangeLogs" // Optional since iOS7
  };
NSError *error;
if ([NSPersistentStoreCoordinator
      removeUbiquitousContentAndPersistentStoreAtURL:[_iCloudStore URL]
                                              options:options
                                                error:&error]) {
NSLog(@"\n\n\n\n\n");
NSLog(@"*         This application's iCloud content has been destroyed         *");
NSLog(@"* On ALL devices, please delete any reference to this application in *");
NSLog(@"*  Settings > iCloud > Storage & Backup > Manage Storage > Show All  *");
NSLog(@"\n\n\n\n\n");
abort();
/*
    The application is force closed to ensure iCloud data is wiped cleanly.
    This method shouldn't be called in a production application.
*/
} else {
    NSLog(@"\n\n FAILED to destroy iCloud content at URL: %@ Error:%@",
                                  [_iCloudStore URL],error);

  }
}
```

The destroyAlliCloudDataForThisApplication method first checks a store exists at the given path. So long as it does, all stores are removed from all coordinators and an iCloud options dictionary is created. This dictionary is given along with the iCloud URL to the removeUbiquitousContentAndPersistentStoreAtURL method. Upon success, you're notified to wipe the application data from all devices. At this point, consider deleting the application entirely to more accurately simulate first time use, if that is your goal.

Update Grocery Dude as follows to implement iCloud reset:

1. Add the code from Listing 15.14 to the bottom of CoreDataHelper.m before @end.

2. Add the following line of code to the loadiCloudStore method of CoreDataHelper.m on the line before return YES;. This will trigger a complete wipe of this application's iCloud data on all devices once the iCloud store loads.

   ```
   [self destroyAlliCloudDataForThisApplication];
   ```

3. Run the application and wait for the iCloud store to be loaded and destroyed. The application should terminate automatically once the abort(); is reached. Figure 15.4 shows the expected result.

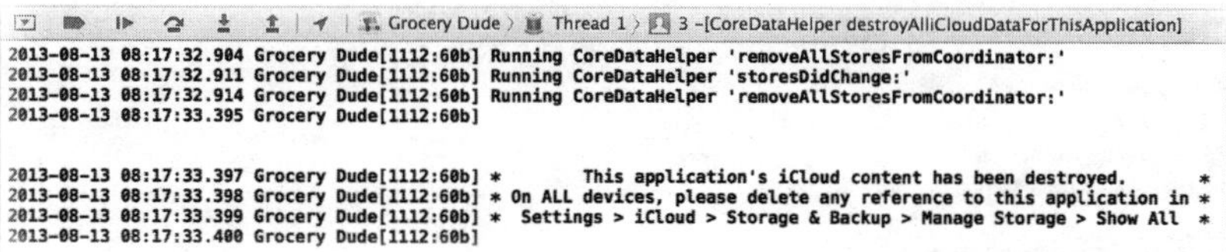

Figure 15.4   iCloud reset

4. Once you receive confirmation that the iCloud content has been destroyed, stop the application and comment out the line of code added to the loadiCloudStore method of CoreDataHelper.m in step 2.

5. Ensure there are no references to Grocery Dude in **Settings > iCloud > Storage & Backup > Manage Storage > Show All** on all devices that synchronize with this iCloud account. The removeUbiquitousContentAndPersistentStoreAtURL method should have taken care of this for you, unless the device in question hasn't received the propagated deletion yet.

6. In Xcode, click **Product > Clean**.

7. Sign in to https://developer.icloud.com/ and ensure there are no files in the Grocery Dude folder.

> **Note**
>
> If you have a device that is refusing to synchronize after you have reset its iCloud data, try resetting all settings via **Settings > General > Reset All Settings**. This approach won't delete any application data, and it can resolve the "Error attempting to read ubiquity root url" error message.

Configurations

Although inappropriate in Grocery Dude, it's good to be aware of Core Data configurations. A configuration allows you to assign different entities to different stores. This can be useful if you need to separate data that should be stored in iCloud from data that is best stored locally. For example, static or even rapidly changing device-specific data (such as a location) would be best placed in a Non-iCloud store. So long as it is unnecessary to replicate that data to other devices, it should stay local. A configuration is created using the Model Editor, as shown in Figure 15.5.

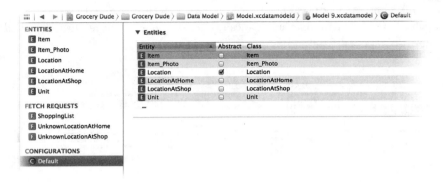

Figure 15.5   Core Data configurations

Configuration creation requires a similar approach to creating an Entity or Fetch Request template. The default configuration can't be deleted, so if you wanted to divide your entities into iCloud and Non-iCloud configurations, you'll need to create two new configurations. Once these are created, you can then drag each entity into an appropriate configuration.

To use a configuration, pass the configuration name when adding a persistent store to a coordinator with `addPersistentStoreWithType`. For example, the `loadStore` method currently passes `nil` as the configuration name, which just uses the default configuration. Instead of `nil`, pass the configuration name.

A key point to be aware of when using configurations is that you are separating your data into separate stores. Relationships between objects in separate stores are not supported, so you will need to work around this constraint.

Finishing Touches

Since Core Data has been integrated with iCloud, the Dropbox backup-and-restore process will have no visible effect with iCloud enabled. This is because the iCloud store is in use instead of the Non-iCloud store that Dropbox is configured to work with. In reality, the only data resident on each device is an iCloud "cache," and not the actual data stored behind the iCloud service. This means that even if users lose their device, they won't lose any data because the store can be reconstructed from iCloud. In addition, restoring an iCloud store would have unpredictable results, so Dropbox backup-and-restore support will be disabled when iCloud is enabled. Listing 15.15 shows the code involved in presenting an alert view, which informs the user that Dropbox is disabled when iCloud is enabled.

Listing 15.15   **DropboxTVC.m: backup / restore**

```
CoreDataHelper *cdh =
[(AppDelegate *)[[UIApplication sharedApplication] delegate] cdh];
if ([cdh iCloudEnabledByUser]) {
    UIAlertView *alert = [[UIAlertView alloc] initWithTitle:@"Not Supported"
                    message:@"This functionality is disabled because iCloud is enabled"
                    delegate:nil
        cancelButtonTitle:nil
        otherButtonTitles:@"OK", nil];
    [alert show];
    return;
}
```

Update Grocery Dude as follows to disable backup-and-restore when iCloud is enabled:

1. Add the following code to the bottom of `CoreDataHelper.h` before `@end`:

   - `(BOOL)iCloudEnabledByUser;`

2. Add the code from Listing 15.15 to the top of the `backup` method of `DropboxTVC.m`.

3. Add the code from Listing 15.15 to the top of the `restore` method of `DropboxTVC.m`.

4. Run Grocery Dude on a couple of devices and enable iCloud in Settings. Don't forget to also sign in to iCloud again if you ever reset the simulator to defaults. You should see that, when changes are persisted on one device, they show up on all other iCloud-enabled devices with Grocery Dude installed.

Summary

Additional features have now been implemented that should keep Core Data and iCloud a little more user friendly. From de-duplication to seeding, each of these techniques goes a step closer to providing the seamless experience that users have come to expect. One final point to note is that it is possible to load the iCloud store when the device is not signed in to iCloud. This is the beauty of the Fallback Store, which is at work under the hood. Still, it doesn't cater to existing Non-iCloud stores, so Grocery Dude has been configured with the additional "iCloud Enabled" setting, allowing you to bypass iCloud and the Fallback Store altogether. To configure `CoreDataHelper` to use an existing store of your own, just ensure that the FILES and PATHS sections return a URL pointing to that store.

Exercises

Why not build on what you've learned by experimenting with adding Core Data and iCloud to a completely new application using the helper classes built throughout this book?

1. Create a new **Single View Application** for **iPhone** in Xcode and name the project **EasyiCloud**.

> **Tip**
>
> If you adapt this procedure to other project types, do not tick Use Core Data.

2. Download and extract the **Generic Core Data Classes** folder from the following URL: http://timroadley.com/LearningCoreData/Generic%20Core%20Data%20Classes.zip.

3. Drag the **Generic Core Data Classes** folder into the **EasyiCloud** group in the **EasyiCloud** project. Ensure that **"Copy items into destination group's folder"** and the EasyiCloud target are ticked before clicking **Finish**.

4. Add a **Data Model** as follows:

    a. Click **File > New > File...** and create an **iOS > Core Data > Data Model**.

    b. Ensure the **EasyiCloud** target is selected and click **Create** to accept **Model** as the filename.

5. Configure **Model.xcdatamodeld** as follows:

    a. Add an entity called **Test** with three attributes: **modified**, **device**, and **someValue**.

    b. Set the **modified** attribute type to **Date**.

    c. Set the **device** and **someValue** attribute types to **String**.

6. Create an `NSManagedObject` subclass for the **Test** entity. Ensure the EasyiCloud target is selected before clicking **Create**.

7. Create an **iOS > Cocoa Touch > Objective-C class** that is a `CoreDataTVC` subclass called `TestTVC` and then replace the code in `TestTVC.m` with the code from Listing 15.16.

Listing 15.16   **TestTVC.m**

```
#import "TestTVC.h"
#import "CoreDataHelper.h"
#import "AppDelegate.h"
#import "Deduplicator.h"
#import "Test.h"


@implementation TestTVC


#pragma mark - DATA
- (void)configureFetch {
```

```objc
    CoreDataHelper *cdh = [CoreDataHelper sharedHelper];
    NSFetchRequest *request =
    [NSFetchRequest fetchRequestWithEntityName:@"Test"];
    request.sortDescriptors = [NSArray arrayWithObjects:
                [NSSortDescriptor sortDescriptorWithKey:@"modified" ascending:NO],nil];
    [request setFetchBatchSize:15];
    self.frc =
    [[NSFetchedResultsController alloc] initWithFetchRequest:request
                                    managedObjectContext:cdh.context
                                      sectionNameKeyPath:nil
                                               cacheName:nil];
    self.frc.delegate = self;
}

#pragma mark - VIEW
- (void)viewDidAppear:(BOOL)animated {
    [super viewDidAppear:animated];

    CoreDataHelper *cdh = [CoreDataHelper sharedHelper];
    [Deduplicator deDuplicateEntityWithName:@"Test"
                    withUniqueAttributeName:@"someValue"
                          withImportContext:cdh.importContext];

}
- (void)viewDidLoad {
    [super viewDidLoad];
    [self configureFetch];
    [self performFetch];
    // Respond to changes in underlying store
    [[NSNotificationCenter defaultCenter] addObserver:self
                                    selector:@selector(performFetch)
                                        name:@"SomethingChanged"
                                      object:nil];
}
- (UITableViewCell*)tableView:(UITableView *)tableView
        cellForRowAtIndexPath:(NSIndexPath *)indexPath {

    static NSString *cellIdentifier = @"Cell";
    UITableViewCell *cell =
    [tableView dequeueReusableCellWithIdentifier:cellIdentifier
                                    forIndexPath:indexPath];
    Test *test = [self.frc objectAtIndexPath:indexPath];

    cell.textLabel.text = [NSString stringWithFormat:@"From: %@",test.device];
    cell.detailTextLabel.text = test.someValue;
    return cell;
}
```

```
- (void)tableView:(UITableView *)tableView
commitEditingStyle:(UITableViewCellEditingStyle)editingStyle
 forRowAtIndexPath:(NSIndexPath *)indexPath {
    if (editingStyle == UITableViewCellEditingStyleDelete) {
        NSManagedObject *deleteTarget = [self.frc objectAtIndexPath:indexPath];
        [self.frc.managedObjectContext deleteObject:deleteTarget];
        [self.tableView reloadRowsAtIndexPaths:[NSArray arrayWithObject:indexPath]
                            withRowAnimation:UITableViewRowAnimationFade];
    }
    CoreDataHelper *cdh = [CoreDataHelper sharedHelper];
    [cdh backgroundSaveContext];
}

#pragma mark - INTERACTION
- (IBAction)add:(id)sender {

    CoreDataHelper *cdh = [CoreDataHelper sharedHelper];
    Test *object =
    [NSEntityDescription insertNewObjectForEntityForName:@"Test"
                              inManagedObjectContext:cdh.context];
    NSError *error = nil;
    if (![cdh.context obtainPermanentIDsForObjects:[NSArray arrayWithObject:object]
                                    error:&error]) {
        NSLog(@"Couldn't obtain a permanent ID for object %@", error);
    }
    UIDevice *thisDevice = [UIDevice new];
    object.device = thisDevice.name;
    object.modified = [NSDate date];
    object.someValue = [NSString stringWithFormat:@"Test: %@",
                             [[NSUUID UUID] UUIDString]];
    [cdh backgroundSaveContext];
}
@end
```

8. Replace the default view with a table view, as follows:

   a. Select **Main.storyboard**.

   b. Delete the existing **View Controller**.

   c. Drag a **Table View Controller** onto the storyboard and then click **Editor > Embed In > Navigation Controller**.

   d. Drag a **Bar Button Item** on to the top right of the **Table View Controller**.

   e. Set the **Identifier** of the new **Bar Button Item** to **Add** using Attributes Inspector (**Option+⌘+4**).

f. Select the **Prototype Cell** and then set its **Style** to **Subtitle** and its **Identifier** to Cell.

g. Select the **Table View Controller** and set its **Custom Class** to TestTVC using **Identity Inspector (Option+⌘+3)**.

h. Hold down **Control** and drag a line from the **Add** button to the yellow circle at the bottom of the **Table View Controller**. Then select **Sent Actions > add**.

9. Turn on the iCloud capability using the approach discussed in Chapter 14.

10. Configure a **Settings Bundle** as follows:

a. Click **File > New > File...** and create a **Resource > Settings Bundle**, ensuring that the EasyiCloud target is selected before clicking **Create**.

b. Select **/Settings.bundle/Root.plist**, expand **Preference Items**, and delete the three items that aren't a Toggle Switch.

c. Set the **Default Value** of **Item 0** to **NO**.

d. Set the **Identifier** of **Item 0** to **iCloudEnabled**.

e. Set the **Title** of **Item 0** to **Enable iCloud**.

f. Add #import "CoreDataHelper.h" to the top of AppDelegate.m.

g. Add [[CoreDataHelper sharedHelper] ensureAppropriateStoreIsLoaded]; to the applicationWillEnterForeground method of AppDelegate.m. This new class method allows greater portability of CoreDataHelper. Further information on its usage is found in CoreDataHelper.h.

11. Add [[CoreDataHelper sharedHelper] iCloudAccountIsSignedIn]; to the didFinishLaunchingWithOptions method of AppDelegate.m before return YES;.

12. Add [[CoreDataHelper sharedHelper] backgroundSaveContext]; to the applicationDidEnterBackground and applicationWillTerminate methods of AppDelegate.m.

13. Update the selectedUniqueAttributes method of CoreDataHelper.m so that it is appropriate to the new data model. To do so, replace the selectedUniqueAttributes method with the one from Listing 15.17.

Listing 15.17 CoreDataHelper.m: selectedUniqueAttributes

```
- (NSDictionary*)selectedUniqueAttributes {
if (debug==1) {
    NSLog(@"Running %@ '%@'", self.class, NSStringFromSelector(_cmd));
}
    NSMutableArray *entities   = [NSMutableArray new];
    NSMutableArray *attributes = [NSMutableArray new];
```

```
// Select an attribute in each entity for uniqueness
[entities addObject:@"Test"];[attributes addObject:@"someValue"];
//[entities addObject:@"Item"];[attributes addObject:@"name"];
//[entities addObject:@"Unit"];[attributes addObject:@"name"];
//[entities addObject:@"LocationAtHome"];[attributes addObject:@"storedIn"];
//[entities addObject:@"LocationAtShop"];[attributes addObject:@"aisle"];
//[entities addObject:@"Item_Photo"];[attributes addObject:@"data"];

NSDictionary *dictionary = [NSDictionary dictionaryWithObjects:attributes
                                                       forKeys:entities];

return dictionary;
}
```

14. Update `entitiesToCopy` in the `mergeNoniCloudDataWithiCloud` method of
    `CoreDataHelper.m` so that it is appropriate to the new data model. To do so, replace the
    line of code with the one shown here:

    ```
    NSArray *entitiesToCopy = [NSArray arrayWithObjects:@"Test", nil];
    ```

15. Run the application on two more devices and then enable iCloud in **Settings >
    EasyiCloud**. No data will be merged into iCloud if `confirmMergeWithiCloud` is
    commented out in the `loadiCloudStore` method of `CoreDataHelper.m`.

16. Tap the + button to create test objects on each device. Once "Using local storage:
    0" appears in the console log, you should see data show up on other devices. The
    expected result is shown in Figure 15.6. If the simulator seems slow to sync, click **Debug
    > Trigger iCloud Sync**.

For your convenience, the EasyiCloud project is available for download from the following
URL: http://timroadley.com/LearningCoreData/EasyiCloud.zip.

Figure 15.6   Easy iCloud

16

Web Service Integration

Everybody is a genius. But if you judge a fish by its ability to climb a tree,
it will live its whole life believing that it is stupid.

Albert Einstein

In Chapter 14, "iCloud," and Chapter 15, "Taming iCloud," Grocery Dude's Core Data stack was integrated with iCloud. A key limitation of iCloud, however, is that its data is constrained to one iCloud account. Because iCloud accounts are deeply intertwined with many aspects of user devices, it is not practical or recommended to share iCloud accounts. This means that iCloud cannot be used to collaborate. For example, assume a husband and wife wanted to contribute to the same shopping list. This isn't currently possible with iCloud. The bottom line is that alternative backend systems need to be considered instead. There are several options available, and you should evaluate them on their own merits. In the interest of not reinventing the wheel, it is recommended that you avoid provisioning your own servers, databases, security, and everything else involved with managing a backend system. This means you can instead rely on tried-and-true frameworks developed by service providers such as StackMob. This chapter will explain and demonstrate the steps to integrate Core Data with StackMob. The decision to use StackMob is driven from its close alignment with Core Data.

Introducing StackMob

StackMob is a company that provides an enterprise-class Backend-as-a-Service (BaaS), which allows devices to share data so long as they can connect to a REST API and authenticate with OAuth2. The StackMob iOS SDK is so tightly integrated with Core Data that once you've replaced the persistent store with a StackMob store, you're almost ready to go.

Note

REST stands for Representational State Transfer and is the software architecture approach for intersystem communication used by StackMob. Think of REST as "The Internet" for application components. If one area of a system needs to access a resource in another area of the system, it uses a URL like you do when visiting a website. This client/server model works well because it allows distributed systems to remain modular. This means each component is self-contained and independently upgradable without fear of breaking something up or downstream.

StackMob will use the existing Core Data Managed Object Model; however, you'll need to configure it so that it works with StackMob. Once the local model is updated, you'll need to configure equivalent StackMob schemas. This is so their backend system knows what objects to expect from the model. A StackMob schema is equivalent to a Core Data entity. To create the schemas, all you need to do is create a managed object for each entity, and the equivalent schemas will be generated automatically.

The StackMob client replaces the need for a persistent store coordinator and provides a managed object context and caching option. At the backend, StackMob will store everything except binary data, which is instead stored in Amazon's Simple Storage Service (S3). Using the S3 service costs money, so photos and thumbnails will not be implemented in this chapter in order to keep the sample project free. An overview of Core Data integration with StackMob is shown in Figure 16.1.

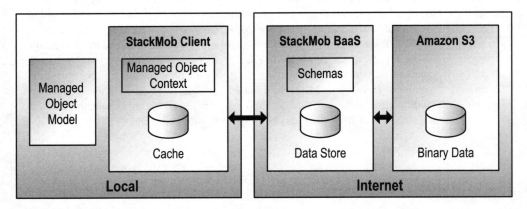

Figure 16.1   StackMob overview

To integrate Core Data with StackMob, you simply add the StackMob iOS SDK and supporting frameworks to an Xcode project. Once everything is integrated, an instance of SMClient can be created and the managed object model supplied to the client in order to get back a persistent store and context to work with. A cache policy is also set to ensure that all fetches are cached in a local store that is available without reliance on network connectivity.

> **Note**
>
> StackMob integration into Grocery Dude will branch off into a new project called Grocery Cloud. The creation of this new base project is covered in Appendix B, "Preparing Grocery Cloud for Chapter 16." Follow the instructions in Appendix B if you would prefer to create the base project yourself. Alternatively, you may download, unzip, and open the base project from http://www.timroadley.com/LearningCoreData/GroceryCloud-AfterAppendixB.zip. Any time you start using an Xcode project from a ZIP file, it's good practice to click **Product > Clean**. This practice ensures there's no residual cache from previous projects using the same name.

The StackMob SDK

To add StackMob support, the first thing you'll need to do is download the StackMob iOS SDK. At the time of writing, the latest version is 2.1.1. There are also several supporting frameworks that Grocery Cloud must first link to in order for StackMob to function correctly.

Update Grocery Cloud as follows to add the required SDK and frameworks:

1. Download and extract the latest iOS SDK from the following URL: https://developer.stackmob.com/sdks. Follow their installation steps, which should resemble steps 2 to 5.

2. Drag the downloaded StackMob directory into the root of the Grocery Cloud Xcode project and ensure that **"Copy items into destination group's folder"** is ticked. Also, ensure that **"Create groups for any added folders"** is selected and that the **Grocery Cloud** target is ticked before clicking **Finish**.

3. Select the **General** tab of the Grocery Cloud target and scroll down to the **Linked Frameworks and Libraries** section. Add the following frameworks, as shown in Figure 16.2:
   - MobileCoreServices
   - SystemConfiguration
   - Security
   - CoreLocation

4. Add -ObjC in the **Other Linker Flags** section found in the **Build Settings** tab of the Grocery Cloud target, as shown in Figure 16.3. (Tip: You may need to click **All** to see all the settings and then search for **Other Linker Flags**.)

5. Add the following lines to /**Supporting Files/Grocery Cloud-Prefix.pch** before the last #endif:

```
#import <SystemConfiguration/SystemConfiguration.h>
#import <MobileCoreServices/MobileCoreServices.h>
```

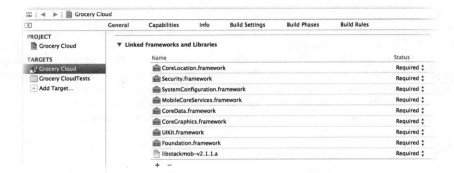

Figure 16.2   Additional frameworks required to support StackMob

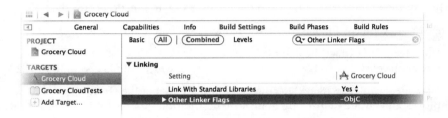

Figure 16.3   `ObjC` linker flag is required by the StackMob iOS SDK.

As mentioned previously, interaction with StackMob web services will be via a StackMob client. Before a StackMob client can be used, an application needs to be defined on the StackMob servers.

Creating a StackMob Application

To create an application on StackMob, you'll need a StackMob or GitHub account. Head over to www.stackmob.com and create an account now. Once you've created an account, you'll be redirected to a page used to set up a new application.

Create an application with the name **grocery_cloud**. You'll be taken to a tutorial, which you may skip. Navigate to the **StackMob Dashboard** and then select **Schema Configuration**. This area allows you to view the existing backend schema for Grocery Cloud. At this point there's only a user schema, as shown in Figure 16.4.

Figure 16.4   A StackMob schema

Managed Object Model Preparation

As shown previously in Figure 16.1, a Managed Object Model is still used to define the application's data structure when using StackMob. However, mandatory changes are required to the existing model before integration can be achieved.

Since version 2 of StackMob's iOS SDK, a feature called **Offline Sync** has been available. This feature allows an application to remain usable when network connectivity is unavailable. Offline writes are cached, and once connectivity returns, changes can be synchronized with the server again.

To support the Offline Sync feature, two new date attributes called `createddate` and `lastmoddate` are required in each entity. These attributes are used for conflict resolution in cases when an offline device has changed data that has also been modified by other means. For brevity, these attributes will be added directly to each entity to avoid the need for a mapping model. In applications that have not yet been released to the public, it is recommended that a new entity called StackMob be introduced as a parent to all existing entities. This simplifies the model design, which is explained in detail in StackMob's own documentation.

In addition to the new date attributes, a new string attribute is required in each entity for the object's StackMob primary key ID. The name of this attribute will be a combination of the containing entity name (all in lowercase) with a suffix of `_id`. For example, the Item entity requires a new attribute called `item_id`.

Update Grocery Cloud as follows to configure the model for StackMob integration:

1. Select **Model.xcdatamodeld**.

2. Click **Editor > Add Model Version...**.

3. Click **Finish** to accept **Model 10** as the version name.

4. Ensure **Model 10.xcdatamodel** is selected.

5. Add an attribute called `createddate` to the **Item** entity and then set its type to **Date**.

6. Add an attribute called `lastmoddate` to the **Item** entity and then set its type to **Date**.

7. Copy the `createddate` and `lastmoddate` attributes from the **Item** entity to the **Item_Photo**, **Location**, and **Unit** entities. Depending on your version of Xcode, the Model Editor may need to be in **Table Editor Style** for attribute copy and paste to work.

8. Add a completely lowercase **String** attribute called `entityname_id` to every entity. For example, in the **Item** entity, create a **String** attribute called `item_id`. Use Figure 16.5 as a guide to the exact attribute name required in each entity.

Another entity called **User** is required for authentication.

Update Grocery Cloud as follows to add a User entity and start using Model 10:

1. Add an entity called **User**.

2. Add an attribute called `user_id` to the **User** entity and then set its type to **String**.

3. Add an attribute called `username` to the **User** entity and then set its type to **String**.

4. Add an attribute called `createddate` to the **User** entity and then set its type to **Date**.

5. Add an attribute called `lastmoddate` to the **User** entity and then set its type to **Date**.

6. Select all entities in **Model 10** and generate `NSManagedObject` subclasses, replacing existing files (via **Editor > Create NSManagedObject Subclass...**). Ensure the **Grocery Cloud** target is ticked before clicking **Create**.

7. Repeat step 6 to ensure relationships are correctly generated in the subclass files.

8. Select **Model.xcdatamodeld** and then set the current model to **Model 10** using **File Inspector (Option+⌘+1)**. The expected result is shown in Figure 16.5.

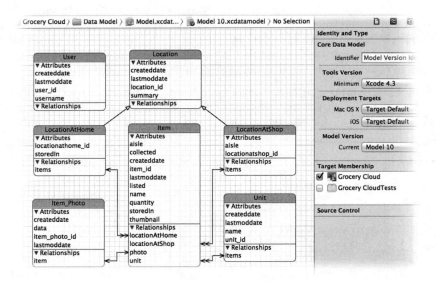

Figure 16.5   StackMob compatible model

> **Note**
>
> Sometimes, creating `NSManagedObject` subclass files causes the same file to be linked twice in Xcode. If this happens, it will cause a Mach-O Linker Error at runtime, and you'll need to delete one of the duplicate references of each subclass file.

Configuring a StackMob Client

Interaction with the StackMob web service occurs via a StackMob client (that is, `SMClient`). A StackMob client requires that a public key be provided when an instance of `SMClient` is created. You can find the development and production keys for a StackMob application using the dashboard shown previously in Figure 16.4. From the StackMob Dashboard, click **Home** to view the public keys for your own **grocery_cloud** application.

To support StackMob, a property for a client instance will be required in `CoreDataHelper.h`, in addition to a new property for the special StackMob persistent store. This store behaves like any other persistent store. To save to it, you'll just access the context for the current thread through the StackMob client. Listing 16.1 shows the two new properties required for StackMob integration.

Listing 16.1   **CoreDataHelper.h**

```
@property (retain, nonatomic) SMClient              *stackMobClient;
@property (retain, nonatomic) SMCoreDataStore       *stackMobStore;
```

Update Grocery Cloud as follows to integrate with StackMob:

1. Add `#import "StackMob.h"` to the top of `CoreDataHelper.h`.

2. Add the properties from Listing 16.1 to `CoreDataHelper.h` beneath the existing properties.

The next step is to update `CoreDataHelper.m` to use the StackMob client. This client will contain the StackMob managed object context(s) and persistent store coordinator. Listing 16.2 shows the code involved in configuring the StackMob client.

Listing 16.2   **CoreDataHelper.m: init**

```
- (id)init {
if (debug==1) {
    NSLog(@"Running %@ '%@'", self.class, NSStringFromSelector(_cmd));
}
    self = [super init];
    if (!self) {return nil;}

    _model = [NSManagedObjectModel mergedModelFromBundles:nil];
```

```objc
    // Use StackMob Cache Store in case network is unavailable
    SM_CACHE_ENABLED = YES;

    // Verbose logging
    SM_CORE_DATA_DEBUG = NO;

    _stackMobClient =      // APIVersion 0 = Dev, 1 = Prod
    [[SMClient alloc] initWithAPIVersion:@"0" publicKey:@"YOUR_APP_KEY"];
    _stackMobStore =
    [_stackMobClient coreDataStoreWithManagedObjectModel:_model];

    __weak SMCoreDataStore *cds = _stackMobStore;
    [_stackMobClient.session.networkMonitor
        setNetworkStatusChangeBlockWithCachePolicyReturn:^SMCachePolicy(
            SMNetworkStatus status
        ){
        if (status == SMNetworkStatusReachable) {
            [cds syncWithServer];
            return SMCachePolicyTryNetworkElseCache;
        } else {
            return SMCachePolicyTryCacheOnly;
        }
    }];

    _context = [_stackMobStore contextForCurrentThread];

    _importContext =
    [[NSManagedObjectContext alloc]
                        initWithConcurrencyType:NSPrivateQueueConcurrencyType];
    [_importContext performBlockAndWait:^{
        [_importContext setParentContext:_context];
        [_importContext setMergePolicy:NSMergeByPropertyObjectTrumpMergePolicy];
        [_importContext setContextShouldObtainPermanentIDsBeforeSaving:YES];
        [_importContext setUndoManager:nil]; // the default on iOS
    }];


    _sourceContext =
    [[NSManagedObjectContext alloc]
                        initWithConcurrencyType:NSPrivateQueueConcurrencyType];
    [_sourceContext performBlockAndWait:^{
        [_sourceContext setMergePolicy:NSMergeByPropertyObjectTrumpMergePolicy];
        [_sourceContext setParentContext:_context];
        [_sourceContext setContextShouldObtainPermanentIDsBeforeSaving:YES];
        [_sourceContext setUndoManager:nil]; // the default on iOS
    }];
    return self;
}
```

Mostly the first half of the `init` method of `CoreDataHelper.m` has changed, as the StackMob client now handles the persistent store coordination. The client is configured with an API version of 0 (Development) as opposed to 1 (Production). No public key is listed in Listing 16.2 because you will need to substitute `YOUR_APP_KEY` with your own application's public key, available from the StackMob Dashboard.

Once a cache policy has been set based on reachability options, the remaining code in the `init` method hasn't changed too much. A new context setting called `setContextShould-ObtainPermanentIDsBeforeSaving` is configured on the import and source contexts as recommended by StackMob, which ensures that permanent IDs for newly inserted objects are created in these contexts. Any time access to a StackMob context is required, it should be accessed via the purpose-built `contextForCurrentThread` method available via the StackMob store.

Update Grocery Cloud as follows to configure the StackMob client:

1. Replace the `init` method of `CoreDataHelper.m` with the code from Listing 16.2.

2. Replace `YOUR_APP_KEY` with your own application's public key, available via the StackMob Dashboard.

3. Comment out all code in the `setupCoreData` method of `CoreDataHelper.m`. This code is no longer required but is left in place so you can more easily experiment with it later.

Saving

There are two ways to save using StackMob: synchronously and asynchronously. To ensure the application remains responsive, asynchronous saving is recommended where possible. The existing `saveContext` and `backgroundSaveContext` methods will be updated to save a StackMob context. Listing 16.3 shows the code involved in these updated methods.

Listing 16.3 **CoreDataHelper.m: SAVING**

```
- (void)saveContext {
if (debug==1) {
    NSLog(@"Running %@ '%@'", self.class, NSStringFromSelector(_cmd));
}
    NSManagedObjectContext *stackMobContext =
    [_stackMobStore contextForCurrentThread];
    if (!stackMobContext) {
        NSLog(@"StackMob context is nil, so FAILED to save");
        return;
    }

    NSError *error;
    [stackMobContext saveAndWait:&error];
    if (!error) {
        NSLog(@"SAVED changes to StackMob store (in the foreground)");
```

```
    } else {
        NSLog(@"FAILED to save changes to StackMob store (in the foreground): %@"
                                                        , error);
    }
}
- (void)backgroundSaveContext {
if (debug==1) {
    NSLog(@"Running %@ '%@'", self.class, NSStringFromSelector(_cmd));
}
    NSManagedObjectContext *stackMobContext =
    [_stackMobStore contextForCurrentThread];
    if (!stackMobContext) {
        NSLog(@"StackMob context is nil, so FAILED to save");
        return;
    }

    [stackMobContext saveOnSuccess:^{
        NSLog(@"SAVED changes to StackMob store (in the background)");
    } onFailure:^(NSError *error) {
        NSLog(@"FAILED to save changes to StackMob store (in the background): %@"
                                                        , error);
    }];
}
```

Update Grocery Cloud as follows to enable StackMob context saves:

1. Replace the `saveContext` and `backgroundSaveContext` methods of `CoreDataHelper.m`
    with the equivalent methods from Listing 16.3.

2. Replace `[[self cdh] backgroundSaveContext];` in the
    `applicationDidEnterBackground` and `applicationWillTerminate` methods of
    `AppDelegate.m` with `[[self cdh] saveContext];`.

3. Add `[cdh saveContext];` to the bottom of the `textFieldDidEndEditing` method of
    `ItemVC.m`.

Any time a new object is created, it should be given a primary key and the object saved immediately. Each method that inserts objects in Grocery Cloud has slightly different code, so this is spelled out in Listing 16.4. The expected placement of this code will be immediately after the existing call to `insertNewObjectForEntityForName`.

Listing 16.4 **Grocery Cloud Object Insertions**

```
// In PrepareTVC.m prepareForSegue
[newItem setValue:[newItem assignObjectId]
        forKey:[newItem primaryKeyField]];
[cdh saveContext];
```

```
// In LocationsAtHomeTVC.m prepareForSegue
[newLocationAtHome setValue:[newLocationAtHome assignObjectId]
                   forKey:[newLocationAtHome primaryKeyField]];
[cdh saveContext];

// In LocationsAtShopTVC.m prepareForSegue
[newLocationAtShop setValue:[newLocationAtShop assignObjectId]
                   forKey:[ newLocationAtShop primaryKeyField]];
[cdh saveContext];

// In UnitsTVC.m prepareForSegue
[newUnit setValue:[newUnit assignObjectId]
         forKey:[newUnit primaryKeyField]];
[cdh saveContext];

// In ItemVC.m ensureItemHomeLocationIsNotNull
[locationAtHome setValue:[locationAtHome assignObjectId]
                forKey:[ locationAtHome primaryKeyField]];
[cdh saveContext];

// In ItemVC.m ensureItemShopLocationIsNotNull
[locationAtShop setValue:[locationAtShop assignObjectId]
                forKey:[locationAtShop primaryKeyField]];
[cdh saveContext];

// In ItemVC.m imagePickerController:didFinishPickingMediaWithInfo
[newPhoto setValue:[newPhoto assignObjectId]
          forKey:[newPhoto primaryKeyField]];
[cdh saveContext];
```

Update Grocery Cloud as follows to ensure all new objects are given a primary key:

1. Add the line of code for each method shown in Listing 16.4 to the line after the call to `insertNewObjectForEntityForName` found in the same method.

Note that some classes out of scope of this chapter have not been updated (for example, `CoreDataImporter`).

Underlying Changes

At the time of writing, there's no StackMob notification that can be observed to trigger a table view refresh in response to a change in underlying data. For example, with iCloud, `NSPersistentStoreDidImportUbiquitousContentChangesNotification` can be observed. As a workaround, a `viewDidAppear` method will be added to trigger a refresh on each table view. Listing 16.5 shows the code involved.

Listing 16.5 `PrepareTVC.m, ShopTVC.m, UnitsTVC.m, LocationsAtHomeTVC.m,` and
`LocationsAtShopTVC.m: viewWillAppear`

```
- (void)viewDidAppear:(BOOL)animated {
if (debug==1) {
    NSLog(@"Running %@ '%@'", self.class, NSStringFromSelector(_cmd));
}

    [super viewDidAppear:animated];
    [self configureFetch];
    [self performFetch];
}
```

Update Grocery Cloud as follows to ensure the table views are refreshed with the latest data
when they appear:

1. Comment out `[self performFetch];` in the `viewDidLoad` method of all
   table view controller classes (that is, `PrepareTVC.m`, `ShopTVC.m`, `UnitsTVC.m`,
   `LocationsAtHomeTVC.m`, and `LocationsAtShopTVC.m`).

2. Add the method from Listing 16.5 to the top of the VIEW section of all table
   view controller classes (that is, `PrepareTVC.m`, `ShopTVC.m`, `UnitsTVC.m`,
   `LocationsAtHomeTVC.m`, and `LocationsAtShopTVC.m`).

A `UIRefreshControl` will be added to `CoreDataTVC` later in the chapter so the user can manually trigger a refresh.

Automatic Schema Generation

The backend StackMob servers require that a schema be configured for each entity that needs
to be synchronized. The naming convention between an entity and its equivalent schema
differs slightly. These differences are explained in the "StackMob Core Data Coding Practices"
section of the StackMob iOS SDK Reference, which is available from the StackMob website. It's
not too critical that you learn the differences at this stage because the schemas are generated
automatically during the development phase. Generating a schema is as easy as creating a new
object because that's exactly how schemas (and relationships) are generated. Listing 16.6 shows
a new method that will be used as a one-off to generate the equivalent StackMob schemas for
each entity.

Listing 16.6 `AppDelegate.m: generateStackMobSchema`

```
- (void)generateStackMobSchema {

if (debug==1) {
    NSLog(@"Running %@ '%@'", self.class, NSStringFromSelector(_cmd));
}
    CoreDataHelper *cdh = [self cdh];
```

```
NSManagedObjectContext *stackMobContext =
[cdh.stackMobStore contextForCurrentThread];

// Create new objects for each entity
LocationAtHome *locationAtHome =
[NSEntityDescription insertNewObjectForEntityForName:@"LocationAtHome"
                            inManagedObjectContext:stackMobContext];
LocationAtShop *locationAtShop =
[NSEntityDescription insertNewObjectForEntityForName:@"LocationAtShop"
                            inManagedObjectContext:stackMobContext];
Unit *unit =
[NSEntityDescription insertNewObjectForEntityForName:@"Unit"
                               inManagedObjectContext:stackMobContext];
Item *item =
[NSEntityDescription insertNewObjectForEntityForName:@"Item"
                               inManagedObjectContext:stackMobContext];
Item_Photo *item_photo =
[NSEntityDescription insertNewObjectForEntityForName:@"Item_Photo"
                               inManagedObjectContext:stackMobContext];

// Set Primary Key Fields
[locationAtHome setValue:[locationAtHome assignObjectId]
                forKey:[locationAtHome primaryKeyField]];
[locationAtShop setValue:[locationAtShop assignObjectId]
                forKey:[locationAtShop primaryKeyField]];
[unit          setValue:[unit assignObjectId]
                forKey:[unit primaryKeyField]];
[item          setValue:[item assignObjectId]
                forKey:[item primaryKeyField]];
[item_photo    setValue:[item_photo assignObjectId]
                forKey:[item_photo primaryKeyField]];

// Give each attribute a value so the schema is generated automatically
locationAtHome.storedIn = @"Fridge";
locationAtShop.aisle = @"Cold Section";
unit.name = @"L";
item.name = @"Milk";
item.collected = [NSNumber numberWithBool:NO];
item.listed = [NSNumber numberWithBool:YES];
item.quantity = [NSNumber numberWithInt:1];

// sectionNameKeyPath WORKAROUND (See Appendix B)
item.storedIn = @"Fridge";
item.aisle = @"Cold Section";

// Always save objects before relationships are created to avoid corruption
[cdh saveContext];
```

```
// Create relationships and then save again
item.unit = unit;
item.locationAtHome = locationAtHome;
item.locationAtShop = locationAtShop;
item.photo = item_photo;
[cdh saveContext];
}
```

The code in the `generateStackMobSchema` is nothing that hasn't been demonstrated previously in this book. An object is created for each entity, and the attributes for each are then populated to ensure they're generated within a StackMob schema.

Update Grocery Cloud as follows to generate a StackMob schema for each entity:

1. Add `#import "Item_Photo.h"` to the top of `AppDelegate.m`.

2. Add the code from Listing 16.6 to the bottom of `AppDelegate.m` before `@end`.

3. Add `[self generateStackMobSchema];` to the bottom of the `didFinishLaunchingWithOptions` method of `AppDelegate.m` before `return YES;`.

4. Run Grocery Cloud on a device or the iOS Simulator to generate the StackMob schema automatically. Internet connectivity must be available the first time you do this in order for the schema to be generated automatically. You can safely ignore any "Object will be placed in unnamed section" messages, which are explained in Appendix B.

5. Click **Schema Configuration** on the StackMob Dashboard to reveal the automatically generated schema. The expected result is shown in Figure 16.6.

Figure 16.6   Automatically generated schema

6. Comment out `[self generateStackMobSchema];` in the `didFinishLaunchingWith Options` method `AppDelegate.m`.

Schema Permissions

By default, StackMob schema permissions are open. This means that objects can be Created, Read, Updated, and Deleted (CRUD) by anyone. Although this is useful during development, it is not ideal for Grocery Cloud in production. The intention of Grocery Cloud is to facilitate a common shopping list between a two or more people. To achieve this, user accounts are required to restrict who can do what. If two people need to share a shopping list, they will need to authenticate using the same StackMob user account. As far as the end user is concerned, he or she will actually know of a "user" as a "shared list." A "shared list" will, of course, just be a user account requiring a password.

Update the **grocery_cloud** schemas as follows to limit access:

1. Enter **Schema Configuration** of the StackMob Dashboard.

2. Edit the **item** schema.

3. Scroll down to the **Schema Permissions** section and configure the permission levels shown in Figure 16.7.

4. Click **Save Schema**.

5. Click **Schema Configuration** to return to the list of schemas.

6. Repeat steps 2 to 5 for the **item_photo**, **locationathome**, **locationatshop**, and **unit** schemas.

Schema Permissions ⓘ

> Read about how schema permissions work.

Logged In Permissions are currently only available when using StackMob SDKs that support OAuth 2.0

Action	Permission Level
Create	Allow to any logged in user ▾
Read	Allow to sm_owner (object owner) ▾
Update	Allow to sm_owner (object owner) ▾
Delete	Allow to sm_owner (object owner) ▾

Figure 16.7   Schema permission levels

With permission levels now in place, user accounts are required to work with data. As such, a new interface will be added that allows users to create a "shared list" (user account). Any objects that have been created up until now will still have open permissions. If you try to create or edit an object, access will be denied and context saves will fail.

Authentication

The permissions structure has been put in place to allow people to read, update, or delete only what they have created. This means that different people can maintain their own list without their items being visible to others. Because the concept of a "user" and a "shared list" is the same, if you want to share a list, you just tell someone the shared list name and password. To support this, a new interface will be implemented to allow a shared list to be created or logged in to.

Update Grocery Cloud as follows to implement a **More** tab for list sharing:

1. Select **Main.storyboard**.

2. Drag a **View Controller** on to the storyboard beneath **Navigation Controller – Shop**.

3. Select the new **View Controller** and click **Editor > Embed In > Navigation Controller**.

4. Hold **Control** and drag a line from the center of the **Tab Bar Controller** to the new **Navigation Controller**; then select **Relationship Segue > view controllers**.

5. Set the **Identifier** of the new **Tab Bar Item** to **More** using **Attributes Inspector** (**Option+⌘+4**).

6. Set the **Navigation Item Title** of the new **View Controller** to **Shared Lists**. Figure 16.8 shows the expected results.

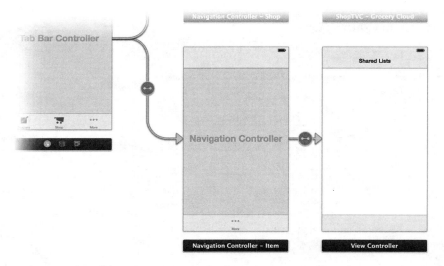

Figure 16.8   Shared lists `LoginVC`

From now on, the new view will be referred to as the LoginVC view, as this will be the name of a new custom class created specifically for it. This view will first be updated with new interface elements so the user can authenticate and create a shared list "account."

Update Grocery Cloud as follows to update the LoginVC view:

1. Drag two **Text Fields**, two **Buttons**, and one **Label** anywhere on to the LoginVC view.

2. Configure both Text Fields as follows using **Attributes Inspector (Option+⌘+4)**:

   - Set **Alignment** to **Center**.
   - Set **Border Style** to **Line** (represented by a rectangle with a solid border).

3. Set the placeholder text of one of the text fields to **Shared List Name** and the other to **Password**.

4. Set the **Password** text field to **Secure** by ticking **Secure**.

> **Tip**
>
> Secure is located beneath the keyboard.

5. Set the **Height** of both text fields to **44** using **Size Inspector (Option+⌘+5)**.

6. Set the **Width** of both buttons to **120**.

7. Set the text of one button to **Create** and the other to **Enter** using **Attributes Inspector (Option+⌘+4)**.

8. Set the **Alignment** of the label to **Center**.

9. Set the text of the label to **Create or Enter a Shared List**.

10. Arrange the view as shown in Figure 16.9. Widen the text fields and label to the edge guides in the process.

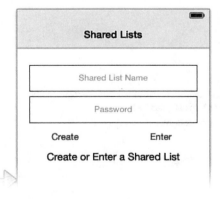

Figure 16.9   An updated shared lists LoginVC

11. Select the Shared Lists view and click **Editor > Resolve Auto Layout Issues > Reset to Suggested Constraints in View Controller**. If this does not resolve the auto-layout issues, you may have to manually configure the constraints as per the final project available at the end of the chapter.

Securing the User Class

When a user authenticates, his or her password would usually be transmitted in clear text. To prevent this, customizations are required to the User `NSManagedObject` subclass. These customizations ensure that the sensitive traffic is encrypted so long as User objects are created with the `initIntoManagedObjectContext` method shown in Listing 16.7.

Listing 16.7 **User.h**

```
#import <Foundation/Foundation.h>
#import <CoreData/CoreData.h>
#import "StackMob.h"
@interface User : SMUserManagedObject
@property (nonatomic, retain) NSString * username;
@property (nonatomic, retain) NSDate * createddate;
@property (nonatomic, retain) NSDate * lastmoddate;
- (id)initNewUserInContext:(NSManagedObjectContext *)context;
@end
```

The code from Listing 16.7 was provided by StackMob in their "Creating a User Object" tutorial, which is available by searching their website. The implementation of this class is shown in Listing 16.8.

Listing 16.8 **User.m**

```
#import "User.h"
@implementation User
@dynamic createddate;
@dynamic lastmoddate;
@dynamic username;

- (id)initNewUserInContext:(NSManagedObjectContext *)context {
    self = [super initWithEntityName:@"User"
      insertIntoManagedObjectContext:context];
    return self;
}
@end
```

Update Grocery Cloud as follows to ensure that user object creation is secure:

1. Replace the contents of User.h with the code from Listing 16.7.

2. Replace the contents of User.m with the code from Listing 16.8.

> **Note**
>
> If NSManagedObject subclasses are regenerated, the custom User class code will be lost. Any time you need to regenerate these files, remember to update this class with the code from Listing 16.7 and Listing 16.8.

Introducing LoginVC

The next step is to add the code that will drive the Shared List view. As mentioned previously, the custom class that will drive this view is called LoginVC. This class will handle the creation and authentication of a shared list (that is, user account). The header code involved is shown in Listing 16.9.

Listing 16.9 **LoginVC.h**

```objc
#import <UIKit/UIKit.h>
@interface LoginVC : UIViewController <UITextFieldDelegate>

@property (strong, nonatomic) IBOutlet UITextField *usernameTextField;
@property (strong, nonatomic) IBOutlet UITextField *passwordTextField;
@property (strong, nonatomic) IBOutlet UILabel *statusLabel;
@property (strong, nonatomic) UIActivityIndicatorView *activityIndicatorView;
@property (strong, nonatomic) UIView *activityIndicatorBackground;

- (IBAction)create:(id)sender;
- (IBAction)authenticate:(id)sender;
@end
```

The LoginVC view will have a username (shared list name) and password text field. It will also be a UITextField delegate, so the keyboard can be dismissed when the user is finished with either text field. In addition, there will be a label for showing status and an activity view used to show what is happening. The create and authenticate methods will be used to create a new account or sign in to an existing account.

Update Grocery Cloud as follows to create the LoginVC class:

1. Select the **Grocery Cloud View Controllers** group.

2. Click **File > New > File…**.

3. Click **iOS > Cocoa Touch > Objective-C class** and then click **Next**.

4. Set **Subclass of** to `UIViewController`.

5. Set the class name to `LoginVC`.

6. Click **Next** and then ensure the Grocery Cloud target is selected before clicking **Create**.

7. Replace the contents of `LoginVC.h` with the code from Listing 16.9. You may be warned that the `create` and `authenticate` methods aren't implemented yet if you click `LoginVC.m`.

8. Select **Main.storyboard**.

9. Ensure the **Shared Lists View Controller** is selected and then set its custom class to `LoginVC` using **Identity Inspector** (**Option+⌘+3**), as shown in Figure 16.10.

Figure 16.10   Custom class: `LoginVC`

The next step is to link each text field, button, and label to the appropriate properties in the `LoginVC` header. This will allow them to be referenced by the implementation of `LoginVC`.

Update Grocery Cloud as follows to link the new user interface elements to code:

1. Double-click `LoginVC.h` so that it opens in a new window.

2. Select **Main.storyboard** and position `LoginVC.h` near the **Shared Lists View Controller**.

3. Hold down **Control** and drag a line from the Shared List Name text field to the `usernameTextField` property in `LoginVC.h`.

4. Hold down **Control** and drag a line from the Password text field to the `passwordTextField` property in `LoginVC.h`.

5. Hold down **Control** and drag a line from the **Label** to the `statusLabel` property in `LoginVC.h`.

6. Hold down **Control** and drag a line from the **Create** button to the `create` method in `LoginVC.h`.

7. Hold down **Control** and drag a line from the **Enter** button to the `authenticate` method in `LoginVC.h`.

Now that the interface is linked to the code, `LoginVC` can be implemented. The starting code required in `LoginVC.m` is shown in Listing 16.10.

Listing 16.10 **LoginVC.m**

```
#import "LoginVC.h"
#import "CoreDataHelper.h"
#import "AppDelegate.h"
#import "User.h"

@implementation LoginVC
#define debug 1

#pragma mark - VIEW
- (void)updateStatus {
if (debug==1) {
    NSLog(@"Running %@ '%@'", self.class, NSStringFromSelector(_cmd));
}
    CoreDataHelper *cdh =
    [(AppDelegate *)[[UIApplication sharedApplication] delegate] cdh];

    if([cdh.stackMobClient isLoggedIn]) {

        [cdh.stackMobClient getLoggedInUserOnSuccess:^(NSDictionary *result) {
            self.statusLabel.text =
            [NSString stringWithFormat:@"You're using '%@'",
                                            [result objectForKey:@"username"]];
        } onFailure:^(NSError *error) {
            self.statusLabel.text = @"Create or Enter a Shared List";
        }];

    } else {
        self.statusLabel.text = @"Create or Enter a Shared List";
    }
}
- (void)viewDidLoad {
if (debug==1) {
    NSLog(@"Running %@ '%@'", self.class, NSStringFromSelector(_cmd));
}
    [super viewDidLoad];
    [_usernameTextField setDelegate:self];
    [_passwordTextField setDelegate:self];
    [self hideKeyboardWhenBackgroundIsTapped];
```

```objc
    [self updateStatus];
}


#pragma mark - WAITING
- (void)showWait:(BOOL)visible {
if (debug==1) {
    NSLog(@"Running %@ '%@'", self.class, NSStringFromSelector(_cmd));
}
    if (!_activityIndicatorBackground) {
        _activityIndicatorBackground =
        [[UIView alloc] initWithFrame:CGRectMake(0, 0, 100, 100)];

    }
    [_activityIndicatorBackground
                setCenter:CGPointMake(self.view.frame.size.width/2,
                                    self.view.frame.size.height/2)];
    [_activityIndicatorBackground setBackgroundColor:[UIColor blackColor]];
    [_activityIndicatorBackground setAlpha:0.5];
    _activityIndicatorView = [[UIActivityIndicatorView alloc]
                initWithActivityIndicatorStyle:UIActivityIndicatorViewStyleWhite];
    _activityIndicatorView.center =
                    CGPointMake(_activityIndicatorBackground.frame.size.width/2,
                            _activityIndicatorBackground.frame.size.height/2);

    if (visible) {
        [self.view addSubview:_activityIndicatorBackground];
        [_activityIndicatorBackground addSubview:_activityIndicatorView];
        [_activityIndicatorView startAnimating];

    } else {
        [_activityIndicatorView stopAnimating];
        [_activityIndicatorView removeFromSuperview];
        [_activityIndicatorBackground removeFromSuperview];
    }
}


#pragma mark - ALERTING
- (void)showAlertWithTitle:(NSString*)title message:(NSString*)message {

if (debug==1) {
    NSLog(@"Running %@ '%@'", self.class, NSStringFromSelector(_cmd));
}
    UIAlertView *alert = [[UIAlertView alloc] initWithTitle:title
                                                message:message
                                                delegate:nil
                                        cancelButtonTitle:nil
                                        otherButtonTitles:@"Ok", nil];
```

```
        [alert show];
        [self showWait:NO];
}

#pragma mark - VALIDATION
- (BOOL)textFieldIsBlank {
if (debug==1) {
    NSLog(@"Running %@ '%@'", self.class, NSStringFromSelector(_cmd));
}
    if ([_usernameTextField.text isEqualToString:@""] ||
        [_passwordTextField.text isEqualToString:@""]) {

        [self showAlertWithTitle:@"Please Enter a Shared List Name and Password"
                         message:@"If you don't have a Shared List you can create
➥one by filling in a Shared List Name and a Password, then clicking Create"];
        return YES;
    }
    return NO;
}

#pragma mark - DELEGATE: UITextField
- (BOOL)textFieldShouldReturn:(UITextField *)textField {
if (debug==1) {
    NSLog(@"Running %@ '%@'", self.class, NSStringFromSelector(_cmd));
}
    [textField resignFirstResponder];
    return YES;
}

#pragma mark - INTERACTION
- (void)hideKeyboardWhenBackgroundIsTapped {
if (debug==1) {
    NSLog(@"Running %@ '%@'", self.class, NSStringFromSelector(_cmd));
}
    UITapGestureRecognizer *tgr =
    [[UITapGestureRecognizer alloc] initWithTarget:self
                                            action:@selector(hideKeyboard)];
    [tgr setCancelsTouchesInView:NO];
    [self.view addGestureRecognizer:tgr];
}
- (void)hideKeyboard {
if (debug==1) {
    NSLog(@"Running %@ '%@'", self.class, NSStringFromSelector(_cmd));
}
    [self.view endEditing:TRUE];
}
@end
```

The new code is initially broken into six sections:

- The **VIEW** section contains methods used to update the status label with the status of the shared list and configure the initial view.

- The **WAITING** section contains a method used to toggle an activity indicator in cases where network calls are necessary.

- The **ALERTING** section contains a method used to wrap a standard UIAlertView. This simply reduces the amount of code required because there will be quite a few calls to create alert views in the future.

- The **VALIDATION** section is used to alert the user when either text field is blank and he or she tries to create or authenticate to a shared list.

- The **DELEGATE: UITextField** section contains a method that is used to hide the keyboard when either text field loses focus.

- The **INTERACTION** section contains two methods that are used to hide the keyboard when the background is touched.

Update Grocery Cloud as follows to begin the implementation of LoginVC:

1. Replace all code in LoginVC.m with the code from Listing 16.10.

Two additional methods are required in LoginVC.m that are already mentioned in LoginVC.h. Their absence will currently be causing an incomplete implementation warning. Listing 16.11 shows the implementation of the create method, which is the first of the two methods to be placed in a new ACCOUNT section of LoginVC.m.

Listing 16.11   **LoginVC.m: create**

```
#pragma mark - ACCOUNT
- (IBAction)create:(id)sender {
if (debug==1) {
    NSLog(@"Running %@ '%@'", self.class, NSStringFromSelector(_cmd));
}
    CoreDataHelper *cdh =
    [(AppDelegate *)[[UIApplication sharedApplication] delegate] cdh];
    NSManagedObjectContext *stackMobContext =
    [cdh.stackMobStore contextForCurrentThread];

    [self showWait:YES];
    if ([self textFieldIsBlank]) {
        return;
    }

    // ENSURE NETWORK IS REACHABLE
    if (!cdh.stackMobClient.networkMonitor.currentNetworkStatus ==
                                        SMNetworkStatusReachable) {
```

```objc
            [self showAlertWithTitle:@"Failed to Create Shared List"
                        message:@"The Internet connection appears to be offline."];
        [self updateStatus];
        return;
    }

    // ENSURE USER DOESN'T EXIST
    NSFetchRequest *fetchRequest =
    [[NSFetchRequest alloc] initWithEntityName:@"User"];
    [fetchRequest setPredicate:[NSPredicate predicateWithFormat:@"username==%@",
                                        self.usernameTextField.text]];

    [stackMobContext executeFetchRequest:fetchRequest
                            onSuccess:^(NSArray *results) {

        if ([results count] == 1) {
            // USER ALREADY EXISTS
            [self showAlertWithTitle:@"Please choose another Shared List Name"
                        message:[NSString stringWithFormat:@"Someone has
already created a list with the name '%@'",_usernameTextField.text]];
        } else {

            // CREATE USER
            self.statusLabel.text =
            [NSString stringWithFormat:@"Creating Shared List '%@'...",
                                        _usernameTextField.text];
            User *newUser =
            [[User alloc] initNewUserInContext:stackMobContext];
            [newUser setUsername:_usernameTextField.text];
            [newUser setPassword:_passwordTextField.text];

            [stackMobContext saveOnSuccess:^{

                // USER CREATED SUCCESSFULLY
                [self updateStatus];
                [self showWait:NO];
                [self authenticate:self];

            } onFailure:^(NSError *error) {

                // USER CREATION FAILED
                [stackMobContext deleteObject:newUser];
                [newUser removePassword];
                [self updateStatus];
                [self showWait:NO];
                [self showAlertWithTitle:@"Failed to Create Shared List"
                            message:[NSString stringWithFormat:@"%@",error]];
```

```
        }];
    }
} onFailure:^(NSError *error) {

    // UNSURE IF USER EXISTS
    [self showAlertWithTitle:@"Failed to Check if Shared List Exists"
                     message:[NSString stringWithFormat:@"%@",error]];
    }];
}
```

The commenting in Listing 16.11 should go a long way toward explaining what is happening at each step in the code. First, the activity indicator is displayed as the account creation begins. The method will return prematurely if the text fields are blank or the network is unavailable. A check is then performed to see if the user already exists; if not, a new user is created. If the existing user check or user creation fails, the user will be notified and the method will return. If the user creation succeeds, the user will be notified and the authenticate method will be triggered.

Update Grocery Cloud as follows to implement the create method:

1. Add the code from Listing 16.11 to the top of LoginVC.m, just before the VIEW section.

The final method required in LoginVC.m is called authenticate. Listing 16.12 shows the code involved in this new method.

Listing 16.12   **LoginVC.m: authenticate**

```
- (IBAction)authenticate:(id)sender {
if (debug==1) {
    NSLog(@"Running %@ '%@'", self.class, NSStringFromSelector(_cmd));
}
    if ([self textFieldIsBlank]) {
        return;
    }
    CoreDataHelper *cdh =
    [(AppDelegate *)[[UIApplication sharedApplication] delegate] cdh];

    self.statusLabel.text =
    [NSString stringWithFormat:@"Connecting to Shared List '%@'...",
                                    _usernameTextField.text];
    [self showWait:YES];

    // ensure new objects are saved prior to an account switch
    [[cdh.stackMobStore contextForCurrentThread] saveOnSuccess:^{
```

```
    [cdh.stackMobClient loginWithUsername:_usernameTextField.text
                             password:_passwordTextField.text
                            onSuccess:^(NSDictionary *results) {

        [self showAlertWithTitle:@"Success!"
                         message:[NSString stringWithFormat:
   @"You're now using Shared List '%@'", [results valueForKey:@"username"]]];
        [self updateStatus];
        [self showWait:NO];

        [[NSNotificationCenter defaultCenter]
                          postNotificationName:@"SomethingChanged"
                                        object:nil
                                      userInfo:nil];
    } onFailure:^(NSError *error) {

        if (error.code == 401) {
            [self showAlertWithTitle:@"Failed to Enter Shared List"
                             message:@"Access Denied"];
        } else {
            [self showAlertWithTitle:@"Failed to Enter Shared List"
                             message:[NSString stringWithFormat:@"%@",
                                        error.localizedDescription]];
        }
        [self updateStatus];
        [self showWait:NO];
    }];
} onFailure:^(NSError *error) {
    NSLog(@"Failed to save context prior to account switch");
}];
}
```

The `authenticate` method displays an activity indicator and updates the status label prior to commencing work. It also exits prematurely if either text field is empty. The context is saved prior to a login attempt just in case there is data from an old list that is yet to be persisted. Provided this save succeeds, the StackMob client method `loginWithUsername` method is called. The most common failed response will be 401, which means access has been denied. This error is specifically handled in the login failure code. Should authentication be successful, the status is updated, the activity indicator is hidden, and a `SomethingChanged` notification is sent so that the table views are refreshed.

Update Grocery Cloud as follows to implement the `create` method:

1. Add the code from Listing 16.12 to the bottom of the ACCOUNT section of `LoginVC.m`, just before the VIEW section.

2. Delete Grocery Cloud from your device, click **Product > Clean**, and then run the application to reinstall it.

3. Select the **More** tab and create a Shared List by entering a list name and password; then clicking **Create**. The expected result is shown in Figure 16.11.

Figure 16.11   Successful creation of a shared list (that is, user)

4. Return to the **Prepare** tab and create a new item. As you create the item, also create a new home and shop location. Once you've done that, assign the new locations to the item using the picker views. If your new item does not show up, try switching tabs to trigger a refresh.

Maintaining Responsiveness

Even with caching enabled, it is inevitable that calls to the network will be required at some point. In LoginVC, an activity indicator is displayed whenever a network call is required using showWait. A similar approach needs to be implemented for when each table view performs a fetch. The code in the WAITING and ALERTING sections of LoginVC will be reused and the performFetch method updated in CoreDataTVC.m in order for this to be achieved. At the same time, a UIRefreshControl will be implemented that enables the user to manually call performFetch by swiping down on any CoreDataTVC-driven table view.

The updated `performFetch` method is shown in Listing 16.13.

Listing 16.13   **CoreDataTVC.m: performFetch**

```
- (void)performFetch {
if (debug==1) {
    NSLog(@"Running %@ '%@'", self.class, NSStringFromSelector(_cmd));
}
    if (self.refreshControl.refreshing) {
        [self.refreshControl endRefreshing];
    } else {
        [self showWait:YES];
    }
    if (self.frc) {
        [self.frc.managedObjectContext performBlock:^{

            NSError *error = nil;
            if (![self.frc performFetch:&error]) {

                NSLog(@"%@ '%@' %@",self.class, NSStringFromSelector(_cmd),
                                                            error);
                if ([error.domain isEqualToString:@"HTTP"] && error.code == 401) {

                    [self showAlertWithTitle:@"Access Denied"
                    message:@"Please Create or Enter a Shared List on the More tab"];
                } else {
                    if (error) {
                        [self showAlertWithTitle:@"Fetch Failed"
                                        message:[NSString stringWithFormat:@"%@",
                                                error.localizedDescription]];
                    }
                }
            }
            [self.tableView reloadData];
            [self showWait:NO];
        }];
    } else {
        NSLog(@"Failed to perform fetch: The fetched results controller is nil.");
    }
}
```

Update Grocery Cloud as follows to ensure table views show an activity indicator:

1. Copy the `activityIndicatorView` and `activityIndicatorBackground` properties from `LoginVC.h` to `CoreDataTVC.h`, placing them after the existing properties.

2. Copy the WAITING and ALERTING sections from LoginVC.m to CoreDataTVC.m, placing them just before the existing FETCHING section. These sections contain the showWait and showAlertWithTitle methods.

3. Replace the performFetch method in CoreDataTVC.m with the method from Listing 16.13.

4. Add the code shown in Listing 16.14 to CoreDataTVC.m on the line above the FETCHING section.

5. Run the application again to test that the activity indicator is displayed while table view fetches are performed.

Listing 16.14   **CoreDataTVC.m: viewDidLoad**

```
#pragma mark - VIEW
- (void)viewDidLoad {
    [super viewDidLoad];
    UIRefreshControl *refreshControl = [UIRefreshControl new];
    [refreshControl addTarget:self
                       action:@selector(performFetch)
             forControlEvents:UIControlEventValueChanged];
    [self setRefreshControl:refreshControl];
}
```

Summary

Congratulations, you've now configured a backend service and have integrated it with an existing Core Data application! There are a still few areas requiring additional refinement that are excluded from this chapter to keep it as succinct as possible. For example, the transition from PrepareTVC to ItemVC still lags when a network call is made. The code also needs to be refactored to display an activity indicator while items are inserted or retrieved from the network. Still, you should now be in a good position to apply the StackMob framework to your own applications.

If you need photo (binary data) support, you'll need an Amazon S3 "bucket." To create an S3 bucket, you'll first need to sign up for an Amazon Web Services (AWS) account at http://aws. amazon.com/. As you create an Amazon AWS account, you'll need to provide a valid credit card number. Pricing can be viewed at http://aws.amazon.com/pricing/s3/ and varies based on the region the bucket is placed in. Search the StackMob website for the "Upload to S3" tutorial for further information.

Exercises

Why not build on what you've learned by experimenting?

1. Examine the StackMob contents by visiting **Schema Configuration** and clicking **View Data** for the item schema.

2. Create a new **Shared List** and populate it with some new items. Again, view the data on the **Schema Configuration** page for the item schema. Notice how the `sm_owner` schema field indicates what shared list (that is, user) owns and can therefore read, update, or delete each row.

3. Enable StackMob debug by setting `SM_CORE_DATA_DEBUG` to `YES` in the `init` method of `CoreDataHelper.m`. Run the application again and examine the console log. You should see a lot of verbose logging giving greater visibility of what's happening under the hood.

For your convenience, the final Grocery Cloud project is available for download from http://timroadley.com/LearningCoreData/GroceryCloud-AfterChapter16.zip.

A

Preparing Grocery Dude for Chapter 1

This appendix details the steps required to build the Grocery Dude sample application from scratch. Grocery Dude will be developed across the course of this book, and as each chapter introduces topics on Core Data, you'll expand Grocery Dude to practice what you've learned. These instructions require at least Xcode 5 and iOS 7.

New Xcode Project

The creation of the base Xcode project isn't related to Core Data, so the instructions to build it are tucked away in this appendix. If you prefer, you may skip the creation of this project and begin Chapter 1, "Your First Core Data Application." A link to the Xcode project created as a result of this appendix is available in Chapter 1.

Create the initial Grocery Dude Xcode project as follows:

1. Open Xcode and click **Create a new Xcode project**.

2. Choose the **iOS > Application > Single View Application** template and click **Next**.

3. Set the project options shown in Figure A.1, substituting Tim Roadley with your own developer name, and then click **Next**.

4. Select an appropriate directory for the new project, ensure **Create git repository** is not ticked, and then click **Create**.

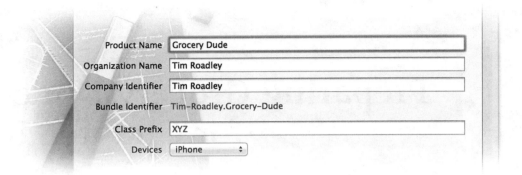

Product Name	Grocery Dude
Organization Name	Tim Roadley
Company Identifier	Tim Roadley
Bundle Identifier	Tim-Roadley.Grocery-Dude
Class Prefix	XYZ
Devices	iPhone ‡

Figure A.1   Project options

Storyboard Design

The initial storyboard will be a simple configuration made up of a View Controller and Table View Controller embedded in a Navigation Controller.

Update Grocery Dude as follows to create the initial storyboard:

1. Select **Main.storyboard**, which is located in the Xcode Group called **Grocery Dude**.

2. Drag a **Table View Controller** from the **Utilities** pane onto the storyboard, placing it to the left of the existing **View Controller**. You can toggle the **Utilities** pane by pressing **Option+⌘+0 together**.

3. Ensure the new **Table View Controller** is selected.

4. Tick **Is Initial View Controller**, as shown in Figure A.2 at the bottom right. If you can't see these settings, make sure the **Utilities** pane is open at the **Attributes Inspector** tab. You can do this by selecting **View > Utilities > Show Attributes Inspector** or by pressing **Option+⌘+4** together.

5. Ensure the **Table View Controller** is selected and then click **Editor > Embed In > Navigation Controller**.

6. Drag a **Bar Button Item** on to the top right of the **Table View Controller**.

7. Select the new **Bar Button Item**.

8. Change the **Identifier** to **Add** in the **Bar Button Item** section of **Attributes Inspector**, as shown in Figure A.3.

9. Hold down **Control** and drag a line from the **Add** button to the center of the **View Controller**, and select **Action Segue > push**.

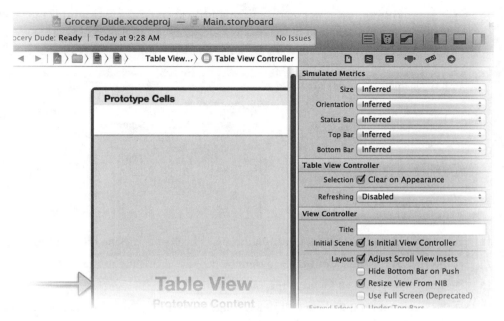

Figure A.2   Setting the initial View Controller

Figure A.3   Setting a Bar Button Item identifier

10. Select the new action segue and then set its **Identifier** to `Add Item Segue` using the **Attributes Inspector**, as shown in Figure A.4.

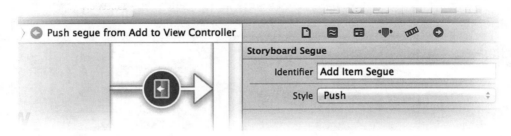

Figure A.4   Add Item Segue

11. Set the **Title** of the **Table View Controller** to **Items** by double-clicking the title area.

12. Set the **Title** of the **View Controller** to **Item** by double-clicking the title area.

13. Select the **Prototype Cell** found in the **Table View**.

14. Set the **Style** of the **Table View Cell** to **Basic** and the **Identifier** to `Item Cell` using **Attributes Inspector**, as shown in Figure A.5.

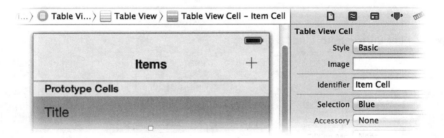

Figure A.5   Item Cell

15. Arrange the storyboard as shown in Figure A.6.

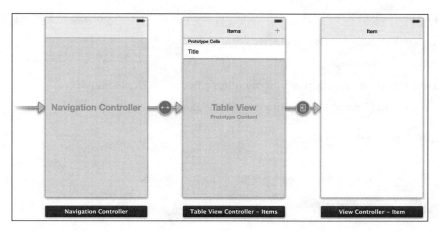

Figure A.6   The initial storyboard

App Icons and Launch Images

Like any iOS app, Grocery Dude needs icons and images to make it look unique.

Update Grocery Dude as follows to configure the appropriate app icons:

1. Download and extract http://www.timroadley.com/LearningCoreData/Icons_Images.zip.
2. Select **Images.xcassets**, which is an **Asset Catalog** that will contain the application images.
3. Select **AppIcon**.
4. Drag **AppIcon_29pt.png** into the **iPhone 29pt** placeholder.
5. Drag **AppIcon_40pt.png** into the **iPhone Spotlight 40pt** placeholder.
6. Drag **AppIcon_60pt.png** into the **iPhone App 60pt** placeholder.

Figure A.7 shows the expected results.

Figure A.7   App icons

Update Grocery Dude as follows to configure the appropriate launch images:

1. Ensure **Images.xcassets** is still selected.

2. Select **LaunchImage**.

3. Drag **LaunchImage_2x.png** into the **iPhone Portrait - 2x** placeholder.

4. Drag **LaunchImage_R4.png** into the **iPhone Portrait - R4** placeholder.

Figure A.8 shows the expected results.

Figure A.8   Launch images

The sample project is now ready for Chapter 1. Feel free to run Grocery Dude on the iOS Simulator or an iOS device to examine your handiwork so far! Note that the deployment target is iOS 7 and previous versions of iOS aren't supported with Grocery Dude.

Preparing Grocery Cloud for Chapter 16

The StackMob integration to be discussed in Chapter 16, "Web Service Integration," will be implemented into a new project called Grocery Cloud. This appendix shows how to prepare the Grocery Cloud starting project using Grocery Dude from the end of Chapter 12, "Search." Nothing in this appendix is related to Core Data, which is why it has been placed in an appendix. It is not essential that you follow this appendix, seeing as the Grocery Cloud starting project is downloadable from the link given in Chapter 16. The following instructions assume you're using Xcode 5 or above.

Renaming Grocery Dude

The first step is to rename Grocery Dude to Grocery Cloud, so there's no confusion between the two projects.

Rename Grocery Dude to Grocery Cloud as follows:

1. Download and unzip **Grocery Dude** from the end of Chapter 12 using the following URL: http://www.timroadley.com/LearningCoreData/GroceryDude-AfterChapter12.zip.

2. Rename the directory containing the project from Grocery Dude to **Grocery Cloud**. Don't rename the Grocery Dude directory within the newly renamed Grocery Cloud directory just yet.

3. Double-click the **Grocery Dude.xcodeproj** file in the Grocery Cloud directory, which should open the project in Xcode 5 or above.

4. Click **Product > Clean** to ensure there's no residual cache from other projects.

5. Ensure the **Project Navigator** is visible (⌘+1) and then slowly click the project name twice and rename it to **Grocery Cloud**, as shown in the top left of Figure B.1. As soon as you've renamed the project, a window will appear as shown on the right of Figure B.1.

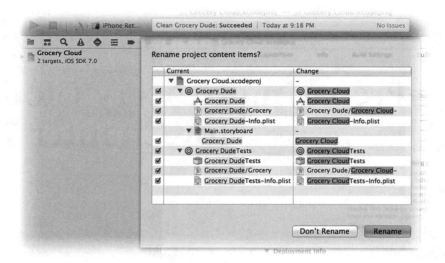

Figure B.1   Renaming Grocery Dude to Grocery Cloud

6. Click **Rename**. If you are prompted with an alert informing you that **Main.storyboard** has changed, click **Revert**.

7. Rename the **Grocery Cloud** > **Targets** > **Grocery Cloud** > **Info** > **Bundle display name** from `${PRODUCT_NAME}` to **GroceryCloud**.

Repointing File Paths

The next step is to change the path where the Info.plist and Precompiled Prefix Header files are expected to reside once the renaming exercise is complete.

Update Grocery Cloud as follows to repoint file paths:

1. Select the **Build Settings** tab of the Grocery Cloud target and ensure **Basic** is selected, as shown in Figure B.2.

2. Change the directory that **Grocery Cloud-Info.plist** and **Grocery Cloud-Prefix.pch** are located in from **Grocery Dude** to **Grocery Cloud**, as shown in Figure B.2.

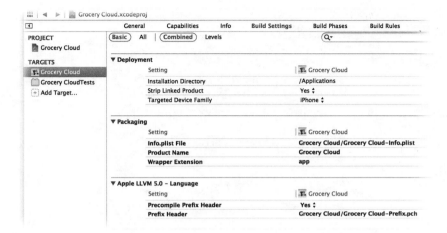

Figure B.2   Changing expected file paths

Renaming Groups and Tests

Xcode groups are used to organize the project class files. The next step is to rename these groups so they match the new project name.

Update Grocery Cloud as follows to rename the Xcode groups:

1. Rename each of the groups in the project so they all begin with **Grocery Cloud**. Then rename **Grocery_DudeTests.m** to **Grocery_CloudTests.m**, as shown in Figure B.3.

2. Right-click the top **Grocery Cloud** group shown in Figure B.3 and select **Show in Finder**.

3. Rename the **Grocery Dude** directory shown in Finder to **Grocery Cloud**. Some files in Xcode will now display red because their parent path is invalid.

4. Rename the **Grocery DudeTests** directory shown in Finder to **Grocery CloudTests**. Some more files in Xcode will now display red because their parent path is invalid.

5. Return to Xcode and select the **Grocery Cloud** group shown near the top of Figure B.3. Open the **Identity and Type** section of **File Inspector (Option+⌘+1)** and then click the icon shown in Figure B.4.

6. Choose the **Grocery Cloud** directory that sits alongside **Grocery Cloud.xcodeproj** to represent the **Grocery Cloud** Xcode group. The files that were previously red beneath the **Grocery Cloud** group should return to black.

7. Repeat steps 5 and 6; however, this time repoint the **Grocery CloudTests** group to the renamed **Grocery CloudTests** directory.

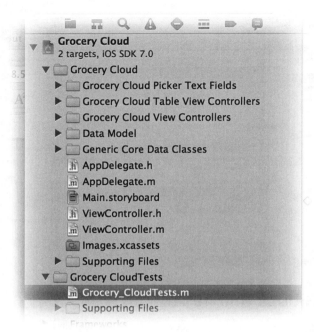

Figure B.3   Renaming Grocery Dude groups and tests to Grocery Cloud

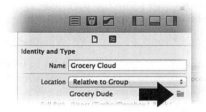

Figure B.4   Repointing the Grocery Cloud group

Renaming the Scheme

The project scheme is currently called **Grocery Dude**. This should be renamed to **Grocery Cloud** to maintain consistency throughout the project.

Update Grocery Cloud as follows:

1. Click **Product > Scheme > Manage Schemes....**

2. Slowly double-click the scheme name and rename it to **Grocery Cloud**, as shown in Figure B.5, and then click **OK.**

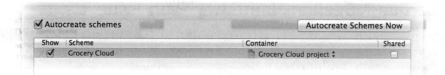

Figure B.5   Renaming the scheme to Grocery Cloud

Updating the Artwork

Grocery Cloud will have a different icon and default splash screen than Grocery Dude to help distinguish between the two projects.

Update Grocery Cloud as follows to replace the existing artwork:

1. Download the updated artwork from the following URL: http://www.timroadley.com/ LearningCoreData/Icons_GroceryCloud.zip.

2. Select the **Images.xcassets** asset catalog.

3. Select **AppIcon**.

4. Drag **AppIcon_29pt.png** into the **29pt** placeholder to replace the existing icon.

5. Drag **AppIcon_40pt.png** into the **40pt** placeholder to replace the existing icon.

6. Drag **AppIcon_60pt.png** into the **60pt** placeholder to replace the existing icon.

7. Select **LaunchImage**.

8. Drag **LaunchImage_2x.png** into the **2x** placeholder to replace the existing image.

9. Drag **LaunchImage_R4.png** into the **R4** placeholder to replace the existing image.

Disabling Camera and Image Support

To keep Chapter 16 concise and Grocery Cloud free on the App Store, image support will be removed from Grocery Cloud. To this end, the thumbnail generation triggered in the viewDidAppear methods of PrepareTVC.m and ShopTVC.m needs to be commented out. The code won't be removed, so you may experiment with adding image support yourself later.

Update Grocery Cloud as follows to disable image support:

1. Comment out the viewDidAppear method in PrepareTVC.m and ShopTVC.m.

2. Add the following code to the bottom of the viewDidLoad method of ItemVC.m:

```
self.cameraButton.hidden = YES;
self.photoImageView.hidden = YES;
```

Workaround: Section Name Key Path Issue

StackMob provides a framework that will be used in Chapter 16 to integrate Core Data with their backend web service. A known limitation of the StackMob framework is that you cannot set a relationship as the key path used to divide a UITableView into sections. Unfortunately, this functionality is fundamental to Grocery Cloud. To work around this issue, two new string attributes will be added to the Item entity. These attributes will be populated with item locations from their equivalent relationship, and will be used instead to section the table view. Note that until the workaround code has a chance to run, you may see the error "Object will be placed in unnamed section" in the console log.

Update Grocery Cloud as follows to work around the section name key path issue:

1. Select **Model.xcdatamodeld**.

2. Click **Editor > Add Model Version...**.

3. Click **Finish** to accept **Model 9** as the new model name.

4. Ensure **Model 9.xcdatamodel** is selected.

5. Create a new **String** attribute in the **Item** entity called **storedIn**.

6. Create a new **String** attribute in the **Item** entity called **aisle**.

7. Regenerate and overwrite the existing NSManagedObject subclass files for all entities by selecting all **Model 9 entities** and then clicking **Editor > Create NSManagedObject Subclass...** and then follow the prompts. Ensure the Grocery Cloud target is selected before clicking **Create**.

8. Ensure **Model.xcdatamodeld** is selected.

9. Set the **Current Model Version** to **Model 9** using **File Inspector (Option+⌘+1)**.

The code to copy an item's related location names to the equivalent attribute from the Item entity is shown in Listing B.1.

Listing B.1 **PrepareTVC.m: cellForRowAtIndexPath**

```
// StackMob Relationship sectionNameKeyPath Workaround
[self.frc.managedObjectContext performBlock:^{
    if (!item.storedIn ||
        ![item.storedIn isEqualToString:item.locationAtHome.storedIn]) {
        item.storedIn = item.locationAtHome.storedIn;
        NSLog(@"sectionNameKeyPath WORKAROUND (See Appendix B):");
        NSLog(@"item.storedIn is now = '%@'", item.storedIn);
    }
    if (!item.aisle ||
        ![item.aisle isEqualToString:item.locationAtShop.aisle]) {
        item.aisle = item.locationAtShop.aisle;
```

```
        NSLog(@"sectionNameKeyPath WORKAROUND (See Appendix B):");
        NSLog(@"item.aisle is now = '%@'", item.aisle);
    }
}];
```

Update Grocery Cloud as follows to work around the section name key path issue:

1. Add #import "LocationAtHome.h" to the top of PrepareTVC.m.

2. Add #import "LocationAtShop.h" to the top of PrepareTVC.m.

3. Copy the code from Listing B.1 to the bottom of the cellForRowAtIndexPath method of PrepareTVC.m before return cell;.

4. Repeat steps 1, 2, and 3 for ShopTVC.m instead of PrepareTVC.m.

Now that the reliance on locationAtHome.storedIn and locationAtShop.aisle has been removed, the sectionNameKeyPath reference in the configureFetch methods needs to be updated.

Update Grocery Cloud as follows to ensure sectionNameKeyPath does not rely on a relationship:

1. In the configureFetch method of PrepareTVC.m, replace the two occurrences of locationAtHome.storedIn with storedIn.

2. In the configureFetch method of ShopTVC.m, replace the two occurrences of locationAtShop.aisle with aisle.

Summary

The starting project for Chapter 16 has now been created. Note that the persistent store local to the device won't be used anymore. If you already have a copy of Grocery Cloud on your device, perhaps from the App Store, it is recommended that it be removed before beginning Chapter 16. If you did run the application now, you would see a lot of console log entries as the sectionNameKeyPath workaround is applied.

As one final touch before beginning Chapter 16, search the Xcode project for the word "Dude" and replace it with the word "Cloud."

Index

A

D

L

N-O

P-Q

W

X-Z

More Resources for Mac and iOS Developers

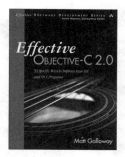

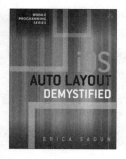

Developer's Library

informit.com/devlibrary

ESSENTIAL REFERENCES FOR PROGRAMMING PROFESSIONALS

The Core iOS 6 Developer's Cookbook, Fourth Edition

Erica Sadun

ISBN-13: 978-0-321-88421-3

The Advanced iOS 6 Developer's Cookbook

Erica Sadun

ISBN-13: 978-0-321-88422-0

Programming in Objective-C, Fifth Edition

Stephen G. Kochan

ISBN-13: 978-0-321-88728-3

Other Developer's Library Titles

TITLE	AUTHOR	ISBN-13
Objective-C Phrasebook, Second Edition	David Chisnall	978-0-321-81375-6
Test-Driven iOS Development	Graham Lee	978-0-321-77418-7
Cocoa® Programming Developer's Handbook	David Chisnall	978-0-321-63963-9
Cocoa Design Patterns Applications for the iPhone	Erik M. Buck / Donald A. Yacktman	978-0-321-53502-3

Developer's Library books are available at most retail and online bookstores. For more information or to order direct, visit our online bookstore at **informit.com/store**.

Online editions of all Developer's Library titles are available by subscription from Safari Books Online at **safari.informit.com**.

Addison
Wesley

**Developer's
Library**

informit.com/devlibrary